Riot on
Sunset
Strip

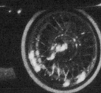

Riot On Sunset Strip
Rock'n'Roll's Last
Stand In Hollywood
Domenic Priore

A Jawbone Book
Second Edition 2015
Published in the UK and the USA by
Jawbone Press
2a Union Court
20–22 Union Road
London SW4 6JP
England
www.jawbonepress.com

ISBN 978-1-908279-90-3

EDITOR Tom Seabrook
JACKET DESIGN Mark Case

Every attempt has been made to locate names of people in
bands who left behind music during the mid-1960s LA scene.
We are in search of any stories, interviews, photographs,
art, recordings, movies, or television appearances for further
texts and documentary projects extending from the subjects
discussed in this book. All suggestions can be sent to the
author, Domenic Priore, at itsboss9@aol.com.

Printed in the Czech Republic by PB Print UK

1 2 3 4 5 19 18 17 16 15

Contents

by Arthur Lee

" Hey Folks, this is Arthur Lee. I'm the one who kicked the door open for all these guys like Jimi Hendrix, Sly Stone, Bill Graham, The Grateful Dead, The Doors—all these want-to-be rock stars that you are so familiar with. This guy Domenic wants me to start his story off, so here goes. "

The Byrds were happenin'. Bob Dylan was happenin'. And it was the most beautiful time in my life. It has not always been purse first and ass last in my book. We shared, we cared, and we tried to represent peace and love. It's too bad that people that are caught up in calling people bitches and mfers weren't there to see what life can really be like. I look and listen to these hip-hop and so-called rap artists. Some are very talented, but all most of them do is preach hate. Love On Earth Must Be.

The Strip was like a home away from home to me. After the gigs I usually didn't have a place to stay, but the people in those days could always find a place for me. I'd go to a party after shows and I was welcomed by all, especially white people. When Martin Luther King Jr was walking down the street hand in hand in Montgomery, Alabama, and Tennessee, trying to tell people it's too bad you're judged by the color of your skin rather than substance, I was already ahead of the game; I was putting it to shame.

The people were like: "If I got it, you got it." And if I got it, here it is, come and get it. It was all about sharing. But if I was a regular nine-to-five negro instead of walking around with one shoe on and one shoe off, I'm sure I wouldn't got the recognition that a person being black would get. You got to take a chance to get a chance in this world, and I took a chance. And guess what I got? A chance.

The music was about getting along. The music is the key, but God is above that. I call him Love, I use his name, but mostly I'm a human being, just like you. The flesh is weak, but life goes on. The music was the inspiration for the music that I hear today. There was the birth of folk-rock: that's what I listened to. I'm glad I was there to help shape the music that I hear today.

I was there to bust the door open for other black entertainers: I came from South LA, where blacks and whites were joined together. There were no Crips, no Bloods. I came to Hollywood to send LOVE.

And Love I got.

Arthur Lee,
Los Angeles,
August 2004

Making it on the Strip

by Jerry Hopkins
of the *Los Angeles Free Press*

I have a theory about the Sunset Strip. I say it is not real. It is plastic. I say the Strip is manufactured in Japan and shipped here in small parts, then it is reassembled by a committee of pot smokers.

If you are not convinced I will tell you about the time I watch a lady named Szou dance all by herself at the Trip wearing a Gypsy Boots T-shirt for a dress. Or the time a friend of mine walks into a lady's apartment and she is sitting cross-legged on the floor pasting feathers on a picture of The Rolling Stones.

I can also tell you about a concert I go to and I see janitors clean up after, and they find six pair of little girl's panties under a layer of jelly beans. And another time I see folks lined up for a block outside Barney's Beanery, it is past midnight and these people are standing in line to see an art exhibit.

Do you believe this? Not me, I don't.

Almost every day I see something like this I don't believe. I see people like Vito, who is a sculptor and a father-like figure for the teenyboppers and who also is the husband of the lady in the Gypsy Boots T-shirt. I see Kim Fowley, who is a singer and who does Mick Jagger type things with his fingers when he dances.

Others I see include Earl Leaf, who carries a camera everywhere and who is the world's oldest teenager, and Teri Garr, who is an actress and a dancer, in her Hollywood pad is a big poster from a 1930s movie and she likes to wear antique shades and a T-shirt that says "Chiquita Brand Bananas."

There is also Wallace Berman, who is a talented artist and who has worn his hair very long for almost 20 years now, and a pretty brunette lady she judges how happy she is by how many Top 40 record stars she balls the last month or so. Phil Spector is around, too, and so is 'Wild Man' Fisher, a songwriter who jumps up and down a lot.

Of course there are groovy people like Roger McGuinn and Zal Yanovsky. Roger is wearing those Byrd glasses so long now his eyes are rectangular, and Zolly is the fellow with The Lovin' Spoonful. His face is made of rubber and his feet when he is playing and singing they seem to be going off in different directions to leave the rest of him hanging there.

Places I see these people usually are the Trip, the Fred C. Dobbs', Canter's, Bido Lito's, Ben Frank's, and Barney's Beanery.

Sometimes I go to the Whisky A Go Go, which Time magazine might say is where the action WAS and which might be back 'in' any time now. Every now and then I stop in at the Fifth Estate to see a movie, or just go to Barry Friedman's pad, which is Barbara Burns's old place and is a small house with a sunken bathtub in the middle of the living room. Barry is a fire-eater with a circus when I meet him three years ago. Now he is producing records and organizing new groups.

If you will forgive me a moment I sound like Time magazine again, this is where it is happening and these are some of the people it is happening to. The important thing is the music and to dance. It is like the Peanuts cartoon that has Snoopy bouncing up and down and he says: "To dance is to live." To dance, and to stand around sharing secrets and digging each other.

Next few weeks I will tell you some true stories about these people. Oscar Levant, who is a hipster a little removed from this group, says you strip away the phony tinsel from Hollywood and you find the real tinsel underneath. I say you strip away the phony plastic and you find real vinyl.

A couple of nights ago I am with Artie Kornfeld, who is one of The Changin' Times. He comes out of The Trip and he looks up and down at things. He says to his partner Steve Duboff: "I get this feeling it is not real. I get this feeling somebody is going to say 'strike the set' and it will all disappear somehow."

Not a chance, Artie. There is another shipment due in from Japan day after tomorrow.

CHAPTER ONE

Going to a go go

"Discotheque music may be interpreted as the pulsebeat of today's youth. These social dances are a revolt against tradition and the restrictions of authority; resulting movements are expressions of youthful desires for freedom. Throughout the history of social dance, young social dancers have won the right to dance the 'in' dances of their day and to consider their versions the right ones. The discotheque dances of the 1960s are part of our American heritage and belong in a serious study of American social dance.**"** JOHN G. YOUMANS, SOCIAL DANCE

On Sunset Strip in 1965 and 1966, a thriving, celebratory scene appeared out of nowhere, exploded in a dazzling array of visceral creativity, and then, just as suddenly, vanished. So much incredible music, art, and social revolution came from one place in one time that it's difficult to grasp how it all happened so fast. The fruits of LA's teen megalopolis, and the remnants it left behind, transformed the mid 1960s Sunset Strip into a fascinating artistic Mecca. During this moment, something actually displaced movies as the center of action in Hollywood: rock'n'roll.

This new LA nightlife comprised a heady mix of modernist design, pop art, and beat aesthetics, interlaced with elements of rock'n'roll from the late 1940s to the mid 1960s. Teens could interact freely and creatively with budding youth icons in clubs that had previously been the exclusive domain of the rich and famous of the 1930s and 40s movie industry. Economics were now fluid, new ideas rampant, ephemera colored the atmosphere, and society itself seemed extremely changeable.

This was great news for Sunset Strip's artistic community, which began to collaborate with other forces: television, radio, independent cinema, and fresh forms of consumerism beginning to hit the newly minted teen market, symbiotically altering mass media in surprising ways. In 1964, the musical pendulum swung from New York City to this fresh, idealistic locale on the West Coast, with The Beach Boys, Phil Spector, Elvis Presley, and The Beatles—whose headquarters in the USA was the Capitol Tower on Vine Street—all having a base in Hollywood. (The sea change was confirmed when the influential music television show *American Bandstand* moved from Philadelphia to Los Angeles in March.) This environment would soon foster the rise of independent cinema through an auteur movement acclaimed as the 'New Hollywood' group of directors, among them Arthur Penn, Francis Ford Coppola, Martin Scorsese, and Stanley Kubrick.

"The striking thing about the folk-rock craze," the poet Allen Ginsberg wrote, "has been its miraculous spirituality and intelligence. We are perhaps in an impasse of racial history and spiritual evolution wherein, with electronic networks linking consciousness together, divine lyric statements do emerge from individual souls that move youthful hearts to an understanding deeper than hysteria. Miraculously, intentions and lyrics of popular music have evolved to include true poetics. The art form escapes from stereotype, cant, and hypocrisy and does touch the common experience we all thirst for."[1]

But across the span of three months, from November 1966 to January 1967, a series of curfews, crackdowns, and harassment by local authorities resulted in unrest, youth riots, and, ultimately, the closing of the clubs themselves. The strife between the Strip's patrons, city officials, the LAPD, and County Sheriffs culminated in confrontations on the street, effectively dismantling this vibrant hub of US culture.

The ensuing exodus afforded San Francisco the opportunity to assume the mantle at the center of the counterculture by mid 1967. Few will recall that LA is where Alan Pariser, Ben Shapiro, Lou Adler, John Phillips, and other frustrated Striplings organized the Summer Of Love's most significant event, the Monterey Pop Festival. Ben Shapiro set up office for the festival at 8428 Sunset, the original site of his jazz club, the Renaissance. It then metamorphosed into Stratford On Sunset, a British Invasion-styled club that featured mod-approved soul acts during the Strip's rock'n'roll heyday. But by mid 1967 the tudor-motif Stratford, known as the 'Castle On The Strip,' was just one of Sunset's many shuttered clubs.

Alan Pariser took on Monterey Pop as a project after the success of his first concert promotion, the CAFF Benefit. Community Action For Facts And Freedom held a show on February 22nd 1967 at the Valley Music Theatre as a final attempt to keep Sunset Strip open to youth culture. The CAFF Benefit featured The Byrds, Buffalo Springfield, The Doors, Hugh Masekela, Peter, Paul & Mary, and several speakers who gave credence to the new movement.

In the years preceding 1967, Sunset Strip had been the original setting for a counter-cultural epicenter. With its direct access to the international media, this 1.7-mile stretch of curvy LA highway defined social values and tastes for American youth and beyond, much as the arrival of motion pictures had decades earlier. The Beatles' stunning debut—and tremendous audience share—on *The Ed Sullivan Show* in February 1964 had upped the ante for rock'n'roll on television. Shortly thereafter, a wide range of music television shows started up in Los Angeles: *Shindig!*, *Where The Action Is*, *Shivaree*, and *Hollywood A Go Go* beamed rock'n'roll to television sets across the USA, and to many parts of the globe in syndication. LA kids could keep up with the local beat by tuning in to *Shebang*, *Groovy*, *Boss City* and *9th Street West* on hometown channels, while ABC's *The Hollywood Palace*—a West Coast addendum to Ed Sullivan's variety format—gave CBS a run for its money. These programs allowed artists of folk, blues, rhythm and blues, surf, garage, and various other strains of rock'n'roll an instant widespread audience.

On the Strip and areas outlying its centrifugal force, modernist architecture added a celestial feeling to the drive-in restaurants, underground theaters, and coffeehouses, not to mention more than 35 psychedelic/mod nightclubs catering to the scene. It was here that such groundbreaking bands as The Byrds, Love, The Seeds, The Standells, The Bobby Fuller Four, The Mothers Of Invention, Buffalo Springfield, and The Doors played regularly for an intimate, appreciative audience not only intent on dancing, but also hungry for sociopolitical change. These club-level bands were instantly heard on radio—and seen on television—as they radiated non-conformist ideals to youth culture.

Although the rest of the world may not quite have appreciated its cultural relevance, LA's peculiar historical and musical significance had long been in the works. Both country & western and rhythm & blues gained a strong foothold in Los Angeles by virtue of Oklahoma farmers' dust bowl migration to Southern California in the 1930s, and in South Central's jump-jazz scene of the 1940s. The saxophone-based rhythm & blues of Big Jay McNeely and hillbilly-bop of

The Maddox Brothers & Rose are but two examples of how LA helped to spawn rock'n'roll at its outset.

During the mid 1950s, rhythm & blues vocal groups in Los Angeles such as The Platters and The Penguins were second in number only to those in New York City, while rockabilly, shunned in Nashville, flourished within LA's country & western environment. The bohemian vendetta of West Coast jazz helped break the color lines of the LA Musicians' Union in 1953, and this integration soon followed into the nightclubs of Hollywood. By the early 1960s Los Angeles had a dizzying mix of music, as exemplified by the Ash Grove on Melrose Avenue. Opening on July 15th 1958, the all-ages club would book Bill Monroe & His Bluegrass Boys one week and John Lee Hooker the next. Ravi Shankar appeared at the club in 1965, only weeks apart from John Coltrane's performance at Shelly's Manne-Hole.

History has, for the most part, dealt the Sunset Strip of the mid 1960s a bad hand. Most commentaries focus on Hollywood's film culture, with many—including *Hollywood: The First One Hundred Years* and *Sunset Boulevard: America's Dream Street*—opting to dismiss the revolutionary music that emerged from the area as an unpleasant interruption. But by 1965, Sunset Strip had become the USA's last central outpost for rock'n'roll in its original, primitive, dance-worthy, and socially groundbreaking form.

As The Beatles emerged to become a global entertainment phenomenon, deserted showbiz nightclubs on the Strip became enclaves for enthusiastic kids forming bands. In mid 1964, hot on the heels of The Beatles, The Rolling Stones' single 'It's All Over Now' broke in San Bernardino, leading to their first trip to the USA and a raunchy appearance on *The Hollywood Palace*. That summer, the Stones' raw energy combined with Bob Dylan's acerbic protest songs, providing bands on the LA scene with a renewed sense of momentum, focus, and direction. After the Payola Scandal of the late 1950s, which culminated in the imprisonment of the influential disc jockey Alan Freed, the arresting sounds of Chuck Berry, Jerry Lee Lewis, and Little Richard all but disappeared from the airwaves. Here, at last, was rock'n'roll to believe in again.

"In the spring of 1965, The Byrds took to the air," Paul Jay Robbins wrote in the Monterey Pop Festival program. "Their launching pad was the Sunset Strip and their hymn sounded from the total collective consciousness of a new breed of people. The Strip, so long a tinsel turkey, had become a flaming phoenix and the light was seen around the world. … It has gone far from then and there, but those days and nights in 1965 were both crucible and catalyst for what followed, and who. We strolled the Strip as though it were the hallway of our common apartment house. We grew, our music grew; our elusive anthem delighted and inspired us."

As the Los Angeles music industry boomed in the three years following The Beatles' arrival in the USA, bands and promoters in San Francisco sought to catch up with their own audiences, drawing worldwide attention that culminated in a much-hyped 1967 Summer Of Love. In common histories, San Francisco is touted as the focus of mid to late 1960s American music, unjustly overshadowing the fact that LA's flourishing pop culture was responsible for originating many of the ideas that would later take hold in the Bay Area.

Take, for example, the formative psychedelic poster art of Rick Griffin, whose style was honed at *Surfer* magazine while Griffin was living in the South Bay area of Los Angeles. Another famous San Francisco poster artist, Stanley Mouse (from Michigan), developed his style working alongside LA illustrators Von Dutch, Ed 'Big Daddy' Roth, and Robert Williams. Ron Cobb of *The Los Angeles Free Press* is now considered the significant transitional link between the crazed comic book art of early-1950s *Mad* artists Harvey Kurtzman, Basil Wolverton, and Wally Wood and the quintessential San Francisco poster art of the Fillmore and Avalon Ballrooms.

When Kurtzman made an attempt to create a hip version of *Mad* called *Help!*, he chose a student from Birmingham High School in Los Angeles named Terry Gilliam as his associate editor. Gilliam studied art at Occidental College in LA and absorbed Sunset Strip culture while working at *Help!*. His talents were finally exposed to a larger audience from 1969 onward as the Californian member of the UK television comedy troupe Monty Python.

Los Angeles was ahead of the game at other important counterculture signposts. The gels and oil lamps projected on walls at psychedelic concerts rose out of the LA beat scene, as developed by Christopher Tree in 1959 at the Insomniac Cafe in Hermosa Beach. This spread in 1967 through Buddy Walters, who had been working with the West Coast Pop Art Experimental Band in LA during 1965–66. Walters took these light show effects on tour with The Animals and The Jimi Hendrix Experience, and to the Monterey Pop Festival; his visual innovations gained their legend from there.

Based on civil rights activities such as 'sit-in' demonstrations and 'teach-in's, Peter Bergman of Los Angeles comedy troupe The Firesign Theater coined the term 'love-in.' This arrived in reference to events such as the first Renaissance Pleasure Faire, which debuted in 1964 as a folk music event put on by LA underground radio station KPFK. Bergman also appeared on this radio outlet as part of the Elliot Mintz radio show *Head Shop*. After helping to form CAFF, Mintz went on to become the media representative for John Lennon and Yoko Ono. Elsewhere, the terms 'flower power' and 'flower children' were coined by LA garage-punk group The Seeds. Most significantly, the political fervor of folk-rock and the dynamics of psychedelia were both pioneered by The Byrds on Sunset Strip with 'Mr Tambourine Man' in 1965 and 'Eight Miles High' in 1966.

"There's a reason why it happened here in California rather than anyplace else," notes The Byrds' David Crosby. "This is the newest, been settled in the shortest period of time part of this country. And the newest part, frankly, ... of the civilized world, just about. It has almost no folkways and mores, it almost has no societal inertia, it has almost no weight of history. Therefore it can be shifted around in terms of conceptual changes, changes in value systems, changes in lifestyle; changes in, particularly, value systems. It can happen in a place like that far more easily than in a place where life has been rigidly structured for a very long time."[2]

Despite this, the legendary San Francisco scribes Jann Wenner of Rolling Stone and Ralph Gleason of *The San Francisco Chronicle* routinely dismissed things Los Angeles as "plastic." Gleason, on his PBS show *West Pole; An Essay Of The San Francisco Adult Rock Sound*, introduced the program with this offhand remark: "San Francisco is the city where rock'n'roll changed from teenage entertainment, where it grew up and became *music*."

For self-appointed rock pundits like Gleason and Wenner, most rock'n'roll preceding Haight-Ashbury psychedelia was deemed superficial and irrelevant, yet many performers on the 'Frisco scene had similar (albeit often hidden) LA roots. Janis Joplin's first residence in California—after migrating from Texas—was the Venice Beach beatnik environment of 1962, where she first smoked reefer and sang in coffeehouses. The Grateful Dead made a career move to Los Angeles in 1966 in order to hold acid tests and court Warner Brothers Records. In 1989, Frank Zappa neatly summarized San Francisco's snobbery toward LA:

"The scene in Los Angeles was far more bizarre. No matter how 'peace-love' the San Francisco bands might try to make themselves, they eventually had to come south to evil 'ol Hollywood to get a record deal."[3]

This Northern-Southern California discord is more explicitly illustrated in Ellen Sander's *Trips*: "It should be mentioned that San Francisco and LA have, for some strange reason, a heavy antagonism between them which was not overcome by the love movement. San Francisco is too smug and self-centered for LA; the worst implication you could put on something in or from San Francisco is to call it an LA trip. But when the hippies from Golden Gate Park got to the Strip, they found a scene freakier than their own. The Byrds had changed the street: celebrities, Mary Travers, Odetta dancing, starlets, writers, Michael J. Pollard, were all grooving. Dylan would often stop by and play with them. Those nights at Ciro's were the talk of both coasts' underground, and they hadn't even hit the road yet."

The aggressive nature of garage-punk was derived from the 1950s wild man archetype. In mid 1960s LA it ran parallel with the city's artistic community and its rampant attitude of political dissent. The Strip's situationist punk scene was in direct conflict with the passive, non-participation politics of Ken Kesey and The Merry Pranksters in San Francisco. "The visit (to the Artists' Tower Of Protest on Sunset Strip) by Kesey and The Merry Pranksters had mixed significance," says art historian Francis Frascina. "For many, they represented an oppositional drug culture, as did Dr Timothy Leary, who promised that the kids who had taken LSD would not fight any war or join any corporation. For others, Kesey, in converting thousands of young people to acid, began to undermine, if not destroy the organized political culture of the West Coast. The proselytizing of both Kesey and Leary was aimed at what they regarded as the traps of the old 'political games.' To the consternation of many, the influence of the drug culture, advocated by Kesey and Leary, began to deflect radicals from campaigns for civil rights, workers' rights, and the withdrawal of the United States from Vietnam. In the eyes of some theorists, Kesey and Leary's recommendations were of potential assistance to the state in its regulatory dissuasion of active and organized dissent. This view had been considered by RAND Corporation into its range of social controls."[4]

The sum total of the polarized north-south approach to societal change in California was best captured at the Teen-Age Fair, an event held annually at the Hollywood Palladium. Beginning at Pacific Ocean Park in 1962, the Fair's main draw was its 'Battle Of The Bands' and, curiously, the promotion of new commercial products for the youth market. On the surface, a gritty teenage rock'n'roll event—featuring local garage bands such as The Primadons, The Piranhas, The Vibrators, The Psy-Kicks, and The Racket Squad—twinned with the forces of big business could be perceived as a 'plastic trip' by outsiders. But that term could hardly be applied to the winner of the 1965 contest, Captain Beefheart & His Magic Band. This collision of rock'n'roll and commerce launched what we now call 'youth culture,' for better or for worse, as major companies began to target culturally savvy kids.

This was a relatively new phenomenon. Until the 1950s, teenagers were not a separate consumer market. It had taken corporations some time to court a culture that embraced something as foreign to them as rock'n'roll, but now sections of the adult population in big cities were in the throes of taking fashion and lifestyle cues from youth. In London, The Rolling Stones came up with a rhythm & blues theme for a Rice Krispies cereal ad that was instant pop art for television. A garage-punk band such as Paul Revere & The Raiders, meanwhile, would bring their own brand of cool to General Motors' television commercials for its new Pontiac Judge and Chevrolet Porcupine and SS 396 cars by the end of the decade.

This youth culture provided a valuable testing ground for new ideas and fresh approaches to marketing. Startup companies and their products were big attractions at the Teen-Age Fair: independent, youth-driven ventures proffered Hobie Surfboards, Yardley Of London's mod-look makeup, or Ed 'Big Daddy' Roth T-shirt and car designs. Backyard recreation items such as Wham-0's Frisbee, Slip 'n' Slide, Water Wiggle, or Superball—all of which offered a cheap, risqué thrill—mingled with wild new automotive hi-fi gear from Madman Muntz. Pre-teens could usurp the vibe at the Super Kids Circus at Pan Pacific Auditorium, where Mattel premiered Roth/Griffin-esque toys such as Creepy Crawlers, Incredible Edibles, and Thingmaker, with TV ads put together by Terry Gilliam. Pillsbury even pitched their Happy Face powdered drink range. These mavericks successfully forced major companies into the rock'n'roll frame of mind.

Pop culture itself was flowing into something—in the LA surf vernacular of the time—more 'righteous.' New York social observer Tom Wolfe covered the Teen-Age Fair in a short story for Esquire magazine, which then grew into his first book, *The Kandy-Colored Tangerine-Flake Streamlined Baby*. The Byrds, expanding on the folk movement, gave rock'n'roll a social consciousness that immediately spread to others. The corporate world soon realized that, in order to appeal to the US youth market, it would have to adopt, however superficially, the liberal values of rock'n'roll, which espoused racial mixing and uninhibited sexuality. With the civil rights movement in full swing, 'changing the world' for the better suddenly seemed very realistic.

In this environment, rock'n'roll culture formed into a powerful export commodity. Hollywood aligned itself with London as the Sunset Strip quickly fused with the cult of The Beatles and the explosion of pop art and mod fashion. The Byrds were touted by The Beatles as their favorite American group, and were a direct influence on the folksy sound of *Rubber Soul*. On the afternoon of August 24th 1965, The Beatles took their first voluntary acid trip with The Byrds and Peter Fonda at 2850 Benedict Canyon in Beverly Hills. (The group's first experience of the drug had come after their drinks were spiked at the home of a British dentist.) The Rolling Stones, meanwhile, recorded their landmark single '(I Can't Get No) Satisfaction' at RCA's Music Center Of The World on Sunset Boulevard, just blocks from a scene on which Brian Jones was not only a regular, but also a role model. The signature fuzz-tone of 'Satisfaction' would, within months, lead directly to the sound of garage-punk.

These alliances between Britain and Los Angeles took many more forms on the Strip scene. Them, Van Morrison's group from Belfast, Northern Ireland, found their single 'Gloria' banned in most of the United States for its provocative innuendo—"She comes up to my room/She makes me feel *all right*"– but LA radio stations played it freely. 'Eight Miles High' by The Byrds would also be dropped from national airplay in early 1966 based on the trade paper The *Gavin Report* claiming it was a drug song. Even 'God Only Knows' by The Beach Boys was banned in most radio markets for being 'blasphemous.' But Los Angeles radio stations ignored these 'recommendations' and all three records became tremendously popular on the local scene.

'Gloria'/'Baby Please Don't Go' was a double-sided smash in LA, topping the charts for several weeks on both KRLA's Tunedex and KFWB's Fabulous 40 Survey. Them's 18-night run at the Whisky A Go Go in May 1966 was unprecedented for an engagement by a group from the UK, and earned them a base of acceptance in the USA. (A live album drawn from the two-and-a-half week stand was mooted, but never emerged.) Following its exposure in LA, 'Gloria' became a garage band standard, and remains one of the signature songs of the decade. A cleaned-up version was recorded by The Shadows Of Knight, from Chicago, in 1966.

The Yardbirds' double-time rave-up style was copped by many of the best LA garage bands. Likewise, Yardbirds guitarist Jeff Beck found the city so seductive that he left the group to stay with Mary Hughes, an actress who featured prominently in ads for American International Pictures' beach party movies. And were it not for Brian Wilson's amiable rivalry with The Beatles, the interwoven grooves of *Pet Sounds*, *Revolver*, *Smile*, and *Sgt Pepper's Lonely Hearts Club Band* may never have been achieved.

By the fall of 1966, the revolutionary glee of Sunset Strip had begun to clash heavily with the town's conservative elements. There was a misbegotten property sale and a plan to build a 14-mile Laurel Canyon Freeway (Route 170) through the area. The plan never saw the light of the day, but still prompted LA County Supervisor Ernest E. Debs to take draconian measures against the Strip's nightlife. With the city of Beverly Hills fighting the overcrowding nature of Debs's plan every step of the way, he used militaristic tactics in an attempt to clear the Strip of its vibrant rock'n'roll culture and make room for skyscrapers that were never built.

With a convenient 10pm curfew to enforce, police brutality instigated youth picketing, which in turn led to mass arrests and a major riot on Saturday, November 12th 1966. The tactics of local authorities outraged parents: the LAPD and County Sheriffs handled these demonstrators in a way they felt the perpetrators of the previous year's Watts Riots should have been dealt with. In the months that followed, clubs such as the Trip and Pandora's Box were torn down, and the teen nightlife boom quickly faded. When the smoke cleared in early 1967, Hollywood was a very different town, and one where the throbbing pulse of a vital music scene had become difficult to find.

It took just a few months to dismantle the achievements that marked Sunset Strip among the major musical epicenters of the mid 1960s. The bands that did survive were, for the most part, cut off from the teenage nightclub thrill that had spawned their initial energy. Not even the smallest portion of the Strip would seem vital again until the emergence of the punk rock scene in the late 1970s, and even that brief eruption was cleared away in the 1980s to make way for a more corporate hard rock sound that could only have thrived during the Reagan era. The face of Sunset Strip has changed again from that nadir in recent years, but the emphasis remains with big money, well out of reach to organic, grass roots creativity.

What happened in the Los Angeles of 1965 and 1966 has given our world immeasurable color and contributed to much positive social change. For one fleeting moment, all of the progress made in the allied arts during the 20th century came to a head in one crystalline apex. The possibilities were boundless. In that specific epoch, bands on Sunset Strip stood for something—stopping wars before the hydrogen bomb kills us all; pursuing civil rights; defending the landscape; raising questions about the food we consume—all to a frantic dance beat in modernist nightclub settings. It's important to reflect on this, so that we may counter ignorance and ambivalence in the here and now.

CHAPTER TWO

That's the Hollywood nightlife

" *The Sunset Strip is the Via Veneto of Los Angeles, with wall-to-wall restaurants, nightclubs, taverns, and clubs.* **"** *VENTURE*, JUNE 1965

Like Route 66, Sunset Boulevard had existed for centuries as a Native American trail. The term 'Strip' was first applied to it early in the 20th century to identify the stretch of unincorporated land separating Hollywood from Beverly Hills. In the early years of the local film industry, a special mystique took hold near the intersection of Sunset and Crescent Heights where the Garden Of Allah apartment complex and the Chateau Marmont hotel were built.

The Garden Of Allah was commissioned in 1921 by the actress Alla Nazimova, and became home over the years to many celebrated figures, including the author F. Scott Fitzgerald; the Marmont was built in 1929 and modeled on the Château d'Amboise in the Loire Valley, France. Bordering the north and south side of Sunset Strip, these two structures could be perceived as a gateway of sorts to the promise and grandeur that lay in the hills just to the west.

In 1924, a pair of colonial-style buildings on either side of Sunset were commissioned by the landowner and entrepreneur Francis S. Montgomery Sr, the grandson of a French immigrant, Victor Ponet, who had relocated during the late 19th century period when impressionist painters were capturing California 'en plein air.' These two blocks of boutiques and restaurants became known as Sunset Plaza; one of the buildings later turned into the Strip's first top-rate nightclub, La Boheme, and was an instantly popular home of illicit drinking and gambling during the Prohibition era.

LA architecture and pop historian Jim Heimann notes that venues just outside of Los Angeles proper "thrived by offering the forbidden delight of public dancing along the coastline." As early as 1905, ballrooms such as the Ship, the Egyptian, the Bon Ton, the Venice, the Cinderella Roof Ballroom,

Danceland, the Three O'Clock, and the Sunset Inn opened in the cities of Santa Monica and Venice.

Around the same time, movers and shakers from New York City began to arrive in Los Angeles to exploit the booming movie industry. The best watering holes were opened in and around Culver City, adjacent to the MGM studio lot: Fatty Arbuckle's Plantation and Frank Sebastian's Cotton Club were hot spots in the 1920s. These were viable alternatives to the Alexandria Hotel, the original movie star hangout downtown. Inside the Ambassador Hotel on Wilshire Boulevard, the Cocoanut Grove set the gold standard in 1921, while across the street the Brown Derby restaurant captured the town's spirit of freewheeling, facetious humor by having a roof in the shape of the hat that provided its name.

After the repeal of Prohibition in 1933, the previously desolate Sunset Strip enjoyed a wave of renewed interest. Club Ballyhoo, billed "Hollywood's newest and smartest café," opened at 8373 Sunset. Nearby, the shortlived Club Seville housed a vast fish tank beneath the see-through dance floor of its Crystal Marine Room. The Centaur Cafe began operating out of a house just along the street, further solidifying Sunset Strip as the fashionable new place to drink spirits. The Strip gained momentum in 1934 when Billy Wilkerson, publisher of *The Hollywood Reporter*, bought La Boheme and transformed it into the Trocadero. Wilkerson reinforced the film industry by providing a comfortable place where thespians could mingle and pose for 'candid' glamour photographs, promotional exclusives that would then turn up in the *Reporter*.

In these early incarnations, Sunset Strip nightclubs were the exclusive domain of the movie industry and the very rich, who gathered to strike deals and woo investors. Landowners preferred to keep the area apart from the city of Los Angeles, intentionally leaving the region open to vice-related revenue. Two larger homes in the district became high-class gambling joints, known as the Clover and Colony Clubs; bootlegged liquor had gone hand in hand with organized crime and murder. Thirty years later, the marijuana, long hair, and LSD experiments of the 1960s would seem tame by comparison. According to the writer David Clark: "A great deal of indignation has been expressed lately over the youth influx on Sunset, with many complaints that the young people have ruined the 'traditionally high-class and genteel nature' of the area. Ralph Story's reply on his local morning television show was perfect. He offered a display of photos and news clippings showing what the Strip had really been like years ago. It seems that gangster Mickey Cohen once owned a haberdashery on Sunset, and it was often the scene of gangland wars. One overturned bus and a few demonstrations by the current youth crowd look fairly placid next to machine-gunned black limousines and crime czars lying bullet-riddled on the pavement."[1]

The darker side of these 'good old days' began to emerge when it was revealed that Chief Of Police James 'Two Gun' Davis and Earl Kynette of the Police Intelligence Unit had taken part in the fatal bombing of private investigator Harry Raymond's car on January 14th 1938. The incident had ties to Los Angeles Mayor Frank L. Shaw. Clifford Clinton, the owner of Clifton's Cafeteria downtown, had employed Raymond to expose the rampant corruption among the police and politicians of Los Angeles. The Mayor's brother, Joe Shaw, had been in charge of setting up the dirty work, handing out favors, and taking bribes. In an attempt to curtail the scrutiny, Clinton's own basement had been bombed out by mobsters on October 27th 1937, and telephone threats were made to his wife. Earl Kynette was convicted of the Harry Raymond bombing and sentenced to a prison term.

Reformers took this as a cue to rally public support and rid Hollywood of organized crime. In a special recall election, Frank L. Shaw was voted out of office and replaced by reform Mayor Fletcher Bowron, who stamped out gambling in the area. The 'respectable' criminals involved retreated to the Southern Nevada desert, where they built up a new 'Strip' all of their own in the quaint village of Las Vegas.

* * *

The transformation from Sunset Strip to Vegas took about ten years. Billy Wilkerson again led the way, opening Ciro's, the pinnacle of Hollywood nightlife splendor, in 1940. In January 1941, Felix Young and Charlie Morrison upped the competitive ante by opening the Mocambo, a plush room adjacent to Wilkerson's Trocadero with a Latin American vibe. A contemporary report described the Mocambo as "a cross between a somewhat decadent Imperial Rome, Salvador Dali, and a birdcage." The arrival of comic genius Preston Sturges's split-level nightclub/restaurant, Players, next door to Chateau Marmont shortly thereafter was the icing on the cake. The Trocadero, Ciro's, the Mocambo, and Players gave old-world sophistication a modern West Coast spin and displayed Sunset Strip as the epitome of early 20th century élan.

El Rancho Vegas and the Last Frontier, featuring old West gambler motifs, were the first large casinos in Southern Nevada on a strip of road once called the Los Angeles Highway. As glamour took precedence over gambling on Sunset Strip, a short-lived Colony Club was opened out in Las Vegas. The momentum picked up when Wilkerson—truly the innovator of both the Sunset and Vegas Strips—bought land on the Los Angeles Highway in 1945 to build the Flamingo Hotel, an expansion of his previous successes with the Trocadero and Ciro's in Hollywood. To pursue this new investment, Wilkerson sold Ciro's to Herman Hover, who managed the club during its legendary heyday.

Excitement on Sunset Boulevard was no longer confined to the Strip. Earl Carroll's Vanities opened near the southeast corner of Sunset and Vine in 1938, followed closely by the Hollywood Palladium across the street in 1942. The work, respectively, of local architects Gordon Kaufman and Frank Don Riha, these two venues were at the southern tip of a major center for restaurants and jazz that ran two blocks north to the corner of Hollywood & Vine. The area represented the peak of dreamland, Art Deco Hollywood.

Earl Carroll's Vanities featured the world's largest revolving stage, a 60-foot turntable braced on its outer lip by another 20-foot circular stage that could turn in the opposite direction. A huge neon image of the dancer Beryl Wallace was framed by Carroll's phrase: "Through these portals pass the most beautiful girls in the world." Back in New York City, Carroll had been in direct competition with Florenz Ziegfeld of *Follies* fame. Because Carroll paid a higher wage, his chorus line featured the best-looking women. His glamorous Hollywood venue became a spectacular showcase of hopeful ingénues and future starlets.

The Hollywood Palladium opened out of necessity. The Palomar Ballroom, famous as the 1930s jazz venue where Benny Goodman, Gene Krupa, and Anita O'Day popularized the swing craze, was destroyed by fire on October 2nd 1939. According to KKJZ disc jockey Chuck Cecil, the Palomar had also been known as the Patio and Rainbow Gardens in the years since it was built, in 1925, at Third Street and Vermont. *The Los Angles Times* financed the Hollywood Palladium in order to fill the Palomar's void, with bandleaders Tommy and Jimmy Dorsey— who had played a big part in breaking both Frank Sinatra and Elvis Presley— providing gala opening night entertainment.

Meanwhile, out in Las Vegas, a variety of distractions slowed down construction of Billy Wilkerson's Flamingo. In lieu of payment on Wilkerson's gambling debts, gangster Benjamin 'Bugsy' Siegel was dispatched to take over the operation and, as a result, was credited with 'creating' Las Vegas. But the futuristic glamour that made the Nevada town a hit clearly evoked the style of Wilkerson's previous Hollywood ventures. The Flamingo was soon followed by the Desert Inn, Sahara, Sands, Tropicana, and Stardust, all of which, in their original designs, followed the model Wilkerson had perfected on Sunset Strip. Siegel, on the other hand, quickly found himself in over his head financially and was murdered in Beverly Hills, allegedly on the order of his boss, Meyer Lansky.

Another prominent mobster, Mickey Cohen, was then assigned to the new Sunset Strip rackets of the 1940s and 50s: prostitution and nightclub extortion. The initial demand for the former was created by World War II soldiers on leave—the first large group of non-glitterati to show up on the Strip. Crime in Hollywood then began to take on an even sleazier face. Extortion rackets eventually made it difficult for the Mocambo and Ciro's to remain open. The non-fatal shooting of Cohen on June 19th 1949 took place at 9039 Sunset, then known as Sherry's. (It was later renamed Gazzarri's, while a different Sherry's opened up near the corner of Sunset and Crescent Heights.)

Back at Ciro's, Herman Hover had hired an excellent booking manager, George Schlatter, who would later produce the sensational television hit *Laugh In*. Hover and Schlatter turned Ciro's into a howling entertainment success. In its prime, the club was defined by its biggest draw, the comedy team Dean Martin and Jerry Lewis. Ciro's was also responsible, in part, for desegregating Hollywood. The Will Mastin Trio's 1951 opening slot for Janis Paige on Oscars night broke Sammy Davis Jr as a major star: he was called out for so many encores that Paige was never able to take the stage. Nat 'King' Cole also swooned Sunset Strip from the Ciro's stage in the 1950s en route to becoming one of the era's finest singers. But the seeds for racial integration had been planted years before all this in other parts of the town.

On Central Avenue, in South Central Los Angeles, two music genres prospered in the late 1940s: jump blues—epitomized by The King Cole Trio, Louis Jordan & His Tympani Five, Big Joe Turner, Roy Brown, Wynonie Harris, and Amos Milburn, as well as others who'd moved to Los Angeles—and jazz. Club Alabam and the Last Word sat across from one another, near the Downbeat. The interchange of musicians from both styles made for an intense scene (as covered in the CD/book set *Central Avenue Sounds: Jazz In Los Angeles 1921–1956*). These artists initially found it difficult to work outside of LA's black community. Then, in the early 1950s, the Johnny Otis Show began to showcase the rhythm & blues sound in venues such as the Shrine Exposition Hall and El Monte Legion Stadium. Otis introduced younger artists such as Etta James and Little Esther as well as rhythm & blues vocal groups including The Hollywood Flames and The Penguins. The songwriting team of Jerry Leiber and Mike Stoller emerged around the same time, helping to mark Los Angeles out as one of the true birthplaces of rock'n'roll.

Rockabilly, too, was more than welcome on Los Angeles-based country & western television programs such as Tex Ritter's *Ranch Party* on KTTV. Hillbilly shows also prospered in LA after the remarkable Saturday night success of *The Spade Cooley Show* on KTLA in 1948, followed by Cliffie Stone's *Hometown Jamboree* and KTTV's *Cal's Corral*, emceed by future television car salesman Cal Worthington. (Worthington later hired a rockabilly singer, Sammy Masters, to give voice to his theme song, 'Go See Cal.') KTLA added *Western Varieties* on Friday nights, as well as Gene Autry's *Melody Ranch*. KTTV's five-hour program from Compton, *Town Hall Party*, featured live half-hour sets by both Gene Vincent & The Blue Caps and Eddie Cochran & The Kelly Four. Nashville would never be as friendly to the new rockabilly sound that came in the aftermath of Elvis Presley & The Blue Moon Boys.

The most raucous homegrown personality of early 1950s Los Angeles was Big Jay McNeely, whose rhythm & blues sax workouts emerged from the shards of the 1940s scene on Central Avenue. Segregation—and fear—limited McNeely's formative brand of rock'n'roll to venues outside Hollywood, but he was a tremendous hit at El Monte Legion Stadium and toured nationwide. An appearance in Seattle during the late 1950s left an indelible impression on a young Jimi Hendrix, whose biographers, Harry Shapiro and Caesar Glebbeek, recall: "McNeely's act was a blueprint for the game plan that Jimi would use later on."

These left-of-center presentations—which, for McNeely, included performing at a drive-in promotional gig on roller skates, while wearing the cape from the movie *Quo Vadis*—did not come without trouble. Johnny Otis recalls how "the Los Angeles police hounded us in the early days. As the music grew in popularity, more white kids came to our dances, sometimes—God forbid—even dancing with black and Chicano teenagers. At first, the cops would stand around glaring at the kids and harassing them with bullshit questions, checking their IDs, and so on. This was damaging enough, but eventually they began to use ancient blue laws against us."[1]

The laws in question were Los Angeles Municipal Codes, drafted "to insure that teenagers were not exploited by commercial enterprise" (Section 103.118, July 11th 1950). Ordinance 5860 (effective February 27th 1959) prohibited "dancing in public eating places, if not accompanied by parent, guardian, or spouse," and Section 45.03a—dating back to 1875 and last amended in 1904—could impose youth curfews. Memos from the Board Of Police Commissioners show that such disciplinary action was synonymous with the emergence of rhythm & blues: "Due to numerous problems at teenage dances in the Los Angeles area prior to and during the year 1947, the Los Angeles County Juvenile Officers Association and the Metropolitan Welfare Council requested the Los Angeles Youth Committee to study the need of regulating teenage dances." Johnny Otis recalls police taking undue advantage of these laws to curb racial mixing: "These tactics completely disrupted our dances, and we were unable to continue promoting dances in Los Angeles." Because of these provincial hassles, the biggest rock'n'roll shows of the 1950s were all held at El Monte Legion Stadium, 13 miles to the east of Los Angeles proper.

* * *

The gilded age of 1930s and 40s Sunset Strip had not been conducive to musical excitement. Segregation had confined hot jazz and rhythm & blues to Club Alabam, the Last Word, and the Downbeat on Central Avenue, the Californian Club and the Oasis near Western Avenue, or downtown at the Million Dollar Theater and the 5/4 Ballroom. Covertly, rock'n'roll began seeping onto Sunset Boulevard in the 1950s through engagements by Louis Prima and Keely Smith with Sam Butera & The Witnesses. These shows were held at the Moulin Rouge, which replaced Earl Carroll's Vanities after Carroll's death in 1948.

Louis Prima was the biggest draw at the Moulin Rouge, but few of his audience knew he was performing the brash 1940s New Orleans sound dubbed rhythm & blues. He had been successful during the big-band era with a manic version of his 'Sing Sing Sing,' so the adult audiences jammed into the Moulin Rouge considered him to be a jazz act. Prima's jumpy rave-ups became the center of excitement in 1950s Hollywood. By this time, the Hollywood Palladium showcased the last gasps of the big-band era, which now meant the light-hearted dance orchestra of Lawrence Welk—a world apart from Charlie Barnet, Benny Goodman, or Count Basie with Lester Young at the Palomar Ballroom in the 1930s.

One of the key figures in the journey towards a fully integrated Hollywood night scene was the jazz vocalist Billy Eckstine. He subverted the booking policies of the time when he formed a silent partnership during the late 1940s with British actor Louis Hayward to open the Chanticlair, which gave black musicians a license to play on the Strip for the first time. This two-story hepcat joint and others like it played a major role in breaking down the local Musicians' Union segregation barriers.

The first step was when Eckstine invited the great jazz musician Charles Mingus to play bass in his band, which at the time featured 18 members—all of them white. Shortly thereafter, an amalgamation of musicians formed an interracial symphony orchestra. Rhythm & blues historian Tom Reed describes how "Marl Young, Benny Carter and others in the (black) Musicians' Union held meetings with the National Association for the Advancement of Colored People (NAACP), civic leaders, and Union officers." On January 14th 1953, after a long battle with the Unions' conservative elements, the all-white Musicians Local 47 was integrated with members of the black Local 767. The main black newspaper in the area, *The California Eagle*, celebrated with the headline 'Musicians Outlaw Jim Crow Union.' (The Jim Crow laws, which concerned racial segregation in public places, were enforced in a number of southern states between 1876 and 1964.)

While this integration took place, small jazz clubs were taking off in areas away from the Strip such as Mid-Wilshire. Boogie-woogie pianist and scat-man Harry 'The Hipster' Gibson turned on Billy Berg—the owner of Billy Berg's on Vine, just south of Sunset—to Charlie Parker and Dizzy Gillespie, while Chet Baker began sitting in with Gerry Mulligan at the Haig on Kenmore near the Wilshire Brown Derby and the Ambassador Hotel's Cocoanut Grove. (The Haig was owned by Richard Bock, who founded the Pacific Jazz label, and whose World Pacific studio was used early on by The Byrds among others.) Between sets, Baker would regularly appear with Charlie Parker a few blocks away at the Tiffany. Club Oasis made its own impact on Western Avenue by booking harder rhythm & blues acts such as Ruth Brown, Dinah Washington, The Treniers, and Cab Calloway.

In 1954, Billy Eckstine sold the Chanticlair to Gene Norman, who renamed the club Crescendo but retained its open door policy. Six years earlier, Norman had run the short-lived Hollywood Empire on Vine Street, at which, during its four-month existence, Louis Armstrong, Duke Ellington, and Louis Jordan all played to mixed audiences. With Norman at the helm, the Crescendo gained a high profile by emphasizing musical thrill over shallow ostentation of other Sunset Strip clubs. On the same evening, Lester Young or the Modern Jazz Quartet might be setting the pace for bebop at the street-level Crescendo, while Lord Buckley, Lenny Bruce, Mort Sahl, or Woody Allen stretched comic boundaries upstairs at the Interlude. (In 1958 the leading exponents of exotica, Les Baxter and Martin Denny, met for the first time at the Interlude.)

Located in the center of Sunset Strip, between La Cienega Boulevard and the Sunset Plaza, the Crescendo and Interlude began to shake up the environment. "Ciro's was down the street," Gene Norman recalls, "and that was more like a boutique club. It was mostly a place to get dressed up and go for a social evening. Next door to me was the Mocambo, which was the same thing. At the beginning, people would say 'Go to the Crescendo? Well, no (hoity toity) we'll go to the Mocambo.' They can have the snob appeal, I was trying to play to the people."

The difficulties with segregation were clearly apparent: police chief Edwin W. Parker made special efforts to bust white women for entering clubs where the entertainment and clientele were primarily black, and to separate interracial couples seated together. This did not go uncontested within entertainment circles: Marilyn Monroe persuaded Charlie Morrison, owner of the Mocambo, to allow Ella Fitzgerald to sing there by promising to sit in the front row for each performance. Thereafter, Morrison found performers such as Eartha Kitt indispensable to the Mocambo during the 1950s. This defiance then began to spread to the Las Vegas Strip, where Marlene Dietrich flouted the Flamingo's racism by entering the casino with Pearl Bailey and Lena Horne on each arm.

The high-profile integration of Hollywood nightlife presaged the 1954 Supreme Court decision to declare segregated schools unconstitutional. The bravery of various nightclub operators, musicians, and female movie stars in the face of LAPD and County Sheriff practices was later echoed in national civil rights events, such as when President Eisenhower called in units of the 101st Airborne Division for a daily convoy of jeeps, mounted with machine guns, to escort nine students to Little Rock Central High School in Arkansas during 1957, or when President Kennedy called in the Federalized National Guard to oppose Governor George Wallace and allow a black student, James Meredith, into the University of Alabama in 1963.

As alto sax man Buddy Colette points out: "That was before the civil rights law had ever been passed. So again, the musicians were ahead of a lot of the stuff that followed." The mixed musicianship of West Coast jazz eased the problems faced by interracial audiences in Hollywood nightclubs. Duke Ellington, Julie London, Ornette Coleman, Pérez Prado, Lionel Hampton & Illinois Jacquet, Dave Brubeck, and Billie Holiday now played regularly at jazz clubs throughout town. Sociologist and historian Mike Davis dubbed the Los Angeles of this period "the most integrated music scene in the United States."[3]

With segregation still rampant in film industry circles, movie glamour spots were beginning to fade fast on Sunset Strip. Ciro's closed its doors in December 1957 after Herman Hover ran into trouble with the IRS. When the Mocambo too ran into financial difficulties in 1959, Ben Shapiro, who was then working as Miles Davis's manager, seized the opportunity and reopened the building as the Renaissance. The original Renaissance—a split-level hillside home once owned by the Barrymore family across from Ciro's, featuring a basement painted by Venice beat/pop artist John Altoon—was, according to legend, shut down by police after a controversial appearance by Lenny Bruce. Now relocated to the shell of the old Mocambo, the Renaissance followed the Crescendo's lead, bringing the finest jazz to the Strip, including Miles Davis, John Coltrane, and Elvin Jones.

The venerable Garden Of Allah was on its last legs, but for a time it became a seedy crash pad for decadent jazz characters. "It had a bar on one side and a bandstand that faced a sunken dance floor," recalls the artist Frank Holmes. "Sliding glass doors were used to ventilate the dance floor, and opened up to a swimming pool that was all lit up with some palm trees and lawn chairs around it. Around that was a string of cabins that you could rent. It was pretty notorious." The record producer Kim Fowley adds that "all the actors wanted to go smoke opium at the Garden Of Allah … I was the lookout. So they march [in] and guess who has the shit? [Actor/screenwriter] Robert Benchley, the same guy who'd fallen into the Allah's Black Sea swimming pool with all of his clothes on … and after being fished out coined the phrase 'get me out of these wet clothes and into a dry Martini.' They went into his place and they all laid on the floor and smoked opium."

* * *

With West Coast jazz reaching dizzying heights in the 1950s, several coffeehouses opened in Hollywood. The Unicorn was a folksy, beat-poet place between Clark and Hilldale; then there was the Bit on the corner of Sunset and Gardner, which opened in 1959 with a performance by Les McCann; and Cosmo Alley opened in a brick-walled back room behind the Ivar Theater in downtown Hollywood. The bohemian Chez Paulette, across from the Mocambo and Crescendo, became a favorite of the new Hollywood rebel cult, including Marlon Brando, James Coburn, James Dean, and Maila Nurmi, then ubiquitous as television's first horror host, 'Vampira.' Suzanne Pleshette, Sally Kellerman, and Madeline Rue waited tables at Chez Paulette, where Barry Feinstein, who later took the fisheye-lens photograph used on the cover of The Byrds' *Mr Tambourine Man*, poured the joe.

James Dean, Maila Nurmi, and fellow actors John Gilmore and Jack Simmons were known as the 'Night Watch' on Sunset Strip. "Many of the all-night jams at Googie's, the bikes and stunts, were construed by reporters as crazy antics to shock and deride Hollywood," recalled Gilmore. "Jimmy [Dean] was reveling in the publicity, creating a language of physical and psychological impact, a dangerous image that radiated from the screen and tabloid papers."[4] A compelling 1957 documentary called *The James Dean Story* (which features graphics by David Stone Martin, a soundtrack by Chet Baker and Bud Shank, and film work by a young Robert Altman) shows Dean and his environment: Ciro's, the Melody Room, Googie's, Schwab's, Villa Capri, the Moulin Rouge, Wallich's Music City, the Fox Theater, and NBC's radio studio on the corner of Sunset and Vine. More footage from this period can be seen in the short *While The City Sleeps*, which catches some of the late 1950s' missing links: Wil Wright's Ice Cream Parlor, the Crescendo, and the Renaissance, with Miles Davis on the marquee.

The transition of Sunset Strip from elitist showplace to artistic center was almost complete. Modeling themselves on the Crescendo's success and mirroring its excitement, smaller places began to open on Sunset during the 1950s, among them the Summit, the Sea Witch, Pandora's Box, and the Purple Onion, which featured an invaluable exterior painting by Burt Shonberg, the proprietor of beat hangout Café Frankenstein in Laguna Beach. For one engagement, Purple Onion manager Ray Klein commandeered a teenage Kim Fowley as an 'escort' to make sure that Thelonious Monk would not get lost between sets on runs for booze, dope, and women. Fowley recalls the decor inside the Purple Onion: "It was adobe chic and very dark inside, with lamps, stupid lamps, like Tennessee Williams's glass menagerie, and adobe pastiche everywhere. All the white guys had horn-rimmed glasses, all the women had no tits and hairy armpits, and there's me with pimples."

It made a refreshing change to see that Sunset Strip now harbored a beat scene to rival the one thriving out in Venice Beach. By the time the 1950s rolled around, this slowly crumbling seaside knockoff of Italian culture envisioned by Abbot Kinney in 1905 had become just the right setting for a low-rent art community. As documented in Lawrence Lipton's 1959 book *The Holy Barbarians*, the action centered around an espresso bar called Venice West (which remained open until 1966) and the Gas House, which was chased down by local authorities in 1960 despite support from 1920s film stars including Stan Laurel and Groucho Marx.

The principals had been painters: John Altoon, Wallace Berman, Ben Talbert, Mike Angeleno, Fowad Magdalani, and Tony Landreau. Gas House proprietors Al Mathews and artist Eric 'Big Daddy' Nord played host to the poetry of John Thomas, Frankie Rios, James Ryan Morris, Charles Foster, Alexander Trocchi, Tony Scibella, and Stuart Perkoff, who also made a hilarious appearance on Groucho Marx's game show *You Bet Your Life*. Jimmy Alonzi tinkered with light shows, Julie Meredith sang folk songs, and there was in-house sculpting by Tati. Just before the opening of Venice West, Perkoff scrawled Wallace Berman's equation "art is love is God" on the main wall, providing the proper operative vibe. Trocchi's *Cain's Book* and Perkoff's *The Suicide Room* were among the few published books to have come from this group of beats; their work primarily appeared in magazines and broadsides. A posthumous anthology of Stuart Perkoff, *Voices Of The Lady: Collected Poems*, was finally published in 1998, and contains previously unpublished 1950s and 60s works such as *The Venice Poems* and *Round About Midnite*.

In among all this was the Lighthouse in Hermosa Beach, home to Howard Rumsey's Lighthouse All-Stars, a defining crew of West Coast jazzmen who had split from the Stan Kenton band. Aware of the value of keeping the next generation involved and interested, the Lighthouse had a special section for younger listeners. Across the street, the Insomniac cafe and bookstore offered various alternatives to jazz, including folk. Van Dyke Parks played acoustic sets there, while Frank Holmes—who later provided the cover art for The Beach Boys' unreleased *Smile* album—mixed the coffee.

Sean Bonniwell, who played there as part of the folk combo The Wayfarers before forming The Music Machine, recalls: "There was 24-hour entertainment … someone was on the Insomniac stage every one of those hours. Sonny Terry & Brownie McGhee, Howlin' Wolf, Bill Cosby, The Smothers Brothers, Eden

Ahbez, mimes, acrobats, and anyone else who would show their ass for a quarter. It was vaudeville, but it was crazy. It was said by all who played there, if you could survive the Insomniac, you could survive show business."

Folk clubs, such as the New Balladeer and Ledbetters in Westwood, were beginning to prosper. The Troubadour opened originally on La Cienega Boulevard in the 1950s, next door to the Coronet Theatre, a meeting ground for people who were curious about movies beyond the Hollywood mainstream. This was the place to be introduced to underground European Cinema, or catch a screening of an early Kenneth Anger film, and also featured readings by leading authors such as Aldous Huxley and Gerald Heard. The Ferus Gallery and Warner Playhouse were nearby on La Cienega, as were the jazz joints Losers and El Toril. The intensity level increased when Gazzarri's, Jack Martin's AM-PM Discotheque, and the Hole In The Wall boutique opened in the early 1960s, along with a profusion of art galleries, including Ed Kienholz's Now Gallery.

Although the Troubadour was born into this environment, the Ash Grove on Melrose wound up being the most down-to-earth place in town. The key element was that it had no age limit—kids of 14 and up were admitted to hear a range of artists from topical singer Pete Seeger to blues legend Lightnin' Hopkins. The folk music boom in the early 1960s took in acoustic blues as well as protest songs, fostering a sense of rebellion akin to that of 1950s rock'n'roll. Ash Grove attendees were the beneficiaries of the care that went into making a great club. "Although the Ash Grove is nominally a place for entertainment," notes John Cohen in *Sing Out!* magazine, "it has more often taken a role somewhere between a community cultural center and a university extension course. There were traditional jazz nights, a film series, modern dance programs, an art gallery, a book and record store, and flamenco concerts." Ash Grove proprietor Ed Pearl adds: "The keynote for me is love and respect for the music and people, rather than pure entertainment, or escape, or being impressive. In other words, one can lose oneself in music and people here, and have as much of a total experience as possible."[5]

Thus far, attention to rock'n'roll in Hollywood had been minimal, and its beat almost impossible to find live and in person. During the early 1950s, KPOP disc jockey Art Laboe started holding live radio broadcasts from Scrivner's drive-in at the northwest corner of Sunset and Cahuenga. His shows were infused with the sprit of a new music that was taking the country by storm, making teenagers dance and their parents nervous. Chuck Berry, Jackie Wilson, Little Richard, and many others showed up for interviews, drawing crowds of fans to the parking lot, desperately waiting to catch a glimpse of their idols. Laboe's show became the most popular in LA radio history, and a valuable promotional tool for its presenter's live shows at El Monte Legion Stadium.

The Strip's major nightclubs were still deep in the Hollywood glamour era and as such were no place—yet—for these rockin' teens. But there were a few exceptions: Elvis Presley & The Blue Moon Boys headlined at Hollywood's futuristic Pan Pacific Auditorium, described by the author Sam Hall Kaplan as "having four flagpole pylons shaped like giant fins," which "hinted at speed and energy."[6]

Presley's half-hour set shook tinseltown. Capitol Records soon discovered Gene Vincent and the flamboyant shouter Esquerita—a key influence on Little Richard—and put them on its roster. Liberty Records was quick to sign Eddie Cochran & The Kelly Four, and arranged a gig a block away from Scrivner's at Jimmie Maddin's jazz club (formerly the Summit). "Cochran had his own little group that he brought in," recalled Maddin. "It was on a Sunday afternoon, and KRLA was a partner in the deal. They called it KRLA Hop, and they brought a different deejay in there each Sunday. I was recording for Liberty at the time, which made the Cochran booking easier. KRLA Hop was there four or five months, it was a great promotion, they did great business, made money."[7] As the Red Velvet, this same room remained a fixture well into the mid 1960s.

The first nightclub on the Strip itself regularly to feature rock'n'roll acts was the Sea Witch, which became a consistent hangout for Eddie Cochran and his songwriting girlfriend, Sharon Sheely. The nascent scene also featured Texan rockabilly singer Jett Powers, who released three singles—'Go Go Girl,' 'Teen Age Quarrel,' and 'Loud Perfume,' all of which feature on the retrospective compilation *California License*—before reinventing himself as P.J. Proby. During the late 1950s and early 60s, he made a living by recording publishing demos for Liberty Records, and many of these songs ended up as Elvis Presley album tracks. Powers also played in a Sea Witch house band that included among its members future Canned Heat bassist Larry Taylor, eventual Mothers Of Invention guitarist Elliot Ingber, former Teddy Bear Marshall Leib, and lead guitarist Derry Weaver, who later added his signature riffs to The Beach Boys' 1962 version of 'Moon Dawg.'

Del-Fi recording artist Larry 'Mojo Workout' Bright was another steady

Sea Witch performer, and so too during 1957–9 were Wesley Reynolds & The House Rockers. The songwriter Baker Knight, who wrote Ricky Nelson's 'Lonesome Town,' also turned up for gigs from time to time. In 1960 and 1961, the instrumental house band Gerry McGee & The Cajuns took over. The Cajuns later released a dual-artist swamp-pop 45 on Sage Records, backing Jackie DeShannon—who they had previously performed with at the club—on the flip side, 'Just Another Lie.'

"The place was packed, lined up around the block," remembered Gerry McGee. "Lot of celebrities, actresses would come in there and stuff, it was a jumpin' place." The Enchanters' 'Café Bohemia' on Orbit (later included on the *Jungle Exotica* compilation) was a pure Sea Witch environment disc. "The first record I made was with Richard Clasky," says Sea Witch stalwart Larry Taylor. "He did a record called 'Image Of A Girl' with a group called The Safaris, sort of like [The Teddy Bears'] 'To Know Him Is To Love Him,' but real crude. We did ['Cafe Bohemia'] in his house and we used the shower as an echo chamber."

LA's early rock'n'roll community was still very small. The majority of the gang could be found on La Cienega Boulevard at the original Smokey Joe's Cafe, later immortalized in a Leiber & Stoller hit sung by The Coasters. Beat-jazz, folk, and rock'n'roll audiences were only just beginning to mingle and interact on Sunset Strip. Nestled between the original location of the Renaissance and Pandora's Box, the Fifth Estate coffeehouse sat on property owned by Petersen, publishers of *Hot Rod*, *Teen*, *Surfing*, and other youth-oriented magazines. Legendary jazz photographer William Claxton was an art director and advisor for Petersen at the time. "There was a room in the back for folk-singing," recalls scene regular Hammond Guthrie, "and another housed a small art gallery. The main salon had an espresso machine and a diverse lending library with a small fireplace, off which was a cinema room where silent European films were shown. The clientele at the Fifth Estate was a much more eclectic group than the frenetic crowd over at Fred C. Dobbs's … the Fifth Estate was far and away the hippest scene I'd encountered."

The Fifth Estate's beat ambiance nurtured the birth of the independent *Los Angeles Free Press*, which had an office in the coffeehouse's basement. Published by Art Kunkin, the *Free Press* started out as the program for the inaugural Renaissance Pleasure Faire, a folk music event held in 1964. Lawrence Lipton of Venice West became a steady contributor to the *Free Press*, along with new, hip writers such as Paul Jay Robbins and Jerry Hopkins.

Jazz flourished in this environment. By the early 1960s, basketball star Wilt Chamberlain and deejay Tommy Smalls opened Basin Street West, where many jazz live albums were subsequently recorded. Shelly's Manne-Hole, on Cahuenga near Hollywood Boulevard, opened in 1960 and became LA's leading jazz venue. Formerly the Lamp, it was run by the well-respected drummer Shelly Manne, whose status in the jazz world drew various legendary performers to sit in from time to time with the house band. Wes Montgomery performed there around the time of 'Bumpin' On Sunset,' his 1966 tribute to the Strip, and it was also where Sergio Mendes first got it going with Brasil '65. A contemporary report in *Venture* magazine notes that: "For jazz buffs, Shelly's Manne-Hole in Hollywood, where only beer and wine are served, works on a rotating band policy: Shelly's own group plays a couple of nights a week, visiting combos move in on other nights. Some of the greatest modern jazz played anywhere can be heard here."[8]

In 1962 Steve Allen produced a television show called *Jazz Scene USA*, on which the Shelly's Manne-Hole logo could be seen behind host Oscar Brown Jr. Exquisitely shot by future *TAMI Show* director Steve Binder, *Jazz Scene USA* was actually taped live in a studio, but was designed to give the audience an impression that concerts were being transmitted directly from the Manne-Hole. The show opened and closed with a montage of LA venues, including a couple recently set up by two prominent members of the Martini set, Dean Martin and Jerry Lewis. No longer a performing duo, they launched competing supper clubs on Sunset Strip, Dino's Lodge and Jerry Lewis' Restaurant. The Ad Lib Room opened on May 3rd 1965 with Jack Costanzo running a Wednesday Latin night and Red Norvo regularly filling the room with vibraphone sounds, while Redd Foxx opened the popular Jazz Go Go club in South Central, showcasing top black comedians as well as jazz and naked ladies.

Plush burlesque joints began to crop up all over Sunset Strip, with the Classic Cat, the Largo, Seventh Veil, and Body Shop adding a lascivious edge to the area. In 1964, the Largo was notable for the topless waitresses employed in its upstairs restaurant, the Phone Booth (itself inspired by the Condor Club in San Francisco's North Beach). That year's topless craze reached its crest with William Claxton's exquisite photo of his wife, Peggy Moffitt, modeling Rudi Gernreich's famed topless bathing suit. By 1966, Losers', a legit jazz club on La Cienega Boulevard, would be advertising a 'topless LSD review,' thereby cashing in on two Strip fads at once.

This diverse array of entertainment did not resonate well with the Hollywood establishment, which was confounded by the disappearance of silky, showbiz performers. "The big billboard in front of Chateau Marmont, at the entrance to Sunset Strip, was taken over by the Sahara Hotel in Las Vegas in the late 1950s," according to historian Marc Wanamaker. "It was a sign that the Strip was on its way out, coinciding with the end of the studio system and the old Hollywood era." For the narrow, bourgeois elite, the writing was on the wall. "There was definitely a feeling of death on the Strip," adds pop vocalist Andy Williams. "Las Vegas had set a salary standard for new talent that the nightclubs could not come near matching. Rock'n'roll was coming in big. It was the end of the era of small, intimate clubs. Things had changed to people performing in large palaces, or in very small rooms, doing dinner theater."[9]

The proliferation of the beat scene and black performers on Sunset Strip had stirred the reactionary perspective of LA County Supervisor Ernest E. Debs, who had begun to concoct a master plan for the area in the late 1950s. Deciding that jazz was 'depressing' the area, Debs hoped that property values would drop and allow major corporations to pick up the land cheaply. Positioned adjacent to the moneyed Beverly Hills region, the Strip seemed to Debs a natural location for the construction of a new financial district. He proposed the building of a new Laurel Canyon Freeway (Route 170) to bring commuters into the area. Among the initial investors were the 9000 Building and Continental Bank, which built a ten-story tower between La Cienega and Sunset Plaza in 1963. Within six months, however, it had been sold on to Playboy Inc, becoming both the magazine's West Coast base of operations and a Playboy Club. Things were not going to plan.

Although a lot of old money seemed to have fled to Las Vegas, Sunset Strip was now home to exciting creativity and a nightclubbing boom, all taking place right under the nose of the establishment. The Strip had already entered the annals of pop history when Edd 'Kookie' Byrnes took the role of a hep-talkin' parking lot attendant at Dino's Lodge in the ABC television hit *77 Sunset Strip*. (The address of Dean Martin's lounge-restaurant was, in fact, 8524 Sunset Boulevard, but that proved less easy to snap your fingers to.) Produced by Warner Bros, the show ran for six seasons from 1958–1964, feeding the cascading aura of Hollywood nightlife—albeit in a somewhat watered-down form—into the national consciousness. But despite Byrnes's teen appeal and that of the rockabilly crowd at the Sea Witch, the youth-orientated sounds of rock'n'roll remained a minor blip on the Hollywood radar, the focus of which remained on bebop-jazz, beat idealists, swingers, folkies, and burlesque raunch.

When the twist craze broke at the Peppermint Lounge in Manhattan, both Chubby Checker and Joey Dee & The Starliters successfully negotiated stints at the Crescendo. Hollywood club owners felt compelled to keep up with New York high society, and in doing so allowed rock'n'roll to sneak into the nerve center of Los Angeles. Between 1962–1964, house band covers of rhythm & blues standards—'What'd I Say,' 'Louie Louie,' 'Money,' 'Shout,' and the rest— were dependable dance floor favorites. The emphasis on new, twist-orientated clubs such as the Peppermint West and PJ's provided a venue for the latest dance sensations. Closer to home, musicians in the outlying areas of LA had been devising their own indigenous forms of rock'n'roll: jump and vocal group rhythm & blues from South Central, the reverbed guitar sounds of surf instrumental bands from the South Bay and Orange County, and hard-edged garage-soul by East LA Chicano outfits. These styles were adopted by Hollywood house bands, who left a legacy of wild surf/soul performances of well-worn rock'n'roll standards on disc.

One surprising result of this new scene was that singing cowboy film star Gene Autry, the owner of the Los Angeles Angels, felt compelled to move the baseball club to the much safer confines of Anaheim in 1966, partly to keep his players away from the Hollywood nightlife. Prior to that, the sportsmen were constantly out on the Strip; one, no-hitter sensation Bo Belinsky, was regularly to be found shacked up with a cast of buxom teen movie starlets such as Mamie Van Doren, Ann-Margret, and Tina Louise at the Continental West Hotel (which, in a strange twist, was also owned by Gene Autry).

Shows featuring the groundbreaking rock'n'rollers of the time were still taboo and took place in areas outside of Los Angeles. KRLA deejay Bob Eubanks, a crafty promoter in his early days, opened two clubs called the Cinnamon Cinder in the nearby townships of Studio City and Long Beach. "It was because of the Cinnamon Cinder that we got The Beatles," Eubanks points out, "because we were buying talent from the agencies at the time. When the major concert promoter in town, Lou Robin, turned The Beatles down, they came to me. Robin had been used to getting Frank Sinatra or Ella Fitzgerald for $10,000 and here come The Beatles asking for $25,000. Because of my work in radio, I knew what was going on. So I hocked my house and we did the Hollywood Bowl." The pompous Hollywood establishment was about to crumble. By showcasing major acts heard on rock'n'roll radio stations, the Cinnamon Cinder provided fierce competition to Hollywood nightclubs, which were offering nothing more than solid cover bands.

A reaction was inevitable. The young thespian crowd of Hollywood had been content to dance to the light social-consciousness of Trini Lopez, who had a huge hit in 1963 with his cover of The Weavers' 'If I Had A Hammer.' Lopez was a regular performer at PJ's, the most popular twist club in town, located two blocks south of the Strip on Santa Monica Boulevard and described by *Venture* as "another 'in' spot that swings virtually through the night." Lopez's best-selling LP *Trini Lopez Live At PJ's* kicked off that rash of albums recorded at local clubs, including three more cut at PJ's by The Standells, The Bobby Fuller Four, and The Sin Say Shuns. Sid & Marty Krofft also got their break at the club before becoming a hit at the New York World's Fair and on *The Ed Sullivan Show*, and then with their psychedelic children's shows *H.R. Pufnstuf*, *Lidsville*, and *The Bugaloos* in the early 1970s. At PJ's, "starlets on their way up, young actors of the Method school and the younger echelons of the television and movie industry jam its front and back rooms to talk and drink and lend an ear to such jazz combos as that of Eddie Cano. They all seem to know each other, and the casual visitor may feel a bit out of it. But they're fun to watch."[10]

The most famous house band album was by an Italian kid from Baton Rouge, Louisiana, born John Henry Ramistella. After recording his 1957 debut single, 'Little Girl,' at Cosimo Matassa's legendary J&M Recording Studio in New Orleans—where Roy Brown, Big Joe Turner, Fats Domino, and others all cut groundbreaking records—Ramistella changed his name to Johnny Rivers at the suggestion of the New York deejay Alan Freed, the man who coined the phrase 'rock'n'roll.' A succession of edgy Rivers singles followed, and Ricky Nelson covered 'I'll Make Believe' in 1961. (Rivers was drawn to the Strip's rockabilly crowd through his friendship with Nelson's guitarist, James Burton.)

In 1963 at Capitol Records, Rivers recorded 'Double C—Cinnamon Cinder,' a tribute to the club that got the teenage nightclub craze rolling. His first gig of note came that year at a small club on the northwest corner of La Cienega Boulevard at Beverly, called Gazzarri's. He'd started there with the same format that brought Trini Lopez success at PJ's: guitar and vocal, backed only by drummer Eddie Rubin. At this point, Gazzarri's was similar to—but not quite as popular as—PJ's and Peppermint West. Rivers began to attract large crowds with an approach that was more tuned to rock'n'roll music than Lopez. Rivers asked Bill Gazzarri, the club's owner, if he could hire a bassist to fill out his sound, but Gazzarri was reticent to stump up the extra cash. As a result, a frustrated Rivers accepted an offer from Elmer Valentine, who was looking to open a twist club of his own.

* * *

"For the uninitiated, 'discotheque,' a French word for record library, is a place where people go to dance the jerk, twine, monkey, swim, frug, watusi, and so on and so forth. There is no 'live' music, rather a record spinner selects popular tunes of the day in accordance with the varying moods of the dancers."—Liner notes to *Latin Au Go Go* by Orquesta Joe Cain.

In 1947, Compton MacKenzie published *Whisky Galore*, a novel about a freighter carrying 10,000 cases of whisky wrecked near a drink-starved island during World War II. Two years later the British director Alexander Mackendrick turned it into a movie of the same name; renamed *Tight Little Island* in the USA, the film was also dubbed into French, for which it was given the title *Whisky A Go Go* ('à go go' translates literally as 'in abundance'). A comedy classic, it inspired the name of a bar in Juan-les-Pins, near Cannes, which became one of the first discotheques. This first Whisky A Go Go was apparently modeled on the Ginza club in New York City, which pioneered the concept of girls dancing freestyle on an elevated platform in full view of the dance floor.

On a trip to the Cannes Film Festival, Elmer Valentine, the manager of PJ's, paid a visit to the club and saw girls dancing in cages. On his return to LA, he and his business partners opened their own Whisky on Sunset Strip (with the blessing of the Juan-les-Pins club's owners). The Hollywood take on the club was located on the edge of the Strip, just before Beverly Hills, where there were only a handful of other music venues at the time. One was a beatnik-folk club called the Unicorn, run by Herb Cohen—soon to become Frank Zappa's manager—who also owned a coffeehouse in a backstreet near Hollywood and Vine called Cosmo Alley. The nearby Melody Room was a regular lowbrow haunt for actors Jackie Coogan and Caesar Romero—then best known for their roles as Uncle Fester and The Joker—and featured performances by lounge acts such as Esquivel and The Bobby Troup Trio, and early rhythm & blues combo Billy Ward & The Dominoes. The Classic Cat and the Largo were also close by, but the area was best known for its posh restaurants: *Dragnet's* Jack Webb hung out at the Cock'n'Bull, Glen Campbell and

Bobby Darin could often by found in the various bistros, and Marilyn Monroe had met Joe DiMaggio on a blind date at Villa Nova Italian Cuisine.

The Whisky A Go Go made its debut on Sunset Strip on January 11th 1964 and was an immediate success. British disc jockey Jimmy Saville, the host of the television chart show *Top Of The Pops*, came over to cover the event for the BBC, while on March 20th *Time* magazine ran a Julian Wasser photo alongside a story about the new discotheque craze. A live album from the club, *Johnny Rivers At The Whisky A Go Go*, popularized both the venue and the singer, who had hits with covers of Chuck Berry's 'Memphis' and 'Maybellene.'

The Sea Witch might have featured rock'n'roll earlier, but its success was much more localized. With the Whisky A Go Go, excitement centered on the fact that this was a full-time, high profile rock'n'roll venue at which all were welcome, and that it was kicking off a major trend dubbed 'Go Go' dancing by *Time* magazine. Four of Johnny Rivers's first six albums exploited the fact that they were recorded at Whisky A Go Go, the best of them being *Recorded Live (And Then Some)! Johnny Rivers ... And I Know You Wanna Dance*, and international acclaim came to both Rivers and the club. According to *Playboy* magazine: "Los Angeles has emerged with the biggest and brassiest of the discos—Whisky A Go Go, a frenetic watering hole inspired by its more docile Parisian namesake. Two short-skirted maidens demonstrate the latest dance in a nine-foot-square glass-enclosed booth dangling 30 feet above the floor. When the live musicians take five, the girls convert the place into a true discotheque, playing record requests made from strategically located floor telephones on a $35,000 stereophonic sound system."[11]

When Rivers took to the road, former Sun Records artist Billy Lee Riley filled in at Whisky A Go Go. Riley is best known for 'Flying Saucers Rock'n'Roll' and 'Red Hot,' recorded alongside His Little Green Men, and was next to cut a live album at the club. A promo film of Riley's churning take on Tommy Tucker's 'Hi-Heel Sneakers' captures the smoky, sweaty, dance bohemia that had now become part of the Hollywood fabric. *Otis Redding In Person At The Whisky A Go Go* was later cut at the club and is now considered its most important live document, but in 1964 the main attraction was an attractive female deejay in a slit-skirt dress, spinning an abrasive set of rhythm & blues from a specially constructed platform above the stage.

That girl was Patty Brockhurst, who played records from a cage-like veranda high above the dance floor on Whisky A Go Go's opening night. Once the records were spinning, she was inspired to dance, unprompted, strictly because she dug the sounds. From her perch, the impact of this visual enticement stirred the Hollywood audience. The records she played were far more riveting than the fare at nearby burlesque houses. Because the Whisky A Go Go had been designed in the mode of a French discotheque, the sexual element fitted in naturally as a teenage rock'n'roll version of Les Folies Bergère.

This was a completely unintentional phenomenon. Brockhurst's cool was contagious; the patrons of the Whisky enjoyed a child-like feeling that they were getting away with something 'even hotter' than those at other places on the Strip. This, in turn, blew away any remaining Hollywood inhibitions and unleashed the true wildness of rock'n'roll. Go Go proprietors Shelly Davis and Elmer Valentine quickly noted this, installing more cages and hiring two more girls to maintain the momentum. One of these new recruits, Joanie Labine, designed the outfit that became the trademark for an instant, international phenomenon: the go-go girl. Her white dress with bare midriff and fringing was copied throughout popular culture for the next few years.

Go Go nightclubs were soon springing up all over the planet, with Whisky franchises opening in New York, San Francisco, Chicago, and even Hong Kong, while movies and television variety shows adopted the Go Go motif until the end of the decade. As Frank Zappa recalled: "During this period in American Musical History, anything with 'Go Go' pasted on the end of it was *really hot*. All you were required to do, if you were a musician desiring steady work, was to grind your way through five sets per night of loud rhythm tracks, while girls with fringed costumes did the twist."[12]

Joel Hill Scott of The Strangers (later The Joel Scott Hill III), who had been cutting rockabilly records since 1960—among them 'Caterpillar Crawl' and 'Sticks'n'Stones'—adds: "We were lucky enough to land a residency at a new club on Santa Monica Boulevard called the Action. It opened with a great flourish—loads of publicity and capacity audiences … and that was when Hollywood, especially Sunset Strip, was just beginning to change from its old cocktail lounge image to a more rock'n'roll-oriented scene. We got a good thing going at the Action, because we knew so many of the local musicians, and they were always coming along to jam with us. We were resident there for a while, making good money—and on our night off, every Monday, they'd put on this other group called The Mothers—with Frank Zappa and Henry Vestine."

Places like Jack Martin's AM-PM on La Cienega opened up during this rolling nightclub trend to meet the demand created by the Whisky A Go Go. An album, *The Regents Live At The AM-PM Discotheque*, was released on Capitol Records by the club's house band, who would later nail the same job at It's Boss (and were not the same Regents of 'Barbara Ann' fame). "That was a common part of the strategy in opening a new club in Hollywood," says the LP's producer, David Axelrod. "We recorded that album on a remote [studio]. You'd have all these expensive restaurants on La Cienega, and then there'd be this rock'n'roll club. Jack Martin's AM-PM was the kind of place where you could order steak sandwiches, and a fistfight would break out every ten minutes. A lot of tough guys went there, so it didn't last very long."

* * *

The area of Sunset Strip surrounding the Whisky A Go Go soon became a new center for rock'n'roll nightlife in Los Angeles. A new Gazzarri's opened nearby in June 1965; the old one on La Cieniega became Gazzarri's Broadway A Go Go. The London Fog and the Galaxy added two more rock'n'roll nightclubs to the north side of the street between Clark and Hilldale, which was bordered by the Whisky A Go Go on the east and a casual diner, the Hamburger Hamlet, on the west. Also on the same block was Sneeky Pete's, described by Hollywood gossip columnist Louella Parsons as "a colorful little dinery" where "Dillinger's gun hangs over the bar and the walls are covered in the likenesses of guys and dolls of the 1920s and 30s." The Art Graham Trio regularly provided a musical backdrop that took in tango, samba, jazz, and pop.

The three-block strip now had four rock'n'roll clubs, two lounges, two burlesque showcases, and an underground movie theater, Cinematheque-16; it also housed the offices of the Philles and GNP-Crescendo record labels and Dick Clark Productions and several restaurants, including the youth-orientated Beef'n'Beer, Ribs A Go Go, and a Belgian waffle shop, the Olde Worlde. The 9000 Building just east of Doheny and Sunset had become a magnet for various music industry offices, while Gaiety Delicatessen across the street was invariably filled with teen-scene movers and shakers during its lunch rush.

But the heart of the Strip remained at its traditional center, near Sunset and La Cienega. Ciro's re-opened in 1964 under the management of Frank Sennes, who attempted to emulate the Whisky's success by renaming his club Ciro's

LeDisc. The opening night bill included performances by The American Beetles and George & Teddy, poached from the Condor Club in San Francisco, where they had backed topless dancer Carol Doda. The Strip's Phone Booth followed suit by introducing topless waitresses of its own, but not everybody was best pleased. Makeup artist and body-painter Sheryl Carson noted that, "it's kind of sad that you can't get a job as a cocktail waitress anymore unless you're gonna show your knockers."[13]

Across the street from Ciro's LeDisc, Stratford On Sunset (formerly the Renaissance) now featured major rhythm & blues groups and local garage bands, notably an early line-up of Love. West of La Cienega, of course, one would encounter the Sea Witch, Dino's Lodge, the Playboy Club, and the Crescendo. The north side of this enchanted block featured a diner, Ben Frank's, that had become a prime hangout for teenagers, and Fred C. Dobb's coffeehouse, named after Humphrey Bogart's character in *The Treasure Of The Sierra Madre*. Also nearby, in the Sunset Plaza, were the deVoss mod boutique and Wil Wright's Ice Cream Parlor, a regular haunt of Duke Ellington and Brian Wilson, where, according to David Crosby, "you could have arrested all the pot smokers in Los Angeles."

To the east, the spiritual entrance to Sunset Strip was another hub of excitement. The Garden of Allah had been destroyed in 1959 (a bank was built in its place), but the Chateau Marmont remained, flanked by an adult nightclub, the Scene, which fluctuated between "topless efforts and jazz"—as well as hypnotists and female impersonators—"in order to compete with its Sunset Strip neighbors."[14] Diagonally opposite was another longtime showbiz haunt, Schwab's Pharmacy, and Googie's coffee shop and diner; on the same block were Sherry's coffee shop, which doubled as a jazz lounge with a house band led by 'Wall Of Sound' session pianist Don Randi, and Pandora's Box, sat on the triangular traffic island at Sunset and Crescent Heights. A few blocks either side stood a pair of hot-dog stands, the Dog House and the modernist Plush Pup. Next to the Plush Pup was the Jay Ward Animation Studio, outside of which from 1962 was a rotating statue of Rocky & Bullwinkle (Ward's biggest stars) that parodied the chorus girl spinning atop the iconic Sahara billboards across the street. The Strip's entryway was rounded out by the Fifth Estate coffeehouse and the Body Shop, which was now headlined by the burlesque starlet Tura Satana.

Contrary to County Supervisor Ernest E. Deb's plans, by the mid 1960s this winding downtown stretch in the Hollywood Hills had evolved into a place where anyone could, in the words of Petula Clark, "listen to the music of the traffic in the city/linger on the sidewalk where the neon signs are pretty." The movie star exclusivity of the 1930s and 40s had faded in the manner of Norma Desmond's character in Billy Wilder's 1950 epic *Sunset Boulevard*. (Footage of Clark's performance of 'Downtown' at the Moulin Rouge in November 1965 shows the singer reaching out from the stage to touch the hand of Sky Saxon, vocalist in The Seeds, who had just cut their future classic 'Pushin' Too Hard.')

This new Strip set the stage perfectly for the coming onslaught of bands formed by kids inspired by Beatlemania. This combined with the success of the Whisky A Go Go in early 1964 represented a turning point from which hundreds of garage bands in the Greater Los Angeles area took their cue. Byrds manager Jim Dickson recalls how, in 1965, "when we put The Byrds into Ciro's LeDisc, the only thing goin' on at Whisky A Go Go was Johnny Rivers. Elmer Valentine came to me and said: 'You guys are taking all of our business away. How do we get a piece of this? Why don't you come over to Whisky A Go Go and play for a few weeks?' And that's what started Whisky A Go Go getting better bands in there."

Once the doors had opened, Hollywood was quick to develop its own creative rock'n'roll scene, one that would no longer be a poor second to New York City, let alone Central Avenue, East LA, or the beaches of the South Bay and Orange County. Only one scene could favorably compare to that of Los Angeles in the mid 1960s, and that was London, England. Fittingly, Los Angeles would draw some thrilling moments from The Beatles, The Rolling Stones, Them, The Yardbirds, and others. This cross-continental camaraderie occurred just as each city was experiencing its musical and artistic zenith.

CHAPTER THREE

The roots of Los Angeles rock'n'roll

" *Floods of artists from across the globe settled in Mt. Parnassus on the Left Banke of Le Seine. Marcel Duchamp called the convergence 'the first truly international colony of artists we ever had.' Unsurpassed in its convergence of creative energy, the interchange was just unbelievable. Everyone was involved in the arts and it produced really extraordinary effects.* **"** BILL MACLEISH, *THE LOST GENERATION*

When most people think of rhythm & blues in the 1960s, the unified sound of Motown springs to mind. Los Angeles R&B was very different, in that all of the acts that emerged had very different styles, and—with no Berry Gordy-type figure around to keep order—there were no rules as to what a black artist 'should' sound like. Some preferred the more frantic style of 1950s rhythm & blues to 60s soul; others forged their own musical identities.

Rhythm & blues in 1940s Los Angeles provided a more crucial link to the development of rock'n'roll than is generally recognized. The R&B labels Specialty, Kent, Modern, Aladdin, and Imperial were all based in the city, and there were several good venues to play in both South Central and downtown. Los Angeles offered a more open-minded opportunity than Kansas or Omaha would for Big Joe Turner and Wynonie Harris. Mississippian Ike Turner and Arkansas native Louis Jordan both moved to greener pastures out west as LA became the city in which many formative rock'n'roll acts would settle.

Los Angeles rhythm & blues was born out of the 1940s scene on Central Avenue, where jump jazz—more stripped-back and kinetic than big band or bebop—provided the link between 1930s jazz and blues and 1950s rock'n'roll. The King Cole Trio were an early exponent of this sound with their pioneering piano-based boogie-woogie, while saxophone honkers such as Big Jay McNeely, Joe Houston, and Chuck Higgins carried the momentum into the 1950s.

The most famous song to emerge from LA's fertile rhythm & blues scene is 'Hound Dog,' written by two white teenagers from the Fairfax district, Jerry Leiber and Mike Stoller, and recorded first, in 1953, by Big Mama Thornton and then, three years later, by Elvis Presley. But there are many others of a similar caliber: The Johnny Otis Show donated hits to two LA natives, Etta James ('Roll With Me Henry,' 'Good Rockin' Daddy,' 'Tell Mama,' and 'Seven Day Fool') and Little Esther ('The Deacon Moves In' and 'Release Me').

Founded in 1949, The Hollywood Flames, best known for 'Buzz Buzz Buzz,' were LA's first exponents of the rhythm & blues vocal-group sound. Over the years the group featured singers including Bobby Day ('Rockin Robin'), the composer of 'Little Bitty Pretty One' by Thurston Harris and 'Over And Over,' later made famous by The Dave Clark Five. Earl Nelson was another Flames alumni; he later scored hits with 'Harlem Shuffle,' recorded alongside Bob Relf as Bob & Earl, and 'The Duck,' as Jackie Lee. Gaynel Hodge, who later recorded 'Alley Oop' with Kim Fowley and Gary Paxton, was also in The Hollywood Flames for a time. According to rhythm & blues deejay and historian Tom Reed, black artists in Los Angeles took this chameleon-like approach "because the R&B singers weren't getting paid right for their records, [so] they just kept on recording under different names to take what money they could get out of the business. So it's hard to get a handle on just who was behind what, and therefore impossible to define or summarize the scene in a simple manner."

The Platters were easily the most popular rhythm & blues group to hail from the Los Angeles area. Many of the group's singles are now considered to be classics of the era, from their debut hit, 'Only You,' through to 'Smoke Gets In Your Eyes' and 'The Great Pretender.' Meanwhile, The Coasters—as in West Coast—started life in LA as The Robins, for whom Leiber & Stoller penned 'Riot In Cell Block 9' and 'Smokey Joe's Café.' The renamed group had two further hits, 'Searchin'' and 'Youngblood,' before relocating to New York City.

Perhaps the finest rhythm & blues performer to emerge from LA was Sam Cooke, whose hits ranged from the 1958 romantic ballad 'You Send Me' to the thoughtful social commentary of 'A Change Is Gonna Come' (1964). By the early 1960s, Cooke had begun to build an empire of publishing and production interests, and was eager to discover promising local talent. He opened a storefront in South Central Los Angeles called the Soul Station, where local youths could develop their playing, producing, and promoting skills. (A young Sonny Bono brought Cher here as he tried to launch her as a solo star.)

Bobby Womack signed to Cooke's SAR label in 1961 as a member of The Valentinos, who went on to have hits with 'Looking For Love' in 1962 and 'It's All Over Now' in 1964. A cover version of the latter, which Womack had co-authored, soon became the first US hit by The Rolling Stones. Womack later established himself as a session guitarist for artists such as Otis Redding and Aretha Franklin. But by then the focus and potential of SAR had come to an abrupt end, following the apparently accidental, fatal shooting of Cooke in December 1964. The momentum of LA rhythm & blues continued, but it had lost one of its main organized centers.

As Los Angeles's harder-edged answer to Chubby Checker, Round Robin & The Parleys were a local favorite at the height of the twist craze. The group's 1963 hit 'Do The Slauson' was named for a cruising strip in South Central where one of two Wich Stand coffee shops served as a prime teenage hangout. It inspired similar efforts such as 'The Slauson Shuffle' by East LA group The Romancers and 'Harlem Shuffle' by Bob & Earl, who noticed that 'Do The Slauson' had only hit locally, so intentionally expanded their geography to corner airplay on the East Coast.

The definitive early LA sound came together in a session for Round Robin's 'Kick That Little Foot Sally Ann,' a song written by Phil Sloan and Steve Barri and arranged by Jack Nitzsche. The backing vocals are by The Blossoms, with Darlene Love laying down a wail at the close that's more than a match for Plas Johnson's sax solo during the middle break.

Round Robin continued to make hits during the mid 1960s, including 'The Roundest Of Them All,' on which he boasts of being rounder than Chubby Checker and Fats Domino over a pounding mix of twist music and Bo Diddley. The arrangement was by H.B. Barnum, a former member of The Dootones who later worked his magic on Sonny & Cher's 'I Got You Babe.' Robin surpassed 'The Roundest' in 1965 with 'I'm A Wolf Man,' a fuzz-toned garage-punk effort written by Baker Knight, a Sea Witch regular who had written many of Ricky Nelson's hits.

Without a doubt the most influential local R&B group was Don & Dewey. Guitarist, bassist, and electric violinist Don 'Sugarcane' Harris and guitar and keyboard player Dewey Terry cut their first disc, the frenetic 'Jungle Hop,' for Specialty Records in 1957. According to LA Weekly's Johnny Whiteside, they mixed "the gospel passion of Sister Rosetta Tharpe, the soul grit of James Brown, the tortured blues of Guitar Slim, and the lusty carnival rock'n'roll of Little Richard … with a howling force that could only have come from the streets of Los Angeles." Although the duo barely broke through on their own, their songs were hits for a number of other artists. Dale & Grace charted with 'I'm Leaving In Up To You' in 1963, while East LA's The Premiers hit the Top 20 with 'Farmer John.' The Righteous Brothers based a good deal of their act on Don & Dewey, hitting with no less than three of their ravers: 'Koko Joe,' 'Justine,' and 'Big Boy Pete.'

Among the nationally popular dance crazes to broke out of the Los Angeles rhythm & blues community was 'The Jerk,' as performed by The Larks. The group was an extension of Don Julian & The Meadowlarks, who'd been making records as far back as 1954, such as 'Heaven and Paradise,' 'I Got Tore Up,' 'LSMFT Blues,' and 'Boogie Woogie Teenage.' As the 1950s turned into the 60s, the group went through many line-up changes and, by 1964, Julian had decided just to call his group The Larks. After coming home one day and seeing his niece grooving to 'Dancing In The Street' by Martha & The Vandellas, he asked her: "Girl, what's that you're doin'?" She replied: "The jerk. C'mon, I'll teach it to you." This exchange then formed the opening line of Julian's record.

The Olympics were another story all together. Their 'Hully Gully' was a huge go-go hit, and one of the most enjoyable dance crazes of the 1960s. The Olympics turned up all around town, from Maverick's Flat on Crenshaw to a 1967 show at the Cheetah, where they shared a bill with The Merry-Go-Round. Initially, on records such as their 1958 debut hit, 'Western Movies,' The Olympics' sound was more closely aligned to 1950s vocal rhythm & blues than 60s soul. But in 1965 their version of 'Good Lovin'' became a huge turntable hit at the Teen-Age Fair, and subsequently charted strongly on LA radio. A cover by The Young Rascals was a big national hit in early 1966, the same year than The Olympics attempted to tap into the hit sounds of the moment with the vibes and Motown-style backing vocals of 'Mine Exclusively.'

* * *

Perhaps the best encapsulations of LA rhythm & blues came on 'Papa-Oom-Mow-Mow' and 'The Bird's The Word' by The Rivingtons. Humorous and insanely rocking, both were picked up nationally; 'Papa-Oom-Mow-Mow' became an anthem for Cleveland horror host Ernie Anderson (better known as Ghoulardi). The Beach Boys liked the song so much that they covered it on two live albums, as well as performing it on *Shindig!*, despite having plenty of their own tunes to plug, while The Trashmen turned The Rivingtons' hits into a Number 4 *Billboard* smash called 'Surfin' Bird.' Liberty Records signed The Rivingtons to an LP deal for *Doin' The Bird*, which includes wild versions of 'Long Tall Sally' and 'Mama-Oom-Mow-Mow' (an edgier version of its hit predecessor). Like many Los Angeles vocal groups, The Rivingtons' stock-in-trade came out of the wilder style of the 1950s R&B scene, during which time the group was known as The Sharps. Their earliest sessions—including those for 'Tapun Tapun,' which remained unreleased until the 1970s—were recorded for the Combo label at the tail end of the decade.

The Vibrations were another LA act that carried the 1950s rhythm & blues vocal-group sound into the 1960s. Reminiscent of The Coasters in both their sense of humor and counterpoint singing style, The Vibrations first record of note was 'The Watusi,' a wild raver complete with crazy vocal interactions. This came in complete contrast to the smoother soul records that would dominate black music in the 1960s. It's particularly noteworthy that The Vibrations recorded the original version of 'My Girl Sloopy' (and on Atlantic, no less). The song was quickly covered by The Yardbirds in England, and then made successful, as 'Hang On Sloopy,' by The McCoys in the USA.

"Its got that Indian tom tom *fuck* beat, much like 'I Want My Woman' by The Emperors, which is also a caveman standard," garage-punk musician Shelly Ganz notes of The McCoys' version. "The build/rave-up plus scream in the middle defines the hit version of 'Hang on Sloopy' as the epitome of 1960s punk." Alongside 'Louie Louie,' 'Papa-Oom-Mow-Mow,' and 'Good Lovin',' 'My Girl Sloopy' is among the best examples of how rhythm & blues 45s that hit locally in LA later became standards when covered by white garage bands across the nation.

Assuming a position right in the middle of LA's rhythm & blues community was the deejay The Magnificent Montague, who took the scene by storm from the moment he began broadcasting on KGFJ in February 1965. That August he hosted the Stax Records Revue at the 5-4 Ballroom, just as tensions between the poverty-stricken communities of South Central Los Angeles and the authorities seemed to be coming to a head. In his autobiography, Montague recalls being onstage on a balmy Sunday evening, trading his catchphrase—'Burn, Baby!

Burn!'—with the crowd between frantic performances by Rufus and Carla Thomas, William Bell, The Mad Lads, and The Mar-Keys, as well as Booker T. & The MGs, who backed each of their label-mates. "So here comes [Wilson] Pickett, and how does he top this? Like any great performer, he amps up the drama. Girls in the crowd are already screaming out for 'Midnight Hour' [which had just been released], but he teases them, asking them if they believe the midnight hour is 'the right time.' There was so much energy in moments like this in LA that sometimes I just wanted to stand back and watch."[1]

Before long, Montague's signature cry leapt beyond its musical roots when it was adopted by the crowd at the Watts Riots. "All of a sudden I hear that chant on the TV news," Montague recalls. "This is crazy. I'd been screaming 'Burn, Baby! Burn! on the radio for two years—'63 in New York and '64 in Chicago. … I didn't know it yet, but 'Burn, Baby! Burn!' is going to become institutionalized as a radical chant and a political rant … Nobody would ever shout it the innocent way it was supposed to be used, to praise another person's performance."

As well as giving the world 'Burn, Baby! Burn!,' Montague also pulled off something of a coup at the time of the Stax Records Revue when he talked the label into allowing Booker T. & The MGs to sit in on record sessions with some local players during the Memphis group's stay in Los Angeles. The sessions resulted in a pair of pure soul LPs on Imperial Records—both of which were credited to The Packers—and a hit single, 'Hole In The Wall,' which featured Booker T. on piano, Steve Cropper on guitar, Earl Grant on bass, Al Jackson on drums, Leon Haywood on organ, Packy Axton on saxophone, and The Magnificent Montague himself on congas.

Refreshingly, a number of small labels in Los Angeles during this time had begun to think in terms of both black and white kids, who had, essentially, been listening to the same radio stations during the first rock'n'roll era. Del-Fi Records formed two new subsidiaries during the mid 1960s: Mustang, home to The Bobby Fuller Four, and Bronco. Barry White—then a 22-year-old producer, arranger, and session player of growing renown—took control of Bronco, aiming to use it to create a Los Angeles equivalent of the Motown sound. Among the hits he produced were 'It May Be Winter Outside' by Viola Wills, which pitches itself somewhere between Phil Spector and Motown, and the mean dance floor grooves of Felice Taylor's 'Under The Influence Of Love,' Brenda Holloway's 'Echo' and 'Hey Fool,' and 'This Thing Called Love' by Johnny Wyatt. (Wyatt also recorded the wonderfully ridiculous 'Everyone's Goin' Mod.') Another Bronco act of note was The Versatiles, who would soon find much wider success as The Fifth Dimension. The label also issued several 45s by Barry White as a performer, which hinted at the bright future that lay ahead of him.

When Northern Soul hit big in the UK during the mid 1970s, old 45s on Mirwood Records became a hot commodity. The label put out albums by both The Olympics and Jackie Lee, while its subsidiary Mira countered with Sunset Strip jazz from The Afro Blues Quintet and The Leaves' classic 'Hey Joe.' But perhaps the coolest interracial, genre-crossing label of them all was Double Shot Records, which issued hits by both Count Five ('Psychotic Reaction') and LA's most popular soul singer, Brenton Wood ('Gimme Little Sign' and 'The Oogum Boogum Song'), in a neat juxtaposition of the twin markets of garage-punk and R&B/soul. Another Double Shot act, Kent & The Candidates, combined the two genres succinctly on their garage-soul single 'Trouble.' Led by drummer/vocalist Kent Sprague, the group often played at the Haunted House on Hollywood Boulevard and appeared in the Bob Hope comedy *How To Commit Marriage*.

Double Shot was also home to Compton's Señor Soul, the band that pioneered the funk-tinged soul sound that would later bring international success to War. The key figure in both groups was flute/organ/sax-player Chuck Miller, who had started out in 1962 in The Creators. At one point future Love saxophonist/flautist Tjay Cantrelli was a member, as was vocalist Johnny Hamilton. Little Johnny Hamilton & The Creators made their biggest impact with the 1965 single 'Burn,' which foreshadowed the Watts Riots by turning Magnificent Montague's on-air call-out, 'Burn, Baby! Burn!,' into a musical anthem.

During 1965, Miller began performing with The Afro Blues Quintet Plus 1. This loose and ever-changing aggregation of musicians often played in high-profile, low-key environments, from Sunset Strip coffeehouse the Living Room—adjacent to It's Boss—and Maverick's Flat in South Central, to a steady Sunday afternoon gig at Shelly's Manne-Hole in downtown Hollywood. The group's 1966 debut, *Introducing The Afro Blues Quintet Plus 1*, was described by Harlan Ellison in *Cad* magazine as taking in folk-rock, calypso, African drum chants and "lilts of Puerto Rico." By the time of sessions for the group's fourth and final album in January 1968, their material ranged from Lee Hazlewood's 'Some Velvet Morning' to Bob Dylan's 'Too Much Of Nothing.'

Gradually evolving into Señor Soul, the group signed to Double Shot and scored a hit with 'Pata Pata,' before making the instrumental full-length *Señor Soul Plays Funky Favorites* (1968), a collection of 1966-vintage grooves like 'Sunshine Superman' reassessed in a latin-soul style. A second album, *It's Your Thing*, and the single 'El Loco' followed shortly thereafter on Whiz Records, demonstrating a newly Hammond organ-dominated funk feel. By the time of the final Señor Soul single, 'Don't Lay Your Funky Trip On Me,' the group's line-up was essentially that of War, following the reunion of Chuck Miller and Willie Briggs with members of The Creators. After backing Los Angeles Rams star Deacon Jones as Nite Shift, War recorded 'Spill The Wine' with Eric Burdon, formerly of The Animals, in 1969 and had numerous other hits over the next decade including 'Cisco Kid,' 'The World Is A Ghetto,' and 'Low Rider.'

The Soul Runners scored a hit in early 1967 with 'Grits And Cornbread,' released on the MoSoul label. The group featured Bernard Blackman on guitar, Melvin Dunlap on bass, James Gadson on drums, Raymond Jackson on trombone, and John Rayford on tenor saxophone. With the arrival of vocalist Charles Wright, formerly of the rhythm & blues vocal group The Twilighters, The Soul Runners became The Watts 103rd Street Rhythm Band, signed to Warner Bros, and made a self-titled debut album. The group peaked on the live follow-up, *Together*, which was recorded at the Haunted House. Then came a run of great singles, from the avant-garde funk of 'Do Your Thing' to 'Love Land,' featuring falsetto vocalist James Gadson, and 'Express Yourself.' The original Soul Runners line-up subsequently became Bill Withers's backing band on three early-1970s albums.

Billy Preston had a more showboat appeal, typified by the title of his 1966 Capitol album, *The Wildest Organ in Town*. Something of a child prodigy, Preston had performed an organ duet with the host of *The Nat King Cole Show* during the late 1950s. In 1962 Sam Cooke issued Preston's debut, *Sixteen Year Old Soul*, on his Derby imprint. Following the hot single 'Greazee' and a second album, *Hymns Speak From The Organ*, Preston landed a regular gig on ABC television's *Shindig!* Two more albums, *The Most Exciting Organ Ever* (Vee Jay, 1964) and *Early Hits Of 1965* (Exodus), presented him as a pop-gospel version of Jimmy Smith. Signing to Capitol, Preston released a tough, Sly Stone-produced cover of 'In The Midnight Hour' before earning a headlining stint at the Trip in February 1966 (as documented on 1967's *Club Meeting*). Preston then began an association with The Beatles—who he'd met in Hamburg in 1962—that saw him play on 'Get Back,' 'Let It Be,' and 'Revolution' as well as cut solo material for the group's Apple Records label. He recorded a number of solo hits in the early 1970s, including 'Outta Space,' 'Will It Go 'Round In Circles?,' and 'Nothing From Nothing.'

By and large, however, the Los Angeles rhythm & blues scene had all but disintegrated by the turn of the decade. It's difficult to say whether any of these artists could have sustained their momentum if Sam Cooke had been around to provide the scene with a greater focus. As it stood, nobody was able to unify or define the diverse styles of the time, let alone cover all the bases. This might explain why Brenda Holloway, the only Los Angeles-based artist to sign to Motown, fell out with the Detroit label. Chicago-based rock'n'roll journalist James Porter notes: "She's out in full-color mod LA in the mid 1960s and is impressed with this new psychedelic sound and wants to get a piece of the action in some way. Berry Gordy, back in gray Detroit where the brothers still wear processed hair, laughed the idea off, saying she should stick with the standard soul songs that Motown was giving her." (Holloway did at least cut 'Every Little Bit Hurts' for the label, and was one of The Beatles' opening acts at Shea Stadium in 1965.)

The LA artists came from totally different musical backgrounds, be it the stompin' abandon of Ty Wagner, the vocal group rhythm of The Olympics, The Afro Blues Quintet Plus 1's melting pot of latin, jazz, folk-rock, and soul, or the smooth grooves of Dobie Gray. Gray had been a regular on the circuit after breaking out with 'Look At Me' in 1962. Three years later he laid out one of the cornerstones of cool with 'The In Crowd,' a song that was also a smash as a jazzy piano instrumental by Chicago's Ramsey Lewis Trio. Also in 1965, Gray released 'See You At The Go Go,' in tribute to Whisky A Go Go; he later fronted the rock group Pollution, and had a huge solo hit in 1973 with 'Drift Away.'

* * *

"Let's Take A Trip Down Whittier Boulevard! *¡Honk! ¡Honk!* ¡Arriba! ¡Arriba! ¡Ha-ha-ha-ha-ha-ha!"

In East Los Angeles, there was no greater rallying cry than the one hollered by organist Ronnie Figueroa at the start of Thee Midniters' 'Whittier Blvd,' one of the most important tracks ever cut in Los Angeles. The song was a jumped-up pound-out of The Rolling Stones' instrumental theme '2120 Michigan Avenue' featuring garage band organ, Dick Dale-style lead guitar, and the profound sound of the group's soulful horn section. Arranged by Romeo Prado, the horn refrain has the feel of a showstopping Hollywood finale; lying underneath was the tough garage/beat backing so familiar to devotees of 1960s punk.

Thee Midniters started out as The Midnighters, but were asked to change their name by Hank Ballard's group, thereby inaugurating the garage-rock tradition of using 'Thee.' The group had several personalities, and were able to whip out psychedelia and emotional ballads too when it suited them. Vocalist Little Willie G. provides a definitive garage-soul moment on 'The Town I Live In,' an effective cover of an obscure 1962 recording by McKinley Mitchell. The group's own 'Dreaming Casually' takes the romanticism of East LA streets and opens up the possibility of "letting your mind go and seeing what happens," according to bassist Jimmy Espinoza.

Thee Midniters released four albums between 1965 and 1968: an eponymous debut on Chattahoochee followed by *Love Special Delivery*, *Thee Midniters Unlimited*, and *Giants* on their own Whittier Records. A cover of Marvin Gaye's 'Stubborn Kind Of Fellow' demonstrated their ability to give Motown material a Rolling Stones raunch without sacrificing the soulful nature of the original. In Thee Midniters' hands, Larry Williams's 'Slow Down' and 'Money' by Barrett Strong took on a righteous edge. (Both songs had previously been re-energized by John Lennon and his fellow Beatles.) The group also offered up a nervy, terrifying take on 'Johnny B. Goode' and a punked-up reading of Them's 'Gloria,' which, combined with original material such as 'Looking Out A Window' and 'Thee Midnite Feeling,' marked them among the most powerful *Nuggets*-style bands.

Thee Midniters came to represent a completely different style of music particular to East LA, where cruising Whittier Boulevard in a lowrider had become a familiar rite of passage. The Chicano community had become very enamored with the idea of 'playing it cool.' The lowrider is the antithesis of the hot-rod, made (more) famous by Jan & Dean and The Beach Boys: the aim was to create a stunning bachelor pad inside the largest, vintage, luxury car available, cut the shock absorbers, and lower the axles as close to the ground as possible (hopefully without scraping the pavement). Plush purple-velvet interiors were popular in East LA, along with plenty of tapestry and dangling tassels; the priority with lowrider drivers was romance, and accoutrements of love came first. A car club plaque was a permanent fixture in the back window, as were the contrasting symbols of death—usually in the form of skulls—and a Sacred Heart.

There was an overriding attitude of juvenile delinquency at rock'n'roll dances in East LA, which was also borne out in records from the area. Most of the action took place at the Golden Gate Theater, on the corner of Atlantic and Whittier, and Kennedy Hall, located at 451 South Atlantic Boulevard. (Thee Midniters posed in front of Golden Gate's marquee on the sleeve of the debut album.) The Montebello Ballroom at 12th and Whittier had been a prime music venue since the 1920s and was later used for rock'n'roll shows on occasion. Other much-loved dance places were lodged in neighborhoods such as St Alphonsus Hall (one block east of Atlantic), Little Union Hall (four blocks south of Olympic), and Big Union Hall, located in the city of Vernon. The Paramount Ballroom in Boyle Heights was a breakout place for the East LA sound.

Rhythm & blues was the chosen music of East Los Angeles. The Chicano community regularly had to deal with its own warring teenage gangs, but tended to treat black culture with respect and reverence. Jump-jazz was popular among Mexican-American youths in the 1940s, as was the tough but romantic vocal group style during the 1950s. 'Earth Angel' by The Penguins remains an anthem in East LA, as does 'Angel Baby' by Rosie & The Originals, a group from National City, located between San Diego and Tijuana.

This connection to rhythm & blues explains why a song by New Orleans artist Chris Kenner, 'Land Of A Thousand Dances,' first broke in East Los Angeles in 1965 when it was covered by Cannibal & The Headhunters. The group added the trademark "na, na-na na-na" chorus that has since become a defining 1960s moment. What started out as an improvised hookline by vocalist Frankie Garcia ended up becoming a commonly used chant during civil rights marches. Cannibal & The Headhunters maintained their 1950s-style rhythm & blues vocal-group sound during the 1960s because it remained the 'in' sound in the Ramona Gardens housing project where they grew up. The group had the ability to expand on the concepts of songs such as The Flamingos' classic 'I Only Have Eyes For You,' applying dreamy 1960s production techniques to 1950s-style harmonies on their third single, 'Please Baby Please.'

Similarly, The Blendells' 1964 cover of Stevie Wonder's 'La La La La La La' gave the song a dirty guitar raunch reminiscent of Herbie Hancock's 'Watermelon

Man.' The muted-trumpet solo is an excellent cheap-sounding send-up of Herb Alpert's voguish adoption of Mexican-style horn-playing. An important aspect of the record's charm is the vocal phrasing, which could only have come from the local vernacular. The grinding sound of 'Dance With Me,' meanwhile, confirms Chicano rhythm & blues as no more than kids with guitars, drums, and horns, not slick session cats, as had played on the recordings that inspired the East LA groups' sound.

One reason that a rock'n'roll *band* sound took precedence in the area—as opposed to the vocal-group aesthetic—was that, in Ritchie Valens, the Mexican-American community had its own Elvis Presley. His hits, including 'La Bamba,' 'Donna,' and 'Come On Let's Go,' had an important social impact, and encouraged his label, Del-Fi, to sign Chan Romero, best known for 'Hippy Hippy Shake' (1959). Following in the 1950s tradition, Romero worked up audiences at El Monte Legion Stadium, where sets by Handsome Jim Balcom, The Mixtures, and The Romancers became notable cultural events in the teenage-Chicano community.

Among the earliest Mexican-American rock'n'roll recording artists was jump-blues artist Lalo Guerrero, who in 1955 released 'Tin Marin De Do Pingue'—a dead ringer for 'Rock Around The Clock.' More successful with the kids, however, was Little Julian Herrera, who emerged a year later. Herrera was in fact of Eastern European heritage, and was born on the East Coast. After running away from home at a young age he was adopted by a Mexican-American family before being snapped up by Johnny Otis's Dig Records on the strength of his powerful stage presence. The haunting ballad 'Lonely Lonely Nights' and 'Symbol Of Heaven' (1957) were both huge local hits.

In 1958 deejay Art Laboe signed Herrera to his Starla label and found the singer a permanent band. But the ensuing 'I Remember Linda,' recorded with his group The Tigers and backed by a cover of Little Richard's 'True Fine Mama,' ended up being Herrera's last release for a while: his career ground to an abrupt halt when he was imprisoned for statutory rape. Six thousand people turned up for his 1963 comeback show at El Monte Legion Stadium, but he only made one more single, a surf-styled reworking of his own 'Lonely Lonely Nights.'

This was not the first time the worlds of rhythm & blues, Chicano, and surf had become intermingled in Los Angeles. The best early example of this local cross-pollination is the story of the Rillera brothers, Barry and Rick, from

Santa Ana, who formed a dance band called The Rhythm Rockers in 1955. A year later, they started working with a young black singer, Richard Berry. One evening, while listening from backstage as the Rillera brothers played a cover of Rene Touzet's 'El Loco Cha Cha,' Berry penned his own take on the song: 'Louie Louie.'

When The Kingsmen had a hit with Berry's song in 1963, The Rilleras were still playing at their regular haunt, the Harmony Park Ballroom, this time as part of Dick Dale's Del-Tones, adding the Mexican edge to Dale's famed recording of 'Misirlou.' After playing sax with the Del-Tones, Barry Rillera joined The Trademarks, a surf group featuring his younger brother Butch on drums and led by lead guitarist Gary Moulton. Together they recorded the magnificent single 'Baha-Ree-Bah (Parts 1 & 2),' as issued by Jubal Records. The brothers also knew Bill Medley and Bobby Hatfield from their times at Rendezvous and Harmony Park, and as such were later invited by the duo to play on their early hits as The Righteous Brothers, including 'Koko Joe' (1962), 'My Babe,' and 'Little Latin Lupe Lu' (both 1963).

Meanwhile, an entirely new scene was just about to break out of East Los Angeles. The Romancers took over as the house band at El Monte Legion Stadium during the summer of 1962 and set the pace for a wave of East LA groups that would soon follow in their footsteps. Led by Max Uballez—vocalist, rhythm guitarist, and prolific songwriter—The Romancers began their recording career with the singles 'You'd Better'—credited to Maxamillian—and 'Rock Little Darlin'' before signing to Del-Fi Records for the albums *The Slauson Shuffle* and *Let's Do The Swim*.

By this stage the group included guitarist Andy Tesso, whose raw, straightforward playing proved highly influential on many of the East LA groups that followed, such as Thee Midniters, The Blendells, and The Premiers. As well as inspiring many of the scene's younger players, he also gave guitar lessons to many Chicano kids. The Romancers, Premiers, and Blendells became a kind of amorphous East LA talent-pool, which proved essential given the variety of interchangeable gigs that local musicians would encounter.

"Vietnam wrecked a lot of the stuff that was going on," says Tesso, who was drafted into the service during the war's initial escalation. After Tesso's departure, The Romancers continued with an Etta James/Harvey Fuqua cover, 'My Heart Cries,' and the garage-styled 'She Took My Oldsmobile.' The group then combined with frontman Max Uballez's brother, Robert, and a new guitarist, Richard Provincio, to form The Smoke Rings, releasing the amped-up garage-punker 'Love's The Thing' on Linda Records. Max Uballez also wrote a number of local hits for the scene's other groups, including 'Annie Oakley' and 'Feel Like Dancing' for The Premiers, 'Don't Let Her Go' and 'The Fat Man' for Cannibal & The Headhunters, the Farfisa-organ-driven 'Like You Do' for The Back Seat, and 'Beaver Shot' for The Atlantics.

Another prominent East LA group of the time was The Mixtures, named for the diversity of races that made up their membership. With an Irish-Italian, a Hawaiian, a Puerto Rican, an African American, and several Mexicans in their ranks, the group was a virtual United Nations of rock'n'roll. "We had the Latin feel, the black-soul feel, and the white surfing sound," recalls sax man Delbert Franklin. "It made us a good group: we were a conglomeration of everything." The Mixtures' songs ranged from the raucous rhythm & blues of 'Tiki' and the local instrumental hit 'Olive Oyl,' to garage-soul on 'Hey Joe' (released as The Summits). Despite living 100 miles away in Oxnard, the group headlined KRLA's Friday night dances at the Rainbow Gardens in Pomona. Like The Romancers' Max Uballez, Chick Carlton—a guest on The Mixture's live album, who had earlier released the punched-up rock'n'roller 'So You Want To Rock' with his first group, The Majestics—wrote songs for other local groups, including 'I'm In Love With Your Daughter' for The Enchanters and 'Devil In Disguise' for Cannibal & The Headhunters.

San Gabriel combo The Premiers, meanwhile, had a national hit in 1964 with their reading of the Don & Dewey rocker 'Farmer John,' named for a local hot-dog manufacturer. The single was produced by Billy Cardenas, who played an integral role in the East LA scene as the manager of many of the key groups, and was recorded at Stereo Masters on Melrose Avenue. "I was interested in live sounds," explains Eddie Davis, the founder of several local labels including Faro, Linda, and Rampart. "So I suggested that we record 'Farmer John' live. We got a crowd and took them over to the studio and we just overdubbed the music with a party going on. … All those voices screaming … they were a girls' car-club called the Chevelles that used to follow The Premiers. They would scream and holler for The Premiers."[2]

The liner notes to the subsequent *Farmer John*, issued by Warner Bros, explain that the rest of the album was cut live at the Rhythm Room in Fullerton. This shortlived club had been opened in an old Cal Worthington garage by Davis, who rigged the venue for live recordings, but was unable to put his audio set-up to much use before civic pressure forced him to stop hosting rock'n'roll shows there. The *Farmer John* sleeve also extends thanks to both the Chevelles and Crystals car clubs, demonstrating the tight-knit links between these two local scenes. After touring nationally with Cannibal & The Headhunters in 1965, The Premiers made one of LA's most frightening garage-rock records, 'Get On This Plane,' which was produced by The Romancers' Max Uballez and Larry Tamblyn of The Standells for the Faro label.

There was a direct pipeline for national hits to break out of East Los Angeles. Local musician Richard Rosas, who played with Mark & The Escorts (and, later, Neil Young & The Blue Notes) explains: "Eddie Davis and Billy Cardenas would produce your records on their label, Faro. Billy Cardenas would have you booked all over, places like Kennedy Hall, Montebello Ballroom, the Big Union Hall in Vernon, Garfield High School, and St Alphonsus, which Frank Zappa later sang about on *Apostrophe*. There'd be seven or eight bands playing at each place, and people would go from one side of town to the other, maybe playing to three or four crowds a night. … Godfrey had a radio show, and so did Huggy Boy, and they used to play all the bands from East LA. If your record took off, Davis and Cardenas would let a bigger company pick it up, and you went out on tour, like Cannibal & The Headhunters. They were sent to New York City to play the Apollo, went on The Beatles' tour in 1965, and came back here and opened for them at the Hollywood Bowl."

Mark & The Escorts were one of many popular teenage bands roving these dance halls. Named for lead guitarist Mark Guerrero and fronted by vocalist Ricky Almaraz, the group recorded several singles, including 'Get Your Baby' and 'Dance With Me,' for GNP-Crescendo Records in 1965, before changing their name to The Men From S.O.U.N.D. a year later. Another similarly youthful East LA act was The Salas Brothers, who were backed on singles such as 'Darling (Please Bring Your Love)' (1963) and 'One Like Mine' (1965) by the instrumental quartet The Jaguars (who had a hit with 'Where Lovers Go'). Steve and Rudy Salas later achieved wider success as Tierra.

Another familial teen band, Ronnie & The Pomona Casuals, cut an album, *Everybody Jerk*, for Donna Records in 1964. As well as including the first East LA rendition of 'Land Of A Thousand Dances,' the album features seven songs on the theme of the jerk, including two—'Slow Jerk' and the title track—written by Arthur Lee, then gigging with his pre-Love group The LAGs. The scene offered up a girl group that year, The Sisters, who sang at dance halls such as the Big Union and the Little Union and had a local hit with a crude cover of The Dixie Cups' 'Gee Baby Gee.' Arthur Lee was again involved, turning up at sessions for 'Gee Baby Gee' and 'All Grown Up' with his future Love-mate, Johnny Echols. Both songs were produced by Billy Cardenas—"the Phil Spector of East Los Angeles," according to one of the three Sisters, Ersi Arvizu. "He found all the talent, and recorded the groups with his own sound," she says. The Sisters only recorded seven tracks in total—they're all included on *Del-Fi Girl Groups: Gee Baby Gee*—but were a rare match for New York's Shangri-Las, if not in terms of hit records, then at least in their commanding appearance.

Lil' Ray Jimenez worked the East LA circuit for years after moving into the city from the farming town of Delano in 1959 at the age of 13. He recorded for a number of labels but found little success of note aside from the local hit 'I Who Have Nothing,' released on Atco with a B-side, 'I Been Tryin',' that was notable as the first Arthur Lee song on record. More famous was Chris Montez, who wasn't an East LA native but lived near The Beach Boys in Hawthorne between 1961 and '63, and would, on occasion, drop by the Wilsons' house to jam. Inspired by Richie Valens, Montez debuted in 1962 with 'Let's Dance' and 'Some Kinda Fun' before touring Britain the following year with The Beatles, who gradually overtook him as headliners as their 'Please Please Me' surged up the charts. After a brief lull, Montez was signed by Herb Alpert to A&M Records, for whom he cut three 1966 hits, 'Call Me,' 'The More I See You,' and 'There Will Never Be Another You.'

East LA was in tune with the self-deprecating humor displayed by numerous Hollywood garage bands, too, as evidenced by The Sunday Funnies' camp send-up of psychedelia, 'A Pindaric Ode,' released in 1967. The flipside to minor local radio hit 'Whatcha Gonna Do,' 'A Pindaric Ode' lays out a bed of squeaky organ, fuzz-toned guitar, breezy vocal harmonies, and a backward-tape fadeout alongside a mildly facetious spoken-word vocal.

The scene in East Los Angeles had remained prosperous and continuous since the 1950s. As such, there was little need for bands from the area to play elsewhere until they had achieved a radio hit. Concert promoter and record producer Eddie Davis recalls that he had similar reasons to Johnny Otis for not turning his attentions to Hollywood: "The law [in LA] didn't allow teenage dances for people under 18 unless it was for charity. … I went to jail because I gave a dance at the Shrine Exposition Hall. Eighty per cent of the attendance was under 18. The police stopped the dance. I paid a fine and nothing even happened. It went away."

There were, however, three Mexican-American groups that did manage to play consistently on the burgeoning Hollywood nightclub scene. Tony, Vic & Manuel recorded a great house band album for Reprise in 1965, *A Go Go Hollywood Night Life*, which featured original instrumentals such as 'That's The Hollywood Night Life' alongside covers including 'Whole Lotta Shakin' Goin' On.' As The Sinners, the group was a regular fixture at the original Gazzarri's on La Cienega, and could be seen constantly on television show *Hollywood A Go Go*, which had a close association with the club. They also backed Jan & Dean on their 1963 LP *Surf City* and cut three Jan Berry-produced singles as The Matadors on Colpix Records.

Jim Doval & The Gauchos, a Chicano group from Chicago, Illinois via Fresno, landed a steady house band gig at the Crescendo and cut a house band album as well as appearing on ABC television's *Shindig!* and *Shivaree*. "The very first band that made an impression on us was called The Gauchos," recalls Chris Hillman of The Byrds. "They were a straight-ahead rock'n'roll showband with long hair, which was rare in 1964. The Byrds all came from a folk background, and so rock'n'roll was really new to us."[3] The Mothers Of Invention were also influenced by Jim Doval & The Gauchos—Frank Zappa briefly borrowed Doval's idea of a rhythmically solid two-drummer line-up.

Hollywood's most prominent Mexican-American group of the mid 1960s also arrived via Fresno. Pat and Lolly Vasquez, who would find fame during the 1970s as Redbone, started out in the early 1960s as The Avantis, recording three surf masterpieces: the throbbing 'Wax 'Em Down,' the heavy-riffing 'Phantom Surfer,' and the sly 'Gypsy Surfer.' The duo also cut an album for Del-Fi, *Hotrodder's Choice*, as The Deuce Coupes, while Lolly provided the lead guitar parts on two of the most memorable 1960s instrumentals, 'Let's Go' by The Routers and 'Outer Limits' by The Marketts.

At the dawn of the Sunset Strip rock'n'roll era, the Vasquez duo landed a house band gig at the Purple Onion, adjusting their surnames to become the more nightclub-friendly Pat & Lolly Vegas. There, they backed a duo called

Caesar & Cleo who, during their tenure at the Purple Onion, also changed their names, rechristening themselves Sonny & Cher. Having already written for Dobie Gray and The Routers, Pat Vasquez composed 'Niki Hoeky' for P.J. Proby and 'February Sunshine' for The Giant Sunflower and, with Lolly, performed 'The Robot Walk' in the low-budget Arch Hall Jr movie *The Nasty Rabbit*.

By 1965 Pat & Lolly Vegas had become the main attraction at the Haunted House, a magnificently hip psycho go-go funhouse located near Hollywood and Vine. The residency earned the duo an appearance in the film *It's A Bikini World*, in which they perform 'Walk On (Right Out Of My Life)' accompanied by a moon-walking go-go girl. The movie was released in conjunction with *Pat & Lolly Vegas At The Haunted House*, produced by Leon Russell and Snuff Garrett. By that time, Lolly Vegas's guitar playing had earned him many admirers, including the Whisky A Go Go's house photographer, George Rodriquez. "I never understood why people thought Hendrix was the greatest guitar player," says Rodriguez. "All that showy stuff, the playing with the teeth, and the acrobatics, he didn't need to do all of that. Now Lolly Vegas, that guy could *really* play guitar. He could blow Jimi Hendrix away, with ease."

* * *

The coastline of the Greater Los Angeles area is among the best places to surf in the world. Malibu and Rincon are two spots that stand out, while the consistency of surf-riding waves in Southern and Baja California allow a person to surf most days of the year. Although Hawaii remains a surfer's paradise without compare, the surfboard reached its design peak in 20th century Los Angeles, gradually evolving from the thick, heavy, wooden structures of the 1930s to something lighter and less cumbersome by the mid 1950s. The advent of these new nine-and-a-half-foot polyurethane boards meant that you no longer had to be a strongman to surf: you could even be a scrawny teenager. At the time, teenagers were wholly absorbed in the sounds of rock'n'roll, at exactly the moment when transistor radios arrived, ready to bring music to the beach.

Also growing in popularity were films of different surfing locales, usually narrated live by the film-makers—among them Bud Browne, Greg Noll, John Severson, and Bruce Brown—who would rent a theater or link up with a local college or high school to reach grass roots audiences. They would splice together reel-to-reel audio tapes of Hawaiian music, West Coast jazz, and popular contemporary rock'n'roll instrumentals by Duane Eddy, Link Wray, The Fireballs, Johnny & The Hurricanes, and The Wailers. Flamenco-guitar music was used in scenes from Baja California and Mexico. (By using instrumentals, the filmmaker could narrate without the fear of intrusion by unrelated vocals.)

Teenagers who attended such screenings were most affected by the rock'n'roll tracks featured. The mainstream beach movie *Gidget*, released in 1959, was based around Kathy Kohner, the teenage surfing daughter of author Fred Kohner. The first rock'n'roll record to exploit its popularity was 'Moon Dawg' by The Gamblers ('Moon Doggie' being one of *Gidget*'s characters). The instrumental song featured a rippling lead guitar line by Derry Weaver, offset by a sturdy rhythm played by Elliot Ingber, who later performed on The Mothers Of Invention's *Freak Out*. The Gamblers' bassist was Larry Taylor, who would later join Canned Heat, while future Beach Boy Bruce Johnston pounded the keys. Released on the jazz label World Pacific, 'Moon Dawg' set the pace for an onslaught of surf-related instrumentals over the next few years. It was covered by a number of artists, most notably The Beach Boys, who added mysterioso wordless vocals to their 1962 version, on which Derry Weaver reprises his lead guitar role.

From way up in the central-Californian beachside town of San Luis Obispo came the rhythm & blues-instrumental group The Revels, who had been performing locally since 1957. In 1960 they released their second single, 'Church Key,' which features a decidedly Duane Eddy-esque guitar line and a grinding sax part. Suddenly California was producing a slew of hot instrumentals. Next up was 'Underwater' by The Frogmen (from Westchester High, just south of Venice Beach), which became a regular presence on local radio during the spring and summer of 1961. Then came The Belairs and Dick Dale & His Del-Tones, both of whom drew huge, steady followings at their own self-promoted dances. The Belairs' hit-in-waiting was a Sonny Bono-produced track, 'Mr Moto,' that bore all the hallmarks of the coming surf guitar boom. Dick Dale & His Del-Tones had a more aggressive sound, with Dale double-picking the strings of his guitar like a locomotive.

Dale had learnt this double-picking technique from Joe Maphis while struggling as a singer on the LA rockabilly circuit; coupling it with Duane Eddy's tone and Link Wray's raunch and adding in a fierce intensity of his own, he came up with a more powerful guitar sound than had ever been heard before. Dale also dug into the music of his Lebanese heritage, giving an exotic classicism to songs such as 'Misirlou,' 'The Victor,' and 'The Wedge'—all popular within the surfing community. In an era of the Spanish Moors, the infusion of Arabic people to Spain brought a similarly melodious flair to flamenco guitar-playing. With Mexico so close to Los Angeles and flamenco stylings providing a soundtrack to Baja footage in surfing films, these guitar motifs, tacked onto a rhythm & blues backing, became an instinctive charge for surfers.

Dick Dale & His Del-Tones filled the Rendezvous Ballroom in Balboa every week during the summer of 1961, while The Belairs opened the Belair Club in Redondo Beach. (After the group split, the venue would be renamed the Revelaire, and would later briefly serve the folk-rock scene as the Third i, with an opening night show featuring The Turtles, Buffalo Springfield, and The Everpresent Fullness.)

In the fall of 1961, Dale released his first hit record, 'Let's Go Trippin'.' The Belairs' 'Mr Moto,' meanwhile, was a local hit at the same time as a vocal record, 'Surfin',' appeared by some kids from Hawthorne calling themselves The Beach Boys. Beneath its fine vocal harmonies—reminiscent of early Jan & Dean hits such as 'Baby Talk'—was little more than stand-up bass and a drum that sounded like someone had put a coat over the bottom of a trash can (which was precisely what Brian Wilson had done). 'Surfin' Safari' broke The Beach Boys nationally in 1962 with the exotic intrigue of its lyrics and one of the most memorable guitar-breaks of the decade. The following year's 'Surfin' USA' brought the surf trend to its zenith: soon, vocal surfing songs were more popular across America that the instrumental movement that had so captivated local kids in Los Angeles.

Back in Los Angeles, however, the real excitement was only just beginning. The Belairs split off into three different factions. Guitarist Paul Johnson formed P.J. & The Galaxies, but was writing enough great, original tunes also to be able to supply hits to his former bandmates: drummer Richard Delvy and keyboardist Jim Roberts, now working together in Hollywood in The Challengers, and lead guitarist Eddie Bertrand, now fronting Eddie & The Showmen. The latter group kicked up a storm as the house band at the Retail Clerks' Union Hall in Buena Park—the hottest place in town to see surf bands by 1963—and cut some of the most intense surf records of the period: 'Squad Car,' 'Scratch,' 'Mr Rebel,' and 'Faraway Places.'

Among the regulars at the Retail were The Lively Ones, who knocked out audiences with their stunning live energy. Their Del-Fi debut, *Surf Rider*, is a definitive surf LP and was the top seller at Wallich's Music City in Hollywood during the summer of 1963. Other groups hosted by Eddie & The Showmen at the Retail included The Chantays, both The Surfaris and The Original Surfaris (two entirely separate groups), The Pyramids, and The Beach Boys. The Retail was in direct competition with the Harmony Park Ballroom in Anaheim, where Dick Dale & His Del-Tones took up a Friday night residency. Harmony Park gave its Sunday night residency to Laguna Beach group Dave Myers & The Surftones, who had a hit with their reverb-drenched cover of 'Church Key.'

The competition between the Retail and Harmony clubs extended to the two venue's audiences, leading to fights when one entered the other's turf. It even prompted animosity between Dick Dale and Eddie Bertrand, starting a feud that would not be resolved until, 20 years later, the former bandleaders met, by chance, at Newport Beach. (Asked more recently if there had been anyone else on the surf scene that he considered important, Dick Dale immediately mentioned Eddie & The Showmen.)

Back up in San Luis Obispo a group called The Sentinels picked up where The Revels left off with full-on flamenco-tinged rock'n'rollers such as 'Latinia' and 'Tor-Chula,' while out in Riverside a group of science-fair geeks calling themselves The Tornadoes had a one-off hit with 'Bustin' Surfboards.' A suburb northeast of Los Angles called Glendora, meanwhile, was a real hornet's nest, with its own nightspot in neighboring Azusa called A Teen Canteen. The venue gave birth to a number of bands, including The Surfaris, whose 'Wipe Out' is an out-of-tune masterpiece right up there with 'Louie Louie.'

The tiny city of Downey, southeast of downtown LA, was another example of how mid-century suburbia in the area could be pretty damned cool. Eddie Cochran lived there, and is buried in nearby Cerritos, while as well as a drive-in movie theater and an expansive Tahitian Village entertainment complex, the city boasted its own recording studio and record label during the early 1960s. The first hit to be released on Downey Records was 'Boss' by the rhythm & blues instrumental group The Rumblers, who took their name from Link Wray's 1958 hit 'Rumble.' Next up on Downey was the surf shot heard around the world, 'Pipeline' by The Chantays. Alongside 'Wipe Out,' 'Pipeline' was the biggest hit of the surf instrumental genre. (Dick Dale's 'Misirlou' only reached its current status in contemporary culture when it was included on the soundtrack to that landmark of independent cinema, *Pulp Fiction*, in 1994.)

'Penetration' by the Long Beach group The Pyramids, with its understated lead guitar leaps and pulsating bass rhythm, was another huge surf hit in early 1964, and led to the group making a memorable appearance in the Annette & Frankie movie *Bikini Beach*.

Throughout the Greatest Los Angeles area and beyond, surf instrumental music was high on the minds of most teenage musicians into rock'n'roll. The surf sound spilled right back into the rhythm & blues community from which it sprang in records by The Mixtures, The Jaguars, The Atlantics, and Thee Midniters. Even Beverly Hills gave birth to a super-cool surf combo in the shape of The New Dimensions, whose members went on to form seminal Sunset Strip bands such as The Sounds Of The Seventh Son, The East Side Kids, and The West Coast Pop Art Experimental Band.

Some of the best surf records actually came from the Midwest: Bobby Fuller made some great surf sides while still living and recording in El Paso, Texas, while The Trashmen took surf to excessively wild proportions from Minneapolis, Minnesota, by cobbling together The Rivingtons' 'The Bird's The Word' and 'Papa-Oom-Mow-Mow' to create 'Surfin' Bird.' The Astronauts, from Boulder, Colorado, had the most liquid sound of all on their 'Baja,' although it did help that they recorded in one of LA's most advanced studios, RCA's Music Center Of The World, where The Rolling Stones later cut 'The Last Time,' 'Satisfaction,' and 'Paint It Black.'

The aggressive guitar-attack, tone, melody, and sound of surf-rock singles (and their moody flipsides) would flow into guitar riffs by mid-1960s bands in an unconscious manner. Despite many years of dismissive attitudes toward the surf sound by post-San Francisco rock-music scribes, few could deny the surf-instrumental's staying power. Surf-style riffs drove The Beatles' 'I Feel Fine,' The Rolling Stones' 'Satisfaction,' and The Monkees' 'I'm A Believer,' while countless garage-punk records would feature surf guitar lines. The force and power of surf guitar had, by 1965, become immersed as a firmly established element in the rock'n'roll dialogue. Teenagers in surf bands conjured up that sound from a distinctive culture all of their own.

* * *

In the 1950s, the bebop-loving beat generation first landed on Sunset Strip through the folk music scene surrounding the Unicorn. This was a moment of transition, with all manner of folk and folk-blues artists coming to play on Hollywood's glamour street, including The Weavers, Odetta, Oscar Brand, Bob Gibson, Josh White, Big Bill Broonzy, Ramblin' Jack Elliot, Jesse Fuller, Cisco Houston, and Sam Hinton. At the same time, the Troubadour on La Cienega, the Ash Grove on Melrose, and the Insomniac Café in Hermosa Beach cultivated protest music, which would mushroom during 1965–66.

Bud Dashiell and Travis Edmonson launched a formidable recording career in LA during the late 1950s. They first appeared on a 1958 World Pacific Records live compilation *Saturday Night At The Coffee House: A Night At The Ash Grove*, which also featured Barbara Dane, Rolf Cahn, and Lynn Gold; the cover photograph of the model Peggy Moffitt was taken inside the Insomniac. Bud & Travis were especially good at Mexican boleros, and contributed an acoustic-folk version of 'La Bamba' to the album right around the same time that Ritchie Valens recorded his classic hit version. The duo's second album, *Spotlight On Bud & Travis* (1960), gave them their only *Billboard* Top 30 hit, 'Cloudy Summer Afternoon.'

With their two-part harmonies, acoustic guitar, and spare percussion, Bud & Travis's records still sound fresh, with a focus on the timbre and quality of each man's voice: dark, rustic, and full of range. They next released two live albums from the 3,000-seater Santa Monica Civic Auditorium—*In Concert* and *In Concert, Part 2*—the size of venue reflecting how popular the duo had become in the Greater LA area. Their subsequent albums showcase songs that stretch beyond the traditional folk idiom, such as 'Golden Apples Of The Sun,' as popularized by Judy Collins. Their *Naturally* (1960) featured a cover photographer by Barry Feinstein that foreshadowed his later work on The Byrds' *Mr Tambourine Man* (1965). Bud & Travis became associated with the less traditional, less purist Troubadour crowd. A follow-up live album, this time from Washington DC's Cellar Door, was released in 1964, while on their final album together—*The Bud & Travis Latin Album*, released the following year—they recorded only Spanish-language songs.

Barbara Dane had been singing folk songs in public since 1946, when she appeared on the same bill as Pete Seeger in her home town of Detroit. She moved to San Francisco in 1957, and had become a regular in Los Angeles by 1959, recording an album live at the Ash Grove that year. (Fifteen songs from that session were issued in 1961 as *When I Was A Young Girl*.) As well as being a fine guitar-picker, Dane had a moody, smoky voice well-attuned to both folk and blues.

Judy Henske was the best-known figure to break out of the scene at the Unicorn, where she opened for comedians such as Woody Allen and Lenny Bruce during a nine-month engagement (her relationship with Allen inspired elements of his 1977 movie *Annie Hall*). A native of Chippewa Falls, Wisconsin, Henske arrived in LA by way of San Diego during the late 1950s. She stepped beyond the commonly held definition of folk, pre-empting both The Stone Poneys and Jefferson Airplane with torch-song adaptations of Fred Neil's 'Just A Little Bit Of Rain' and the traditional 'High Flying Bird.'

Henske recorded her debut single, 'That's Enough,' as Judy Hart in 1962, before joining future Modern Folk Quartet vocalist Cyrus Faryar in Dave Guard & The Whisky Hill Singers, with whom she cut an album for Capitol. In 1963 she recorded *Judy Henske* and *High Flyin' Bird* for Elektra and also appeared on ABC television's *Hootenanny* and the folk-exploitation movie *Hootenanny Hoot*. (*Hootenanny* has since come to be considered by many as the moment at which folk sold out after ABC refused to air many of the genre's most important artists because of their political views, leaving all smile and no guile.) After making *Little Bit Of Sunshine, Little Bit Of Rain* (1965), Henske recorded *The Death Defying Judy Henske* in 1966 with producer Jack Nitzsche, who dubbed her 'Queen Of The Beatniks.'

Nitzsche also worked that year with another mainstay of the LA folk club circuit, Bob Lind, on the hit single 'Elusive Butterfly,' which had a breezy, rolling flavor that proved highly influential on Glen Campbell's breakthrough hits, 'Gentle On My Mind' and 'By The Time I Get To Phoenix.' Other Lind tracks were later recorded by The Blues Project, Marianne Faithfull, and The Turtles. Nitzsche produced a second Lind LP, *Photographs Of Feeling*, after which the singer "left the hype and hysteria of the Hollywood scene," according to the liner notes of his next project, *Since There Were Circles* (1968). By this stage Nitzsche had moved on to work with Neil Young of Buffalo Springfield; Judy Heske, meanwhile, busied herself making *Farewell Aldebaran* in collaboration with Jerry Yester of The Modern Folk Quartet for Frank Zappa's Straight label.

Perhaps the most prolific artist to come out of the early LA folk scene was Hoyt Axton, whose mother, Mae Boren Axton, co-wrote 'Heartbreak Hotel.' Originally from Oklahoma, Hoyt played the nightclubs of San Francisco's

North Beach during the late 1950s, and recorded his debut single, 'Georgia Hoss Soldier,' for Nashville's Briar label in 1961. He showed up for Hoot Night at the Troubadour (now on Santa Monica Boulevard) in March 1962, where Doug Weston recognized his talent and helped to promote him. Later that year, a 24-year-old Axton recorded his first LP, *The Balladeer Recorded Live At The Troubadour*, for Horizon Records, one of several of the Troubadour's expanding business interests, which also included the Davon Music publishing company.

'Greenback Dollar' was the most widely heard of Axton's songs during this period, hitting Number 21 on the *Billboard* chart in a version by The Kingston Trio in 1963. It was also reworked in a hot rock'n'roll style by Dick Dale & His Del-Tones on the surf group's first album for Capitol. Axton's visibility increased when ABC television's *Hollywood And The Stars* featured a documentary about him called *The Story Of A Folk Singer*. Axton also made two albums of his own in 1963, *Thunder 'N Lightnin'* and *Saturday's Child*—a dramatic cover of the title track was later recorded by Nancy Sinatra. In 1964 he recorded the garage-sounding *Hoyt Axton Explodes*, which was followed a year later by *Mr Greenback Dollar Man* and *Hoyt Axton Sings Bessie Smith*. Axton also marked 1965 with an appearance on an episode of *Bonanza* entitled 'Dead And Gone' in which he played a criminal working on the Cartwright family's Ponderosa ranch and found time to sing seven songs.

Axton's performing career slowed after that, but his profile was raised in the late 1960s and 70s by a string of covers by more famous artists. Steppenwolf recorded 'The Pusher'—which was used as the lead track on the *Easy Rider* soundtrack—and 'Snowblind Friend,' while Three Dog Night cut versions of 'Joy To The World' and 'Never Been To Spain' and Ringo Starr released a rendition of 'The No No Song.' By this stage Axton had resumed his recording career, and continued to make solid country-rock albums for many years on the Columbia, Capitol, A&M, and MCA labels.

At the Ash Grove, a bastion of traditional folk, The Dillards—led by guitarist-vocalist Rodney Dillard and his banjo-playing brother Doug—aimed straight for the genre's mountain core: bluegrass. Originally from Salem, Missouri, the group came to Los Angeles in November 1962 and settled into the Melrose Avenue club, where they were discovered by World Pacific and Elektra record producer Jim Dickson. Their version of the Buddy Knox rockabilly hit 'Somebody Touched Me,' which featured on their 1963 debut *Back Porch Bluegrass*, demonstrated the same revival-meeting spirit that would color the country-rock movement at the Troubadour in 1968.

Back in 1963, this kind of sound landed The Dillards a regular spot on *The Andy Griffith Show*. According to Richard Kelly's book about the show: "Griffith, who frequently played guitar on the show, and who enjoyed bluegrass music, arranged to have The Dillards on the show to provide an atmosphere of genuine country music. [Cast as] the Darling family, they represented a weird set of mountain folk who occasionally descended on peaceful Mayberry with their superstitions, jugs of moonshine, and bluegrass. Their essential function was to provide a comic menace to the town."[4] Mitchell Jayne of The Dillards notes: "It wasn't until we got on this Andy Griffith show that [people back home] ever really thought we'd amount to anything, because although they may not believe in us at home, they *really* believe in Andy Griffith at home. Everybody at home has little plastic statues of Andy Griffith on their dashboard."[5]

Next came *Live … Almost* (recorded at the Mecca, and featuring a version of Bob Dylan's 'Walkin' Down The Line') and a pair of collaborations with Glen Campbell, both called *12 String Guitar* and released under the pseudonym The Folkswingers. *Pickin' And Fiddlin'* (1965) featured guest fiddle-player Byron Berline, who later found work with Bill Monroe's Bluegrass Boys in Nashville and alongside Doug Dillard and The Byrds' Gene Clark—now recording as Dillard & Clark—back in Los Angeles.

In 1965 The Dillards switched to Capitol and started to move in the direction of folk-rock, influenced no doubt by their associations with Jim Dickson and The Byrds (for whom they opened on tour the following year). The group appeared on the TV shows *Shindig!*, *Hollywood A Go Go*, and *Where The Action Is* and recorded songs such as the full-on folk-rock 'Each Season Changes You' with members of The Leaves. Not particularly interested in this supposed pop-direction, Doug Dillard left the group to record a solo work, *The Banjo Album*, with Gene Clark and future Flying Burrito Brother Bernie Leadon. He would also form Dillard & Clark and appear in The Byrds' live group of 1968 (for the tour in support of the excellent, bluegrass-flavored *Sweetheart Of The Rodeo*). The Dillards replaced him with journeyman banjo-player and vocalist Herb Pedersen for their folk-rock masterwork, *Wheatstraw Suite*. The Eagles' Bernie Leadon would later praise the "meticulous" three-part harmonies on this "beautiful album," which featured versions of Tim Hardin's 'Reason To Believe' and Rising Son Jesse Lee Kincaid's

'She Sang Hymns Out Of Tune.' The Dillards then recorded the majority of the soundtrack to *Bonnie And Clyde* (only 'Foggy Mountain Breakdown' was by Earl Scruggs), backed Glen Campbell on 'Gentle On My Mind,' and cut their own rock'n'roll-inflected *Copperfields* (1969).

Bluegrass became a hot commodity at the Ash Grove during the early 1960s. Two formidable local groups were among the top draws: The Country Boys (who later became The Kentucky Colonels) and The Golden State Boys (who evolved into The Hillmen). Both were blessed with remarkably talented singers and pickers, several of whom would later find wider popularity in The Byrds.

As children, Roland and Clarence White played on radio shows as The White Brothers. With the addition of banjo-player Billy Ray Latham, stand-up bassist Roger Bush, and fiddler Bobby Slone they grew into The Country Boys, appearing on *The Andy Griffith Show* in February 1961. After recording for Sundown and Republic the group signed to Nashville-based Briar International, changing their name to The Kentucky Colonels in time for their full-length debut, *The New Sounds Of Bluegrass America*. The group's early work, like much of Briar's output, stuck to straight-up folk-bluegrass; a 1963 session with Eric Weissberg and Marshall Brickman formed the bulk of the soundtrack to the 1972 movie *Deliverance*.

The true versatility of The Kentucky Colonels came to the fore after they signed to LA's World Pacific label for the groundbreaking *Appalachian Swing!* (1964). Clarence White mixed the traditional hillbilly-pickin' sound with the contrasting styles of Django Reinhardt, Chuck Berry, and Elvis Presley sideman Scotty Moore, stepping out to the fore and using his guitar in a way that had previously been the realm of mandolin, fiddle, or banjo players in bluegrass bands.

The group's intensity rose further on their next recordings, on which they backed dobro lead guitarist Tut Taylor on his *Dobro Country*. They can be seen and heard in the hokey hillbilly movie *The Farmer's Other Daughter*; various live recordings of the Colonels at Ash Grove and an unreleased studio album that emerged from this period appear on the Rounder, Sierra Briar, and Shiloh labels.

With the onset of folk-rock, the Colonels recorded a couple of electric tracks ('Everybody Has One But You' and 'Made Of Stone'), introducing a sound that Clarence White would develop further on solo recordings for Bakersfield International, which were produced by long-time LA player Gary Paxton.

During these sessions, White began a recording partnership with drummer and harmonica player Gene Parsons, with whom he patented the Parsons/White String Bender, which gave their recordings a unique pedal-steel-meets-Fender Telecaster sound. Recording variously as The Reasons, Nashville West, and 'Cajun' Gib & Gene, White and Parsons were involved in the making of numerous pioneering country-rock records of the 1960s, including Rick Nelson's *Country Fever* and The Gosdin Brothers' *Sound Of Goodbye*.

Vern and Rex Gosdin first came to prominence on television as members of The Golden State Boys. Chris Hillman of The Byrds recalls seeing the group performing regularly on *Cal's Corral*: "I loved watching them on the show, and later I got the chance to be in the band." The group, which had debuted with the excellent 'Always Dreaming,' changed its name to The Hillmen after his arrival, but only made one Jim Dickson-produced LP before disbanding. Shortly afterward, Hillman joined The Byrds as bassist, but also found time to produce the first single by The Gosdin Brothers, 'One Hundred Years From Now,' for which he brought in Clarence White to play electric lead guitar. White and Gene Parsons then played on a number of other fine Gosdin Brothers 45s, such as 'She Still Wishes I Were You' and 'Hangin' On' (1967). The group then signed to Capitol records, for whom they recorded *Sound Of Goodbye* and a breezy folk-country-pop take on Donovan's 'Catch The Wind' (both 1968).

Verve/Folkways group The New Lost City Ramblers, who hailed from New York City, were another favorite on the Hollywood club circuit. The Ash Grove was their regular haunt, largely because multi-instrumentalists Mike Seeger and John Cohen from the group worked in collaboration with the club's owner, Ed Pearl. Regularly cited as a defining influence by folk-rock artists, Seeger helped to spur diversity and musical interaction in the collaborative LA folk music scene.

Much has been said about the networking that went on in folk clubs, and the many associations forged during this period. The poet Rod McKuen could be found on the Strip making beatnik-folk music at the Unicorn; at the Troubadour on Santa Monica, you'd have Mason Williams ('Classical Gas') and top session-player Jimmy Bond hanging out with comedy duo The Smothers Brothers (and later collaborating on *The Smothers Brothers Comedy Hour*); The Pair Extraordinaire and San Francisco duo Joe & Eddie would record live albums at the Ice House and the Mecca, in Buena Park, where The Dillards had cut similar discs; Chris Hillman studied the mandolin playing of The Dillards' Dean Webb at Ash

Grove; and Bob Dylan played his first LA solo show in 1964 at Wilson High School in Long Beach, near the Golden Bear in Huntington Beach, where Hoyt Axton performed regularly.

* * *

During the summer of 1964, two maverick radio stations in the Inland Empire—the Southern Californian region to the east of Los Angeles proper, encompassing San Bernardino and Riverside Counties—started playing rough and tumble records by The Rolling Stones, who had yet to make an impact in the USA. Because their signals were transmitted in direct proximity to the LA radio market, KFXM and KMEN were able to operate in similar ways to pirate radio stations in the UK, and as such could break records not yet playlisted in the central city. The Stones quickly became the template for countless American garage-punk bands of the 1960s, so when 'Satisfaction' hit the following June, Sunset Strip was already rife with bands ready to use the group's fuzz-tone sound as a springboard.

The wealth of great bands that came out of San Bernardino and Riverside is testament to the head start Inland Empire kids and their LA counterparts received. Between early 1966 and mid 1967, a young deejay from Liverpool, England, by the name of John Ravenscroft—much more famous later on as John Peel—appeared regularly on KMEN, giving the station a direct link to the new wave of British groups. "Local radio outlets had caught on to the popularity of the British groups," recalls *Ugly Things* magazine editor Mike Stax, "but there were also imports in hip shops, and just hip kids picking up on the trends from the UK. The Southern California kids were just more tuned in than many other parts of the country."

A couple of days prior to their San Bernardino debut in June 1964, the Stones—encouraged to make the trip to the USA by Phil Spector and Gene Pitney—performed a roughneck version of 'I Just Want To Make Love To You' on *The Hollywood Palace*. Comic insults were hurled at the group by Dean Martin, who compared them to "Jackie Coogan and Skippy" and claimed the group had "challenged The Beatles to a hair-pulling contest." (Perhaps the first comparison wasn't too far off the mark: years after starring with Charlie Chaplin in *The Kid*, Coogan haunted the Melody Room on Sunset and was busted several times for marijuana possession during the 1950s, before playing a dope-peddler in 1958's *High School Confidential*, and Uncle Fester in *The Addams Family* from 1964–66.)

The earliest group from the San Bernardino/Riverside area to take up the Stones' mantle was The Bush, who also supported the British group on their third visit to Los Angeles. The Bush only released three singles but were tremendously popular on radio and with local kids, almost certainly inspiring more groups to head off in a similar direction. 'Who Killed The Ice Cream Man' was a Number 1 hit on KFXM, while other Bush songs, including their endearing take on 'Don't You Fret' by The Kinks, have since appeared on garage-punk compilations. "You'd hear these records in LA, broadcast out of San Bernardino," remembers Strip scenester Pam DeLacy, an Orange County resident who veered between Hollywood and San Bernardino on weekends, depending on who was playing where. "There was a lot going on in the Inland Empire. They would have big shows at the Swing Auditorium. Dick Dale got a lot of people going out there in the first place, and I remember seeing him share a bill with The Bobby Fuller Four, plus The Bush and The Whatt Four from Riverside."

Riverside combo The Mustangs were most likely not aware that the sustained guitar chords on a song of theirs, 'That's For Sure,' mirrored what Pete Townshend of The Who was doing in the mod London of 1965. But a year earlier Mick Jagger had already told a local newspaper that San Bernardino was "just like England." The Mustangs rose from the ashes of several surf groups and went straight for the British Invasion sound, making liberal use of a Gibson Maestro fuzz-tone box (as heard on 'Satisfaction').

But if any one band could be said to embody the impact of The Rolling Stones on LA-area teens it was The Hysterics, also from San Bernardino. Their 'Everything's There'—"you've got the eyes, you've got the hair, everything's there, ohhh yeeaaahhh!"—was a powerful portrayal of the feeling of knowing a girl who has, inarguably, 'got it.' The group had a typically short shelf-life, releasing just two singles, 'Won't Get Far' and 'That's All She Wrote.' The second of these was originally a country number by Ernest Tubb, and has a primitive, almost infantile musicality. The British Invasion may have provided the impetus for a lot of these bands, but many of them transformed that vitality into their own environment, taking in local references—often country & western—along the way. Native American sounds also cropped up, such as the tom tom beat of Hank Williams's

'Kawliga' or The McCoys' 'Hang On Sloopy'—a centuries-old beat that came from the very spirit of the land.

A crucial example of US groups' reduction of British bands' embellishment came from the Texan combo Zakary Thaks, who infused driving rock'n'roll with a polka drumbeat on their legendary single 'Bad Girl,' which evoked Tex-Mex accordion music. "The Brits gave American roots music a new timbre, but the Yanks took that wood, whittled it, and warped it with Chili Dogs," explains garage-punk musician Shelly Ganz. "You could never get such twisted adaptations from the studied English groups, who had learned about rhythm & blues at art college."

US teens in 1960s garage bands came to rock'n'roll more directly by way of their culture of wild radio deejays, hot-rods, carnivals and cotton candy, and prime drive-in fare like *Ghost Of Dragstrip Hollow* and *Dracula Vs. Billy The Kid*. "The British were more refined, and you can hear this contrast in the records of The Shadows and Link Wray," says Ganz, "or on '19th Nervous Breakdown,' from The Rolling Stones to The Standells. Count Five's 'Psychotic Reaction' and 'Peace of Mind' may have been influenced by The Yardbirds and The Who, but there's this discordant, primitive thing going on that the Brits didn't have. Then The Seeds are at another level. For Americans, this music was a logical outcropping from the 1950s, and in a sense, they surpassed the British groups. Take the existing surf and frat bands and couple it with The Beatles and The Rolling Stones, and you get a song like 'Hey Tiger' by The Topsy Turbys in 1965. The best of Americana sprung from its leisure time, and with American garage records, it all goes back to the carnival, which you can hear in the organ sounds."

Perhaps the coolest-looking band in the area was The Misunderstood, who released a local single called 'You Don't Have To Go.' In April 1966 the group recorded enough material for an album at Gold Star Studios—with KMEN disc jockey John Ravenscroft taking the role of producer—before attempting to make their mark on Sunset Strip with gigs at Pandora's Box. "We were a pretty energetic group," recalls rhythm guitarist Greg Treadway. "I remember hitting my head several times jumping up, because the roof there was so low."[6] The Misunderstood's performances had a pronounced experimental bent. Mike Stax recalls how the group expanded and electrified The Yardbirds' take on Mose Allison's 'I'm Not Talkin',' stretching it to six minutes of "half-time, double-time, and warp-speed segments, brake-squealing stops and starts, and a feedback section that mirrored their scene-stealing live gimmick of exiting the stage with their instruments howling against their amplifiers." The group's amps were rigged so that, when they fed back, their light show would flash in response. According to Stax: "They pulled this stunt off at Pandora's Box, stunning everyone, including the barman, who is said to have closed the bar in order to observe the spectacle."

The Misunderstood were well aware of the effect this was having, because they had jury-rigged it themselves. "All future light shows were run by people outside the band," recalls lead guitarist Rick Brown, "but our lights were exactly in time with the music, being lit up by the music itself. The lights were plugged into the extension outputs of the three guitar amps. It was completely visual music." Guitarist Glenn Ross Campbell—who had played in surf group The Goldtones and, with The Answers, recorded an anti-Vietnam War song, 'Fool Turn Around,' in 1965 prior to forming The Misunderstood—remarked at the time: "We are just trying to go beyond sounds to present an exciting, visual act. We are giving [the audience] a flying carpet, a vehicle to leave this dimension."[7]

The group's close association with Ravenscroft—who also served as their manager for a time—led them to relocate to England during the summer of 1966, where they recorded songs such as 'Children Of The Sun.' *The New Musical Express* took note of the "strange sounds, oscillations, and reverberations" of the forward-thinking Fontana single 'I Can Take You To The Sun,' adding that it was "extremely well done … A really penetrating performance that grips from start to finish—with pounding drums and weird effects from the slide guitar. Absorbing lyric and tempo changes. On the flip, 'Who Do You Love,' a wild, frenzied tempo, with a Jagger-like spirited vocal backed by incredible way-out noises. It's like The Stones dabbling in Psychedelia!" Sadly, the group was soon torn apart by the US draft board. Campbell returned to Riverside in early 1967, where he and Rod Piazza's group The Mystics combined to form House of DBS, later known as The Dirty Blues Band. (He returned to the UK to form a new line-up of The Misunderstood in 1969.)

More typically, the stories of Inland Empire bands followed that of Merrell & The Exiles. The group was led by Merrell Fankhauser, who in the mid 1960s left behind a surf group, The Impacts, in the picturesque beach-town of San Luis Obispo, moving to the arid desert surroundings of Lancaster to form a new, British Invasion-styled group. Merrell & The Exiles' 'Please Be Mine' charted locally and was played on Hollywood radio stations, and they appeared on television shows in Los Angeles and San Diego. Other radio stations across the USA started to take note of the single, but the band's label, Glenn Records, couldn't afford to promote it or press more copies. Meanwhile, hits-in-the-making such as 'She's Gone' and 'Shake My Hand' stayed in the can.

Exiles guitarist Jeff Cotton and drummer John French went on to join Captain Beefheart's Magic Band, while Fankhauser formed a group called Fapardokly (an amalgamation of the first two initials of each member's name). Between 1965 and 1967 the group recorded numerous moody, pysch-folk songs, including 'Tomorrow's Girl' (originally an Exiles single) and 'Gone To Pot' (a direct lift from The Byrds' 'Eight Miles High'). Another song, '!The Music Scene!' was somewhat ahead of its time in its astute lyrical observations of the unscrupulous aspects of the Hollywood record industry.

Other notable Inland Empire-based bands included The Torquays, who hit the local charts a couple of times in 1966 with The Kinks-esque 'Stolen Moments' and 'Harmonica Man (From London Town).' The following year, Riverside's Whatt Four made a cool, fuzzed-out pysch-pop single, 'Dandelion Wine,' while Warden & The Fugitives put out the primal 'The World Ain't Changed,' on which the title line is repeated over and over, with growing anger, above a grungey 'Satisfaction'-style riff.

Former members of The Bush and The North Side Moss pooled to form the harmonic pysch-pop group The Light, combining elements of The Music Machine and Buffalo Springfield, with whom they played twice at the Swing Auditorium. Buffalo Springfield liked the group so much that they convinced The Light to move into central Los Angeles, where they recorded a lone single for A&M, the Lefte Banke-styled 'Music Box.' As psychedelia approached, the moodier side of the San Bernardino/Riverside teen sound reared its head on 'Shattered' by Good Feelins.

Ken & The Fourth Dimension and The Avengers were both from Bakersfield, a city 100 miles northeast of LA, and were both fronted by Ken Johnson, formerly of the surf group Kenny & The Sultans (who released one single, 'With Vigor,' in 1963). With The Fourth Dimension, Johnson made 'See If I Care,' which pitted a 'Last Train To Clarksville' jangle against raucous organ, fuzz-tone, and snarling vocals, then hit his stride on The Avengers' monumental garage-punk cut 'Be A Cave Man' (1965), displaying a sense of humor somewhere between

Frank Zappa and Jay Ward with the lines: "You gotta pull her by the hair, hold her tighter than a grizzly bear/Be a cave man, keep her in line." The Avengers followed up with the Farfisa-organ-led 'Shipwrecked' and 'You Can't Hurt Me Anymore' before bowing out with 1966's 'It's Hard To Hide.' Johnson's six perfect singles all featured impressive B-sides, a couple of which showed him to be equally adept at folk-rock balladry.

* * *

There is no better indicator of the way Los Angeles became the center of the (American) rock'n'roll universe in 1964 than a pair of closed-circuit television extravaganzas shot in town. *The TAMI Show* (1964) and *The Big TNT Show* (1965) were shown in theaters by American International Pictures, and confirm the jolting effect of The Beatles' arrival in the USA on American youth culture.

The TAMI Show (short for 'Teen Age Music International') opened with a wild performance by Chuck Berry, backed by a Jack Nitzsche-led rock'n'roll orchestra and a coterie of go-go dancers led by Toni Basil and Teri Garr. Taped on October 28th and 29th 1964 at the Santa Monica Civic, the show continued with a litany of current styles: British Invasion acts, such as Gerry & The Pacemakers and Billy J. Kramer & The Dakotas; the cream of Motown, including The Miracles, Marvin Gaye and The Supremes; surf acts The Beach Boys and Jan & Dean; girl-group superstar Lesley Gore; and an early, long-haired garage-punk group from Massachusetts called The Barbarians. Already stunned, the audience is then whipped into a frenzy by James Brown & The Famous Flames and the show's closing act, The Rolling Stones.

The follow-up to *The TAMI Show*, *The Big TNT Show* was held at the Moulin Rouge, on the southeast corner of Sunset and Vine, and displays the pivotal changes that had occurred by 1965. Youth culture had come to the fore; and so had social consciousness. The opening credits thrust the viewer into the visual excitement of the Strip in 1965 and '66 to the clanging, chiming tune of The Modern Folk Quartet's 'This Could Be The Night,' produced by the show's musical director, Phil Spector; The Ronettes are seen doing a turnaround rock'n'roll ballet dance in front of Chateau Marmont at night, with the blinking, flashing neon of the Imperial Gardens Restaurant in the background; The Lovin' Spoonful leap and frolic in front of a strip nightspot before knocking down an ad for their own *Do You Believe In Magic*; Bo Diddley's bassist Chester 'Dr Boo' Lindsey aims the neck of his instrument as if he's shooting the audience with a rifle.

Go-go dancers are seen in a rehearsal hall, shaking in black nylons, white boots, heavy kiss-curl bangs, and thick eyeliner; teenage knees and calves jump on pavements and on wooden nightclub floors; Petula Clark receives the royal treatment prior to a gig; there's a nighttime shot of Ben Frank's glittering neon, and one of the Trip, which advertises an upcoming Marvin Gaye engagement. Large groups of kids are seen riding Honda bikes and antique cars down Hollywood Boulevard; Donovan warms up in his hotel; The Byrds are seen outside the Moulin Rouge in sunny Californian daylight, and then inside, onstage; there are live highlights of Bo Diddley and Ike & Tina Turner; Phil Spector is shown rehearsing with Joan Baez; hordes of gallivanting mod kids chase through the Strip, some in pursuit of David McCallum, the man from U.N.C.L.E., who arrives to kick off the show.

The film's closing message requests that the viewer "be sure to tune in for next year's show," but next year never came. *The Big TNT Show* captures that final, tantalizing moment.

CHAPTER FOUR

Progenitors of the broader social consciousness

**" **_Disappearing into smoke rings of his own mind,_
it immediately took lyrics from moon, croon, spoon,
June, I-love-you, high school romance stereotypes, into
psychological investigations into the nature of consciousness
itself. Into the nature of identity, which is his specialty.
Into making many masks of identity, even referring
ultimately to the tambourine man himself, who is what?
Historical poetry, the tradition of minstrelsy, the trickster
hero, which has been, again, a persona of Dylan
all the way through. **" ** ALLEN GINSBERG

In 1963, KRLA radio deejay Bob Eubanks found a way to answer the insatiable call for rock'n'roll hit-makers to play gigs in and around the lucrative central plexus of Los Angeles, opening nightclubs—for teenagers—in nearby Studio City and Long Beach. "There was a club in New York called the Peppermint Lounge," Eubanks recalls. "They were doing big business. At that time the law stated in LA County that you could not have dancing with liquor unless you served food. There were very few places for people to dance, so we opened these young adult nightclubs, 18 to 25, no booze. From 'Peppermint' we went to 'Cinnamon' and Cinder was the only thing we could come up with that went with Cinnamon."

Making use of his radio contacts, Eubanks started booking the sort of cutting-edge bands that young rockers were craving, instead of the slick teen idols that clogged the hit parade during the early 1960s. "We had some big acts play there. The Beach Boys, Chuck Berry, Ike & Tina Turner, Stevie Wonder, The Supremes, Johnny 'Guitar' Watson, The Rivingtons, Bobby Day, The Coasters, The Righteous Brothers, Jan & Dean, The Byrds, and they would all play the two clubs in one night. We'd go on at 9:30 in Long Beach and play through 10:30, and then they would drive and go on at 11:30 in Studio City and go until 12:30. We started something [not knowing] how big it was going to get."

The Cinnamon Cinder was a surprise hit and provided an alternative to the predictability of covers bands in Hollywood twist-joints. It put kids in the Greater LA area within reach of the action, removing the need to trek out to El Monte Legion Stadium, a long haul for anyone in Hollywood, Santa Monica, or the San Fernando Valley. The Long Beach Cinder drew audiences in from Orange County and the southern half of LA County; the rest could hit the one in Studio City. (There was also, briefly, a Cinnamon Cinder in Alhambra, and on Fairfax, opposite Farmer's Market.)

As his venues remained within LA city limits, however, Eubanks still had to deal with police harassment. His recollections are similar to those of Johnny Otis and Eddie Davis: "The cops were so tough on us. They didn't want dance places, because it was going to cause them trouble. Now there was a place in Hollywood called the Red Velvet, but that was a 21 and over, serve booze kind of thing. Ours was under 21, so they didn't want kids dancing and they made it very difficult. We solved that problem in Long Beach because we hired a Long Beach Police Officer to be our doorman, and took care of all that. The LAPD wouldn't let us hire off-duty Police Officers. They tried to nail us for 'dirty dancing,' which was such a bizarre thing. It was just always on pins and needles."

There was a hit record named after the club by The Pastel Six, written and sung by A&R man Russ Regan, who'd given The Beach Boys their name. Eubanks recalls how regular radio plays created a swarm around his club, adding: "As soon as 'Cinnamon Cinder' went off the charts, Elvis Presley released 'Return To Sender,' and everybody thought it was 'Cinder'. So we got another huge amount of publicity off of that." The financial windfall at the Cinnamon Cinder was noticed nationally as well as locally, providing the final drop of water that burst the dam for teenage rock'n'roll to appear on Sunset Strip.

The opening of venues such as the Whisky A Go Go in the center of the city was long overdue. Hollywood twist-clubs such as PJ's, Peppermint West, Purple Onion, and Gazzarri's had been playing it safe with their percolated brand of cover band rock'n'roll. With Johnny Rivers at the helm, the Whisky in its infancy was still not that much more daring. But the combination of its central location and the sight of go-go dancers looming provocatively on the dance floor as Patty Brockhurst, Joanie Labine, and others spun 45s from above, forced other clubs in the area to think again. The time had come for some rock'n'roll headliners to shake things up. No one, however, could have predicted what was about to unfold at the Strip's geographical center, Ciro's.

A month after the Whisky opened in January 1964, The Beatles arrived in New York City, bringing with them the total mayhem of Beatlemania, which ensured that radio stations would not be returning to the teen crooners of 1959–60. Rock'n'roll had been thriving in America in the form of James Brown, surf groups, girl groups, Phil Spector, and Motown, but since these were all issued on local, independent labels they were downplayed by the national media. Rock'n'roll's rebellious edge had been smoothed and smothered on radio since 1959, with an unsettling number of mediocre, middle-of-the-road acts clogging up the national hit parade in its place.

Many young people had instead gravitated toward folk music during this time. Folk put the angst and aggression of rock'n'roll into a more traditional context, which seemed more palatable to the adult market. The countercultural intent of folk was often softened in the public arena, most notably by the ABC television show *Hootenanny*. Pete Seeger, Joan Baez, and many of the giants of folk refused to appear on the program because of this perceived lack of credibility. There were, however, great loads of kids running around with banjos and harmonicas, looking for ways to forge a new sound. "I used to hang around the Gate Of Horn and the Old Town School Of Folk Music in Chicago," said Roger McGuinn—still known at the time by his original name, Jim McGuinn—in 1965. "I remember early Odetta, Frank Hamilton, Pete Seeger when it was really beautiful. The interest in American culture with Pete Seeger and The Weavers grew to an in-group thing on a bigger level like jazz, sports cars, and hi-fi. It went with that and it grew with that up to complete international acceptance and then the mass-media thing killed it. But the good elements from it have been salvaged … to grow into new things, to be synthesized."

McGuinn and his future Byrds cohorts Gene Clark and David Crosby all had big-label experience behind them by 1964, each of them having played in *Hootenanny*-style folk-exploitation combos. McGuinn had worked in coffeehouses in Greenwich Village, and arranged songs on the superb *Judy Collins #3*. Another soon-to-be Byrd, Chris Hillman, was involved in recordings by the bluegrass combos The Scottsville Squirrel Barkers and The Hillmen, whose sound would also prove influential in the future.

The Byrds met at the Troubadour, a prominent folk club that started out in the La Cienega district before relocating, in 1961, to Santa Monica Boulevard. Local folkies such as Hoyt Axton and Bob Lind appeared regularly at the venue, while on one occasion Roger McGuinn played acoustic versions of Beatles songs. This proved hard for the crowd's purist elements to swallow, but encouraged Gene Clark to start playing with McGuinn.

The duo of McGuinn and Clark was soon joined by Crosby, who had been playing regular solo folk gigs along the Californian coastline, and Hillman. This nascent Byrds line-up—then known as The Jet Set—was given time to grow by producer Jim Dickson at World Pacific Studios, where they benefited from being able to hear themselves back on tape. Having previously worked at the jazz club the Renaissance, Dickson was the manager of the bluegrass groups The Dillards and The Kentucky Colonels, and had produced comedy albums by Lenny Bruce and Lord Buckley. World Pacific, meanwhile, was the highly influential recording center for the West Coast jazz imprint of the same name. Starting out as Pacific Jazz, the label developed the careers of Chet Baker and Gerry Mulligan; owner Dick Bock added the 'World' after signing Ravi Shankar—whose raga stylings were later an influence on The Byrds—in the late 1950s.

David Crosby found The Byrds' fifth member, Michael Clarke, playing bongos on the beach, and enlisted him as the band's drummer partly because of his close resemblance to The Rolling Stones' guitarist Brian Jones. In August 1964, McGuinn, Clark, Crosby, and Dickson went to see the Beatles movie *A Hard Day's Night* at the Pix Theater on Hollywood Boulevard and had their minds collectively blown (they returned for several further screenings). George Harrison's 12-string Rickenbacker guitar and his playing at the close of the movie's title song were an immediate and integral influence on the formative sound of The Byrds.

As inventive as folk-rock sounded to some, its roots could actually be heard in the jangly guitars and smoky harmonies of songs such as 'Don't Throw Your Love Away' and 'Needles And Pins' by early British Invaders The Searchers. The Byrds covered The Searchers' arrangement of 'When You Walk In The Room'—a song written by a friend of The Byrds, LA folk/pop singer Jackie DeShannon—during early rehearsals. (Over in San Francisco, The Beau Brummels were developing their own version of the very same Searchers sound, mirroring The Byrds experiments in Los Angeles.)

Dickson landed The Byrds a one-single deal on Elektra on the strength of demos cut at World Pacific. The label's president, Jac Holzman, attempted to cash in on the British Invasion boom by crediting the single to The Beefeaters. The Beatles-esque A- and B-sides, 'Don't Be Long' and 'Please Let Me Love You,' were among the first rock'n'roll releases on the then folk-based Elektra (which would later put out albums by Love and The Doors). The single sold poorly, however, leading Holzman to decline picking up the option for any further records.

Undeterred, The Byrds continued to record originals. 'The Airport Song' was inspired by time spent by the group in the Los Angeles International Airport Theme Building (now known as the Encounter), where they would drink and watch planes land. It was Crosby's first lead vocal for the group, and had a smooth groove that complimented Gene Clark's moodier songs well. Clark and McGuinn's 'You Movin',' meanwhile, was recorded with Wall Of Sound session men Larry Knechtel and Hal Blaine on bass and drums. 'Tomorrow Is A Long Ways Away' and 'You Showed Me' both feature sparse acoustic backings and make good use of Michael Clarke's bongos; 'You Showed Me' ended up being one of the final hits recorded by The Turtles five years later.

In November 1964 The Byrds signed to Columbia Records, thanks in no small part to the influence of Ben Shapiro, who as well as being the proprietor of the Renaissance during the late 1950s and early 60s was also Miles Davis's manager. Shapiro was introduced to the group by his daughter, Michelle; he had Davis make the call to Columbia that piqued the label's interest.

The Byrds found the key that would set them apart from the rest in the form of a Bob Dylan demo that defined the free spirit of the age and framed existential mysticism as rebellion. Jim Dickson had heard Dylan perform 'Mr Tambourine Man' and asked him for a demo of the song, which Dylan had recently cut with Ramblin' Jack Elliot. David Crosby wasn't initially keen on the song, so Dickson took it to The Kentucky Colonels' brilliant young guitarist Clarence White—who, of course, would end up in The Byrds a few years later—but he too declined to record it. With the Colonels, White had just cut the landmark *Appalachian Swing!* album, which re-examined and expanded the guitar-interplay dynamics of mountain music, and was not interested in pursuing protest songs. When Bob Dylan next passed through town, Dickson went back to The Byrds and asked them to give the song another try. This time, they agreed. A decade after Sam Phillips, Elvis Presley, Scotty Moore, and Bill Black explored rockabilly at Sun Records, it was laboratory time at World Pacific for the progenitors of the broader social consciousness.

"I'd been given free rein [at World Pacific] for producing a guitar album by Glen Campbell that had taken the label out of the red," recalls Dickson. "Dylan came in to jam with The Byrds at the studio for a couple of hours on a variety of tunes. His interaction and encouragement led McGuinn to finally take over and sing lead on 'Mr Tambourine Man.'" In the months to come, McGuinn's arrangement would turn the music world on its head.

The Byrds continued to rehearse and develop their sound at a dance studio owned by sculptor Vito Paulekas at 303 North Laurel Avenue, just off Beverly. Paulekas's dance troupe—which included his sidekick, Carl Franzoni, alongside such colorful characters as Karen Yum Yum and Johnny Fuck Fuck—became an integral element of The Byrds' early mystique, instigating a groovy, improvisatory dance style that was quickly imitated by a growing number of teenage beatniks (who had begun to refer to themselves as 'freaks').

"[Paulekas] let two bands rehearse in the studio when housewives weren't learning how to do sculpting and/or clay," notes Kim Fowley. "One was called The Byrds, the other was called Love. They both came out of his basement. Then [they moved] on to a ballet studio, which is now the Groundling Theater on Melrose. That's the first time The Byrds ever played outside of Vito's basement. They were then booked into Ciro's LeDisc, a few hundred people showed up, and you know the rest." (The Byrds' official debut actually took place in the front bar room of the Troubadour, then known as the Folk Den.)

According to *Hit Parader* magazine: "What The Byrds did to Ciro's was unbelievable. They made it *thee* place for young Hollywood. ... There were queues up and down Sunset Strip of desperate teenagers clamoring to get in. The dance floor was a wild and wonderful mad house. A hard core of Byrd followers—wayward painters, disinherited sons and heirs, bearded sculptors, coltish, misty-eyed nymphs with hair all over the place—suddenly taught Hollywood to dance again."

"We were well-known for dancing to other groups," Carl Franzoni recalls. "Jim Doval & The Gauchos from Fresno ... had horns and everything in their band, they were like a Top 40 band that played near Ciro's, at the Crescendo. Vito hired The Byrds for a teenage dance on Melrose Avenue. A lot of teenagers came from Fairfax High and Blessed Sacrament. Tons. So they go there, and the dance was for 'Stop the War in Vietnam.' There were signs everywhere, Vito made these signs and put them up. The next night was at Ciro's, first night at Ciro's, and we walk in this place, it's a totally red room, lots of light, the best dance floor in Hollywood, its about 40 feet by 60 feet. All the stars in Hollywood are there … these guys have never played for them. We stepped on the dance floor, and from then on it was music and dance for months and months."[1]

Drugs had not yet become a huge part of the Ciro's culture: many attendees had not even tried marijuana, let alone anything harder. Unlike the glazed-eye 'guitar boogie' dancing that burnt-out hippies later became associated with, the music of The Byrds and Love still had that go-go beat essential to the excitement of Sunset Strip. As such, the dancing was more frantic: when bands played in the smaller confines of clubs such as Ciro's LeDisc, Gazzarri's, the Sea Witch, or the Trip, songs such as 'I'll Feel A Whole Lot Better' and 'Can't Explain' took on a tougher attitude. The author and artist Eve Babitz notes: "It would have been hard to keep up that level of energy, had drugs been the primary motivation."

"We were trained dancers," recalls Carl Franzoni. "Vito had studied with some really fine dance teachers in Hollywood. We had a formal place we went to, and the people right after us were Toni Basil and David Winters. They were the shit, big-time dancers, and they would sit and watch us, and take what we were doing and add it into their stuff." What was going on in Hollywood was so unheard of that The Byrds actually paid nine regular dancers from Clay Vito to tour with them once 'Mr Tambourine Man' hit the charts, so crucial were they to the Byrds experience. "The tour itself was really something," says Franzoni. "The first place was Denver. We went into Minnesota, Youngstown, Ohio, Dayton, Ohio, stuff like that. Here we are, in Montana, bus stops across the street from a little Western-looking diner. Those people went from crying to screaming to laughing. Here we're these crazy-looking long-haired people walking in … they'd never seen anything like that."

The Byrds' impact hit the Strip harder, faster, and more profoundly than the Whisky A Go Go phenomenon had the previous year. Shortly after the group's debut at Ciro's LeDisc on March 26 1965—the highlight of which was when Bob Dylan popped up for the encore—the emphasis in Strip nightclubs' booking policies went directly to long-haired, countercultural bands that reflected the influence of Dylan, The Beatles, and The Rolling Stones. Slicker, more predictable house bands in the Johnny Rivers mode began to take a back seat.

"The Byrds were, in my estimation the best dance band that Hollywood ever saw," says Carl Franzoni, "because they made people dance with that kind of music. Those guys were forever fighting with each other, but when they got up there, they really cooked. Love weren't the dance band that The Byrds were and neither was Frank Zappa. The combination of [the band-members], the different factions of what kind of music they came from, it just was such a fantastic blend that it was so folk, from all different parts of the United States. I always think of dancing to 'The Bells Of Rhymney' and like, it's a church, you know? So when they brought that kind of music in to Minnesota, Iowa, places like that, those kids were just: 'Wow, where did *you* come from?' They could have started their own church with that kind of music they were playing."[2]

Derek Taylor recalls The Byrds' impact on Hollywood on the BBC television special *All You Need Is Love*, which first aired in 1975, describing how Peter Fonda booked the group to perform at a birthday party for his sister, Jane, in 1965: "[It] was in itself very unusual for anyone in movies to know anything about rock'n'roll … it was my job to make sure all of The Byrds met Peter Fonda, and Jane Fonda, and Henry Fonda as well, who was not to be too upset by the appearance of The Byrds. Well, I hadn't thought about it before, but all of The Byrds' followers knew no rules; they got high, and went anywhere The Byrds went, and they crashed the party, looking absolutely terrible (for those days). Henry Fonda [was] quite astounded, like: 'What's this? What is going on?'" Taylor panicked, and appealed to The Byrds' manager Jim Dickson to calm the situation. Dickson's response, however, was simple: "This is New Hollywood. They want this madness. That's why they got The Byrds here. This is the beginning, where the worlds meet, again."

When The Byrds debuted 'Mr Tambourine Man' at Ciro's LeDisc on March 26th 1965—with Bob Dylan there in support—one of Hollywood's most exquisite landmarks found itself at the threshold of a social revolution. The Byrds had successfully electrified Bob Dylan. According to music journalist Ellen Sander: "Almost immediately after The Byrds' 'Mr Tambourine Man,' Dylan took off on a mass commercial level. His time was bursting with overdues and The Byrds were merely the last in a series of 'booster rockets,' as McGuinn would later put it."

Bob Dylan was already the stuff of folk legend, and his 'Blowin' In The Wind' had made a huge impact on commercial radio by way of Peter, Paul & Mary's 1963 hit cover. Dylan's folk songs appealed to a small but enthusiastic cult, but pop music in general did not quite feel his overwhelming influence until The Byrds recorded 'Mr Tambourine Man.' A day after The Byrds' performance of the song at Ciro's LeDisc, Dylan already seemed aware of the potential impact of his absorption of rock'n'roll, telling Paul Jay Robbins of *The Los Angeles Free Press*: "You can make all sorts of protest songs and put them on a Folkways record. But who hears them?"

On June 5th The Byrds' 'Mr Tambourine Man' hit Number 1 on *Billboard's* Hot 100. Ten days later, Dylan entered the studio to record 'Like A Rolling Stone,' clearly influenced by the new sound of the Strip. According to Ellen Sander, the single, released on July 20th, "clawed its ways through charts and airwaves. Its sheer power, its visceral intensity, was a frontal attack, echoing that memorable concert at Newport that same year, where with that very song he had blown the scene apart. Next came the landmark LP *Highway 61 Revisited*, which completely resolved Dylan's change in style."

Amid the controversy of Dylan going electric—Pete Seeger even tried to chop Dylan's amplifier leads with an axe at Newport—many initially forgot that he had always aspired to the jeans and leather jacket sensibilities of rockabilly and the rhythmic verse of Chuck Berry. Back when he was still known as Robert Zimmerman in his hometown of Hibbing, Minnesota, Dylan played in rockabilly combos like The Golden Chords and The Rockets. The Rockets demoed a Zimmerman co-write, 'Big Black Train,' at Minneapolis's legendary Kay Bank Studio, where The Trashmen cut 'Surfin' Bird' and The Castaways recorded 'Liar Liar.' Dylan's aim was to be a piano-pounding hellraiser in the mould of Little Richard or Jerry Lee Lewis. "[He] did a good job on Little Richard songs," recalls Jim Propotnick, a member of both The Golden Chords and The Rockets, "and I thought he kind of looked like him with his hair standing straight up."[3]

With hardcore rock'n'roll on its way out following the Payola scandal of the late 1950s, Zimmerman adopted a Woody Guthrie approach to music, entering—and conquering—the New York City folk circuit. "When I was going to [the] University Of Minnesota, Bob Zimmerman looked me up," says Propotnick. "I went down to check [him] out, and saw all kinds of beatniks sitting around drinking espresso and eating tiny little sandwiches. It just wasn't my thing, and also his style of music had changed considerably."

Folk's popularity grew just as rock'n'roll radio was being flooded with the bland teen idols that began to usurp R&B and rockabilly, by way of *American*

Bandstand, from 1958 onward. But by the mid 1960s Dylan wanted to re-immerse himself in rock'n'roll. Tracks such as 'Subterranean Homesick Blues' melded the lyrical constructions of Dylan's folk years with his Chuck Berry roots. When he then introduced The Beatles to pot at the Delmonico Hotel in New York City on August 28th 1964, the combined smoke and inspiration in the room would reverberate 3,000 miles away in Hollywood, where The Byrds developed their synthesis of these two great musical forces.

Roger McGuinn had been a contemporary of Bob Dylan on the New York folk scene, so for Dylan to be drawn into The Byrds' environment was hardly surprising. After making his LA debut in support of Joan Baez at the Hollywood Bowl in October 1963, he returned for his first solo shows late the following year. By the latter part of 1965 he was popular enough to headline the Hollywood Bowl and Civic Auditoriums in Santa Monica, Long Beach, and Pasadena. In April 1966 D.A. Pennebaker's Dylan documentary *Don't Look Back* was previewed in Hollywood; during the same month Dylan was in the audience as Otis Redding cut a live album at the Whisky A Go Go. When in town, Dylan would stay right on the Strip at the Hollywood Sunset Hotel, and once met with Phil Spector at Fred C. Dobbs' coffeehouse. (Local lore maintains that hearing Ronnie Milsap's version of Ray Charles's 'Let's Go Get Stoned' on the jukebox at Dobbs' inspired Dylan to write 'Rainy Day Women #12 & 35,' the opening track on his 1966 double LP *Blonde On Blonde*.)

The actual Dylan myth was not something that he could have cultivated on his own: it came from the way that his catalog could be sorted through a wide variety of bands that felt as though *their* instrumental and vocal arrangements of Dylan's material could be as revealing as The Byrds' take on 'Mr Tambourine Man.' A new lyrical consciousness suddenly began to spread across the airwaves, starting a trend that would continue until the end of the decade. In 1969, *Village Voice* writer Al Aronowitz concluded: "There are very few songs written today that don't have [Dylan's] influence, directly or indirectly, as far as lyrics go."

* * *

The Byrds recorded their 'Tambourine Man' on January 20th 1965 with Columbia Records producer Terry Melcher, the son of Doris Day and an established singer-producer in the Brian Wilson mould. During 1963 and '64 he had created and sung on hits by The Rip Chords ('Hey Little Cobra' and

'Three Window Coupe') and Bruce & Terry ('Summer Means Fun'); the Bruce in question, Bruce Johnston, was hired in 1965 to replace Brian Wilson in the live incarnation of The Beach Boys.

Like Wilson, Melcher shied away from performing, opting instead to produce the first two Byrds albums as well as material by a new group from the Pacific Northwest, Paul Revere & The Raiders. On 'Mr Tambourine Man,' Melcher backed McGuinn's 12-string Rickenbacker guitar with a selection of Phil Spector's session men: Leon Russell on electric piano, Hal Blaine on drums, Larry Knechtel on bass, and Jerry Cole on rhythm guitar. Among the keys to the popularity of this, The Byrds' debut single, were a rhythm guitar lick reminiscent of 'Don't Worry Baby' by The Beach Boys and the effervescent vocal harmonies of Gene Clark, David Crosby, and Roger McGuinn.

Although studio musicians had helped break The Byrds on this first 45, Melcher decided to bring in the other band-members for the rest of the subsequent *Mr Tambourine Man* album in an effort to replicate the sound heard live at Ciro's LeDisc. The Byrds' World Pacific demos had been ragged and informal, warmly displaying Clark and McGuinn at their most prolifically collaborative. Melcher chose to highlight these same songs on The Byrds' Columbia debut. Clark sang most of them in a woodsy timbre, bringing an intensely personal feel to the music that would be greatly missed after his departure from the group in 1966. David Crosby would later remark to *Rolling Stone* magazine that The Byrds were a tighter live act with Clark, because of the focus he provided: "He's an emotional projector on a huge, powerful level. If you get him on a good [night] he can take everybody, anywhere in the vicinity, on a good trip."

The *Mr Tambourine Man* LP captured the watershed moment of The Byrds in sound; likewise, the album's liner notes, penned by A&R man Billy James, evoke the vitality of the scene at Ciro's LeDisc. The Byrds' next single was another Dylan song, 'All I Really Want To Do,' but was overshadowed by a version by Cher, who'd heard the song at Ciro's. "That [song] was stolen away from us," remarks McGuinn, although The Byrds' version benefits from his glorious guitar playing, as does their version of Pete Seeger's 'The Bells Of Rhymney,' a highlight of *Mr Tambourine Man*. Among the other choice cuts are Clark's riveting ballad 'Here With You' and a version of Jackie DeShannon's 'Don't Doubt Yourself, Babe' complete with throbbing Bo Diddley beat and trance-inducing echo.

Mr Tambourine Man includes two further Dylan compositions, 'Spanish

Harlem Incident' and 'Chimes Of Freedom,' which contains the kind of lyric that gave real purpose to the freak scene with its references to "warriors whose strength is not to fight" and "refugees on the unarmed road of flight." McGuinn's cracked lead vocal drove straight to the heart of Sunset Strip in 1965, while Crosby provides not only a beautiful backing vocal, but also a conviction to match that of the songs.

On The Byrds' next single, 'Turn! Turn! Turn! (To Everything There Is A Season),' the key, final hookline is Crosby's: "A time for peace/I swear it's not too late." For some, these lyrics were merely poetic; others recognized them as having been taken from the Bible: Ecclesiastes 3:1–8. This message came through the ages, not just from some long-haired beatnik. Many who had previously taken a cynical or negative attitude toward rock'n'roll suddenly realized— and understood—what youth culture was trying to put across; sympathetic 'establishment' people began to embrace what kids were starting to broadcast. Like 'Mr Tambourine Man,' 'Turn! Turn! Turn!' was a groundbreaking moment in popular culture.

The standout cuts on The Byrds' second album, *Turn! Turn! Turn!* (released in the final weeks of 1965), are Gene Clark's romping 'The World Turns All Around Her' and McGuinn's adaptation of a song that Dylan had demoed with different lyrics, 'He Was A Friend Of Mine.' The latter song became a full-on tribute to John F. Kennedy; at the Monterey Pop Festival, Crosby blasted the Warren Report in his introduction. Two Clark solo compositions—'Set You Free This Time' and 'If You're Gone'—strengthened the record's emotional character. The Byrds had by now begun to make serious inroads on television programs in both Britain and the United States, popping up on *The Ed Sullivan Show*, *Ready Steady Go*, *Top Of The Pops*, and *Shindig!*

Strangely, however, The Byrds did not go down particularly well on their first trip to the UK during July and August 1965. The group had a cool, anti-showbiz stance that kids in 1960s Hollywood understood inherently, but that audiences in the UK just didn't get. "[The Byrds] were folkies, and used to playing in front of a small, intimate audience," notes LA scenester Paul Body. "They were great in that setting, but in a larger place, they lost it. The harmonies would get lost in the wash of the bigger sound systems, and the direct connection with the audience was lost as well."

Even so, nobody could deny the greatness of the records: both The Beatles and

The Rolling Stones took notice. Gene Clark recalls: "[John Lennon] particularly liked our group. Of course, he liked Dylan too. He thought that there was something in all this; that was a little more than just another rock'n'roll group. He liked the fact that we used the Dylan songs, and he liked our own material, so one night … [he] and George came to see us. Afterward we got together and started talking and ended up, because we were in London, spending time with them."

Upon their return to Los Angeles the group staged a huge concert dubbed *The Byrds Ball* at the Hollywood Palladium. The expectations and controversy that had met The Byrds in the UK did not seem to matter back home. The concert became a celebration of both The Byrds' international impact and the LA scene's ability to innovate on the same level as had the British. The Byrds—and Los Angeles—had raised the odds by spiking the youthquake with social revolution. Derek Taylor notes: "If The Beatles began 'it,' then The Byrds too began their 'it,' and it is to Roger McGuinn and his four errant, elegant brilliant friends that we and you, us, and the American nation and young people should offer a nod of thanks for nudging us, and not so slightly, in a new and better direction."[4]

Only a year earlier, McGuinn, Clark, and Crosby had sat in a movie theater learning all they could from *A Hard Day's Night*. Now, with The Beatles crossing the Atlantic for their second US tour in late August 1965, John Lennon and George Harrison could be found in the control booth while The Byrds recorded a version of Dylan's 'It's All Over Now, Baby Blue.' KRLA started playing a dub of this session almost immediately, but it was soon pulled from the airwaves and not released, with The Byrds declaring that all the attention in the studio had made them nervous.

Nevertheless, by the time *Rubber Soul* came out in December 1965—just before *Turn! Turn! Turn!*—The Byrds' impact on The Beatles was obvious. The suede coats the band wore on the cover and the fisheye-lens photograph are both reminiscent of *Mr Tambourine Man*. *Rubber Soul* is regularly cited as the turning point in The Beatles' career; the moment where they took on more introspective songwriting and a thematic studio vision. Such breakthroughs as the sitar on 'Norwegian Wood (This Bird Has Flown)' can be traced directly back to The Byrds' involvement with Dick Bock at World Pacific. According to Clark: "I think they picked up on a lot of things, like another approach. *Rubber Soul* did come out of the time we spent with The Beatles. You could tell that there was definitely a little bit deeper thinking that went into their lyrics and their approach to the recording."

The Byrds' friendship with The Beatles had solidified on August 24th 1965, when the two groups convened to drop acid at The Beatles' rented house in Benedict Canyon. (This would be the British group's first voluntary LSD experience, although they had, apparently, been surreptitiously 'dosed' by George Harrison's dentist prior to this.) Peter Fonda recalls how they all "ended up inside a huge, empty, sunken tub in the bathroom, babbling our minds away. I enjoyed just hearing John speak … there were no pretensions in his manner. He just sat around, laying out lines of poetry and thinking—an amazing mind. It was a thoroughly tripped out atmosphere, because they kept finding girls hiding under tables and so forth. At one point, Paul, George and I were talking about death, and I was explaining that I had once died on the operating table. 'I know what it's like to be dead,' I said, and just then John walked past and said, 'Who put all that shit in your head?' That exchange turned into the song 'She Said She Said' from *Revolver*."[5]

Fonda would star in both *The Wild Angels* (with Nancy Sinatra) and *The Trip*, a new breed of teen exploitation film developed by Roger Corman at American International Pictures. He could also be seen playing music occasionally at the Sea Witch, where he had covered Kim Fowley's 'The Trip.' Jazz trumpeter Hugh Masekela then produced a single for Fonda called 'November Night' in 1966, written by a new arrival to Los Angeles: Gram Parsons. Fonda set up a cameo for Parsons' group, The International Submarine Band, in *The Trip*; they then cut an album, *Safe At Home*, with Nancy Sinatra's producer, Lee Hazlewood, for his LHI imprint, which had been funded by Nancy's dad, Frank. So, in effect, Frank Sinatra was paying for Gram Parsons to record at the suggestion of Peter Fonda, who had been spending his time tripping with The Beatles and The Byrds.

* * *

The following January, for the second year in a row, The Byrds unveiled a sound that would spread like wildfire: in this case, psychedelia as a pop music form. While there may have been fuzz-tone guitar before The Rolling Stones recorded 'Satisfaction,' it would never become so prevalent without that 45. Similarly, there were abstract recordings before 'Eight Miles High,' but none of them kicked off a psychedelic craze.

Prior to 'Eight Miles High,' there were no pop records with incessant, hypnotic basslines juxtaposed by droning, trance-induced improvisational guitar. The Byrds, however, were blending rock'n'roll with John Coltrane-style jazz. The vocals gave the impression that a haunting, mysterious secret is about to be revealed. The song was written about the group's first plane trip to London, the "rain gray town known for its sound." Gene Clark recalls: "I actually wrote the song … in a hotel room when we were on tour with The Rolling Stones; over dinner, actually, one night with Brian Jones and myself, just having a conversation."

The crunching flipside, 'Why,' went off in another direction, creating guitar patterns that emulated the sitar ragas by Ravi Shankar that The Byrds had first heard at World Pacific. Shankar had made an appearance at the Ash Grove in 1965 within weeks of John Coltrane playing at Shelly's Manne-Hole. The combined work of these two artists intersected beautifully on 'Eight Miles High'/'Why,' the last single The Byrds would record with Gene Clark. The single's ethereal qualities were, in part, the work of RCA engineer Dave Hassinger, who later gave a similar sound to Rolling Stones discs such as 'Paint It Black.'

'Eight Miles High' and 'Why' represented such a sonic departure that The Byrds brought a sitar to a press conference to explain it. "They've got a new sound going called raga-rock, and you can hear it in their latest Columbia single, 'Eight Miles High,'" reported Sylvie Reice of *The Los Angeles Times*. "They describe it as 'an abstraction of music by classical composer-performer Ravi Shankar and jazz saxophonist John Coltrane, adapting to The Byrds' rock'n'roll.' Shankar, according to David Crosby, one of the Byrds, 'is the number one boss of Indian music—and he influences anybody who hears him.'"

Hit Parader reported on the press conference by explaining: "Sitar-like sounds can be produced on a 12-string guitar, as recently demonstrated by The Byrds, by tuning the E-string to the key of D to produce the modal chord. The bottom three strings provide the drone sound and the upper strings are bent to play the melody." Mike Bloomfield, lead guitarist of The Paul Butterfield Blues Band, added to The Byrds' comments in a later *Hit Parader* article about Hindu music, saying that his interest lay "in the drone quality of the music. Like the sound a bee makes: a steady hum. It is the simplest pattern in music and it is a challenge to improvise a free melody around the one basic drone."

The Byrds most controversial record, 'Eight Miles High' put a serious dent in their future on the hit parade. It was already on its way up the charts when Phil

Gavin of the influential radio trade paper *The Gavin Report* killed the momentum by declaring the song to be "about drugs." Roger McGuinn has always denied suggestions that 'Eight Miles High' is a drugs song. Gene Clark, however, is more forthcoming: "A piece of poetry of that nature is not limited to having to be about airplanes, or having to be about drugs. It's partially about drugs, partially about the [plane] trip, and other things, lots of things."

Despite the fact that a lot of radio stations around the country stopped playing it, 'Eight Miles High' remains the psychedelic shot heard round the world, particularly in terms of its bass lines. Soon The Yardbirds' 'Happenings Ten Years Time Ago' would feature those lines beneath the dual guitars of Jeff Beck and Jimmy Page, while The Pink Floyd, under the leadership of Syd Barrett, would take them into the cosmos with 'See Emily Play.'

The Byrds' next single, '5D (Fifth Dimension),' seemed like a revelation of the secrets hinted at in 'Eight Miles High.' Roger McGuinn set the theory of relativity to the swirl of an Irish jig, spinning traditional sounds into a cyclone to the rhythm of his 12-string Rickenbaker and Van Dyke Parks's tingling keyboard fadeout. According to McGuinn: "'5D' is about the fifth dimension, which is a philosophical place. Lord Buckley said that entertainers now are the new clergy, which is about what John Lennon said that he got done in for, only he didn't say it that way ..."[6]

With Columbia A&R man Alan Stanton producing and engineer Ray Gerhardt carrying on his work from the first two albums, The Byrds recorded one of the first ever psychedelic albums, *Fifth Dimension*. The jacket features the group seemingly afloat on a magic carpet, with BYRDS spelt out in a dazzling array of colorful, paisley folk art. "We're trying for an international sound," McGuinn told *Hit Parader*. "The less limitations we can hand them, the happier we are," added Crosby. "You have all kinds of sources: African, South American, blues, folk ... a lot of jazz, a lot of Ravi Shankar."

The overriding feel of *Fifth Dimension* was one of serenity and experimentation. The Byrds' arrangement of Bob Gibson's 'John Riley' brings cymbal crashes and droning guitar to the folk idiom; 'I See You' bends the listener's mind with unexpected changes, timings, and percussion. On 'Mr Spaceman,' McGuinn apparently attempts to communicate with extraterrestrials, hoping they pick up the music via radio waves in space. (The song received enough airplay to make the effort viable.)

Soaking up the vibe at PJ's on Santa Monica Boulevard and Crescent Heights, with Bobby Fuller Four on stage and actress Linda Evans dancing in the white shirt.

Left: Art Laboe, Ricky Nelson, and a horde of rock'n'roll fans at Scrivner's Drive In, late 50s. *Below:* A pair of LPs recorded in Hollywood music hangouts by The Larry Bunker Quartette and R&B sax man Joe Houston, respectively. *Opposite:* Joanie Labine at the Whisky A Go Go, 1964.

■ *Above:* Love on stage at Bido Lito's, 1965.
Right: Sonny & Cher perform at It's Boss during the peak of their hit-making era.
Opposite: Brenton Wood backed by Señor Soul (who later changed their name to War), 1967.

Clockwise from top left: Pat & Lolly Vegas at the Haunted House, 1965; Dick at the Harmony Park Ballroom, Anaheim, 1962; Thee Midniters at Olvera Street, 1966; Dale's 1965 live album from Ciro's; surfers in front of the Golden Bear, Hungtinton Beach.

Above: Them, during their 18-night stand at Whisky A Go Go in May 1966, jam on 'Gloria' with one of their opening acts, The Doors. *Left:* Judy Henske at Barney's Beanery on Santa Monica Boulevard, 1966.

A report on the album by *Los Angeles Times* music critic Pete Johnson notes that The Byrds sound "like a hive full of super-amplified bees," and that the group have pushed rock'n'roll toward "massively overlaid agglomerations of electronic noisemakers." He concludes that the band has taken "a position of leadership in the colonial rebellion against the dominance of the British sound."

What was missing from *Fifth Dimension*, however, was the full participation of Gene Clark. As The Byrds' primary songwriter, Clark's superior earnings irked some of his bandmates. Rather than fight them, he left the band. (At the time, to avoid negative publicity, it was reported that Clark had departed because of his fear of air travel.) As The Byrds started to put together their next LP, *Younger Than Yesterday*, Clark embarked on the making a solo album. Both display the production talents of Gary Usher, a new arrival in the Byrds camp who would oversee some of both parties' best recordings. (Like Terry Melcher, Usher had previously made surf records and beach-movie soundtracks.)

Released in early 1967, *Younger Than Yesterday* opened with 'So You Want To Be A Rock'n'Roll Star,' which pokes fun at the music business (and in particular, some felt, the 'fabricated' success of The Monkees). Hugh Masekela punctuated the words with taunting trumpet licks. The biting commentary was instigated by Chris Hillman, whose 'Thoughts And Words' provided the perfect starting point for some of McGuinn's most complex guitar playing.

David Crosby's 'Everybody's Been Burned' is perhaps his most distinctive Byrds track, and is again offset by sterling guitar work by McGuinn that ranges from pristine jazz licks to a final, sinuous, raga break. Crosby notes that Hillman "did some things on the bass, man, that no one up 'til then had anywhere near enough balls to try. It's a running jazz solo, all the way through the song. Never stops. Nobody else had done that, man, from any rock group."[7] Crosby and McGuinn collaborated on another highlight, 'Renaissance Fair,' which has a melodic hook that seemed later to form the basis of Buffalo Springfield's 'Rock'N'Roll Woman.' (When Neil Young temporarily quit Springfield on the eve of the Monterey Pop Festival, Crosby filled in for him. McGuinn wasn't best pleased, however, and this extension of cross-pollination quickly started to put a strain on his relationship with Crosby.)

Critical reaction to *Younger Than Yesterday* maintained that the group had forged ahead of the pack once again. In *Crawdaddy* magazine, Sandy Pearlman took note of a blend of everything from "magic" and "science fiction" to "technological tongues" and "an African trumpet guy." Pearlman concludes: "Even the most abundant amazing sounds are far too amazing to remain that way for long. They make themselves very familiar. That's how strong the form is. Unique to rock, The Byrds are so formalistic that even when they do something new it's hard to tell."

But despite these artistic successes, tension was mounting anew within the ranks of The Byrds. These creative struggles would, however, lead to one of the group's best albums, *The Notorious Byrd Brothers*. McGuinn, Hillman, and Crosby were all capable of bringing more high-quality material to a session than an LP would allow. Crosby in particular had begun to feel constrained. "David was really wound up, and difficult to work with," notes producer Gary Usher. "He was very opinionated, and it was hard for him to work within a group framework—and The Byrds were a group. David was into another whole situation, another whole scene."

The Byrds were also heading of in another new direction, one that embraced country music and would, for the third time, anticipate a major musical trend. After The Byrds made *Sweetheart Of The Rodeo*, Bob Dylan would follow the group's lead with *Nashville Skyline*, and country-rock would take off. Usher concludes that, during the making of *The Notorious Byrd Brothers*, "David Crosby was heading more and more towards social, esoteric statements like 'Lady Friend,' 'Triad,' songs like that. So it was just a matter of time before the split happened."

Roger McGuinn and Chris Hillman fired Crosby, who used the money from his severance pay to buy a huge schooner, the *Mayan, which he had originally dubbed Lysergia, and* which he docked in Sausalito, thereby solidifying his California-dreamer persona. Crosby immediately got to work producing Joni Mitchell's debut and cutting demos with Buffalo Springfield's Stephen Stills. Four of Crosby's songs made the cut on *The Notorious Byrd Brothers*, but only two—'Tribal Gathering' and 'Dolphin's Smile'—feature his vocals. Gary Usher called on his recording partner from Sagittarius, Curt Boettcher, to supply lead vocal parts on 'Natural Harmony' and 'Draft Morning.'

On *Younger Than Yesterday*, Crosby had resented having to cover Bob Dylan's 'My Back Pages,' while his originals sat in the can. The breaking point during the making of *The Notorious Byrd Brothers* came when the other Byrds chose 'Goin' Back,' written by Carole King and Gerry Goffin, as the band's next single. Crosby was at his most prolific, and frustration mounted. McGuinn and Hillman easily finished the LP without him, but its finest moment was 'Change Is Now,' a roving, bass-driven psychedelic offering that peaked with Crosby's harmonies and a blazing, backwards guitar solo by Clarence White.

The album works as a single entity, weaving together a variety of compelling subjects. 'Wasn't Born To Follow,' another Goffin & King composition, was originally intended for The Monkees; The Byrds' insightful rendition became integral to the 1969 movie *Easy Rider*. The song is used in two different segments of the movie, while the main protagonists (played by Peter Fonda and Dennis Hopper) are based on Roger McGuinn and David Crosby. The success of the Byrds-inspired *Easy Rider* kick-started a new auteur movement in Hollywood. Taking its drive from the mid-1960s Sunset Strip scene, independent cinema emerged with a new generation of directors and movies such as *The Graduate* and *Bonnie & Clyde*. By virtue of the Strip's music scene, 'New Hollywood' proceeded to put the art back into US cinema, and the movie industry back on its feet.

Having left their mark on The Beatles, Bob Dylan, and the entire film industry, The Byrds began to disintegrate amid the conflict surrounding *The Notorious Byrd Brothers*. The original core membership splintered, with drummer Michael Clarke also leaving once the album had been completed. Chris Hillman stayed with The Byrds long enough to collaborate with McGuinn and new member Gram Parsons on *Sweetheart Of The Rodeo*, then left to join Parsons in The Flying Burrito Brothers, with whom he cut the landmark 1969 LP *The Gilded Palace Of Sin*.

McGuinn kept The Byrds rolling with the addition of innovative bluegrass guitarist Clarence White, and recorded 'The Ballad Of Easy Rider' with Gene Parsons on harmonica for the movie's closing scene before making 1970's *The Byrds (Untitled)*, which remains a strong, double-LP statement. Gene Clark, meanwhile, recorded *The Fantastic Expedition Of Dillard & Clark* with banjo player Doug Dillard in 1969, and made a pair of superb solo albums, *White Light* and *Roadmaster* in 1971. David Crosby formed a supergroup with Graham Nash of The Hollies and Buffalo Springfield's Stephen Stills (and later Neil Young). CSN(&Y) may have been in the works all along, as Nash had told *Teen Set* magazine in 1967: "I would love to form a vocal group with Mama Cass and Byrd David Crosby." Crosby himself emerged from CSNY with a superb solo album, *If I Could Only Remember My Name*, in 1971.

Few of The Byrds' contemporaries can claim to have made such a subversive impact on pop culture. The band had a much larger, more positive impact on the world at large than any *Billboard* chart position or album sales or concert attendance figure could possibly measure.

* * *

After The Byrds, the most original band to emerge from the Strip was Love, who also took influence from Bob Dylan's poetic standpoint but (unlike the majority of their peers) did not cover his songs. Bryan MacLean served The Byrds as a roadie in the group's early days, and dated Jackie DeShannon. One evening, while hanging out in the parking lot of Ben Frank's coffee shop, he ran into local musician and songwriter Arthur Lee.

Lee had already been moving through the musical circles of Los Angeles for several years. His first group, Arthur Lee & The LAGs—a play on Memphis group Booker T. & The MGs' name—released an instrumental single on Capitol, 'The Ninth Wave,' at the height of the surf craze in 1963. (The Byrds' Roger McGuinn had also previously cut a couple of surf records there, alongside Bobby Darin, as The City Surfers.) A year later he formed The American Four in response to the British Invasion, and began his first collaborations with guitarist Johnny Echols, who wrote 'Soul Food,' the B-side to the group's 'Luci Baines' (a reference to President Johnson's dance-crazy teenage daughter). Lee wrote songs for East LA rhythm & blues singer Lil' Ray and Ronnie & The Pomona Casuals, and, with Echols, played on recordings by girl group The Sisters.

Lee's pre-Love writing and recording career also included getting Jimi Hendrix on vinyl for the first time. "Hendrix came along after me, you understand," recalled Lee. "After I took off a thousand pounds of beads, the moccasins, and the head band, the whole bit, then here comes Jimi. But see, I didn't know that the same person that I'd played with was Jimi Hendrix, the guy who was causing all the ruckus in London, England, with 'Hey Joe' and all these things people were flippin' out on, 'cause I never knew the guy's last name."

Lee remembered writing the song in question—'My Diary'—for the singer Rosa Lee Brooks and then inviting Hendrix to play a Curtis Mayfield-style lead guitar line. (Brooks's take on the story, as told to rhythm & blues historian Steve Propes, is somewhat different: she recalls meeting Hendrix at an Ike & Tina Turner show at the Californian Club. The following morning, after Brooks had "got to know him intimately," Hendrix "started strumming what he called 'love notes.' Together they made up 'My Diary.')

Impressed by Bryan MacLean's popularity on the Strip and association with The Byrds, Lee invited him to join a band he had recently formed with Johnny Echols called The Grass Roots. According to Love biographer Kevin Delaney: "Echols and Lee grew up together—in fact, their families knew each other in Memphis before both of them were born." The group started rehearsing at Clay Vito before securing gigs at Ciro's LeDisc—less than two blocks from the parking lot where Lee and MacLean first met. After discovering that another band had already called themselves Grass Roots, Lee, Echols, and MacLean settled on a name that summed up the modus operandi of the new movement: Love.

Love are often referred to as the first 'underground' band because of their organic development at Clay Vito, their earthy material, and their popularity within the in-crowd at venues such as Brave New World and Ciro's LeDisc. In reality, Love were part of a creative scene that had spawned The Byrd's commercial success after the first wave of Beatlemania. One of the first longhair bands in America, The Byrds had a charismatic sex appeal that went hand in hand with their musical prowess. Love—hitless and unknown elsewhere in 1965—were seen as more of an 'insider' band.

When Love hit the pop charts a year later with 'My Little Red Book,' the underground concept had already been firmly accepted within the mainstream teen scene. Love's was just a new kind of commercial appeal, but, for the moment, the underground tag helped the group develop an eclecticism that went beyond that of The Byrds. Alongside such seminal acts as The Del-Vikings, The Impalas, and Booker T. & The MGs, Love would become one of the most prominent interracial groups in the history of rock'n'roll. (Lee was driven to experiment with a vast musical hybrid after a number of frustrating experiences early in his career with local black labels such as Sam Cooke's SAR). Just as importantly, however, Love's presence on the scene added momentum to the Sunset Strip movement given its initial resonance by The Byrds.

When The Byrds went off on their first tour in 1965, Love, The Rising Sons, and The Leaves alternated in the vacant slot at Ciro's LeDisc. That July, with a new civic amendment (Section 2076.1) "permitting minors to participate in the dancing at public eating places even if not accompanied by a parent," the venue became It's Boss. These new laws slackened attitudes to public dancing considerably, leading Frank Zappa to note on the *Freak Out! Hot Spots* map he produced in 1966: "It's Boss is teenie-bopper heaven. You only have to be 15 to get in."

The previous month had seen a host of changes on the Strip. The psychotronic-garage den the Haunted House had opened on Hollywood Boulevard with a smoke-snorting monster stage, Batgirl go-go dancers, and a general horror movie motif. The Crescendo/Interlude had become the Crescendo/Tiger Tail and now regularly featured The Turtles. (By the end of the year, the venue would change names again, becoming the Trip.) Gazzarri's opened a second club on the Strip and played host to a steady stream of garage bands, while Pandora's Box started to book similar acts and had no age limit.

Later, in December, the building that was once home to Earl Carroll's Vanities and the Moulin Rouge re-opened as the Hullabaloo. P.J. Proby—barely recognizable from his old days as Jett Powers—headlined the opening night. It was truly the dawn of a new day. In a contemporary issue of *Los Angeles* magazine, Mike Fessier Jr described how "the Strip was suddenly alive with hairy teen hobos and older hippies in nifty belly-button-baring shirts and little girls with mop straight hair and belted hip huggers settled low and cool on their anatomies. The convergence of social types has created a permanent bumper-to-bumper weekend traffic jam in which it now takes some 30 sardine-like minutes to inch along the Strip's 1.7 miles."

The UK's super-hip rock'n'roll magazine *Rave* took immediate notice too, in a story entitled 'An American Scene': "In one of my *Rave* columns, I wrote about the psychedelic effect being created in some of the discotheques on the Hollywood strip. ... All over the country club owners now want to turn their discotheques into psychedelic dens. Why? Because suddenly everyone is aware of LSD and its larger than life effect, and if they're not going to try the drug, then at least they're going to cash in on the trend." Of course, not everybody took kindly to this new way of life on the Strip. According to Fessier Jr, Francis J. Montgomery, who still owned "13 prime acres of Strip land," would have preferred the Strip to be frequented by "people with Cadillacs and Rolls Royces ... more mature people, well heeled."[8]

The new sound of 1965 fell beyond the comprehension of a number of other old-school Hollywood characters such as Frank Sennes, who owned both Ciro's LeDisc and the Moulin Rouge. As such, he offered both venues to people who better understood the dynamics of youth culture. Ciro's LeDisc was taken over by Paul Raffles and Bill Doherty, who had previously worked at PJ's. They immediately fitted out the legendary club with huge pop art paintings and designs, while the futuristic curves of the entrance were given a new prominence by a groovy, bubble-shaped neon sign declaring 'It's Boss' to the Strip. The interior walls became eerie, oversized tributes to vintage comic strips and pop stars in the style of Roy Lichtenstein: Dick Tracy and Little Orphan Annie juxtaposed with various Beatles, Stones, and James Brown silhouettes. Ciro's re-opened as It's Boss in July 1965, with The Regents installed as the permanent house band.

Gary Bookasta acquired the Moulin Rouge, which had not operated as a nightclub since 1960. He retained its original art deco glamour, adding in a twisty of iconic band pictures—including the cover of *Rubber Soul*—which hung from the ceiling. The Palace Guard, featuring 15-year-old drummer Emitt Rhodes and 14-year-old singer David Beaudoin, became the house band. A key prop was acquired when NBC cut *Hullabaloo* from their schedule to make room for *The Monkees*. "When *Hullabaloo* went off the air," recalls Bookasta, "they called me and said 'hey, we've got this building-block set of letters that spell out Hullabaloo, would you like it?' and I said 'Sold!'" The Hullabaloo opened in December 1965 and quickly hosted performances by acts such as The Yardbirds, Them, and James Brown. But as Bookasta notes: "As the Moulin Rouge, Frank Sennes counted on Louis Prima & Keely Smith as the one act he could put in and know he was going to do good business. For us, Love was our biggest regular act."

Love enjoyed a very short prime. *Los Angeles New Times* writer Sara Scribner described best the elusive qualities that set Love apart in a town filled with an outrageous talent overload: "While The Byrds and early Beach Boys captured the sweet sunniness of the California dream, and The Doors slithered down to dig into its dark underbelly, Love is the band that best represented, in music and in life, the true dichotomies, the real psychic split—the sunshine and the noir—of Los Angeles. The story of the band touches upon the mind-boggling heights and the dull dissipation of its city."

The first Love gigs of any impact happened at a little place called Brave New World. Low key with no signage and off the beaten path—two blocks west of La Brea on Melrose—this was an underground club in the truest sense of the word. Love (as The Grass Roots), The Mothers, and The Doors all developed in this appropriately groovy building during 1965 prior to establishing themselves at the more high-profile Sunset Strip bistros. "It was originally operating as a low-profile gay club, then these ahead-of-the-curve combos infiltrated the room with people from the early freak scene," according to musician and scenester Denny Bruce. "Brave New World was the original spawning ground for that era of psychedelia."

Brave New World moved to a new location in early 1966—on Cherokee, off Hollywood Boulevard—and brought the freak bands with it. By then, Love had secured a residency at a tiny place called Bido Lito's on Cosmo Street, between Sunset and Hollywood near Vine, which they used primarily to develop new ideas. As their reputation spread, Love played to a packed Whisky A Go Go and, in December 1966, headlined a bill that also included The Standells, The Turtles, The Seeds, Count Five, and Gene Clark at the Santa Monica Civic.

Love's first impact on record came with Arthur Lee's arrangement of the Burt Bacharach/Hal David song 'My Little Red Book,' which he'd heard performed by Manfred Mann in the film *What's New Pussycat?* Lee delivered the lyrics with a newfound passion, while his band added raw guitar and funky bass to completely transform the original. He mounted a similar attack with his arrangement of 'Hey Joe,' a blues written by Seattle folkie Billy Roberts.

Roberts played up and down the West Coast, stopping in both San Francisco and Los Angeles. After Tim Rose recorded 'Hey Joe' for Elektra, the song was picked up by coffeehouse folk acts such as Dino Valenti and David Crosby before being adopted by The Byrds at Ciro's LeDisc. "[Crosby] would raise the temperature on that dance floor with that one,"[15] recalls dancer Carl Franzoni. Love took on 'Hey Joe' as a sure-fire crowd-pleaser; in their hands the song quickly became, alongside Them's 'Gloria,' the 'Louie Louie' of the Sunset Strip, and was instantly copied by a rash of new bands. "The Leaves more or less copied our style," remembered Arthur Lee ruefully. "They asked our guitar player Johnny Echols for the words. He gave them the wrong words on purpose, they sang the wrong words, and it became Number 1. Such is life."

Arthur Lee's penchant for re-arrangement foretold a brilliant songwriting skill, just as had The Rolling Stones' version of Buddy Holly's 'Not Fade Away.' Once Love signed to Elektra, tracks from their self-titled debut album such as 'Can't Explain' and 'My Flash On You' became Sunset Strip standards. Lee's emotional harmonica playing took precedence on the slower tunes; the tortured 'Signed D.C.' exorcised the pain of dealing with original Love drummer Don Conka's heroin addiction. Bryan MacLean provided a neat counterpoint to Lee's intensity with jazzy originals such as 'Softly To Me.'

The best example of Love's otherworldliness is the first side of their second album, *Da Capo*, released in late 1966. Lee's fiery passion is never more apparent than on the opening 'Stephanie Knows Who,' which breaks into a jazzy solo without losing its rock'n'roll grit. MacLean counters with 'Orange Skies,' a beautiful utopian pastiche unmatched in 1960s music. The best-known track on *Da Capo* is Love's biggest hit, 'Seven And Seven Is,' a driving, rhythmic construction that has no option but to end in an explosion. This, more than any other record, captures exactly the rise and fall of Sunset Strip creativity from 1965–66, boiling it all down into two minutes and 15 seconds. The Doors' 'Not To Touch The Earth' and 'Five To One' echo a similar feeling, but Love nailed it all in one fell swoop.

Alban 'Snoopy' Pfisterer moved from drums to harpsichord on *Da Capo* to make room for the more jazz-orientated Michael Stuart, while the addition of saxophonist and flautist Tjay Cantrelli (formerly of The Creators) helped elevate the music further. Love's line-up was rounded out by Johnny Echols on lead guitar and Ken Forssi on bass. The expanded line-up benefited from recording *Da Capo* at RCA's Music Center Of The World, with engineer Dave Hassinger— who had previously worked on 'Eight Miles High' and 'Paint it Black' combining his skill with producer Bruce Botnick. "People who listen to music today would probably call it jazz-rock," Arthur Lee told *Hit Parader*, "but I don't call it that. It's free music." The Rolling Stones heard an early performance of the side-long closer, 'Revelations,' which purportedly inspired them to stretch out for an extended jam on 'Goin' Home' (from 1966's *Aftermath*).

A few months after *Da Capo*, the original Love's final manifestation arrived with the flowery, baroque *Forever Changes*. Rock'n'roll 45s of the 1950s and 60s could lure kids straight home from school every day to listen to a side over and over, waiting for that great hookline or instrumental break. *Forever Changes* is a rare case of an album-length disc that maintains the seductive qualities of such singles, ebbing and flowing between dreamy orchestration, Herb Alpert-styled brass arrangements, singing as pure as Johnny Mathis (but with more vocal and lyrical bite), and welcome, uproarious intrusions of soulful guitar by Johnny Echols, all underpinned by a constant, pulsating base of acoustic rhythm guitar. The complexity of the music necessitated the generous use of studio musicians from the outset. Lee's 'Live And Let Live' sums up the band—and the time— with the line: "Write the rules in the sky/Ask your leaders, 'Why?'" 'Maybe The People Would Be The Times Or Between Clark And Hilldale' may well be the best distilled encapsulation of what it felt like to be on Sunset Strip during this period. MacLean's reverie in the opening 'Alone Again, Or,' meanwhile, reflects the Strip's twilight in its declaration: "You know that I could be in love with almost everyone."

Sadly, by the time of this masterpiece, various members of Love had succumbed to drug abuse, an unfortunate legacy of the 1960s. The 'summer of love' had left Los Angeles in a state of melancholia, as the disparate lyrics of *Forever Changes* convey so well. With clubs systematically closing after the Sunset Strip riots, Love had fewer places to gig, and the group began to lose their edge as a live act.

The group's disinterest in performing outside of the Los Angeles area had an adverse affect on the successive sales of each LP in America, and allowed some members of the group to wallow in self-indulgence. Lee was left with no choice but to disband the original Love. The group recorded a final single, 'Your Mind And We Belong Together,' in January of 1968. In the Arthur Lee recordings that followed, only 'August,' which captured the essence of LA's most vital month, matched the sound of earlier Love material.

Forever Changes and *The Notorious Byrd Brothers* were recorded at roughly the same time, during the closing moments of 1967, and both embody the final breath of a creative burst that had first emerged from Ciro's LeDisc in early 1965. Both Arthur Lee and Roger McGuinn kept going as The Byrds and Love for a while, but this ran contrary to the essence of prime Sunset Strip rock'n'roll, which was always about collaboration, not individuals. Unity and cross-pollination was the way: the diversity of the crowd—and its coming together through music— led quite naturally to the promotion of universal love on a grand scale.

* * *

As The Byrds became national and international hit-makers in 1965, Love had taken their place as Hollywood's longhair/folk-rock band of choice. The Rising Sons were on the periphery, playing an interesting aggregation of amplified country-blues that emphasized the rural aspect of Muddy Waters and Howlin' Wolf instead of big-city blues of the Paul Butterfield/Mike Bloomfield variety.

Rising Sons co-leader Taj Mahal started out in Cambridge, Massachusetts, in a folk-blues duo with LA native Jesse Lee Kincaid. After learning of folk-rock's stirrings, Kincaid talked Mahal into relocating to Los Angeles, using the availability of a gifted young guitarist by the name of Ry Cooder as an added enticement. "By the time Ry Cooder was 16, 17 years old," recalls Santa Monica musician Louie Lista, "he was already getting so much attention as an outstanding guitar player that he was representing Martin Guitars and Vega banjos at the Teen-Age Fair."

Mahal, Kincaid, and Cooder formed an alliance and brought in Gary Marker to play electric bass, despite the fact that he was more used to jazz-style upright bass. Kincaid played drums initially, but switched back to guitar after the arrival of Ed Cassidy. The group spent a good deal of time honing their sound at the Ash Grove, before signing to Columbia in 1965 after being spotted at the Teen-Age Fair by foresighted A&R man Billy James.

Taj Mahal's singing style covered just about everything from black country-blues and jazzier city-blues to Otis Redding-style soul. He handled Appalachian country styles with equal aplomb. "Taj showed how all those categories really were just created by the early record labels, because they were targeting audiences," notes Lista. "[It all] intermixed, despite the problems of early segregation, the further back you go. Even though he was a very young man then, Taj had that kind of dazzling ability to go from one style to another." Mahal embellished this range with excellent harmonica playing, and with the prodigious Ry Cooder beside him on open-tuned bottleneck guitar brought the complete package to the stage of Ciro's LeDisc.

The Rising Sons became friends with The Byrds, leading Chris Hillman's cousin Kevin Kelly to replace Cassidy on drums by the time of the group's first recording sessions with producer Terry Melcher. These sessions provided The Rising Sons' only single of the 1960s, 'The Devil's Got My Woman.' (Twenty-two Rising Sons tracks were eventually issued by Columbia in the 1990s, while in 2002 Sundazed put out an unreleased album from 1965.)

'The Devil's Got My Woman,' a solid blues featuring excellent work by Mahal and Cooder, was just one of a number of great tracks the group recorded. They cut an eerie, fuzz-laced version of the Goffin & King tune 'Take A Giant Step' (later recorded by The Monkees), while 'Statesboro Blues' was an all-out punk-screamer with Cooder's slide-playing at its wildest, and 'Sunny's Dream' showed Jesse Kincaid to be a fine vocalist and songwriter with its sweetly melancholic pop stylings. Then there were good-time arrangements of Rev Gary Davis's 'Candy Man' and Dylan's 'Walkin' Down The Line,' a hardcore blues take on Willie Dixon's '44 Blues,' and a slow, drifting rendition of 'By And By (Poor Me)' by Sleepy John Estes. The group was also early to recognize the talent of songwriter

Pamela Polland with their heartfelt take on her 'Tulsa County,' while Kincaid sang and arranged a graceful version of Linda Albertano's '2:10 Train.'

But despite The Rising Sons' growing prominence on the Strip—particularly among Rolling Stones fans, who had started to dig deeper into the blues than any previous pop audience—and several national TV appearances—including *The Tonight Show* with Johnny Carson—no further recordings were released by Columbia. The label appeared only to trust The Byrds' version of folk-rock, and didn't know how to sell this authentic, black folk-blues sound in the mid 1960s. Jesse Lee Kincaid did, however, release a magnificent solo 45, an eerie organ-led version of 'She Sang Hymns Out Of Tune,' which would soon be covered by both Hearts & Flowers and Harry Nilsson, while Gary Marker formed a jazzy punk group, The Sound Machine. And both Taj Mahal and Ry Cooder, of course, maintain continued success as solo artists.

* * *

The most exciting manifestation of folk-rock was in its final mutation: folk-punk. The Leaves' rendition of 'Hey Joe' was this short-lived moment's rallying cry, the dying embers of a scarcely realized sound. The Leaves formed during the summer of 1964 at Cal State Northridge in the San Fernando Valley. Bassist and booker Jim Pons first played with frat brothers Robert Lee Reiner (rhythm guitar) and Jimmy Curran (drums) as The Rockwells. None of them could play properly, so they drafted in an 'experienced' surf musician, Bill Rinehart, from nearby Pierce College. Rinehart, who had been playing for six months, coached the group's three-chord repertoire. Pons, a devout fan of Jerry Lee Lewis, booked The Rockwells as the openers for 'The Killer' at Devonshire Downs, an old horseracing track on campus.

Local deejay-impresario Bob Eubanks was impressed by their act, and helped the group secure bookings at bars in the Valley. The college gigs continued, including one with Captain Beefheart & His Magic Band (by which time The Rockwells had become The Leaves). Tom 'Ambrose' Ray took over on drums, with John Beck assuming the role of frontman on harmonica and tambourine. After a stint at a teen club called the Yum Yum Tree in the Valley, The Leaves found a manager in the summer of 1965 and were booked for a three-week stint at the revitalized Ciro's LeDisc.

Denny Bruce explains how The Leaves opened the door for non-Hollywood garage bands: "Love and The Rising Sons, being integrated bands, were more like city groups. The Leaves were from the San Fernando Valley, so for them to play Ciro's meant kids from the Valley felt that they [too] could come into the city, smoke reefer, and be cool. With LA being the diverse place it is, Sunset Strip was now getting a little melting pot vibe going on."

The Leaves were developing strong original material and, with the help of Bob Eubanks, soon secured a deal with Mira Records. Pons and Rinehart—who would be replaced by Bobby Arlin for 'Hey Joe'—came up with several great tunes, including debut single 'Too Many People.' Pons evokes Ray Davies (think 'I'm Not Like Everybody Else') in his rejection of the expectations of the status quo, bemoaning those who are "lookin' to rearrange me." 'Get Off Of My Cloud' by The Rolling Stones and 'I Ain't No Miracle Worker' by The Brogues (from nearby Merced, CA) were driven by this same feeling, suggesting a societal volcano on the verge of eruption. The youth had had enough of being bugged and hassled to conform to hypocritical, conservative values. In the 1950s, rock'n'roll had always been subverted by 'the man,' but this time, the kids were prepared to fight back: their anger and activism would trample the compromise of mediocrity.

The Leaves' next single epitomized this renewal. 'Hey Joe' ignited a swarm of power with one stroke of its monstrous, sustained A chord, with its howling, desperate vocals hell-bent on scaring the living daylights out of the no-gooder who "shot his woman dead." No other version matched the chilling power of The Leaves' rendition; recordings of the song by Love, The Byrds, and The Jimi Hendrix Experience were never as big hits in America. At the time, the best version of a song often did even up as the one that had the most impact on young audiences—and, therefore, the pop charts—and so it was with The Leaves' take on 'Hey Joe,' instantly recognized in Los Angeles and a Number 31 hit nationally. In its wake came 'Goin' All The Way' by Boston-area group The Squires and 'She's Not Just Anybody' and 'The Third Eye' by Santa Barbara's The Dovers. Taken together with 'Hey Joe,' these singles offer the best representation of folk-punk, an idiom that never truly reached fruition after 1966.

The Leaves' full-length debut on Mira Records serves as a time capsule of the transitory folk-punk sound. The material ranges from the harmonica-driven 'Dr Stone' (later given a raucous re-reading by The Beaten Path) to the heart-melting ballad 'Just A Memory,' while a beautiful version of 'Good Bye My Lover' acknowledges folk-rock's debt to The Searchers. With its green paisley cover and black-and-white band photo, *Hey Joe* remains one of the coolest albums of the period. Sunset Strip street-singer Wild Man Fischer declared: "The Leaves Are Happening"—the same phrase graced the marquee when the group played at Ciro's Le Disc.

By the time of second album *All The Good That's Happening* (Capitol, 1967), however, The Leaves were on the verge of dissipation. Rhythm guitarist Robert Lee Reiner had fallen self-indulgently into drug addiction, so the group was forced to pare down to a four-piece. Jim Pons and Bobby Arlin deliver an assortment of fine originals, such as 'On The Plane' and the psychedelic romps 'Lemmon Princess' and 'Twilight Sanctuary,' which combine well with covers of Donovan's 'To Try For The Sun' and Buffy St Marie's 'Codeine.' But once the album had been completed, Pons accepted an offer to join The Turtles, and The Leaves, much like the ones Keely Smith sang about, dried up to "drift by my window."

* * *

Jackie DeShannon was the first established LA artist to be swept up in the rise of folk-rock. According to Jim Dickson, DeShannon was drawn to the music (and style) of The Byrds: "She'd been hanging around with Bryan MacLean a year before he became a founding member of Love, and was turned on to The Byrds by their mutual association. Jackie went around talking them up to everyone and anyone who would listen, and very clearly her connections were good."

Originally a country singer from Hazel, Kentucky, DeShannon found success on several fronts once she hit LA in 1960. Her first singles—such as 'Buddy,' released as Jackie Dee—had the rockabilly wallop of early Wanda Jackson, but by the time she signed to Liberty Records for *Jackie DeShannon* (1963) her style had moved towards folk. The album features great renditions of an unreleased Dylan song, 'Walkin' Down The Line,' as well as the better-known 'Don't Think Twice, It's Alright.' DeShannon also cut a nervy version of Eric Von Schmidt's 'Baby Let Me Follow You Down,' which Dylan had recorded on his debut, too.

DeShannon made her second album a year later alongside producer Jack Nitzsche, who added rock'n'roll and pop elements to her folk stylings. *Breakin' It Up On The Beatles Tour!* is an overlooked work of genius, on which DeShannon pre-dates The Searchers, The Beau Brummels, and The Byrds with a brand new folk-rock sound. Nitzsche brought in a young Ry Cooder to play guitar on the album; Cooder also backed DeShannon live at the Troubadour and at the Melodyland in Anaheim. British group The Searchers soon had a hit with DeShannon's 'When You Walk In The Room,' as well as with a Nitzsche/Sonny Bono co-write, 'Needles And Pins.' (Nitzsche and Bono had previously worked together under Phil Spector.)

Soon everybody from The Righteous Brothers and The Fleetwoods to The Ronettes and Ricky Nelson were recording DeShannon's songs, but the singer herself was still being made to record other people's material. The music business at the time was just not geared toward female artists who looked good, danced and sang well, and wrote hit records. There were only sporadic glimpses of DeShannon in full flow, such as a spellbinding performance of 'When You Walk In The Room' on *Hollywood A Go Go*, during which the singer was able to hold the entire dance floor in her control atop Nitzsche's grand string arrangement.

As the 1960s rolled on, DeShannon penned garage stompers such as 'Too Far Out' by The Liverpool Five, 'Don't Turn Your Back On Me' by Mike Sheridan & The Nightriders, and 'My Group And Me' by LA's own Raga & The Talas (another World Pacific discovery). Lew Chudd at Liberty Records was a strong believer in DeShannon's talent and—showing a then near unheard of confidence in a female artist—had the foresight to set up a publishing deal for her at Metric Music.

Jackie DeShannon lived her life in rock'n'roll circles. In 1964 she was widely reported to have had a fling with John Lennon, went on a double date with Elvis Presley (accompanied by Sharon Sheely and her husband of the time, *Shindig!* host Jimmy O'Neil), and dated British session guitarist Jimmy Page. The future Yardbird is responsible for the blistering guitar break on *Breakin' It Up On The Beatles Tour!*'s 'It's Love Baby (24 Hours A Day).'

When DeShannon moved to Imperial Records in 1965, she hooked up with Burt Bacharach and Hal David, who gave her their most important social statement to date, 'What The World Needs Now Is Love.' (Aware of the musical and societal changes to come, Bacharach offered the similar—if more subtle—song 'The Windows Of The World' to Dionne Warwick.) DeShannon debuted 'What The World Needs Now' on *Shindig!*, and premiered her Bacharach/David follow-up, 'A Lifetime Of Loneliness,' on *Hullabaloo*.

She continued her foray into the pop realm with *Are You Ready For This?*, which mixed her own compositions with Bacharach/David songs, in 1966, and on 1967's standards set *New Image*. A year later she made *For You* and *Me About*

You, which marks the singer's reunion with songwriting collaborator Nitzsche and includes readings of songs by Van Dyke Parks, Tim Hardin, Jimmy Webb, and John Sebastian of The Lovin' Spoonful. Her 1969 album *Laurel Canyon* includes a heartfelt tribute to her hometown, 'LA,' which was accompanied by a promo film that predates by 20 years Randy Newman's more cynical video clip for 'I Love LA.' The DeShannon clip seems like a beautiful dream from a long time ago, but is, in fact, a true reflection of how locals saw Los Angeles at the time.

DeShannon's work with Burt Bacharach offers hints at times of the growing influence of Brazilian music. Bacharach, in New York, was beginning to achieve a similar sound to that of Herb Alpert & The Tijuana Brass back in Los Angeles. With Alpert's A&M label having its headquarters right on Sunset, LA was the entry point for the bossa nova feel that swept through 1960s jazz by way of artists such as Sergio Mendes & Brasil '66. (During this time, Chicano swinger Chris Montez evolved from Ritchie Valens-inspired rocker to cool, casual vocalist on A&M hits such as 'The More I See You' and 'Call Me.')

Groups such as The Byrds and Love developed a similar feeling in their music, too. The freedom of samba rhythms colored John Coltrane's *A Love Supreme*, and from there drove Byrds tracks such as 'Eight Miles High' and 'I See You,' while Love's *Forever Changes* brings Alpert-styled flourishes to a psychedelic context. It was no coincidence that several of the same musicians and engineers were involved in both the Alpert and Love recordings.

"Dizzy Gillespie and Stan Getz brought Cuba and Brasil to the States," notes singer-songwriter and music scribe Danny Weizmann. He recalls how the impact of 'The Girl From Ipanema' by Stan Getz and Astrud Gilberto then expanded the music's impact "from 'serious' jazz to pop hits. [Then came] Les Baxter, Martin Denny, and Herb Alpert. But along the way, the 'romantica' strains also infiltrate The Four Freshmen, Bob Gibson, Bud & Travis, and Bob Dylan-types looking for anti-square exotica. Put it all in the hands of a Californian like David Crosby (who was in Les Baxter's Balladeers for a while) and traditional Latin rhythms such as montuno end up in the cut 'So You Want To Be A Rock'N'Roll Star.'"

With LA's proximity to Mexico, the 1920s movie industry had enjoyed pre-Strip gambling in Tijuana, and Mexican reefer continued to offer a cross-generational experience to 20th century musicians. It should come as no surprise, then, that elements of Latin music became prevalent in Los Angeles. Its lilt had already contributed to the Sunset Strip vibe, notably at the Mocambo, where acts such as Desi Arnaz, Carmen Miranda, and Xavier Cugat had been popular.

The Latin sound then veered into Pérez Prado's jazz stylings, which spread across the fabric of Los Angeles musicians, becoming popular at the Garden of Allah, the Crescendo, and PJ's by way of nightclub regulars Eddie Cano and Jack Costanzo. One clear-cut example of this exists on an episode of *Shivaree* featuring Cano and The Byrds. Each act plays two songs on the show, complementing each other's sound so well that it remains one of the most musically satisfying half-hours in the *Shivaree* archive.

Bongo player Jack Costanzo had been a member of Stan Kenton's Orchestra at the Rendezvous Ballroom in Balboa alongside flamenco/bossa nova guitarist Laurindo Almeida, who recorded a wealth of solo albums and colored records by Henry Mancini, Stan Getz, and Bud Shank (on World Pacific). The mid-1960s LA groove spread to the east coast when The Joe Cuba Sextet hit with 'Psychedelic Baby,' while Esquivel brought new production extremes to the Latin sound from RCA's Music Center Of The World in Hollywood.

"The thing to understand is how insanely popular Sergio Mendes, Herb Alpert, and Astrud Gilberto were during the 1960s," notes Danny Weizmann. "Today, their legacy is quaint, but by the end of the decade I don't think a single suburban home did not have the following LPs: *Getz/Gilberto* [by Stan Getz and Joao Gilberto, featuring Antonio Carlos Jobim and Astrud Gilberto], [Herb Alpert's] *Whipped Cream & Other Delights* and *Herb Alpert & The Tijuana Brass Greatest Hits, Crystal Illusions* [Sergio Mendes], or the single of Hugh Masakella's 'Grazing In The Grass.' This was not some jazzy cabaret side-thing, it was the cultural language of the time that outsold even The Beatles and Cream." These artists foretold the Latin undercurrents in the sound of The Byrds, Love, The Doors—note Jose Feliciano's hit cover of 'Light My Fire' and, moreover, 'What The World Needs Now.'

* * *

Folk-rock may have been the 'next big thing' in 1965, but its roots had grown organically. From the moment the wildness of 1950s rock'n'roll disappeared from radio, the folk scene had absorbed the genre's rebellious spirit, as witnessed by Bob Dylan's gravitation from rockabilly to folk (and then back to folk-rock). This evolutionary process can also be observed in the careers of Simon & Garfunkel, Jackie DeShannon, and others too numerous to mention.

The Everly Brothers made a smooth transition through the mid-1960s music scene with a timeless sound that easily spanned the 1950s/60s chasm. The impact of Phil and Don Everly's move from Nashville to Hollywood in 1964 is rarely given much consideration, but it preceded a run of five killer albums in two years that absorbed and then ran riot with the Strip's ambient energy. *Gone Gone Gone*, *Beat & Soul*, *Rock & Soul*, *In Our Image*, and *Two Yanks In England* were vital, essential groundworks that underpinned the folk-rock movement.

These albums' high quality was due in no small part to the acquisition of lead guitarist James Burton shortly after The Everly Brothers relocated to Los Angeles. Burton's bayou style had been honed to perfection through years of playing for Ricky Nelson and contributing to records such as Dale Hawkins's 'Suzie Q.' Burton's experience made him the perfect replacement for Chet Atkins, who had been the Everlys' Nashville guitarist. Burton and the brothers made recordings together that stand among the most important statements of each artist's career. The Everlys' move to LA also renewed their acquaintance with the hit husband and wife songwriting team of Boudleaux and Felice Bryant.

From their chart breakthrough, 'Bye Bye Love' (1957), through hits such as 'All I Have To Do Is Dream' (1958) and 'Cathy's Clown' (1961), The Everly Brothers maintained a consistency largely unmatched in the rock'n'roll era. The hits began to dry up when they stopped working with the Bryants (because of management issues) but, following a stint in the Marines, the brothers dropped into one of the most fertile environments a musician could dream of: Hollywood, 1964.

Almost immediately, The Everly Brothers became regular performers on ABC television's new rock'n'roll program *Shindig!*, performing hits, covers, and new releases week in, week out. They also appeared on *Hullabaloo* and in a *Where The Action Is* segment filmed at the Trip. The duo employed the cream of LA's remaining rockabilly musicians on sessions: Sonny Curtis and Jerry Allison of The Crickets became regulars, and there were sit-ins by guitarists Glen Campbell and Al Casey, drummers Hal Blaine and Jim Gordon, and keyboardists Leon Russell, Don Randi, and Larry Knechtel.

Though not among the group's biggest hits, the run of 'Gone Gone Gone,' 'The Price Of Love,' 'Love Is Strange,' and 'Man With Money' demonstrates how 1950s rock'n'rollers—with their careers floundering pre-Beatles—could find themselves reinvigorated by the energy and excitement of the new wave of bands. Chuck Berry also had hits in 1964 and '65 with songs such as 'No Particular

Place To Go' and 'You Never Can Tell,' Little Richard returned with 'Bama Lama Bama Loo,' Jerry Lee Lewis unleashed his 'High Heel Sneakers' and the powerful *Live At The Star Club*, and Bo Diddley's awesome presence was felt everywhere after the arrival of The Rolling Stones. (Rockabilly legend Gene Vincent thrived amid the mid-1960s energy in LA as well, prompting a pair of folk-punk singles for Challenge, 'Bird Doggin'' and 'Love Is A Bird.')

Before The Beatles, US radio stations in the early 1960s had cooled to hardcore rock'n'roll, but the UK continued to welcome acts such as Eddie Cochran, Gene Vincent, and Muddy Waters. Aware of this, The Everly Brothers traveled to England to record with The Hollies, for whom they remained a defining influence. The resulting collaboration, *Two Yanks In England*, is a milestone pairing, and is latterly considered among the Everlys' finest works. Refreshed by this artistic triumph, the duo returned to America to record their final hit, 'Bowling Green,' in early 1967.

* * *

Back at the Troubadour, proprietor Doug Weston had begun to experiment with groupings of musicians who regularly appeared at the club. His first such effort was the 1963 LP *Sing Out On The Beach* by The Troubadour Singers—featuring Mason Williams, Jim Helms, and others—on Horizon Records. Weston then groomed The Men in 1964, dubbing them "the first folk-rock chorus and orchestra." The Men later evolved, independently, into The Association.

Another acoustic group with a steady gig at the Troubadour, The Modern Folk Quartet, made a similar move to electric instrumentation in 1965. Adapting their name from The Modern Jazz Quartet, the group formed in the spirit of creative interaction. Cyrus Faryar, Tad Diltz, and Chip Douglas first started playing together in the coffeehouses of Honolulu, Hawaii before hooking up with Jerry Yester upon their arrival in Hollywood, where they cut two acoustic LPs for Warner Bros. Tom Dawes of New York folk combo The Cyrkle notes The MFQ's influence: "They were singing diminished, flatted ninths, jazz chords … really advanced stuff." After they became interested in electrification, the Quartet was most likely to be found at the Action or the Crescendo/Tiger Tail.

Phil Spector saw great potential in the MFQ, who he felt could bring the nascent folk-rock boom into focus. (He had earlier tried—and failed—to sign The Lovin' Spoonful to his Phillies label for the same purpose.) Spector produced a version of Harry Nilsson's 'This Could Be The Night' for the MFQ to use as the theme song for *The Big TNT Show*, the Moulin Rouge concert film featuring performances by The Byrds, Ike & Tina Turner, and others for which Spector acted as musical director. The combination of Spector's dreamscape production and montaged images of teen Hollywood could never be reproduced in a million years.

Despite this, 'This Could Be The Night' and several other magnificent MFQ/ Spector recordings stayed on the shelf. Time was slipping away for the group, still without a record to their name. They eventually signed a two-single deal with ABC/Dunhill, releasing the Jack Nitzsche-produced raga-rock track 'Night Time Girl' and the double A-side 'Don't You Wonder'/'I Had A Dream Last Night.' But in truth the moment had passed, and the group disbanded soon after. (They did, however, end up as the opening act for several of The Velvet Underground's legendary gigs at the Trip. The original openers, The Mothers Of Invention, lost the slot on the first night after Frank Zappa aimed an anti-New York diatribe at the Velvets.)

Chip Douglas had been most responsible for The Modern Folk Quartet's blend of jazzy vocal arrangements and folk harmonics, and carried that idea into his production of The Turtles' classic single 'Happy Together.' That led to him producing The Monkees' third and fourth albums, and Linda Ronstadt's solo debut. Of the other MFQ members, Cyrus Faryar formed The Group With No Name, recorded two solo LPs, and lent his voice to the spoken-word album *The Zodiac Cosmic Sounds* (Elektra, 1967), while Henry Diltz gained recognition as a photographer, shooting the covers for Crosby, Stills & Nash's 1969 debut and The Doors' *Morrison Hotel* (1970).

Soon after The Byrds, Love, The Rising Sons, and The Leaves emerged at Ciro's LeDisc, The Turtles appeared, literally and figuratively, on the opposite side of the folk-rock street (specifically, at the Crescendo/Tiger Tail). Formerly a surf band called The Crossfires, the group copied The Byrds' path to success by adding expressive harmonies and a jingle-jangle beat to a cover of Dylan's 'It Ain't Me Babe' (recorded for a new independent label, White Whale).

The Turtles were an immediate hit in Hollywood and, despite seeming at first to be a much more commercial proposition than, say, Love, were in fact cut from the same cloth. They mastered surf instrumentals, folk-rock, garage-punk, Beach Boys harmonies, and British-style psychedelia, thus encapsulating all the LA bands of the time. The real difference between Love and The Turtles is that

Love melted jazz, folk, rhythm & blues, and garage-punk down into a completely new form of music, while The Turtles kept the diverse elements intact.

The Turtles recorded enough material over the course of five years for nine albums, all of them imbued with a wonderfully wayward quality. The group's biggest hit, 'Happy Together'—a US Number 1 hit—defines the pop music of Los Angeles in the throes of Beatlemania, while 1966's 'You Baby' is an early example of the bubblegum sound. Lead vocalist Howard Kaylan once bemoaned the fact that, "after The Crossfires, it was all a sellout," but in truth The Turtles enjoyed knowing that beneath the carefree vocals lurked a hot band, as adept at haunting psychedelia (on tracks such as 'She'll Come Back') as melodious harmonies.

The Turtles full-length debut, *It Ain't Me Babe* (1965), is a straight-up folk-rock set containing material pulled directly from their 'Crosswind Singers' repertoire, as well as Brill Building material and tracks by LA folkies such as Bob Lind and P.F. Sloan. The move toward blatant, unashamed pop is clearly in motion on *You Baby/Let Me Be* ('66), and complete on the following year's *Happy Together*, as exemplified by the title track and 'She'd Rather Be With Me.' This third album also contains introspective songs, such as White Whale staff-writer Warren Zevon's 'Like The Seasons' and 'Me About You,' which was written, like 'Happy Together,' by Gary Bonner and Alan Gordon of little-known New York group The Magicians. The trail of the smoke on the back of the jacket, meanwhile, hints at the psychedelic overtones contained within.

Next came *The Turtles Golden Hits*, which, contrary to the titular suggestion, features many new recordings, including versions of Goffin & King's 'So Goes Love,' Sloan & Barri's 'Is It Any Wonder,' further offerings from Warren Zevon and Bonner & Gordon, and the almost-hit 'Can I Get To Know You Better.' The cover art is the work of Dean Torrence, better known as half of Jan & Dean, who had recently founded his Kittyhawk Graphics company. (His musical career came to a halt when Jan Berry was involved in a near-fatal road accident.)

By this stage drummer Don Murray, rhythm guitarist Jim Tucker, and bassist Chuck Portz had all left The Turtles, leaving just vocalists Howard Kaylan and Mark Volman and Crossfires guitarist Al Nichol. With the arrival of drummer Johnny Barbata (formerly of The Sentinels and The Joel Scott III) and ex-Leaves bassist Jim Pons, the group embraced psychedelia more fully on *Chanlon Road*, which seemed to take as its starting point The Beatles' landmark double A-side

'Penny Lane'/'Strawberry Fields Forever.' (The album remained unreleased until 1987, when it was assembled and issued by Rhino.)

In 1968 The Turtles took their mastery of numerous musical styles to the limit for the concept album *The Turtles Present The Battle Of The Bands:* 11 disparate songs credited to 11 different pseudonyms and tied together as a spoof Teen-Age Fair-style inter-band contest. Among the songs is a cover of Gene Clark's 'You Showed Me' rendered as a timeless Beatles-style pop hit (and attributed on the album to Nature's Children). Finally, for what would become the final Turtles album, *Turtle Soup* (1969), the group recruited Ray Davies as producer, having all admired The Kinks' *The Kinks Are The Village Green Preservation Society.* The lead vocal parts are split evenly between all of the group members—Kaylan's are notably the strongest, particularly on 'Love In The City' and 'You Don't Have To Walk In The Rain.' Internal squabbles and friction between band, management, and label brought The Turtles to a halt in 1970. Kaylan and Volman (and, later, Jim Pons) joined the latest incarnation of The Mothers Of Invention but, because they were still under contract with The Turtles, had to take on the pseudonym Flo & Eddie (which they continued to use for many years hence).

* * *

The other significant early signing to White Whale, The Everpresent Fullness, came by way of the Revelaire Club (where The Crossfires had once served as house band). Guitarist Paul Johnson opened the club, in Redondo Beach, during the summer of 1962, initially naming it for his surf group, The Belairs. (In October 1966 the venue would take on the psychedelic mantle the Third i for a few short weeks and host The Turtles and Buffalo Springfield.)

In late 1964 Johnson rented out his studio in Redondo Beach (the walls of which were scrawled with Rick Griffin's *Murphy* artwork) to a pair of beatnik folk singers, Tom Carvey and Jack Ryan. "Tom and Jack were fresh out of Big Sur, looking real rustic," remembers Johnson. "They were long-haired, real natural sort of guys, and I was this real straight, squeaky-clean surf musician guy." At the time, Johnson and bassist Steve Pugh had been playing with Davie Allan & The Arrows, whose *Apache '65* album they appeared on, but this new folk project quickly took precedence.

"The naïveté and idealism of the drug thing ultimately proved an exercise in futility," says Johnson, "but from my position at the time, the whole experience was wrapped up in my discovery of this whole new world that Tom and Jack introduced me to. They took me up to Big Sur, gave me some LSD, and all of a sudden I felt like I was initiated into the great brotherhood of 'those who know.'"

With the addition of drummer Terry Hand, the line-up of The Everpresent Fullness was complete. Johnson then took the band to Mike Curb, who had previously produced Davie Allan & The Arrows and was currently putting together garage music for use in teen exploitation films. Johnson recalls Curb "immediately [wanted] to do something with the band. Then we saw him thinking real hard. At one point he leaned over the desk, got this real serious look on his face and asked 'Tell me, does LSD give you power over other people?'" (In later years, Curb, a Republican, would be elected Lieutenant Governor Of California.)

With Curb at the helm, The Everpresent Fullness did what all the other aspiring folk-rock bands of the time were doing: cut a Bob Dylan song, in this case a 12-string-led take on 'It's All Over Now, Baby Blue.' Although this would be the only recording the group made with Curb, it didn't take long for a record deal to appear from elsewhere. Johnson recalls his friend Don Murray of The Crossfires telling him that "'we just got this deal with this new record company that's really hot. The producers are hot, they can get guaranteed airplay, and they assured us that we are gonna be stars. The only hitch is we have to change our name. They want to call us The Turtles.' Sure enough, I'm hearing 'It Ain't Me Babe' on the radio a week later."

Johnson made a beeline to White Whale Records, for whom The Everpresent Fullness proceeded to record the single 'Fine And Dandy'/'Wild About My Lovin'' as well as a rockabilly reading of Richard Farina's 'Leavin' California,' a version of Warren Zevon's 'If You See Her,' and an early take on 'I Know Your Rider.' With rough, reedy vocals and an amped-up backing, the group evoked the good-time sound of The Lovin' Spoonful. They proceeded to play It's Boss, the Hullabaloo, and the Trip, and opened for Jefferson Airplane's LA debut at the Whisky A Go Go in August 1966. The group was even picked to guide *Datebook* magazine through a 'Hip Teen Guide To LA' at the end of the year.

But despite this rush of excitement, few Everpresent Fullness recordings were released before the group's demise (after which an LP package was strung together). Bad luck struck when the writer of 'Fine And Dandy' refused the group to release their Lovin' Spoonful-esque arrangement of the song. There were also problems with White Whale, which Johnson refers to as "the classic encounter between art and commerce. We had very strong ideas about the integrity of what we were trying to do. The Turtles were more of a moldable group, but they were struggling over this same thing that is going on at the core. In a way, that is what the 60s were really all about, the struggle over values. Here you have bands playing in Hollywood during this period, trying to adapt to this paradigm shift that they themselves don't really understand. Yet to one degree or another, they are trying to express something about that shift."

* * *

When teenage bands from the Greater Los Angeles area started playing in Hollywood in 1965 it constituted a takeover. When traditional stars left Sunset Strip's showbiz clubs in search of fatter paychecks in Las Vegas, rock'n'roll filled the vacuum. The song most emblematic of the new generation's shifting attitudes was 'Let's Live For Today.' Originally recorded by The Rokes (who hailed from the UK but were based in Italy), the song was given a folk/raga drone and fuzz-tone power chords by The Grass Roots, who turned it into a 1966 US hit. The timing and sustain of the guitar subliminally underscores the words, as if about to implement, and effect, change. Like The Byrds' 'Turn! Turn! Turn!,' 'Let's Live For Today' leapt beyond the traditional barriers of popular song and helped ease the generation gap.

Although they are now remembered for their early-1970s bubblegum hits, The Grass Roots were, before that, primarily a folk-rock group, founded by one of LA's most brilliant songwriters, P.F. Sloan. Having cut several singles by the age of 15, the prodigious Phillip 'Flip' Sloan hooked up with fellow songwriter-arranger Steve Barri in 1961. The pair wrote Round Robin & The Parleys' 'Kick That Little Foot Sally Ann' (1962) and Bruce & Terry's 'Summer Means Fun' (1964), and also sang backing vocals on many of Jan & Dean's records, including 'The Little Old Lady From Pasadena.' During the final crest of the surf wave in 1964, Sloan & Barri recorded the acclaimed *Tell 'Em I'm Surfin'* as The Fantastic Baggys. They also recorded the poppy 'Summer In New York City' as The Imaginations and the Everly Brothers-esque 'Goes To Show Just How Wrong You Can Be' under the pseudonym The Inner Circle, which foretold the sound of their next project, *Where Were You When I Needed You* (1966) by The Grass Roots.

At this point The Grass Roots was not a band, just Sloan and Barri, consummate songwriters, singers, and record producers. Sloan called in a San Francisco group called The Bedouins and had their lead vocalist Bill 'Steamboat' Fulton overdub his voice onto tracks that Sloan himself had already sung on. Surf vocal writers and producers used this trick regularly. Eager to keep working on new material in the studio, they would release records under all sorts of pseudonyms. If one hit, they would put together an actual band to take it on the road.

The original, Sloan-sung version of *Where Were You When I Needed You*'s title track had already begun to receive local airplay, but it was the Fulton take that became a hit. The Bedouins returned to the studio as The Grass Roots and cut a snarling re-reading of Bob Dylan's 'Ballad Of A Thin Man'—which they renamed 'Mr Jones'—with a Wall Of Sound backing. 'Mr Jones' was tremendously popular in LA, where Dylan's sneering refrain—"Something is happening here, but you don't know what it is"—seemed to be on the lips of every kid in town. The Grass Roots—Fulton, drummer Joel Larson, bassist Dave Stenson, and rhythm guitarist Danny Ellis—performed the song on *Shivaree* backed by superimposed pop art effects that helped popularize the group within the Sunset Strip freedom movement. They also backed The Mamas & The Papas on *Shindig!*, and opened for Barry McGuire and The Byrds at the Trip.

The first Grass Roots album is full of strong material, including 'Only When You're Lonely,' 'Lollipop Train (You Never Had It So Good)' and Sloan's version of 'You Baby' (a huge hit for The Turtles). The 'band' perform on half of the songs, of which 'Ain't That Lovin' You Baby' and 'Tell Me' stand out. Fulton and co argued for more creative input, but as far as Dunhill Records was concerned this defeated the band's purpose; that is, to be an outlet for Sloan & Barri. After further confrontations, the former Bedouins were fired, and Dunhill started looking for a new group to take on the Grass Roots mantle.

That group ended up being The 13th Floor, who had left a demo in Norty's record shop on Fairfax knowing that Steve Barri was a regular customer. Barri liked what he heard and brought the four-piece group (and a brand new vocalist, Rob Grill) to Dunhill to cut a fuzzy three-song demo. The 13th Floor were given a little more leeway than their predecessors—including the choice of whether or not to change their name or stick with the old one—and in fact contributed four of the eleven songs on The Grass Roots' second album, *Let's Live For Today*. Standout tracks such as 'Things I Should Have Said,' 'Tip Of My Tongue,' and 'Out Of Touch' improved the group's standing on the pop scene, while an appearance on *The Hollywood Palace* performing the monolithic title track brought the new line-up into the public eye. By the time of the third Grass Roots album, *Feelings*, the band-members were allowed to write half of the songs, including the cosmic, vibraphone-laden title track. But new P.F. Sloan songs dominate *Feelings'* first side, notably 'Melody For You.'

Sloan's solo work for Dunhill in 1965 and '66 was uniformly excellent and unashamedly Dylan-esque. In 1965 he told KRLA: "Dylan was my catalyst: he woke me up out of my sleep, my ridiculous sleep. But Bob Dylan really deals in images, rather than in words. I come out and say exactly what I mean, I *feel* in images." 'Sins Of A Family,' 'Halloween Mary,' 'From A Distance,' and his own reading of 'Let Me Be' rose like smoke from the platters.

Two more Sloan tunes, 'This Precious Time' and 'Eve Of Destruction,' became hits for Barry McGuire. 'Eve Of Destruction' met with the Dylan's wrath for sounding too much like his own work, but overall Sloan had his own melodic style and sense of arrangement, as well as a warm voice that could reach the stars. He once performed at the Hullabaloo in the middle of a bill that also starred The Modern Folk Quartet and The Mamas & The Papas, on whose 'California Dreamin'' he played acoustic guitar.

As Sloan continued to be kept busy by music publisher Lou Adler, his creative spirit began to drain. At one point, feeling that Dunhill had slighted his first two solo works (*Songs Of Our Times* and *Twelve More Times*), Sloan fled to New York, where he reneged on his Dunhill contract by signing with Atco. The resulting *Measure Of Pleasure* was instantly discontinued on release because of the illicit nature of his deal with Atco. In the end Sloan was just not cut out for the Machiavellian maneuverings of the music industry. The Grass Roots meanwhile, continued to have hits into the next decade, many of them provided by a new songwriting team of Harvey Price and Don Walsh. Songwriter-producer Gary Zekley contributed 'I'd Wait A Million Years' and 'Sooner Or Later,' and the group memorably performed 'Midnight Confessions' on *Playboy After Dark*.

* * *

Most of Hollywood's folk-rock groups seemed, in some way or other, to reach the pop charts. But beneath the surface were other bands that, despite being able to match the best of them on record, were never heard outside the Greater Los Angeles area. The most outstanding group lost in the shuffle was undoubtedly The Dovers from Santa Barbara.

Imagine a combination of The Left Banke's romanticism, the grinding folk-punk attack of The Leaves, the dynamic range of Love, and the 12-string jangle of The Byrds and you start to get an idea of The Dovers' sound. But that wasn't all the group was capable of: they also took in ethereal electric piano, raga rave-ups, the speed of The Yardbirds, and the power of The Who, all wrapped up in a euphoric, ghostly shimmer. They were that good.

Drummer Rick Morinini, saxophonist Tony Rivas, and guitarist Bruce Clawson started out in surf group The Vandells, which then evolved into The Del Mars. David Crosby's boyhood pal Robbie Ladewig joined on bass, bringing with him singer-guitarist Tim Granada. The group's folk-rock songs impressed Tony Cary, a moneyed local who lived on Dover Street (from which came the group's British-sounding name). Cary also financed the group's 45s on his newly formed Miramar label. Soon sax-player Rivas adapted his role to become the group's harmony vocalist, singing high parts and shaking a tambourine in the manner of Gene Clark in The Byrds or Mark Volman in The Turtles.

The Dovers played in Santa Barbara with Thee Sixpence and Ernie & The Emperors at the modernist, 5,000-capacity Earl Warren Showgrounds. They also played at skating rink gigs with The Mixtures, Neil Diamond, and The Rising Sons. Taj Mahal was impressed enough with The Dovers that he invited them to hang with The Rising Sons at their gigs in Hollywood.

The majestic grace of The Dovers' debut, 'She's Gone,' demonstrates exactly why the group stood out from the pack. It melds a Bo Diddley rhythm with folk-rock chords, topped off by tambourine reminiscent of Jerome Green's maraca shaking on early Diddley sides and a fittingly rough shroud of echo on the vocals. The flipside, a stirring, heartbreaking folk-punk ballad called 'What Am I Going To Do,' is no less important. Vocalist Tim Granada, who wrote the song, recalls how the song's origins lay in his feelings for the one girl among a host of hangers-on who actually meant something to him: "I was trying to tell her that I loved her, and she said 'no.' She left, she went south, finally, but it became a lot better song."

'She's Gone'/'What Am I Going To Do' proved a tough act to follow, but the group had high hopes for 'I Could Be Happy,' for which they had signed to Reprise. "Unfortunately, when Dick Clark chose to play it on *American Bandstand*'s 'Rate a Record' segment," Granada recalls, "they chose to highlight another record on Reprise opposite of it, and that was Nancy Sinatra's 'These Boots Are Made For Walkin'. We were blown out of the water."

This came as quite a blow, ultimately forcing The Dovers to take stock and return to Miramar. After finding himself in the midst of a post-gig jam session involving Taj Mahal, Bonnie Raitt, and members of The Chamber Brothers and The Zodiacs, Granada realized he would have to make changes to The Dovers' sound, "or else we were gonna lose it. They were starting to do more things on the bass than the old one, two, one, two—they were starting to get off into syncopation. I realized 'this is where music eventually is going to go.'"

With Randy Busby replacing Rick Morinini on drums and Tony Rivas no longer in the group, The Dovers inaugurated a new rhythmic approach on faster numbers such as 'The Third Eye,' which sets an ominous double-time bass run and snapping drum cracks against a mystical, trembling guitar figure. The group's fourth and final single, 'She's Not Just Anybody,' is built on a similar premise, with an added 12-string guitar hook that rushes like a stream through rocks, rapids, and waterfalls. Granada's vocal on the B-side, 'About Me'—"I got news for *them*"—is characteristic of the group's confidence. Why, then, did such a great band remain hidden? Perhaps things were so swingin' in The Dovers' backyard that they never bothered to notice the outside world.

CHAPTER FIVE

Sometimes good guys don't wear white

❝ *The white tie and glittering evening gown have been replaced by the poor boy, leather jackets and stovepipes. What's this world coming to? Well, for one thing, it doesn't look much like it did. The modern teenagers have their own temples and their own set of rituals to go with it … they gather in the temples to perform ceremonial dances to a rhythm that seems to reach back in time, beyond history.* **❞** MONDO TEENO: THE TEENAGE REBELLION

In 1965, the fuzz-drenched anger of The Rolling Stones' 'Satisfaction' sounded like nothing ever heard before. The combination of that record and the social consciousness of The Byrds and Bob Dylan drove LA kids to write their own songs of anger, powered by riffs lifted straight from Sunset Strip house band material and filtered through Vox Beatles amplifiers—punk rock of the highest order. Bob Cabeen of The Black Sheep vividly recalls the atmosphere on the Sunset Strip sidewalk at the time: "There was barely enough room to push forward through the throng. It was much easier to just let the undulating mass of firm, young flesh sweep you along with it."

Rock'n'roll in Los Angeles had become so arresting because its teen bands pushed things right to the edge. With the LP market still, as yet, failing to dominate, the record industry was still geared toward the dynamics of the three-minute single. Garage-rock was perfect for the format, building to maximum effect within the allotted time; lengthy improvisational jams would have diminished the thrill. (As, indeed, they soon would: when the album format took hold in 1967, post-*Sgt Pepper*, lead guitarists emerged as the focal point in rock groups; self-indulgent soloing became the norm, and the dynamic impact of rock'n'roll 45s diminished significantly.)

The LA scene kept hold of rock'n'roll's original sense of conviction, maintaining a sense of sound design, style, and timing with its tightly structured, well-crafted records. Here, the 1960s revolution had nothing to do with 'dropping out' or growing mellow and stale in a parallel universe of patchouli oil. Garage-punk was directly connected to Little Richard and Jerry Lee Lewis, to Chuck Berry and Eddie Cochran, and to the 1950s scene in which rockers opened up a dialog between black and white kids. These kids, in turn, were united in a quest to overthrow the prevalent attitudes of Victorian/McCarthyist sexual repression.

Unlike other more densely populated cities, Los Angeles's wide-open sprawl allowed for separate musical identities to co-exist without fraternal infighting, such as had occurred between mods and rockers in Britain. Factionalism had no place in the Hollywood rock'n'roll scene, where beatnik surfers and hot-roddin' greasers, Carnaby Street mods and R&B shouters, Chicanos and freaking dancers were all welcomed. The only rivals were the guardians of puritanical, Victorian value systems—and they were to be mocked with an absurdist teenage slant.

Opening in 1954 as a funky jazz joint, Pandora's Box is now best remembered as the rallying point for the 1966 Sunset Strip riots, but it was also the club that best embodied the spirit of 1960s garage-punk. It was managed by William Tilden and owned by the actor Tom Ewell (best known for roles in *The Seven Year Itch* and *The Girl Can't Help It*), and run with a promise of "dancing seven nights a week." Preston Epps, who had hit the charts in 1959 with 'Bongo Rock,' led the main house band for years, playing a combination of jazz, rhythm & blues, calypso, and soul alongside his own 'Bongo' instrumentals. The jazz combo Les McCann Ltd were a steady draw during the 1950s, while folk acts like The Smothers Brothers continued to find a home at the venue through to the mid 1960s.

LA's most famous groups—The Doors, The Byrds—sprang from other clubs on Sunset, such as the Hullabaloo, Ciro's LeDisc, or the mid-1960s Whisky A Go Go. Pandora's Box had no comparable claim to fame, but its location—on a traffic island at the corner of Sunset and Crescent Heights—made it seem like the zero-cool tip of the iceberg. Driving in westward from downtown Hollywood, Pandora's appeared lodged between Schwab's, Googie's, the Chateau Marmont, and the lot that had once been home to the Garden Of Allah; coming in from San Fernando Valley, this pink building with a purple logo was the first sign of Sunset Strip nightlife as you descended the Hollywood Hills. Pandora's Box represented a new dawn of opportunity for rock'n'roll-era teenagers on Sunset Strip following the earlier era of movie star exclusivity. The tiny club carried with it a sense that anyone could play, and that nobody would be shut out of the Hollywood experience; hope, promise, and the realization of dreams beckoned just ahead.

The Beach Boys played at Pandora's Box for a month in October 1962 as part of a series of shows presented by KFWB deejay—and future host of ABC television's *Shindig!*—Jimmy O'Neill. From there, they emerged as a breaking, national act on the strength of 'Surfin' Safari.' Brian Wilson met his wife Marilyn at the engagement, elevating the club's reputation within the pop scene.

Shindig! sprang directly from the energy at Pandora's Box in the early 1960s: O'Neill was the club's host, while its regular house band, The Fencemen, went on to play the same role on the TV show. In 1965 KRLA Beat noted: "It was James F. O'Neill who pioneered the idea of a teenage nightclub, and started a whole new trend in youthful entertainment with the opening of his 'Pandora's Box' in Hollywood." The influence of Pandora's Box on *Shindig!* is clear from the television show's pilot episode, which presents Delaney Bramlett (backed by expatriate Fencemen) as a P.J. Proby-style rock'n'roll torch singer, thereby picking up the mantle from ABC's previous musical show, *Hootenanny*.

Originally from Tulsa, Oklahoma, The Fencemen cut the instrumental singles 'Bach 'n' Roll' and 'Sunday Stranger' for Liberty Records during the time of their 1962 Pandora's Box engagement. As session players, the band-members—notably pianist Leon Russell—were heavily involved in record production during the day, but squeezed in their nighttime Pandora's Box engagement just for almost a year. They'd bring back headliners such as Jan & Dean, Lou Rawls, and Jackie DeShannon, and call in fellow Oklahomans J.J. Cale, Junior Markham, and Delaney Bramlett. At the same time, Russell and his studio pals—who included drummer Hal Blaine, bassist Jimmy Bond, and guitarist Glen Campbell—released *Swingin' 12 String Guitar* as both The In Group and Now Sounds. Russell leads much of the revelry on harpsichord, while raucous versions of 'If I Had A Hammer' and 'Greenback Dollar' seem to pre-empt folk-rock. Russell subsequently became one of LA's most in-demand session pianists, built his own Skyhill studio, and had solo hits toward the end of the decade.

The Fencemen's core members continued to crop up on the LA scene. As David & Lee, vocalist-guitarist David Gates and Leon Russell cut the Everly Brothers-style 'Trying To Be Someone' for Gary Paxton's GSP label, on which they predated the Everlys' own use of James Burton as lead guitarist. Gates later penned The Murmaids' Kim Fowley-produced Number Three hit 'Popcicles And Icicles,' and The Girlfriends' incredible Wall Of Sound-alike 'My One And Only Jimmy Boy.' He then wrote 'Saturday's Child,' as recorded by The Palace Guard and The Monkees, and produced the first two singles by Captain Beefheart & His Magic Band, 'Diddy Wah Diddy' and 'Moonchild.' Finally, in the late 1960s, he formed and led the hugely successful Bread.

Studio guitarist Billy Strange, meanwhile, went on to cut a slew of instrumental albums, and pioneered the fuzz-tone guitar sound that became a hallmark of the garage-punk idiom. After inaugurating the sound on Ann-Margret's 'I Just Don't Understand,' Strange was called into Gold Star Studios by Phil Spector to add his fuzz-tone to 'Zip-A-Dee-Doo-Dah' by Bob B. Soxx & The Blue Jeans. It was Spector's arranger, Jack Nitzsche, who then suggested that Keith Richards apply a similar tone to The Rolling Stones' 1965 monolith 'Satisfaction' during a session at RCA Music Center Of The World.

In June 1965, three years after Strange had begun to develop his fuzz-tone sound on the Pandora's Box stage, the venue started to feature more garage fare when LA's age-limit policies were relaxed. This coincided exactly with the moment when Ciro's became It's Boss, the Crescendo/Interlude re-opened as the Crescendo/Tiger Tail, and both Gazzarri's (on the Strip) and the Haunted House debuted. Unlike these larger venues, Pandora's Box tended to headline with groups who had yet to make a record, such as a pre-fame Love (then performing as The Grass Roots).

Los Angeles' new no-age-limit policy allowed Pandora's Box to hire The Banned for a Friday night residency. "My first impression of the Strip was the Sea Witch," recalls the group's Tony Pascuzzo. "Having moved out from the Bronx as a kid and [been] raised in the Valley … goin' down to the Sea Witch for an audition was a big deal. The Doors had just moved on, and The Lost Souls were playin' there. I recall we couldn't get the gig there unless we knew a tune named 'Hey Joe' and a tune named 'The Trip' [by Kim Fowley]. So we learned those tunes … 'Hey Joe,' everybody was doin' it fast before Hendrix came out with it."

The symbiotic relationship between clubs is evident in Pascuzzo's recollection of how his group subsequently landed steady work at Pandora's Box. The Banned took on the house band job there at the suggestion of Sea Witch booker Bud Smith after Leon Russell's group moved on to the Palomino. A parade of similarly obscure groups alternated with The Banned on Saturdays, among them

The Ants, Us (named in response to the Northern Irish group Them), The King Bees, The Sloths, ESP, The Ladybugs, The Knack, and The Seeds Of Time, whose frontman, the future rockabilly singer and cult-movie actor Johnny Legend, could be found handing out flyers further up the Strip wearing a costume bought on the set of *The Outer Limits*. While none of these bands hit the big time, The Sloths released the raw, uninhibited 'Makin' Love' on Impression and The Knack—not the group famed for 'My Sharona'—cut the excellent 'I'm Aware' for Capitol.

In 1966 Monrovia group World War Three, featuring ace guitarist Jim McGrew, took over as the house band at Pandora's Box. "It was fantastic," says drummer Bobby Figueroa. "A lot of people used to go in just to check the scene out, or to hang out on the front lawn. They didn't have a marquee, but they hung up this tarp on the white picket fence, … [our name] got people's attention, so they made a deal of it, putting it visible to people driving by."

Figueroa was one of many Sunset Strip musicians who would have been too young to play on the old nightclub scene, but had deep roots in LA rock'n'roll. He describes the El Monte Legion Stadium as being a "focal point" during his youth, and recalls how his sisters once filled in with Ike & Tina Turner when "a couple of Ikettes were out sick. So I had a deep appreciation for that style of R&B." This served him and his peers well when British groups arrived in the USA playing rhythm & blues covers. "People [thought] they were hearing them for the first time, cos they never listened to that music before. People'd say 'Oh yeah, that Animals song,' and I'd say, 'No, that's Sam Cooke.'"

The Sea Witch—located right in the center of the Strip next to Dino's Lodge—was another venue that focused on bands just starting out, whose names would be displayed in the portholes of the club's exterior nautical décor. In 1960, Bud Smith booked Gerry McGee & The Cajuns (led by the future Ventures guitarist) as the Sea Witch's house band. The three-piece group—McGee, bassist Larry Taylor, and drummer Bill Lewis—released three singles between 1962 and '63 before backing vocalist/keyboard player Bobby Hart in The Candy Store Prophets. This new group played all over LA in 1964, and subsequently contributed backing tracks to the first two Monkees albums.

Among the other groups to play residencies at the Sea Witch were The Rising Sons, The Seeds, The Doors, and Larry Barnes & The Creation, whose drummer, Fito de la Parra, later combined with Cajuns bassist Larry Taylor as the rhythm section in Canned Heat. Another regular act was Lyme & Cybelle, a male/female folk-rock duo featuring Violet Santangelo and Warren Zevon. The duo cut a handful of records together, notably the raga-crazed 'Follow Me,' but Zevon found more success as a songwriter for White Whale Records, composing songs for The Turtles, The Everpresent Fullness, and others.

The most interesting of the more obscure groups that started out at the Sea Witch was The Sound Machine. Fronted by Clem Floyd and former Rising Son Gary Marker, their one 45 on Canterbury Records, 'Spanish Flash,' is a kind of psychedelic garage-jazz, with a Yardbirds-style rave-up in the middle. Clearly a product of the Hollywood environment, the song is about a girl who is "flashing in Cinerama."

* * *

For garage bands in the Greater Los Angeles area, playing a show on the Strip was a very big deal. Countless fine groups never made it beyond these second-tier clubs, which were relatively easy to get gigs at compared to venues such as It's Boss, the Trip, or the Whisky A Go Go. So important was a stint at Gazzarri's to The Joint Effort that they printed the words "Now appearing at Gazzarri's on the Strip" on the label of their self-released 45, 'The Children'/'The Third Eye.'

The original Gazzarri's on La Cienega featured The Walker Brothers and The Sinners as regular house bands; The Sinners moved across to the new Gazzarri's on the Strip when it opened on June 1st 1965, sharing the bill with The Vendells, while the La Cienega venue became home to The Sons Of Adam. By this stage The Walker Brothers had moved to the UK, where they were well on the way to becoming firm favorites. Nonetheless, their British debut album, *Take It Easy With The Walker Brothers*, betrayed a strong Gazzarri's/East LA influence with its "na na" version of 'Land Of A Thousand Dances' and songwriting contributions from locals David Gates, Dan Seals, and Randy Newman.

According to LA scenester Denny Bruce, The Walker Brothers—who were not, in fact, siblings at all, but a trio of guitarist John Maus, bassist Scott Engel, and drummer Gary Leeds—had to move to the UK so that they could make music in a Righteous Brothers style. "They couldn't have done that here, with the actual Righteous Brothers in the vicinity," notes Denny. In fact, The Walker Brothers had already pre-empted Phil Spector's breakthrough successes with Bill Medley and Bobby Hatfield: in 1964 they cut 'Love Her' with Jack Nitzsche and Nick Venet, which hit the UK Top 20. They followed 'Love Her' with the British chart-topper 'Make It Easy On Yourself' (1965) and the international hit 'The Sun Ain't Gonna Shine Anymore' (1966). As Scott Walker, Engel has since made a number of critically acclaimed solo albums and once hosted a UK television variety show.

Back on the Strip, the new Gazzarri's eventually had three stages, all facing each other in the same room, allowing multiple bands to play on a non-stop, live rotation. On any given night, you could see a selection of mostly obscure garage bands, such as Limey & The Yanks or Popcorn Blizzard (fronted by a singer later known as Meat Loaf), performing timeless 45s that would someday become highly collectable and feature on countless compilations. Out-of-town garage bands would play on bills with The Byrds and Love, such as The Daily Flash, who only made two singles but managed to appear in an episode of cult television spin-off *The Girl From U.N.C.L.E.* The Daily Flash didn't last long, although guitarist Doug Hastings briefly replaced Neil Young in Buffalo Springfield, and once found himself in a post-Monterey Pop Festival jam session at Stephen Stills's Malibu beach pad that also included Jimi Hendrix and various Beatles and Byrds. For Hastings and so many others, LA in the mid 1960s was full of surprises.

* * *

The Standells were the quintessential Los Angeles garage-punk band. Vocalist Dick Dodd mixed a greasy, soulful, rock'n'roll house band delivery with Beatles-esque screams and Rolling Stones swagger (and, in keeping with his sly, cocky vocal style, later married a Playboy bunny); Tony Valentino provided bright, economical guitar licks; and Larry Tamblyn was responsible for the classic Vox organ sound that became a benchmark characteristic of 1960s garage (his brother, Russ Tamblyn, was the star of *High School Confidential* and *West Side Story*).

The Standells rose to prominence as Hollywood's top house band of the dance-crazed early 1960s. Having cut several rhythm & blues records alongside vocal group The Salas Brothers and Eddie Davis, Tamblyn formed a self-contained band of his own with Valentino, drummer Benny King, and bassist Jody Rich. Larry Tamblyn & The Standells' first gig was at the Oasis Club in Hawaii, where they followed strippers and a full Japanese floor show—Kabuki theater and all—with a set of contemporary rhythm & blues hits. Shortly thereafter, the group returned to Hollywood, where they picked up a new rhythm section—bassist Gary Lane and drummer Gary Leeds—and took up a residency at Peppermint West (making use of fake IDs obtained in Tijuana).

LA's answer to New York's Peppermint Lounge, Peppermint West sat a half-block north of Hollywood Boulevard at 1750 Cahuenga next door to the Omnibus coffeehouse and the building that briefly housed the Wild Thing in 1966. The kids seen in the 'What'd I Say' sequence of Elvis's *Viva Las Vegas* were culled from the club's dance floor, while actress Mamie Van Doren recalls grooving to The Standells at the venue with Los Angeles Angels no-hit pitcher Bo Belinsky.

The Standells called the Peppermint West home for over a year, during which time they cut a record called 'The Peppermint Beatle' (1963). Tony Valentino had been hip to The Beatles earlier than most in America through fan magazines from Italy, which he continued to read after he'd moved to America. The far-sighted Standells grew their hair long in 1963 to anticipate the new craze, a full six months before The Beatles' first appearance on *The Ed Sullivan Show*.

In 1964, Gary Leeds left The Standells to join The Walker Brothers and was replaced by Dickie Dodd, who had previously played with surf pioneers The Belairs and Eddie & The Showmen, with whom he recorded five excellent singles for Liberty Records. As the surf boom began to bust, Dodd's fellow Liberty recording artist Jackie DeShannon introduced him to The Standells. He recalls her telling him to "be at PJ's, Tuesday, 5:30. They'll be expecting you."

After Trini Lopez swapped PJ's for Las Vegas and national tours, the piano/ conga jazz combo led by Eddie Cano briefly became the headline act, before being usurped by The Standells (who had been playing the three-room nightclub's second stage). "Right at the front door there was a place for a piano, and a very small, crammed area for a drummer, conga player and guitarist," recalls Dick Dodd. "The Standells would play [in the back room], then take a break, and this guy Jerry Wright would play with his trio, so there was always music. There was never a dead spot."

Situated on the corner of Crescent Heights and Santa Monica Boulevard, PJ's was the most high-profile club in early-1960s Hollywood. Dodd describes the audience as being "trendy, hip, swingy," and sporting "thin ties and sport jackets." He adds: "Sinatra used to come in ... and then we met The Rolling Stones, before we had a hit record. PJ's and Whisky A Go Go were the places to go and be seen, and all the stars would come in. Bobby Darin came in and sat in with us one night."

PJ's can also lay claim to having spawned the style that made the Whisky famous. Johnny Rivers' *Live At The Whisky A Go Go* was clearly inspired by the hit LP *Trini Lopez Live At PJ's*. A Standells *Live At PJ's* set followed on Liberty toward the end of 1964; on it, Dick Dodd sings lead on 'Help Yourself' and 'What Kind Of Fool Am I.' He would soon replace Larry Tamblyn as The Standells' primary vocalist.

By the time their contract at PJ's had expired, The Standells had amassed a backlog of rockin' 45s on a variety of labels, including 'The Shake,' 'You'll Be Mine Someday,' 'Big Boss Man,' 'Don't Say Goodbye,' 'Someday You'll Cry,' and 'The Boy Next Door' (on which Tamblyn adopts the vocal style of the record's producer, Sonny Bono). In 1965 the group met Ed Cobb (formerly of vocal group The Four Preps), who signed them to his AVI label and suggested they record one of his songs, the bluesy 'Dirty Water.' The Standells recorded their new arrangement of the song, complete with improvised vocal intro and an updated guitar riff, at Armin Steiner's Sound Recorders on Yucca Street, just a stone's throw from the Capitol Records Tower near Hollywood and Vine. Capitol had recently formed a new label, Tower, to handle the overspill of rock'n'roll talent emergent in Hollywood in the wake of the British Invasion. Tower picked up 'Dirty Water' and its freak-out flip-side, 'Rari,' from AVI; the 45 quickly broke out as a hit in Florida.

Keen to capitalize on this success, Ed Cobb flew to Seattle—where The Standells had just stopped on tour—to cut *Dirty Water* with the band. The album was completed in a couple of days; one song, 'Little Sally Tease,' was written by Seattle native Jim Valley of Don & The Goodtimes. In the hands of The Standells, 'Tease' has a destructive fuzz-tone sound that parallels the contemporary guitar-smashing aura of The Who. The group immediately set out on a national tour to promote 'Dirty Water,' confident that one of the songs they had recorded in Seattle, 'Sometimes Good Guys Don't Wear White,' could give them a follow-up hit.

'Good Guys' demonstrates how completely Beatles/Stones-mania had taken over LA's rock'n'roll kids with its mocking pay-off line: "If you don't dig this long hair, get yourself a crew cut, baby!" The Standells' own Gary Lane left the group shortly thereafter, in part because he didn't want to swap his house band greaser hairstyle for a Brian Jones-style mop. He was replaced, temporarily, by Dave Burke, who the group ran into while playing in Florida. Back in Hollywood, the group cut a strange album of covers, *The Hot Ones*, which mixed their house band heritage with garage-punk and psychedelic concepts.

Given the abrasive sound of 'Dirty Water' and 'Sometimes Good Guys Don't Wear White,' The Standells were the obvious choice to support The Rolling Stones on the British group's 1966 American tour. Next came 'Why Pick On Me,' which brought a raga-punk urgency to the US charts. The Standells—now with John Fleck, once of Love, on bass—were becoming a major act in their own right. As they and The Byrds left the Hollywood nightclub scene to tour elsewhere, a whole wave of folk-rock and garage-punk bands (and various hybrids thereof) began to develop in their wake.

Like The Byrds, whose 'Eight Miles High' was pulled from radio after being denounced as a drug song, The Standells were stifled by censorship just as they hit their stride. Larry Tamblyn explains how the rise of 'Try It,' which he felt was "destined to become a Number 1 hit … came screeching to a halt" after Texan radio mogul Gordon McLendon—generally considered to be one of the founding fathers of modern radio—appeared on television and "claimed the lyrics were vulgar." (Tamblyn feels that McLendon targeted The Standells because they were "not as big as The Rolling Stones, and thus easier to topple.")

Ironically, 'Try It' had made its television debut on the squeaky-clean Saturday morning show *American Bandstand*, and, as it later turned out, McLendon had a number of lurid skeletons in his own closet. But, for The Standells, the damage was done. The record all but disappeared from radio, although KRLA continued to play it, preceded by a disclaimer from newscaster Richard Beebe: "This song has been banned elsewhere, but here on KRLA we let you be the judge." (KRLA also championed Sammy Davis Jr's sympathetic paean to the teen scene, 'Don't Blame It On The Children.')

The Standells continued to record ever-stronger material. The first eight guitar chords of 'All Fall Down' provide the ultimate example of garage echo, with backward-tape effects piercing the cave-like production, while on the rave-up 'Barracuda,' Dick Dodd drums like he's dropping bombs at full throttle. Perhaps the group's finest moment came with their theme to the exploitation movie *Riot On Sunset Strip*. In *Who Put The Bomp*, music scribe Greg Shaw calls it "one of the most powerful calls to violence rock'n'roll has produced," and notes its "unforgettable guitar riff, every bit as inevitable as Keith Richards on 'Satisfaction,' and actually more effective in the context of the song."

By the time *Riot On Sunset Strip* premiered in early 1967, most of the clubs on the Strip itself had already been closed down. The venues that stayed had to make major compromises and, as such, it became difficult for teenage bands to follow in the footsteps of The Standells. The music scene changed swiftly and considerably; as *The Los Angeles Free Press* put it at the time: "Motown music replaces acid bands at Whisky A Go Go." Motown's Berry Gordy had, in 1967, begun to push The Temptations, The Supremes, and The Miracles toward Vegas-style showbiz pizzazz, in the hope of taking over the adult mainstream market. (This ridiculous back-step weakened Motown for several years, until Marvin Gaye, Stevie Wonder, and the Norman Whitfield-era Temptations, revived the label's credibility at the turn of the decade.)

Subsequently, and much to the band's dismay, Ed Cobb began to push for "a little bit of soul" in The Standells' music. Initially, Cobb had been a great songwriter and collaborator for the group, but gradually became a tyrannical manager. After the radical 'Try It' and 'Riot,' he pushed the group into weak covers of Wilson Pickett's 'Ninety-Nine And A Half' and 'Can't Help But Love You'—perhaps the very reason why garage fans continue to hold an aversion to horns. Dick Dodd sang on these records, but the rest is the work of session players. Cobb coaxed Dodd into a souly solo career, while the remaining Standells watched the once-cool 1960s get sullied by Woodstock mud.

* * *

Before the encroachment of late-1960s rock, Hollywood nightclubs kept faith in the sound of rock'n'roll. Building on the momentum of their PJ's engagement, The Bobby Fuller Four cracked the Los Angeles charts with 'Take My Word,' 'Let Her Dance,' and 'Never Be Forgotten' in 1965 before hitting the national charts with 'I Fought The Law' and 'Love's Made A Fool Of You' in 1966. The group mined a Buddy Holly-esque rock'n'roll sound, broken up by reverb-drenched surf instrumentals on a par with LA's finest of the early 1960s.

Bobby Fuller started his musical career as a drummer in El Paso, Texas, although he regularly crossed the border to bars in Juarez, Mexico, to catch gritty rhythm & blues acts such as Long John Hunter. He started making Buddy Holly-inspired records in 1961 at the age of 19, cutting one of his early singles at the Norman Petty Studio in Clovis, New Mexico—Holly's home base. Soon after that he built a recording studio at the Fuller family home, and started releasing hot sides on his own Exeter label. A promotional trip to Los Angeles in 1963 inspired him to try to mimic in El Paso the kind of frenzy whipped up by Dick Dale & His Del

Tones at the Rendezvous Ballroom in Balboa. Thus Fuller opened his own Teen Rendezvous club, billing himself 'The Rock'N'Roll King Of The Southwest'—a name that would stick even after his move to Los Angeles in the heat of 1964.

Most of the tunes that Bobby Fuller recorded in Hollywood were nurtured and developed in his El Paso studio, and display, in their earlier versions, an obvious raunch and an immediate rockabilly/surf vigor. When he hooked up with fellow lead guitarist Jim Reese—who had previously recorded the eloquent 'Surfer's Paradise' with another group from West Texas, Bob Taylor & The Counts—the effect anticipated the dual guitar assault of later Yardbirds recordings.

The wild sound of The Bobby Fuller Four can be heard on '10,000 Pound Bee,' 'Thunder Reef,' 'Stringer,' 'El Paso Rock,' and their cover of The Wailers' 'Shang-Hied' (retitled 'Shangai'd,') while the group's melodic instrumental work peaked on moodier cuts such as 'The Lonely Sea / Lolita Ya Ya' and 'Our Favorite Martian.' Upon their arrival in Hollywood, Phil Spector showed an immediate interest in recording the group, which demonstrates how big a splash these El Paso boys made when they came to town. Instead, however, they signed to the Del-Fi/Donna label's new Mustang imprint. Bassist Randy Fuller (Bobby's brother) and drummer DeWayne Quirico instinctively understood how their music fitted into the excitement of the mid 1960s. In a contemporary interview with *KRLA Beat*, Randy Fuller declared: "We play West Texas rock'n'roll," to which Quirico added: "The same kind of thing The Beatles have been trying to play and can't." With their southern roots, The Bobby Fuller Four were closer to the source—and better equipped to achieve the right tempo than their British contemporaries in Buddy Holly-worship (The Beatles had been named after The Crickets, and The Hollies also took their name from Buddy).

Los Angeles led the American response to the British Invasion. In this respect The Bobby Fuller Four and Paul Revere & The Raiders (originally from the Pacific Northwest) were LA's most valuable transplants. Fuller's 'Take My Word' parallels—and matches—The Beatles' 'You're Gonna Lose That Girl' (from *Help!*). Beneath his rockin' exuberance was the lyrical sensibility of a sensitive, romantic guy. Among his group's most inspired records, 'Let Her Dance' was underpinned by a circular, reverbed, Duane Eddy-style guitar riff that throbs and throbs beside the chanted background chorus, and soared to the top of the Hollywood sound in 1965. In performance, Fuller would accentuate the song with limber, guitar-slinging punctuation, dropping to his knees with passion.

In 1966 The Bobby Fuller Four hit the national charts twice in a row, first with a version of Buddy Holly's 'Love's Made A Fool Of You,' which reached Number 26 on the *Billboard* Hot 100, and then with 'I Fought The Law,' written by The Crickets' Sonny Curtis, which peaked at Number 9. They played a celebrated run at It's Boss on Sunset Strip, made a number of television appearances, and cropped up, rather dubiously, in *Ghost In The Invisible Bikini*, miming along to somebody else's recording with Vox guitars (which, being devout fans of Fender equipment, they hated).

Bobby Fuller's energy fueled the band, so touring began to limit his creativity. The group's next 45 was a rushed recording of a soul tune, 'The Magic Touch,' produced by Barry White of Bronco Records—not the kind of record Fuller would have chosen to make, but the product of pressure to quickly cash in on recent success. When Fuller did find the time to make the record he wanted, he cut the stunning 'Baby My Heart.'

Before he could fulfill this promise, however, Fuller was found dead in a parking lot near his apartment on July 18th 1966. He had been forced to drink gasoline from a can before being choked with a garden hose. While the LAPD initially declared Fuller's death to be a suicide, this explanation now seems unlikely. Rumors of LSD deals, ill-advised relations with the mistress of a mob-connected club owner, life insurance policy cash-ins, and record label cover-ups still rage. Most indicators point to Fuller's way with women as the most likely cause of his unfortunate demise: like legendary bluesman Robert Johnson, he was cut down in his prime, murdered, apparently, by a jealous adversary.

* * *

One of the most crucial bands of the mid-1960s Hollywood scene, The Knickerbockers, arrived from New York in September 1965 to take the house band job at the Red Velvet on Sunset. Originally a jazz club called the Summit, the venue first started presenting rock'n'roll when it was known as Jimmie Maddin's. Kim Fowley recalls living upstairs in 1959, and "booking KRLA's Teenage Nightclub on Sundays, which was the first thing of its kind … we did the last gig with Eddie Cochran in LA before he went off to England and died." During the Knickerbockers era, Elvis Presley found the club to his liking, and made it a regular hangout, most likely because, of all the rock'n'roll clubs in Hollywood, this was the one that most catered to people refused to let their hair go 'Beatle.' The Red Velvet was, thankfully, the last bastion for pompadours, ducktails, and greasy rock'n'roll.

The Knickerbockers' producer, Jerry Fuller, recalls how the group would back up "all the big acts" as they passed through LA, and would "sound just like the record. No matter who sat in with them, they could duplicate their sound." According to Knickerbockers guitarist Beau Charles, who founded the group with his bassist brother, John: "We came out and took the town by storm … we were knockin' people out in the club. All the big acts would stop buy after doing *Shindig!* or whatever." Acts such as The Everly Brothers, The Bobby Fuller Four, and The Shindogs (featuring noted session guitarist James Burton, who had recently released a fuzzy garage-rock 45 of his own, 'Jimmy's Blues'), found themselves right at home, as did numerous 1950s rhythm & blues singers.

Soon after arriving in LA, The Knickerbockers provided the backing tracks for *Sing And Sync Along With Lloyd Thaxton* and released a covers album, *Jerk And Twine Time* (actually recorded in New York in early 1965), featuring fuzzed-up takes on songs by The Kinks and others. Then came the group's defining moment, 'Lies.' By late 1965, The Beatles no longer sounded as they had on their first recordings, but this 1965 45 had that familiar, longed-for sound, with a John Lennon-like vocal and a hook based on the stunning six-note intro to 'I Want To Hold Your Hand.' The Knickerbockers' label, Challenge Records, misread the single by promoting The Byrds-inflected 'The Coming Generation' as the A-side, but it was 'Lies' that soon took off as a national hit.

The accompanying *Lies* album didn't disappoint, taking in Beatles-esque rockers, trippy fades (courtesy of RCA engineer Dave Hassinger), and pulsating garage-punk. The jacket features humorous one-line endorsements by musical luminaries including Marvin Gaye, Brian Wilson, and The Righteous Brothers, as well as rock'n'roll television hosts such as Lloyd Thaxton and Casey Kasem. The Knickerbockers made numerous appearances on *Shindig!* and, like Paul Revere & The Raiders, featured regularly on *Where The Action Is*, recording the backing tracks for all the solo singers on the program.

The Knickerbockers contract with the Red Velvet made it virtually impossible for them to tour upon the success of 'Lies,' so the group missed the opportunity to capitalize on their hit single's popularity. Of the follow-up releases, 'As A Matter Of Fact' manages to cross The Beach Boys with The Music Machine, while the guitar sounds on 'Stick With Me' predate those of The Nazz and

Jefferson Airplane. But by 1967 there was little room for straightforward, high-energy rock'n'roll performed by musicians with slicked-back hair.

* * *

The Seeds, who broke out of Bido Lito's and the Sea Witch, embodied the evolution of garage in Hollywood's teen hot spots. Keyboardist Daryl Hooper recalls having earlier played all over town, "under different band names, performing other artists' material." But their stint at Bido Lito's was different: "It was an underground club, popular with the Hollywood in-crowd."[1]

In October 1965 the group released the first of three singles on GNP-Crescendo, the label owned by Gene Norman, who had run the Crescendo jazz club on the Strip until 1963. 'Can't Seem To Make You Mine' has an electric piano glissando that predates the sound of The Doors. Hooper notes: "We were the first group with really long hair. We coined the terms 'flower power' for the peace and love movement, 'flower children' for the kids with the long hair, and 'flower music' for our particular sound."

The Seeds' second 45 was originally known as 'You're Pushin' Too Hard' on its release the following March. The key element in the single's success—eerie, insistent electric piano and abrasive fuzz-tone aside—is the performance of The Seeds' lead singer. "For six months, Sky Saxon *was* Mick Jagger, locally," recalls writer and spoken-word record producer Harvey Kubernik. "There were the screaming girls, people were stealing his clothes onstage. He was a serious motivator of the flower-power scene, and an enigma in his connection with an audience."

Saxon had an unusual dancing style that hinted at a higher source of inspiration, while his messianic delivery was backed by music so forceful that few could resist its spell. Debut album *The Seeds* drew attention just for the group's look: unprecedented shoulder-length hair, vests, knee-high moccasin boots, wide belts, and corduroy pants. The rustic, black-and-white cover photograph sold the album to a lot of kids even before they had heard what lay between the grooves. In late 1966, following the underground success of *The Seeds*, GNP-Crescendo had a big hit with a reissued 'Pushin' Too Hard.' (This same process was then repeated by Elektra Records with Love and The Doors, and would become the standard way of selling new bands to the public.)

A few months later came *Web Of Sound*, featuring the double-time builds of 'Pictures And Designs' and the minor hit 'Mr Farmer,' which showcases a keyboard sound not unlike that of the new British group The Pink Floyd. The album also includes the 14-and-a-half minute 'Up In Her Room,' a playful, psychedelic rendering of a teenage mod girl's bedroom complete with bottleneck guitar and sound effects depicting kooky gadgets hanging from the walls. The group took this sound a step further on their third LP, *Future* (1967), which has a cover painting by Sky Saxon showing the group as a pop art puzzle on a hill of flowers with a castle on top. The nymph-like prances of 'March Of The Flower Children,' 'Where Is The Entrance Place To Play,' and 'The Flower Lady And Her Assistant' are laced with beautiful, naïve lyrics of hope driven by punk energy. On 'A Thousand Shadows' the lyrics are even more ambitious (but never ambiguous), while the music retains the taut incision of 1950s rock'n'roll.

The Seeds became one of LA's hottest acts at the peak of the Strip scene. Hullabaloo proprietor Gary Bookasta recalls the group doing "wonderful business for us. We would seat 2,000 easily, even thought it was only licensed to 850. Next to Love, The Seeds became our most important act."

But despite their popularity in Hollywood, The Seeds never took off outside of Los Angeles. GNP-Crescendo had difficulty coming up with enough money to press records for and promote the group on a national scale, forcing The Seeds to watch on as bands such as The Doors brought Sunset Strip to the world. With a string of hot records but little support, frustration began to set in, the band-members began to fall out, and The Seeds' sound dissipated. Sky Saxon recorded a mediocre blues album, *Spoonful Of Seedy Blues*, to fulfill a contractual obligation before the group issued a fitting final statement, *Raw And Alive: The Seeds In Concert* (1968), which shows them to be as stunning in person as their studio recordings suggest.

* * *

Hot on the heels of The Seeds, The Music Machine summed up everything the garage-punk sound came to represent: The organ was full, but concise; the chords were crunchy; the lead guitar was imaginative, yet kept its focus on song structure and impact. The Music Machine achieved a dark, bass-heavy sound by tuning their strings down to D flat, and had a look to match: black Levis, black turtlenecks, dyed-black Beatle hair, and one black leather glove on their right hands. According to vocalist and songwriter Sean Bonniwell: "The glove is a representation of the group, and the bare hand is a representation of the individual."[2]

Like The Byrds, the original members of The Music Machine had major label experience as folk musicians. Sean Bonniwell—who was once invited to form a band with Roger McGuinn, but declined—played on three albums by The Wayfarers at RCA, bassist Keith Olsen had been in Gale Garnett's group, and drummer Ron Edgar played with Curt Boettcher in The GoldeBriars. (The Music Machine copped their all-black attire from the cover of The GoldeBriars' debut.) Bonniwell, Edgar, and Olsen formed rock'n'roll trio The Ragamuffins in 1965 before recruiting organist Doug Rhodes—who came from producer Boettcher's orbit and played on The Association's 'Cherish'—and lead guitarist Mark Landon, who arrived by way of an index-card information board in the instrument store he worked in.

The newly expanded Music Machine picked up a six-week gig in San Jose early the following year but, says Bonniwell: "It was a disaster. Everybody hated us." Fortunately, a break was just around the corner. Producer Brian Ross happened to see the group playing at, of all things, a bowling alley (Hollywood Legion Lanes), and within a week raised $150 to record demos of 'Talk Talk' and 'Come On In.' The tracks were cut at RCA's Music Center Of The World, which both The Wayfarers and The Rolling Stones used for mastering. Bonniwell notes the importance of bassist Keith Olsen, who built the fuzz-tone box that gave 'Talk Talk' its distinctive sound: "Everybody in those days was trying to get a hold of that box, because nobody else could get that fat, round tone."

These recordings ended up being issued by Original Sound Records, the label run by Art Laboe, whose live broadcasts from Scrivner's drive-in during the late 1950s and early 60s constituted LA's first major rock'n'roll events. Original Sound was best known for its rhythm & blues vocal group compilation series, *Oldies But Goodies*, as well as various artists sets such as *KRLA 21 Solid Rocks*, which serve as precursors to *Nuggets* and *Pebbles*. On August 1st 1964 the label's recording engineer, Paul Buff, sold his PAL studio in Cucamonga to Frank Zappa and started building a 10-track studio in Original Sound's office on Sunset. Noting that this was then "the only 10-track going," Bonniwell calls Buff a "genius," adding: "I'd tell him what I wanted and he'd find a way to do it." Buff had previously recorded 'Wipe Out' with The Surfaris, and released the supremely kinetic 'Drums A-Go-Go' as The Hollywood Persuaders, which was used as a link to ad breaks on *American Bandstand*. He, Bonniwell, and producer Brian Ross also worked together on Original Sound recordings for groups including

Pasternak Project, Mad Andy's Twist Combo, and The Friendly Torpedoes (who were actually The Music Machine in disguise).

Art Laboe used his radio contacts to push The Music Machine into the public consciousness. KRLA deejay Bob Eubanks gave 'Talk Talk' its first airing on the night of the group's first performance at the Cinnamon Cinder (which Eubanks owned). Sean Bonniwell remembers an instant reaction: by the second night of the group's weekend engagement, "there was a line waiting to go in and see us." Shortly thereafter, The Music Machine featured as house band on Sam Riddle's daily TV show *9th Street West*. Some of the cover versions the group recorded for the show ended up on their rush-released debut album, including a direct, live-sounding take on The Beatles' 'Taxman,' which replaced the British politicians mentioned in the song, "Mr Wilson" and "Mr Heath," with US Secretary Of State Dean Rusk and President Lyndon Johnson. Also present is a slowed-down reading of 'Hey Joe,' complete with an anguished Vox tremolo at the close, and a version of the ancient blues song 'See See Rider,' which predates the nervous energy of Love's 'Stephanie Knows Who.'

The Music Machine's original material had the feel of a raging fire. "Lyrically, I think I was reflecting the introspective examination of what motivates young people," Bonniwell explains. "For the most part, The Music Machine image was really fierce. The anger and frustration came from the confusion of not knowing who or what to blame for the natural conflict of youth or growing up. They blame the 'society' and the structure of the adult world. If you've got the intelligence and sensitivity to understand yourself in that context, then [a kind of] evolution takes place."

The group's titles alone convey the confident duality of their songs. The follow-up to 'Talk Talk' was 'The People In Me,' while 'Masculine Intuition' addresses interpersonal affairs with an insight that was rare then and remains so now atop an awesome sonic representation of a jail cell closing. 'Point Of No Return' takes on US military involvement in Vietnam, and 'The Eagle Never Hunts The Fly' attacks the type of rich person that lacks empathy with the poor.

The Music Machine's sinister fuzz reached its apex on the group's third single, 'Double Yellow Line,' on which the main organ riff is echoed by surf guitar fed through a Leslie speaker. The rest of the group's second album, *The Bonniwell Music Machine*, is a diverse affair, taking in acoustic ballads, psychedelia, pop, and a shameless garage-soul track. The LA scene ate it all up, with hordes of fans flocking to their live shows. The best of these was at the Hullabaloo, with Richard Pryor as the opening act: when the revolving stage turned around, The Music Machine were lying on the floor, pretending to sleep. Then the group 'woke up' and tore through a set that was even more ominous than ever.

This kind of performance left a deep impression on a young Johnny Legend, who recalls: "At this point in time, everyone agreed that they were the best live group we'd ever heard. The dynamics were just so astounding. That was one of the first times I really noticed how thin the record sounded in comparison." This avalanche of excitement was aided by the band's neat trick of leaving no breaks between songs for the entire set. "We were the first band to play an hour of non-stop, original music," explains Bonniwell. "That's why I called us The Music Machine." He wanted the group's records to have the same effect but, alas, his record label "thought I was just nuts. They said 'there's no way, the radio stations won't play it.' Then *Sgt Pepper* came out."

The Music Machine continued to make groundbreaking records, but a few bad calls slowed their pace. The band turned down a trip to the UK, while their manager foolishly passed on an opportunity to play the Monterey Pop Festival. Another crucial mistake was to give an exclusive debut of 'The People In Me'—the follow up to 'Talk Talk'—to a brand new station. This, according to Bonniwell, "completely alienated [Bill] Drake," who was then "the Godfather of Top 40 radio" with "14 sister stations" from LA to New York. Perhaps because of this snub, Drake never played the single, which "killed it, 'cause that guy had control of the markets." (This was an early example of the multi-station ownership that would ultimately render broadcast radio generic and sterilized. Similar deregulation followed in broadcast news, resulting in no less of a mainstream brainwash than that of Russia during the Cold War.)

* * *

The Standells, The Bobby Fuller Four, The Knickerbockers, The Seeds, and The Music Machine all achieved a degree of success, recording memorable hit singles, making numerous television appearances, and influencing successive generations of bands. But there were countless other combos in Los Angeles at this time making rock'n'roll 45s as fine as anything else the genre could produce. It was impossible to tell which band would create the next big buzz around town, and as each new act made the breakthrough, many more would suffer some unfortunate twist of fate and be kept from a larger audience.

The Humane Society, for instance, seemed at one stage to be headed for success ahead of The Doors. 'Knock Knock,' the B-side to their 1967 novelty-garage hit 'Tiptoe Through The Tulips,' reveals them to be just as pioneering as Jim Morrison's group, but in a different way: The Humane Society's anguished howl and double-time bass runs predate The Germs' punk rock terror by 11 years. The band's members all grew up in Simi Valley, a sparsely populated suburb at the northwest tip of Los Angeles, and honed their sound in various garages around town. "It was almost like a Tom Sawyer kind of existence," recalls rhythm guitarist Woody Minnich. Drummer Bill Schnetzler picked oranges and lemons for a living prior to joining the band. Minnich describes their singer and harmonica player, Danny Wheetman, as being one of the first 'freak-out' artists, who would "go bananas" and "destroy things on stage … it blew people away."

The five-piece group—completed by lead guitarist Jim Pettit and bassist Richard 'Mojo' Majewski—signed a two-single deal with Liberty Records and promptly performed their LA-only hit on *Shebang*. According to Whitman, their producer suggested they release the joke song 'Tiptoe Through The Tulips' as "it would absolutely bring the house down" every time they performed it. Liberty never released a follow-up, however, and the more vital—and representative— 'Knock Knock' was widely ignored until being rediscovered, a decade later, by post-Sex Pistols record collectors (and later included on the expanded version of *Nuggets*).

'Sweetgina' by The Things To Come, from the same time period, features a similar writhing-on-the-floor vocal by keyboardist Steve Runolfsson. His pain is accentuated by groaning, pinched lead guitar by Lyn Rominger, and a tough, solid rhythm from guitarist Larry Robinson, bassist Bryan Garofalo, and drummer Russ Kunkel. This Long Beach quintet rehearsed beneath a poolside porch and played gigs at the Mystic Eye in Riverside. This was fitting, as 'Sweetgina' is a powerful extension of Them's 'Gloria.' Recently discovered tapes demonstrate a depth of sound ranging from cave-dwelling folk-rock to echo-drenched, pop art freak-beat. In their prime, The Things To Come were house band at the Airport Club (later the Marina Palace) in Seal Beach, and played on bills with a diverse array of talent, including Dick Dale, Ike & Tina Turner, Cream, and jazz trumpeter Hugh Masekela. Unfortunately, however, by the time the group hit

Hollywood, the club scene that previously would have fostered just this sort of band was already dying out.

In a similar league to 'Knock Knock' and 'Sweetgina' was The Bees' 'Voices Green And Purple,' perhaps the best aural representation of a psychotic episode ever committed to vinyl. Music writer Greg Shaw's explanation of the song breaks down the secret genius of 1960s punk: "Psychedelic drugs affected different people in different ways. Tim Leary and his intellectual friends were wafted into oriental mysticism, but imagine the effects on kids in punk bands whose mental worlds up to then had revolved around cars, girls, beaches, and detention. They saw the colors, heard the voices, and what else could they do? They freaked out!"

The B-side, 'Trip To New Orleans,' is almost as good, and leaves you wanting more, but this is all the San Gabriel Valley group managed. In the midst of the mid-1960s LA scene, so many groups left no more than a one-shot legacy. Often, only the songwriting credits or an address on the record label hint at the band's identity. Such matters are further confused when, for example, more than one band uses a name such as The Bees. A folk-rock combo, featuring future Byrd John York on bass, also went by the name during 1965–66, releasing a pair of singles, 'Forget Me Girl' and 'Leave Me Be,' on Mira/Mirwood. Vocalist George Caldwell then formed The W.C. Fields Memorial Electric String Band with members of The Preachers and cut a punchy pop take on Tommy Boyce and Bobby Hart's 'I'm Not Your Stepping Stone' (later recorded, more famously, by The Monkees, Paul Revere & The Raiders, and The Sex Pistols).

The follow-up, 'Hippy Elevator Operator,' is reminiscent of The Beatles' 'Paperback Writer,' but, overall, The W.C. Fields Memorial Electric String Band sound like a wild combination of Chocolate Watchband vocalist Dave Aguilar and Count Five's primitive double-time rave-ups. San Jose bands such as these did not conform to the serious 'rock' contingency of northern California, and found themselves cast aside by the leaders of the emergent San Francisco clique. Los Angeles, however, remained eager for garage-punk hits, and the number of them to come from San Jose—hometown of The Music Machine's Sean Bonniwell—is little short of stunning.

The Chocolate Watchband played all over Los Angeles, from Pandora's Box to the Hullabaloo. After cutting 'Loose Lips Sync Ship'—part moody surf instrumental, part abstract freak-out—as The Hogs in late 1966, the group appeared in *Riot On Sunset Strip* with Tower Records label-mates The Standells.

Chocolate Watchband singles such as 'Sweet Young Thing' and '(Are You Gonna Be There) At The Love-In'—which featured in *Riot*'s follow-up, *The Love Ins*—are as Stones-mad as anything that had come out of San Bernardino in 1964 and '65.

While The Rolling Stones themselves were moving away from raw, punky sounds by 1966, The Chocolate Watchband kept at it with 'Let's Talk About Girls.' Then, after cutting the garage-rock LP *No Way Out*, the group surpassed the Stones' forays into psychedelia with *Inner Mystique* (1968). Producer Ed Cobb was by this stage using The Chocolate Watchband as an outlet for his own creativity. Much of *Inner Mystique* is not the Watchband at all, but instead features session musicians hired by Cobb in a similar manner to David Axelrod's creative hijack of The Electric Prunes' *Mass In F Minor* (both albums feature the brilliant guitarist Richie Podolor, who had cut his teeth on surf records by The Super Stocks and The Hondells).

The paradox with both *Inner Mystique* and *Mass In F Minor* is that the music is so good that to dismiss either album because they are not exactly what they purport to be would be foolish. The (supposed) Chocolate Watchband album also closes a noteworthy musical circle: perhaps unnecessarily, Ed Cobb brought in a black American vocalist, Don Bennett, to sing *Inner Mystique*'s 'Let's Talk About Girls.' This leaves us with Bennett taking the role of a Chicano punk singer, Dave Aguilar, whose aim had been to emulate Mick Jagger, whose initial goal was to sound like a black rhythm & blues vocalist. As with The Grass Roots and The Electric Prunes, The Chocolate Watchband ultimately found themselves stifled by the machinations of their producer, but the music itself still holds up very well.

Count Five were given a similarly warm welcome by LA audiences. More than a one-song group, Count Five never succumbed to the music-biz chicanery that brought on the demise of The Chocolate Watchband and others. 'Psychotic Reaction' was their hit, but the howling, echoing fuzz-tone of 'Teenie Bopper, Teenie Bopper' is just as good, while 'Peace Of Mind' is brilliant lyrically. Wary of the transience of the music business, however, the group, led by Irish-born singer-guitarist Sean Byrne, opted for college rather than the pursuit of stardom. Their brief immersion in the LA scene culminated in an appearance at the September 11th 1996 'Freak Out' at the Shrine Exposition Hall alongside The Mothers Of Invention, The West Coast Pop Art Experimental Band, and others.

Also on that landmark bill were The Factory. The group cut two singles for

UNI Records in early 1967, gigged regularly at Bido Lito's, and appeared in a remarkable go-go-themed episode of television comedy series *Gomer Pyle*, in which they performed their psych-pop tracks 'Lost' and 'Candy Cane Madness.' The group was equally adept at cave-like garage numbers such as 'Hey Girl' and dreamy soundscapes, as heard on 'Sleep Tonight' and 'No Place I'd Rather Be.' Frank Zappa produced the group's 'Lightning-Rod Man,' and in doing so initiated a lengthy relationship with lead guitarist and vocalist Lowell George. After the band's demise, George had brief stints in The Standells, Fraternity Of Man, and The Mothers Of Invention before forming his seminal group Little Feat (which included Factory drummer Richie Hayward).

* * *

The Sons Of Adam were one of the most popular almost-famous bands among the Hollywood youth in 1965–66. Aside from appearing in *The Slender Thread* (which starred Sidney Poitier and Anne Bancroft), the group's main haunts were Bido Lito's, Whisky A Go Go, and Gazzarri's on the Strip, where they became the main house band. Guitarist Randy Holden started out in surf group The Fender IV before forming The Sons Of Adam, who recorded two 45s for Decca Records with Gary Usher at the helm. Vocalist Joe Kooken displays earnest, youthful desire on the harmonic garage cut 'Take My Hand' and a stripped down reading of Boyce & Hart's 'Tomorrow's Gonna Be Another Day,' which was later recorded by The Monkees. A crunchy take on The Yardbirds' oft-covered 'Mr You're A Better Man Than I' comes close to the original, particularly in the way Holden's neat guitar solo emerges from the messy garage-noise that surrounds it.

Randy Holden had already left the group by the time they came to record their final single, a version of Arthur Lee's previously unheard 'Feathered Fish,' which was backed with the jumped-up two-chord monster 'Baby Show The World' on an Alamo 45. The remaining members of The Sons Of Adam evolved into The New Wing, while Holden formed The Other Half, who were marketed as hippies but were very much a garage-punk act. Holden's guitar work hit its peak on his new group's 1966 single 'Mr Pharmacist,' which evokes all the hallmarks of the Strip scene with its snotty vocal, rave-up rhythm, and grinding harmonica solo. The Other Half's subsequent eponymous debut album is dominated by Holden's guitar playing and vocalist Jeff Knowlen, whose singing style is pitched somewhere between the angst of The Small Faces' Steve Marriott and the force of Little Richard.

The Greater Los Angeles area had more teen crud combos than you could shake a stick at. Only the great state of Texas can claim to have given birth to so many seven-inch slices of pure genius during the mid 1960s. Unknowns like Long Beach combo Opus 1 would cut mind-blowing records like 'Back Seat '38 Dodge' and then disappear into thin air. The song is driven at racing speed by Pete Parker's Farfisa organ, while Brian Decker's passing guitar chords chime into the night, evoking the cuts and turns of the highway. Lyrically, it was based on the artist Edward Kienholz's 'Back Seat Dodge '38' display, an assemblage of lovers that was banned by the Los Angeles County Museum Of Art in April 1966, and only reinstated when the car's back door was shut. Drummer Chris Christensen recalls how the band had been discussing the art exhibit with Bob Keene of Del-Fi Recordings: "Keene was piqued by the idea of something controversial, so we changed the lyric to [a song called] 'Why Did I Lie' and did a little tweaking on the arrangement." Christensen also notes the effect of "those great Del-Fi echo chambers," which give the song the sound of "a huge, hell-bound train." This single aside, Opus 1's other claim to fame was an appearance on an episode of *The Perry Mason Show*, on which they played Gabe & His Angels.

The Titan label captured several slices of Sunset Strip excitement, notably on The Brain Train's 'Black Roses,' a crude, magnificent Yardbirds-style rave-up that serves of a potent example of how Hollywood clubs could spring a major surprise with unknown groups that packed an unfathomable punch. The record's sonic crush is something only a US garage band could muster, with its warped chord changes and double-time bass run jetting right into a meticulously tight verse. The B-side, 'Me,' features Gregorian chanting and a rhythm sound reminiscent of Love's *Forever Changes*. The five-piece band—which featured two drummers—played all over the Strip circuit from the Sea Witch to the Hullabaloo before evolving into the six-member group Clear Light and recording a folk-rock/psychedelic LP for Elektra, which drew comparisons with label-mates The Doors and Love.

Titan also released 'Put Her Down' by Costa Mesa group The Wooly Ones in 1965. A match for The Avengers' similarly brutal 'Be A Cave Man,' the song juxtaposes choppy guitar with a cavalier lead vocal that explains how boys should never let spoiled girls run rings around them. The Wooly Ones then became The Coming Times for their 1966 folk-pop single 'Keep The Music Playing'/'Pork

And Beans,' released on the Josie label. Research 1-6-12 share sentiment on 'I Don't Walk There No More,' while an earthy simplicity marks 45s by John English III & The Lemon Drops ('I Need You Near'), The Rob Roys ('Do You Girl'), and The Silk Winged Alliance ('Home Town' and 'Flash Back').

The Rumors' 'Without Her' serves as a fine example of how 1965 had the best of the surf and psychedelic worlds, rising in a moody trance to a noisy guitar solo in a manner reminiscent of Jefferson Airplane's later 'Somebody To Love.' (The B-side, 'Hold Me Now,' is a tambourine-shaking punker with a wild, surf-style lead guitar break.) The aptly named Time Of Your Life used a similar tact on 'Ode To A Bad Dream,' building great, blocked harmonies atop cheese-whiz organ before introducing a droning, unrelated guitar sound midway through and closing out with a rhythm & blues-style harmonica jam.

The frenzied 'Visions' by The Looking Glasses (also known as The Clouds) sounds as frightening as a near-death experience, its organ humming to a virtual stop as precision guitar swirls around. The song rises to a fuzz-tone crescendo, matching The Doors in its mood-inducing experimentation. Music critic Greg Shaw notes: "In the UK, this group would've been The Pink Floyd, full of cosmic pretensions and very slickly packaged. Here in the suburbs of LA they were content to evoke weird sounds and freak out a few of their friends at neighborhood parties." The group had earlier cut the punk-fuzz 45 'She Gives Me Time' as The Just Too Much, and later evolved into The Odyssey, releasing the jangly, feedback-laden 'Little Girl, Little Boy' on White Whale Records. A further name change resulted in a heavy, psychedelic version of the Frank Sinatra standard 'It Was A Very Good Year,' credited to Sonoma.

The Puddin' Heads' 'Now You Say We're Through' demonstrates how American kids picked up on the Bo Diddley beat craze reintroduced by The Rolling Stones and tossed it back with double-time fire. (The group shared their name with a mop-topped toy used to make instant chocolate pudding.) In the same vein were The Colony's writhing, hollering 'All I Want' and the rage-drenched anti-drug song 'Acid Head' by The Velvet Illusions, about a girl who "reaches for her box of drugs" rather too often, combining a sense of doom and astral euphoria with an incessant beat.

Garage bands tended to focus their songs equally on their environmental surroundings and more ephemeral things—and sometimes both at once. The Bishops' 'Hollywood Scene' derails the seedy side of the music business atop a cinematic score reminiscent of Jack Nitzsche's production style. 'It's Pop' by LA rhythm & blues singer Billy Page has a similar documentary-style lyric, taking in comic strips, old movies, high grade corn, Beatles flicks, James Bond, the CIA, leather boots, Sonny & Cher, Tom Jones's shirts, and more. The instrumental 'Party A Go Go' by Glenn & The Good Guys covers similar social terrain, with background jabber about karate and "far out" activities punctuated by a funky garage riff.

The Mugwumps (also known as The Mugwump Establishment) hailed from Beverly Hills and cut an unhinged garage-punk version of 'Bald Headed Woman' and a crunching take on Donovan's 'Season Of The Witch.' The group popped up on the *Riot On Sunset Strip* soundtrack album, and can be seen in the movie *Mondo Hollywood*. The David, meanwhile, appeared in the documentary film *From Gramophone To Groovy*, and were constantly inspired by ambitious tonal concepts. They recorded two singles for 20th Century Fox in 1966, of which one, 'Forty Miles,' charted locally. After growing tired of the major label's slow release pattern, the group released their debut LP, *Another Day, Another Lifetime*, on their manager Steve Vail's VMC imprint. The material on the album ranges from string and horn arrangements on the title track to gritty garage-punk on songs such as 'I'm Not Alone'—the common factor throughout is a steady organ hum.

Some groups of the time took more obvious influences and spiked them an unintentional twist: The Green Beans followed their groovy, garage-pop 'Friction' with the punky 'Who Needs You,' which adopts the main riff from The Monkees' 'Last Train To Clarksville.' The Grim Reepers reference The Chocolate Watchband's 'Sweet Young Thing' on 'Two Souls,' while Chicano group The Nightwalkers built their 'High Class' out of the guitar line from Paul Revere & The Raiders' 'Kicks.' The Agents wisely borrowed The Hollies' 'I Can't Let Go' for 'Gotta Help Me,' giving the song a Rickenbacker folk-rock sound and an emotive punk vocal. Others, however, opted instead for the blindingly obvious, such as The Tangents, who cut a throbbing-echo version of 'Hey Joe,' or The Epics, who brought a garage crunch to Richard Berry's 'Louie Go Home.'

Several house band albums that evoke this crowd-pleasing vibe came out of Las Vegas's Teenbeat Club: one such example was by the LA-area band The Starfires. In 1965, a dream setlist seemed almost always to include The Rolling Stones' arrangement of Chuck Berry's 'Around And Around' alongside tracks by Rufus Thomas, Jerry Lee Lewis, Don & Dewey, The Beatles, and East LA's own

Premiers. The Starfire's punky take on P.J. Proby's 'Hold Me' foreshadows their later beat-crazed 45s, such as 'I've Never Lover Her' and 'Cry For Freedom,' a bitter rant against the Vietnam War draft. Vocalist Chuck Butler shifts suddenly from muted drama to maniacal rage. Several of their records were released, tellingly, on the Yardbird label.

Various aspects of the early-1960s music scene seemed to stick with these garage-rockers. Instrumentally speaking, Sunset Strip bands loaded their sound with heavy organ and soul bass riffs, punctuated by surf sax and guitar runs, as heard on The Impalas' 'Oh Yeah' or The Ho-Dads' 'Honky.' The moody, minor-chord spookiness of earlier surf instrumental flipsides permeates 'Sleepy Hollow,' a harrowing, Van Morrison-alike punk snarl by Vegas group The Last Words. Fittingly, the single appeared on Downey Records, the same label that had previously put out the landmark surf-side 'Pipeline' by The Chantays. The Chantays themselves had moved towards garage-folk on their second LP, the keyboard-heavy *Two Sides Of The Chantays* (1964), even going so far as to release two singles from the album under the name The Leaping Ferns in an attempt to distance themselves from their surf past. (The group then also recorded as The Ill Winds, and cut the swarming 'Fear Of The Rain' for Reprise.)

The Chevells' 'Take A Look' opens with surfy guitar and evokes both Elvis Presley and early Beatles records before flying into a climactic raga junket, while the B-side, 'Hootenanny Hoedown,' harks back to the hillbilly rock'n'roll instrumentals popular during the late 1950s. The Ascots' 'Summer Days' dresses ebullient, sunny, beachfront garage in punk minimalism, and The Bootiques' Curt Boettcher-produced 'Did You Get Your Fun' sounds like The Turtles by way of early-1960s girl groups. In a similar vein is clean-cut teen idol Eddie Hodges's Spectorish folk-punker 'Water Is Over My Head' (which was, in fact, a Jack Nitzsche production). The Insects' 'Girl That Sits' sounds like a rougher, more immediately Gerry & The Pacemakers-style beat tune; 'My Race Is Run' by The Motleys—who might in fact have hailed from Canada, but at the very least recorded for an LA label—has a similar Merseybeat-inspired sound.

With its bouncy harmonies, sneaky fuzz, and go-go organ, Fenwyk's breezy, melodic 'Mindrocker' has all the appeal of a dirty *Rubber Soul* cut. Although the group flopped, their most notable song lent its name to the long-running *Mindrocker* series of 1960s garage compilations. Some of their other songs were overdubbed and exploited a year later by East Coast teen idol wannabe Jerry

Raye and included on his album *The Many Sides Of Jerry Raye Featuring Fenwy*ck. The London Knights' 'Go To Him' is evocative of a similar folk-garage style, with chiming, melancholy chords worthy of Buffalo Springfield rising and falling beneath cave-style Gregorian chanting. 'One Of These Days' by The Roosters, too, combined a folk-rock jangle with the angry sound of garage-punk, while The Moon cut a fine Beatles-esque psych album, *Without Earth*.

After leaving The Belairs, surf drummer Richard Delvy became a record producer, and soon turned his attention to garage-rock. He spotted Nova Scotian group The Great Scots, got them a spot on *Shindig!*, and promptly recorded their Beach Boy/garage hybrid 'Show Me The Way' (released under the name The Free For All). Delvy's own band, The Challengers, cranked out albums of rock'n'roll instrumentals at a fairly consistent rate. Of particular note is the Strip-specific *California Kicks*, which contains fuzz-toned surf covers of 'Gloria,' 'Kicks,' and 'One Track Mind.' The group's subsequent live LP *Challengers Au Gogo* was put together, according to Delvy, from "a lot of leftover vocal songs from all our appearances on *Hollywood A Go Go*," while they kept surf music alive with weekly appearances on the sporting television show *Surf's Up*. Keeping up with all the trends of the time, The Challengers even made a fake live album, *At The Teenage Fair*, in 1965.

The Brothers Grim attempted a similar emulation of the Teen-Age Fair Band Battle-sound by dubbing the sound of screaming 'fans' onto their harmonic, Beatles-esque cut 'You'll Never Be Mine.' The record is powered by thick, stomping organ, as are similar cuts such as 'Gotta Hold On' by The No-Na-Mee and 'Don't Do It Some More' by The Cindermen (a Cinnamon Cinder house band). These three singles all show how an organ sound—often that of a Vox Continental—could really push the pace of garage bands into frantic overdrive (or, indeed, sink it into an ominous contralto).

The various changes and experiences these groups went through confirms how much was on offer in Los Angeles at the time. The Ringers, for instance, only left behind four songs of their own (including the H.B. Barnum-produced 'Mersey Bounce'), but drummer Bill Lynn played on a number of Elvis Presley recordings, and guitarist Tom Crockett was friends with both Dennis Wilson of The Beach Boys and Bill Medley of The Righteous Brothers.

Sean & The Brandywines' 'She Ain't No Good' is a reminder that grungy 1960s garage groups remained keen on connecting with a dance audience. So too is The Flower Children's 'Mini Skirt Blues,' which blathers on about "Going to a go go/Workin' with my mojo/Checkin' out those miniskirt blues!" Belinda, a mod boutique next door to the Rocky & Bullwinkle statue on Sunset, encouraged an ever-more defiant Sunset Strip trend in 1966: that of wearing micro-miniskirts with nothing on underneath. Such was the liberating feel of the time.

Folk-rock derived pop music arrived in the form of The Rooney Brothers' disc 'Just A Friend.' Produced by Jerry Fuller (known for his work with The Union Gap and The Knickerbockers), the group was formed by the sons of the actor Mickey Rooney, including *Riot On Sunset Strip* star Tim (another brother, Ted, was in The Sloths). A similarly sprightly 12-string guitar sound rings throughout 'I Don't Want To See You' by His Majesty's Coachmen, which manages to sound like rain falling from dark clouds and to glow with sunshine harmony at the same time. This kind of psychic split was a constant in numerous garage records, such as The Plastic People's Curt Boettcher-produced 'It's Not Right.'

Plugged-in folk singers sometimes hit the middle ground between folk and punk, as with Jacobsen & Tansley's 'Dream With Me,' another Boettcher production that sounds like The Merry-Go-Round transplanted onto a dance floor, or Mike Nesmith's dark, pre-Monkees single 'How Can You Kiss Me' (recorded with John London and Bill Chadwick as Mike, John & Bill). Such stylistic inversions were key to Joyride's folksy duet of The Doors' 'The Crystal Ship,' which gave the song an earnest feel and a very different kind of psychedelic edge. The Band Of Wynand's 'Day-Time, Night-Time' shimmers with the psychedelic levitation of its main inspiration, The Byrds' 'Eight Miles High,' but adds it own organ and guitar effects to an appropriately hypnotic crescendo.

The Black Sheep grew up in Los Angeles and La Cañada, and started honing their folk-punk sound as early as 1964. The group wore black turtlenecks and hung thick chains around their necks to depict suffering. Their material ranges from the organ-fueled anger of 'I Told You' to the folksy 'It's My Mind,' which underpins an a cappella broadside with a climactic, stomping beat. The band played at Pandora's Box, Bido Lito's, It's Boss, and the Trip before splintering into two new groups. Of these, The New Generation were first on the bill at The Seeds' Monster Halloween Freak-Off Dance, and headlined the final show at the Third i.

The Chymes, meanwhile, took on the dark, mysterious side of folk music on their single 'He's Not There Anymore.' The group was discovered by Howard Kaylan of The Turtles, who signed them to Chatahoochee Records. Both sides of their single are up to The Turtles' standard: on the A-side, the group's vocals evoke a happy-go-lucky girl-group sound, while a warm, garagey organ fills the space around the darkness of the lyric. Other girls in the garage included Kim & Grim ('You Don't Love Me') and The 4 Making Do, whose 'The Simple Life' describes the joy to be found in watching *Shindig!* and *Hullabaloo*.

The Deepest Blue were descendants of that other primary source of 1965 punk: The Rolling Stones. Their 'Somebody's Girl' co-opts the guitar riff from the Stones' '19th Nervous Breakdown.' The same song was clearly a formative influence on The Nervous Breakdowns, who cut the rumbling, pounding 'I Dig Your Mind.' Sonny Villegas's 'Help Me, Help You' features wild, forceful vocals and a rave-up middle break that, in fact, doesn't end until the record is over; the flipside, 'I Cry,' is a solid, straight-ahead punker. The thrill of PJ's-style dance crazes is clear in the voice of proto-punk lounge-rocker-turned-b-movie star Vic Lance (star of *Mantis In Lace*) in his delivery of 'I'm Comin' Home.' The sound of Perpetual Motion Workshop's single makes it clear why they 'Won't Come Down,' while the noise and feel of the Strip permeates the dark atmosphere of The Crumpets' 'Mama Baby,' a taunting, Whisky A Go Go rocker reminiscent of Billy Lee Riley. The same vibe is apparent on 'Good Things' by The Todes, who sound as if they have arrived straight from inside the dark, brick-walled corridors of Bido Lito's.

On 'They Say,' The In Set update rhythm & blues with swirling punk organ, an extended, surf-style guitar solo, a truly soulful vocal, and pounding, stomping drums. Lonnie & The Legends' 'I Cried' is driven by a similarly carnival-esque organ riff.) The Innkeepers' 'A Man Can Tell' reaches out to a widow the singer is in love with, surrounding the lead voice with background vocals fed through a Leslie speaker, ever-present fuzz-tone, and a spooky Vox organ. The Children Of The Mushroom's 'August Mademoiselle,' a plea for a girl penned-in by her parents, is reminiscent of The Humane Society's 'Eternal Prison'—both records underscore the pain of the daughter's life with searing guitar-fuzz. (Both groups were from Simi Valley, where tales of parental repression were rife during the mid 1960s.) The Soul Brothers' 'My Love For You' sounds like choppy rhythm & blues by way of the Haunted House's resident garage-soul act, Kent & The Candidates, while Flying Jib regulars The West Coast Branch made a couple of singles in 1966–67 ('Linda's Gone' and 'Colors Of My Life') that emphasize their folk and garage sides. The Dave Travis Extreme's loose-pedal raver 'Last Night

The Flowers Bloomed' combines spy guitars with philosophical, folksy lyrics. An organ ups the tempo at the fade, leaving the listener wondering what kind of breakdown occurred when the song was performed live. Mom's Boys keep their blues off-kilter to begin with on 'Up And Down,' using the traditional form as nothing more than an excuse to quickly break into a double-time freak-out. Their 'Children Of The Night' was another of the tracks chosen to feature on the *Riot On Sunset Strip* soundtrack album in early 1967.

'Till The Break Of Dawn' by Bedpost Oracle is stock fuzz, its distinction coming with a smoky lead vocal and neat use of Iron Butterfly-style organ. A similar tonality permeates The Tracers' maraca-shaking version of Bo Diddley's 'Who Do You Love,' which gives the song a go-go dancing beat and teasing vocal harmonies in the chorus. The same pulsating Diddley-with-harmonies trick is heard on The Dirty Shames' constantly revolving 'I Don't Care.'

The Grains Of Sand's 'Goin' Away Baby' and 'That's When Happiness Began' have since become longtime favorites of the 1960s garage comp world. The organ on the latter, which was produced by Michael Lloyd of The West Coast Pop Art Experimental Band and Kim Fowley, is played faster than its choppy, sped-up guitar rhythm, while the frantic singer sounds as if he's struggling to keep up with the manic pace.

The Sunday Group's bluesy 'Edge Of Nowhere' is emblematic of the way these uninhibited teenage groups would convey their intimate thoughts against an often scary sound that took inspiration from the ugly and cryptic aspects of life. The same mood is revealed in The Caretakers Of Deception's 'X + Y = 13,' a constant battle with optimism. These groups sometimes ended up being unintentionally funny, too, such as when The Gass Co cut 'Blow Your Mind,' an endearingly incompetent rip-off of Barry McGuire's 'Eve Of Destruction.' The record's producer, Jack Nitzsche later squirmed at the memory of the song while being interviewed by Ken Barnes in *Who Put The Bomp* magazine, declaring: "It's awful … please don't play that." Edge, meanwhile, cut the overtly syrupy 'Scene Thru The Eyes,' which does still manage to touch the listener with its undercurrent of naïve passion and oddly timed melodic shifts.

The archetypal LA garage tale of the mid 1960s could well be that of Aftermath, who formed in North Hollywood, named themselves after a Rolling Stones LP, played their first gig at Pandora's Box, worked their way into opening slots at the Hullabaloo and It's Boss, and recorded a trashy version of 'Gloria' that wasn't released until 20 years later. Neil Young caught one show and told the group he really liked the band, but an audition at A&M Records fell through; The Merry-Go-Round beat them out. Aftermath fell apart when their lead guitarist was arrested backstage at the Hullabaloo and thrown into Juvenile Hall for three months: he'd been grounded by his parents, and was caught sneaking out of his house because Aftermath had a gig opening for Don & The Goodtimes that night. For Aftermath, it didn't get any better than playing in the houses that Earl Carroll and Billy Wilkerson built.

* * *

It's inevitable in places such as New York or Hollywood that a few recording careers evolve out of showbiz connections. Because rock'n'roll was so far ahead of mainstream entertainment during the 1950s and 60s, it was much more difficult to sell 'manufactured' acts to youth audiences than it is today. By and large, the era's best records were developed naturally, without interference from the mainstream music business. There were some exceptions, however, in terms of garage and pop 45s than came from more established areas of the entertainment industry, but still managed to tap into the fun spirit of rock'n'roll.

The Hanna-Barbera cartoon empire contributed a few of these by way of their subsidiary label, HBR. One standout is 'Hey You' by The Guilloteens, which soon became an oft-covered milestone of garage-punk. The band came from Memphis, and earned a record contract on the strength of Elvis Presley citing them as his favorite local band. Lead guitarist Louis Paul Jr recalls knowing Elvis "before he was famous," and being given the nickname 'Highschool' by him because of his comparative youth. He notes that Tony Ferra, owner of the Red Velvet Lounge, "booked us on Elvis' word, and we were off to California."

Soon after arriving in Los Angeles, The Guilloteens drew the interest of Phil Spector, who came up with the intro to the group's only hit, 'I Don't Believe,' during a rehearsal. According to Paul Jr, the producer "said it needs something and started humming. I started playing what you heard on the opening of the record, and he said 'that's it!'" The group expected then to sign a deal with Spector, but their manager had other ideas, and took the group to HBR. As disappointing as this might have been, it did result in a memorable appearance on *The Flintstones* as The Guillostones, a custom-designed Hanna-Barbera drumhead, and three further HBR singles: 'For My Own' (1965), 'I Sit Down,' and 'Wild Child' (both

1966). (The group also released 'Dear Mrs Applebee in 1967 on Columbia.)

Prior to scoring a pop hit with 'Roses And Rainbows' in 1965, Danny Hutton worked at Hanna-Barbera, where he made rock'n'roll music for kids' television shows. Perhaps his finest achievement in this field was the *Monster Shindig* LP, on which he ghosted as The Gruesomes, as featured in the cartoon series *Super Snooper And Blabber Mouse*. As a solo artist, Hutton drew up an unusual psychedelic pop rendition of 'Funny How Love Can Be' in 1966, with too fast drums and vocals, pied-piper flute, and occasional pit-stops for strange blasts of harmony and feedback.

Having cut this song, it came as no real surprise when Hutton then hooked up with Brian Wilson upon the formation of The Beach Boys' Brother Records in 1966. (Wilson had earlier offered a song by the name of 'Good Vibrations' to Hutton before changing his mind and recording the experimental track with his own band.) Hutton formed a vocal trio, Redwood, for whom Wilson wrote and performed 'Time To Get Alone' and 'Darlin'.' In the wake of the *Smile* debacle, Wilson had started to withhold some of his best new material from The Beach Boys—who were reticent to take up his more outlandish ideas—and gave it instead to Redwood. With its strange fade-ins and abstract production, 'Time To Get Alone' is cut from the same cloth as songs such as 'Heroes And Villains.'

As with 'Heroes And Villains,' the superior version of 'Time To Get Alone' was not released until the 1990s. In 1967, Mike Love informed Hutton that Redwood could not make albums for Brother, only singles. Unhappy with this arrangement, the group cut demos with Van Dyke Parks (who had collaborated with Brian Wilson on *Smile*) and evolved into Three Dog Night, recording 14 gold-selling albums and 21 *Billboard* Top 40 singles.

Everything seemed possible in the relatively unhindered Los Angeles of 1966, even a garage-tinged album by silver-screen goddess Mae West, on which she was backed by a group called Somebody's Chyldren. *Way Out West* includes covers of 'Day Tripper' by The Beatles, Johnny Kidd & The Pirates' 'Shakin' All Over,' and 'If You Gotta Go' by Bob Dylan; her garage backing band are pictured on the jacket.

The Seeds Of Time's Johnny Legend recalls witnessing an even more flipped-out sidelight of the Hollywood orbit, during an open-mic night at the Wild Thing: suddenly, out of nowhere, Jerry Mathers, "the kid from *Leave It To Beaver*," appeared on stage and started performing garage-punk songs. This wasn't an entirely isolated incident, as Beaver & The Trappers then cut a single, 'In Misery,' for the White Cliffs label. On the B-side, 'Happiness Is Havin',' Mathers sounds like a virtual guru, declaring: "Happiness is goin' about 110/Blowing your mind and coming back down again."

Gary Lewis & The Playboys might have been fronted by the son of comic genius Jerry Lewis, but were adept at a variety of musical styles. Although best known for pop hits such as 'This Diamond Ring' (a Number 1 hit in 1965) and 'She's Just My Style,' they were also capable of grimy surf ('Malibu Run'), garage ('Little Miss Go Go'), and moments of *Pet Sounds*-like grandeur ('Jill'). The group is a prime example of how, with the right ideas, collaborators, and studio knowledge, it was possible to make records that came close to those of such musical luminaries as The Beatles and The Beach Boys—with the significant assistance, in this case, of producer Snuff Garrett and musician/arranger Leon Russell.

The group's success gave their producers money to invest in—and experiment on—future recordings. Russell built a studio, Skyhill, at his home in the Hollywood Hills; shortly thereafter, The Electric Prunes cut 'I Had Too Much To Dream (Last Night)' there with engineer Dave Hassinger. Russell used the studio to produce early recordings by J.J. Cale, who played a regular Sunday afternoon slot at the Whisky A Go Go in 1965. Russell and Cale then joined forces with folk duo The Gypsy Trips—whose Roger Tillison wrote 'Rock'N'Roll Gypsies'—to record *A Trip Down Sunset* as The Leather Coated Minds. Around the same time, Russell also formed a group called The Asylum Choir, with whom he cut *Look Inside The Asylum Choir* (1968), an album awash with backward-tape effects, Leslie speaker echo, and ethereal vocals that featured the poignant 'Welcome To Hollywood.'

Perhaps the most unfathomable garage-rock record of the time, however, was 'Let Me In' by The Second Helping. The scowling, jackhammer vocal is by a certain Ken(ny) Loggins, leading music journalist Greg Shaw to remark, on the sleeve of one of the *Pebbles* compilations, on "another sad commentary on the decline of just about everything since 1966, as if we need any more reminders."

* * *

Sunset Strip ambled slowly into 1967, battered by the effect of the previous year's riots. But while the thriving scene of the previous two years had begun to fragment, garage-rock bands continued to spring up in—or gravitate toward—the area. Of particular note are The Strawberry Alarm Clock, who arrived in LA from Santa Barbara and scored a quick hit with 'Incense And Peppermints.' While the sleeve of the group's debut album (also called *Incense And Peppermints*) shows the band-members in blatantly psychedelic dress, they originally came from the surf world. As The Irridescents, the group cut a seminal surf instrumental version of 'Bali Ha'i'—a song from their parents' *South Pacific* albums—before evolving, post-British Invasion, into a garage group by the name of Thee Sixpence. This second group cut several singles for the All American label, including raunchy covers of Love's 'My Flash On You' and 'Can't Explain,' the downright frightening 'In The Building,' and 'Long Day's Care,' which punctuates a stomping fuzz-tone rhythm with wild harmonica.

Thee Sixpence rose to prominence at the Earl Warren Showgrounds in Santa Barbara, where they shared the bill with area bands such as The Dovers, The Colony, and Ernie & The Emperors. The third of these—originally a blend of Merseybeat and folk-rock sounds—echoed Thee Sixpence's career path by following a local hit, 'Meet Me At The Corner,' with a move to Hollywood and a more psychedelic musical approach, as well as several name changes: first to Ernie's Funnies, and then to Giant Crab. Both acts also signed to UNI Records on the recommendation of much-loved Santa Barbara disc jockey Johnny Fairchild.

Inspired by The Chocolate Watchband, Thee Sixpence then became The Strawberry Alarm Clock, quickly recording their strongest work to date, *Incense And Peppermints*. Strangely, the hit title track was not sung by a member of the group: guitarist Lee Freeman had been slated to perform the lead vocal, but went missing for a couple of hours during the session, so his job went instead to Chris Mumford from Shapes Of Sound. Other songs on the album include 'The World's On Fire,' which blends the hypnotic bassline from 'Eight Miles High' with jazz vibes, garage organ, fuzzy guitar, and unexpected flute flourishes. The group's lyrics, full of metaphor and idealism, go off in search of truth, justice, and serenity on wonderfully garish cuts such as 'Rainy Day Mushroom Pillow' and 'Tomorrow' (which they performed on *Laugh In*). The group's first two albums, *Incense And Peppermints* and *Wake Up ... It's Tomorrow*, uphold a sense of beautiful optimism that would vanish by the end of the 1960s.

For a moment, The Strawberry Alarm Clock offered the false promise of a continued psychedelic movement on Sunset Strip during its final months as a creative center. You could catch them at the Galaxy, then go to get something to eat at Hamburger Hamlet, or the Eatin' Affair, which opened in early 1967 and is referenced, slyly, in Love's 'Maybe The People Would Be The Times Or Between Clark And Hilldale.' The Alarm Clock left a brief legacy in celluloid, too, appearing in *Psych-Out* (1967)—during a 'San Francisco ballroom' scene actually filmed at the Cheetah in Venice—and in a riotous party scene at the beginning of *Beyond The Valley Of The Dolls* (1969).

Several groups arrived in Los Angeles from San Diego County—unsurprisingly, given that it is only a two-hour drive from Hollywood. Among them were The Lyrics, a garage-punk act that had actually laid down their best record, 'So What,' in 1965, before they had made it to the Strip. Upon arrival, they cut two singles for GNP-Crescendo in more of a psych-pop vein, and served as opening act on an early Doors tour.

Of more note are Iron Butterfly, who had a heavy, church organ depth and a fuzz-tone sustain to match. Iron Butterfly started out as The Palace Pages; drummer Ron Bushy had previously been in The Voxmen, who dressed like bikers and played nothing but Vox equipment. The Palace Pages arrived on the Strip in 1966, just as the moment began to slip away. Christening themselves Iron Butterfly, the group soon took up residency at Bido Lito's in more than one sense, living upstairs as well as performing regularly there, and at the Galaxy on the Strip. Johnny Legend describes the original line-up as "one of the best live bands" he'd seen.

Aligning themselves with the right people—particularly in terms of support slots for Captain Beefheart & His Magic Band and Love—Iron Butterfly signed a deal with Atco before 1967 was out and promptly recorded *Heavy* (1968). The group's first single, 'Unconscious Power,' sounds like a Music Machine out-take, 'Gentle As It May Seem' harks back to their garage roots, and 'Iron Butterfly Theme' demonstrates a penchant for expansive instrumental textures.

By the time of Iron Butterfly's second album, *In-A-Gadda-Da-Vida*, only organist Doug Ingle and drummer Ron Bushy remained from the group that made *Heavy*. (Erik Brann replaced Danny Weis on guitar and Lee Dorman came in on bass in place of Jerry Penrod, while no replacement was sought for vocalist Darryl DeLoach.) *In-A-Gadda-Da-Vida* contains a side-long version of the mega-hit title-track, which has a rock'n'roll-nonsense chorus that departed vocalist DeLoach wryly notes is reminiscent of the early-1960s hit 'Papa-Oom-Mow-Mow.' The lengthy 'In-A-Gadda-Da-Vida,' which was written above Bido Lito's and originally called 'In A Garden Of Eden,' hangs together in its extended version because each instrumental section was carefully thought out and arranged in advance, with any improvisation occurring atop an already sound backing. Other tracks on the album include the groovy 'My Mirage' and the Monkees-like 'Flowers And Beads.' The ever-changing line-ups of Iron Butterfly continued to record until 1975 (and during several sporadic reunions), gradually becoming more guitar-heavy with the passing years.

Most of the groups that emerged on Sunset Strip in 1967 had more of a pop edge than their contemporaries from San Francisco. The Love Generation had a hit called 'Groovy Summertime' in 1967, The New Age made mellow, vibraphone-led folk-rock, and Colours pre-empted the McCartney-esque sound of Badfinger by two years with songs such as 'Love Heals.' For a brief moment, exotica innovator Les Baxter dipped a toe in the psychedelic rock'n'roll waters, producing and writing for Mira Records group The Forum. Highlights of their work together include the fuzzy, bongo-laden go-go tune 'Look The Other Way' and the dreamy 'Girl Without A Boy.' The Robbs, meanwhile, were regulars on *Where The Action Is* in 1966, and released the bouncy, folk-harmony singles 'Rapid Transit' and 'Race With The Wind' and a self-produced album.

Another prominent group, The Penny Arkade, didn't release a record during the 1960s, and as such weren't properly heard for another 37 years. Singers Chris Ducey and Craig Smith met when both starred in a 1965 ABC television pilot, *The Happeners*, as folk-rockers looking for a break in New York City. The show wasn't picked up, but Ducey and Smith stuck together, recording a single, 'Isha,' for Capitol. As The Penny Arkade, the duo then recruited bassist Don Glut and drummer Bobby Donaho and caught the ear of The Monkees' Mike Nesmith, who subsequently produced album sessions for the group. Nesmith describes the group as having "the quintessential LA sound," a "strange mixture of country and rock'n'roll and blues and everything, filtered through this sort of LA urban sophistication," unlike anything he'd heard "before or since."

Sessions began during the summer of 1967; over the next year the group and Nesmith recorded enough material for two albums. 'Lights Of Dawn' is a raunchy display of the great blend of Ducey and Smith's vocals; 'Thesis' is dark and moody; 'Country Girl' could easily be a Monkees track. 'Swim' is an amusing acid-tripper, 'Color Fantasy' has a beautiful naivety couched in gloomy guitar chords, 'Voodoo Spell' was, by all accounts, a favorite of Frank Zappa, and the 12-minute mosaic 'Not The Freeze' expands on ideas The Who and Buffalo

Springfield had been developing at the time. As good as their material might have been, however, no label deigned to sign the group, and all of this music went missing until Sundazed issued *Not The Freeze* in 2004.

The Boston Tea Party and The American Revolution—two bands whose very names served as reminders of the recent uprisings on the Strip—also released strong albums in 1967. Hailing from Burbank, The Boston Tea Party had made waves at the Galaxy and the Cheetah with a psych/pop cover of 'Words' and their own 'My Daze.' Their first release was the organ-poppin' 'I Found A Way' (1966), which was swiftly followed by a full-length album. The American Revolution's effort is a beautiful, fully orchestrated pop record, full of great productions—by Mike Curb, Michael Lloyd, and Harley Hatcher—such as 'Show Me Cry' and 'Cold Wisconsin Nights.' Lloyd, a member of The West Coast Pop Art Experimental Band, appropriated the latter song for the Hanna-Barbera cartoon show *Cattanooga Cats*. He did the same with two songs by another group, October County, whose 1967 single, also called 'October County,' is reminiscent of (and a match for) The Turtles' contemporary output.

One of the final groups to perform in an unencumbered garage-punk style in Los Angeles was King Verses, who had moved into town from Fresno upon graduation from high school in June 1967. As such, their sound was decidedly backdated by a year or so: amid love-ins and a growing bias towards psychedelia they dropped into town with gritty, screaming fare such as 'Lights,' 'A Million Faces,' and the tormented 'She Belonged To Me.' King Verses made an appearance on *Groovy* and played at the Hullabaloo After Hours on the fading club scene, but a mooted deal with either Elektra or Dunhill never transpired, the LA scene disintegrated, and so did the band.

Other garage-punk bands had begun to move toward the heavier, less dance-orientated sound that would come to dominate popular tastes. Indicative of this evolution was a changing of the guard at the Hullabaloo: The Beatles-esque folk-rockers The Palace Guard had been the house band throughout 1966, but were replaced, upon splitting, by The Yellow Payges, who might still have embodied the Brian Jones look but displayed the pretentiousness and excess of the new hard rock sound. Similarly, Randy Holden of The Other Half quit that group to join the more bombastic Blue Cheer in San Francisco. Gene Clark laments these "troubled times," noting: "People were going away from the more artistic things at that point ... [hard rock] made it difficult to do really good material and get any backing for it." Like Clark, many observers felt that what had made the music of the 1960s so appealing in the first place was now beginning to disappear in a blaze of over-amplified guitar histrionics.

Some cool combos were still keen to move to Los Angeles in search of success, however. The Tikis from Santa Cruz, for instance, realized that their beachside, sunshine pop sound would be better accepted in LA than in the Bay Area. Upon their arrival in Hollywood the group evolved into Harpers Bizarre, cutting a glorious version of Van Dyke Parks's 'Come To The Sunshine' and Paul Simon's '59th Street Bridge Song (Feelin' Groovy).' *Feelin' Groovy*, the first of the group's four albums, followed, as did a theme tune for the 1967 ABC television show *Malibu U.*

A group known first as The Spiders and then as The Nazz turned up in town for gigs at the Cheetah in late 1967, which were followed by slots in support of Buffalo Springfield and Clear Light. Frank Zappa signed the group to Straight Records, and requested they change their name again to avoid competition with Todd Rundgren's band. The newly renamed Alice Cooper then issued their debut album *Pretties For You.*

Steppenwolf—formerly Sparrow—moved to Los Angeles from Toronto by way of the Bay Area and quickly turned heads with 'Born To Be Wild' and 'Magic Carpet Ride,' which features perhaps the most arresting psychedelic breakdown in the history of AM radio. The cover of the group's debut album was reminiscent of *The Seeds*, while the music contained within was clearly inspired by The Music Machine.

A last glimpse of the condensed creativity that had come out of the Sunset Strip scene appeared on a 1968 Columbia Records LP by The United States of America. An early incarnation, known simply as Joseph Byrd & Group, left a clear impression on *The Los Angeles Free Press*. A report on a performance at Aerospace Hall on February 18th 1966 notes how, during the laboriously titled 'Communist Aggression Music Number One: The Deference Of The American Continent Against The Viet Cong Invasion,' "the musicians played their strange martial music wearing Red Cross helmets." They also performed a version of John Cage's 'Aria And Fontana Mix,' "in which Dorothy Moskowitz sang [over] electronic tape manipulations."

As The United States Of America, the group played a series of gigs at the Whisky A Go Go, showcasing a mode of psychedelia from days gone by: short songs, a strong backbeat, and diverse, ethereal dynamics. By now the Moog synthesizer had usurped the sitar as the experimental instrument of choice among musicians in the know. To this Joseph Byrd added harpsichord, calliope, organ, and piano, while Moskowitz offered smooth vocals and sharp lyrics. Linda Ronstadt later told *Zig Zag* magazine that Moskowitz "knocked me out! She had such fantastic voice control—if you asked her to make her voice sound like an electric razor, she could do it."

The United States Of America went completely against the grain of late-1960s rock by shunning the guitar (the band's Gordon Marron played electric violin and ring modulator instead), but this does nothing to dull the intensity of tracks such as 'The Garden Of Earthly Delights' and 'Coming Down.' Joseph Byrd returned a year later with a new band, Joe Byrd and The Field Hippies. *The American Metaphysical Circus* lacks Moskowitz's vocal contributions, but the group does excel on the raga-laced 'Kalyani' and the Middle Eastern-style romp through 'You Can't Ever Come Down.'

The end of the garage-punk era was confirmed when Canned Heat brought Los Angeles into an era dominated by blues-guitar boogies. Although they had links to LA's recent past—bassist Larry Taylor came from the house band at the Sea Witch and guitarist Henry Vestine played in The Mothers Of Invention, while the band played early gigs at Pandora's Box and the Ash Grove—Canned Heat had no real connection to the arresting garage-punk sound that had so shaken the Strip during the mid 1960s. The group and their peers—notably Spirit and Sweetwater—hailed from the hippie culture in Topanga Canyon; they were part of a new, post-1966 direction that was longer focused on the Strip. As cultural historian Jim Heimann notes: "Traffic to the Strip backed up at Fairfax until September 1967. Afterwards, it was no longer a destination." As hard as it was to accept, the moment had passed.

CHAPTER SIX

Surfink a go go: pop art in 1960s LA

" *Everybody wants to freak out and everybody wants to look different. I usually don't go for bright colors, I'm more partial to purple and lavender. But when I was on acid, I just looked at every crayon, and I just loved each and every color. And at one point I even put a crayon between a piece of bread and made a sandwich out of it, and began eating it. I kid you not. I knew what I was doing, but I just wanted to get the color in me, it was so beautiful.* **"** SHERYL CARSON, *MONDO HOLLYWOOD*

At the height of the Sunset Strip rock'n'roll era, teenagers were swamped with a new style of art that could be found everywhere from gig flyers to T-shirts, restaurant menus to promotional material for shows. This surfink style, as it became known, is characterized by raw, curvy, black-and-white lines shaped into the form of downright ugly cartoon monstrosities. Its simple, understated nature—which meant that near enough anyone could adapt to it, and as such that much of it is unaccredited—tied in neatly with the egalitarian positivity of the era.

At its root, surfink was pioneered by a cantankerous hot-rod artist named Ken Howard, better known to the world at large as Von Dutch. He first arrived at his freeform, curvilinear 'pin-striping' method when asked by a customer to paint the cracks in a bent car door. The contour of the lines gradually morphed into intricate geometric flames, resulting in a design style rich with possibility that would come to fascinate those of an artistic inclination in Los Angeles.

Von Dutch's pin-striping became the gold standard in hot-rod art, and led to him being immortalized on vinyl with the 1959 release of Jerry Madison & The Spacemen's 'Von Dutch, The Mad Martian Pinstriper.' His pinstripe and airbrush techniques were an immeasurable influence on both high and lowbrow art movements in the Greater Los Angeles area. Ed 'Big Daddy' Roth was always quick to cite Dutch as his primary inspiration, while the Ferus Gallery's Finish Fetish and Light & Space exhibitions brought his hot-rod art style to international prominence. (Dutch himself viewed the pretensions of the art world as a distraction, so declined all invitations to exhibit at Ferus.) Since his passing in 1992, the Von Dutch name has become an internationally recognized brand of designer clothing, while art exhibits continue to feature his work on everything from crash helmets, fire extinguishers, and bicycles to rocking chairs, prosthetic legs, and a coin-operated guillotine.

Ed 'Big Daddy' Roth and South Bay kid Rick Griffin brought surfink into the common lexicon. Roth had been inspired by the aggressive animals painted onto US military planes during World War II as a youngster, and funneled these images through Von Dutch's hot-rod/beat sentiment. He introduced his first automotive masterwork, *The Outlaw*, at car shows in 1957, and spent much of his spare time airbrushing T-shirts for his fellow hot-rod enthusiasts.

Roth's unique style helped spread appreciation for surfink well beyond the LA scene during the mid 1960s. He became something of a pop star, recording three comedy/music albums for Capitol that feature great color manifestations of his artwork on their jackets. He also licensed kits for model cars based on his designs; when Mattel released its Hot Wheels toy cars, the 'Beatnik Bandit' model sold out instantly. There were comic books and coloring books, and even a spread in *Life* magazine. Roth's T-shirt business continued to grow, aided by the memorable characters he created for it, such as Rat Fink and Mr Gasser, but his focus remained on building cars (some in collaboration with Ed Newton). Despite pursuing these many and varied commercial avenues, Ed 'Big Daddy' Roth remained true to his original style, opting, later in the 1960s, simply to disappear rather than bend to the indulgences of new, 'psychedelic' art forms.

Rick Griffin, meanwhile, had originally been fascinated by tattoo artists at the funky, trashy Long Beach Pike Amusement Park. Griffin took many of his ideas from tattoo art sheets left over at the Pike since the 1940s, as well as early issues of *Mad*. As a teenager during the late 1950s, Griffin started working for Greg Noll's flourishing surfboard company, creating flyers and on-screen intros for Noll's *Search For Surf* movie series. Noll published a Rick Griffin comic book in 1960, which led to Griffin being hired to draw a comic strip for a new magazine, *The Surfer*, later the same year.

This latest creation, *Murphy*, was hugely popular. Many surf shops and surfboard manufactures started to ape Griffin's style in their advertisements, as did other illustrators. Mike Dormer emerged with his Hot Curl character and produced an elaborate surfink painting for the start of *Muscle Beach Party*. Mike Salisbury and John Van Hamersveld, like Griffin, contributed to *The Surfer*, and with Bill Ogden worked on the *SURFtoons* series of comic books. In this sense, Griffin's early work is just as valid and instrumental as the poster art that made him famous in San Francisco during the psychedelic era.

Surfing and hot-rodding were the points around which Los Angeles youth culture rallied during the first half of the 1960s. The focus of these combined styles flowed directly into the logos of locally produced rock'n'roll shows from KHJ television such as *9th Street West*, *Hollywood A Go Go*, and *Groovy*. What is not often noted, however, is that the insular drive of this art came from beatnik jazz. Prior to designing logos for KHJ, Mike Dormer published a beat magazine in San Diego called *Scavenger*. One of his most formative influences is the work of Chicago-born, Brooklyn-educated David Stone Martin who, during the 1950s, pioneered the serif lettering seen on numerous Verve Records jackets. Martin's signature motif was borrowed by countless graphic designers in mid 1960s LA for use on everything from gig flyers to the title cards of nationally syndicated rock'n'roll television shows.

Hand-drawn serif lettering became something of a stock font style for the beat generation. This was most widely exposed in clubs in the Los Angeles area by the artist Earl Newman, who created posters for the Gas House, the Insomniac Café, and Shelly's Manne-Hole. A few years later, Insomniac employee Frank Holmes's jacket for The Beach Boys' *Smile* album was clearly inspired by Newman's work. The Huntington Beach Surfing Championship used Newman's work for many years, as did the Monterey Jazz Festival.

KHJ television and radio helped spread the surfink serif style like wildfire, plastering it all over events, record surveys, and giveaways. The radio station's nouveau-beatnik artwork was seen as a visual representation of the modern sounds of The Beatles, The Rolling Stones, and folk-rock. Pasadena's KRLA came up with the definitive surfink design with the jacket for the first in their budget compilation series, *KRLA 21 Solid Rocks*: boulders shaped into the form of the station's callout letters are surrounded by iconic references to LA's pop culture, including surfers, garage-rockers, King Kong, Mary Poppins, and a girl in hipsters spray-painting countercultural graffiti. This set the style for the artist

W.T. Vinson to follow on the covers of pre-*Nuggets* garage compilations and LPs by The Fifth Dimension, The Hard Times, and Thee Midniters.

The Los Angeles Free Press was next to take the style on board, hiring animator Ron Cobb to draw political cartoons of, for example, President Johnson addressing a 'Mah fellow Americans' speech to a field of dead in Vietnam, or a television set chasing a housewife into the kitchen. Emerging around the time of the Sunset Strip riots, Cobb's images were heralded as the chronological link between *Mad* magazine and the underground comic explosion led by Robert Crumb's *Zap* in the late 1960s.

Surfink spread into the world of sport, too: publicity material for the Los Angeles Dodgers was rendered in a proto-psychedelic lettering style and with a keen sense of beat-style caricature by the *Los Angeles Herald Examiner*'s political cartoonist, Karl Hubenthal. Examples include the space-age *Out Of This World Series* program from 1965 and the floating fonts used in the team's 1971 yearbook. Cross-cultural pollination was rife among the Dodgers of the time: two players, Jim Lefebvre and Al Ferrara, turned up as policemen in the movie *Riot On Sunset Strip*, while a third, Sandy Koufax—viewed by many as the greatest pitcher in the history of baseball—owned the Tropicana Hotel. (According to Frank Zappa, the Tropicana was a "groupie's paradise," and the hotel of choice for most bands passing through town.) Likewise, baseball games of the period were, according to the writer Eve Babitz, largely attended by people "who looked like they were going to a Dylan concert."[1]

In 1966 *The Los Angeles Times*—a beacon of conservatism until Otis Chandler took over in 1960—introduced a magazine insert called *West*. The magazine was assembled with the intention of bringing *The Times* into an arena that could address the prominent liberal issues that had begun to surface alongside the growing civil rights movement. *West* embraced the psychedelic rock'n'roll era with a lean, sophisticated style. Many of the artists, designers, and writers came from the new scene, giving it a very different feel to previous men's magazines, which were generally biased toward jazz and treated rock'n'roll with condescension.

West gave voice to LA's allied music and arts scenes, and had an unprecedented respect for surfing. Mike Salisbury, who had previously worked for *The Surfer*, came onboard as a key graphic designer and promptly wowed the publishing industry. Former *New York Magazine* and *Rolling Stone* design chief Roger Black notes that Salisbury brought "documentary cultural photography" to the mainstream, while *West*'s Lawrence Dietz hails his "extraordinary visual brilliance." In 1972 *West* featured a comprehensive history of the Teen-Age Fair; by the end of the year, both of these prized local institutions would have departed. During its six-year lifespan, *West*'s parent paper went from having a pronounced right-wing bias to a more balanced tone.

In South Central Los Angeles, Bernard Jackson and J. Alfred Cannon organized the Inter-City Cultural Center with the aim of providing education and support in the impoverished, largely black Watts neighborhood in the wake of the August 1965 riots, which began when an angry mob formed after a highway patrol officer pulled over a man he suspected of driving while intoxicated; the rioting lasted five days and resulted in at least 34 deaths, 1,100 injuries, 4,000 arrests, and $35 million worth of damage. The Center helped foster a new, socially relevant strand of black cinema, best exemplified by Melvin Van Peebles's *Sweet Sweetback's Baadasssss Song* (1971), an acute commentary on racial divides that goes much deeper than the blaxploitation movies it inspired. Van Peebles had earlier won the Critics Choice Award at the 1967 San Francisco Film Festival with his go-go themed movie *The Story Of A Three-Day Pass*. He recalls: "When I went to San Francisco, I came as the French delegate. No one knew I was American, let alone black, so everyone freaked out."[2]

Another facet of the Inter-City Cultural Center was the Watts Writers' Workshop, which was created by the author and screenwriter Budd Schulberg. Among their students were community activist and bebop poet Kamau Daaood, Miles Davis's biographer Quincy Troupe, and author/critic Stanley Crouch. The scene was focused around the Watts Happening coffeehouse, which was opened in an abandoned furniture store on 103rd Street after the riots. On the same street, The Watts Towers Art Center and Watts Towers Theater Workshop opened up in the shadow of the monolithic Watts Towers. From the Arts Center came two assemblage works by Noah Purifoy, *Watts Riot* and *66 Signs Of Neon*, both of which were compiled from debris found on the street after the 1965 riot. (NBC paid a visit to shoot a documentary called *The Angry Voice Of Watts* during the summer of 1966.)

Pop culture continued to flourish throughout Los Angeles's indigenous movements. The designer John Van Hamersveld captured all the best elements of pop psychedelia in his work, which includes his landmark poster for the enduring surf movie *The Endless Summer* (1965). The impact of that design can be seen clearly on his sleeves for a pair of albums released by Capitol Records in 1967: The Beatles' *Magical Mystery Tour* and *Wild Honey* by The Beach Boys.

When clubs on the Strip were forced to close, Van Hamersveld helped organize the Pinnacle Concerts held at the Shrine Exposition Hall between October 1967 and September 1968. Among the headliners during this time were Buffalo Springfield, Sly & The Family Stone, The Pink Floyd, The Jimi Hendrix Experience, and The Velvet Underground. Van Hamersveld created many of the promotional posters for these shows (which remain highly collectable), and subsequently designed jackets for Jefferson Airplane's *Crown Of Creation* and The Rolling Stones' *Exile On Main Street*.

Like Ed 'Big Daddy' Roth's T-shirts, the similarly home-made Rickie Tickie Stickies became a sudden and widespread phenomenon during the mid 1960s. Designer Don Kracke became popular with kids in his Palos Verdes neighborhood, who wanted to know where he'd got the brightly colored, pop art stickers with which he'd covered his Ford station wagon. Encouraged by these local kids' enthusiasm, Kracke started selling the stickers in 1967; by the end of the following year, he'd sold over 90 million of them. They could be found for years to come stuck on the front of schoolbooks, guitar cases, and cars (particularly Volkswagens).

Body painting was a key part of LA's freak scene, and one given prominence in Barry Feinstein's movie *You Are What You Eat*, in which regulars at Vito's Studio are seen turning themselves into walking objects d'art prior to a Mothers Of Invention 'freak out' at the Shrine Exposition on September 17th 1966. The most well-known of the LA bodypainters was Sheryl Carson, who had "a body-painting booth at the Monterey Pop Festival … and would you believe, I painted 'love' on a little monkey's forehead." (Documentary filmmakers tend, unknowingly, to use footage of Carson's creations at Monterey, and of Vito Paulekas and his dance troupe, to demonstrate the wild, psychedelic San Francisco of the Summer Of Love, despite the fact that these people were decorated by artists from Los Angeles.)

The more formally recognized pop art movement reached its LA peak at the Ferus Gallery on La Cienega Boulevard. The core group involved—which included Ed Ruscha, Wallace Berman, John Altoon, Robert Irwin, Billy Al Bengston, Mel Ramos, and Edward Kienholz—mixed their artistic endeavors with surfing, hot-rods, and rock'n'roll dancing at the Strip's nightclubs. Journalist Kirk Silsbee notes: "They didn't isolate themselves from the world around them. The Ferus Group recognized that the designs of the hot-rod and surfing culture were aesthetic choices similar to their own." Bengston was photographed, fittingly, in front of the Whisky A Go Go by *Look* magazine in 1966, while Ruscha produced the wonderfully obsessive *Every Building On The Sunset Strip 1966*, which folds out, accordion-like, to show the Strip in its prime. Kienholz's celebrated sculpture, *The Beanery*, depicts patrons at a bar and grill on nearby Santa Monica Boulevard. Ken Price, another of the Ferus artists, recalls: "All of the artists I knew in the early 1960s could fit in a small back room. Someone said if there was a flash grease fire at Barney's [Beanery] the whole LA art scene would be wiped out."

According to the actor, photographer, and Ferus regular Dennis Hopper, the "high priest" of the scene was Wallace Berman. During the mid 1950s he had produced a series of assemblage publications called *Semina*, one issue of which featured an early excerpt from William S. Burroughs's *Naked Lunch*. In 1964 he began to experiment with reprographic art, creating collages on a Verifax copy machine that would inspire the cover of The Beatles' *Sgt Pepper's Lonely Hearts Club Band* (and, in doing so, reveal the inextricable links between London and Los Angeles during the mid 1960s).

An early admirer of Berman's collages and the whole LA assemblage movement was London-based art dealer Robert Fraser. Fraser's clients included The Beatles and The Rolling Stones, whose guitarist, Brian Jones, shared a number of mutual friends with Berman. "Brian knew Toni Basil," notes Tosh Berman, "who had worked on *The TAMI Show* [which the Stones also appeared on]. This is how Wallace Berman became directly connected to Robert Fraser and therefore to Peter Blake ... who in turn included my father on the Beatles album cover as a tribute to his influence." (He can be seen below W.C. Fields and to the right of Tony Curtis, with a yellowish tint and painted on lips.)

Two years earlier, another noted British pop artist, David Hockney, had relocated to Los Angeles. His *Splash*—as featured on the cover of Reyner Banham's *Los Angeles: The Architecture Of Four Ecologies*—is a quintessential product of 1966. Tosh Berman recalls: "Hockney's work really changed when he came to Los Angeles. The environment and aesthetic life change marked a big difference, in respect to what he had previously done in London."

There were also strong links between the pop art worlds of New York and Los Angeles, with a number of combined exhibitions taking place at galleries such as the Pasadena Museum Of Art, the LA County Museum, and the Guggenheim in

New York. The connection was first established in 1962, when New York pop artist Andy Warhol's first solo gallery exhibition was held at Ferus, displaying his series of 32 Campbell's soup-can paintings for the first time. (A rival gallery across the street mocked the show by displaying a stack of actual cans of Campbell's soup.)

A year later, Warhol came to LA for his second solo show, *Elvis And Liz*, at which he shot a short called *Elvis At Ferus*. He subsequently made his first full-length movie, *Tarzan and Jane Regained, Sort Of* … , in a variety of locations around Los Angeles, including the Venice canals, the hills above Malibu, the Watts Towers, the swimming pool at the Beverly Hills Hotel, and the home of Wallace Berman. New York scenesters Taylor Mead and Naomi Levine play Tarzan and Jane; LA luminaries including Dennis Hopper and his first wife, Brooke Hayward, also make appearances. The wrap party was held at the Santa Monica Pier Carousel. Thoroughly imbibing in the spirit of Los Angeles, Warhol never made another movie with so much light; or, indeed, one so lighthearted.

Ferus held a third Andy Warhol show, *Silver Pillows*, in 1966 to coincide with the arrival at the Trip of his Exploding Plastic Inevitable show, featuring The Velvet Underground & Nico. During its short lifespan—October 1965 to May 1966—the Trip hosted performances by acts such as Marvin Gaye, The Temptations, The Leaves, The Rising Sons, and Sam The Sham & The Pharaohs, and even inspired a song by the Scottish singer Donovan, who headlined at the outset of his psychedelic phase. The Exploding Plastic Inevitable was the last and most spectacular engagement to be held at the club. Having been dismissed following performances at San Francisco's Fillmore Auditorium for being "too negative," the show was more warmly received on the Strip. While there were some doubters—one review in *Los Angeles* magazine likened the event to "nothing so much as Berlin in the decadent 1930s"—it seemed as though the entire Ferus scene plus assorted movie stars and musicians turned up to bear witness to the potent combination of The Velvet Underground's music and Warhol's films, which were projected onto three screens behind the band. *The LA Times* noted that Warhol's genius for publicity was "greater than that of Zsa Zsa Gabor and Jayne Mansfield combined."

Warhol, Bruce Conner, and others would screen their films at Cinematheque-16, a 150-seat theater in the alley across from Madman Muntz that opened on June 9th 1966 with a double bill of the gangster movie *Public Enemy* and Conner's *Vivian*. Cinematheque-16 quickly became the underground movie house on Sunset Strip. Its manager, Lewis Teague, once spoke to *The Los*

Angeles Free Press of plans to "show all of Andy Warhol's films end-to-end for about five days with dancing in the lobby." (Such outré fare, derided by *Herald Examiner* columnist Mike Jackson as "gooey amateur attempts to be avant-garde," was previously screened only at the Fifth Estate coffeehouse on the Strip or at the Cinema on Western near Santa Monica Boulevard.)

The absurdist sense of humor inherent in the LA teen scene is best exemplified by a single 1963 photograph taken by Julian Wasser of Eve Babitz playing chess in the nude with famed, early-20th century, dada artist Marcel Duchamp. Babitz, a brilliant and wholly unself-conscious artist in her own right, subsequently went out with Stephen Stills, which, according to John Van Hamersveld, brought "all the musicians down around the art scene. So you get this tremendous collaboration of interweaved ideas." Babitz went on to design the covers of *Buffalo Springfield Again* and *The Byrds (Untitled)*. The idea of LA's art scene mixing lowbrow and highbrow ideas is given further credence by the fact that the Ferus Gallery closed its doors at around the same time that rock'n'roll was being derailed on the Strip.

The Los Angeles art scene of the mid 1960s maintained a consistent sense of satire. Its artists didn't seem interested in making art for consumption but, rather, as some kind of prophetic or satirical statement about the world they lived in. The movement at large understood how to put a simple face onto a complex condition, using tools that were already to hand in their environment. Both the early Surfink crew and the Ferus group used the same sense of unserious communication to sanctify the evil in the world. Artistically, at this point, Los Angeles became a clear, open space that could identify social inconsistencies to an otherwise cheerfully commercial world, and transform these negative ideas into a newfound positivity and hope. These themes would soon be taken very seriously throughout the international art world.

* * *

The Watts Towers—the product of 33 years of steady work, between 1921 and 1955, by the Italian architect Sabatino 'Simon' Rodia—still stand as a permanent embodiment of the independent artistic spirit of Los Angeles. During the mid 1960s, however, they were rivaled by a temporary display that took a similar form: the Artists' Tower Of Protest. Organized by Walter Hopps, the curator of both the Ferus Gallery and the Pasadena Art Museum, and assembled by conceptual sculptor

Mark di Suvero, the monument stood for three months at the intersection of La Cienega and Sunset. Two-foot square panels were painted by 418 international artists for the exhibit and joined together on 15-foot-high scaffold to form a continuous, 100-foot-long billboard that arced like a Cinerama screen.

Rising above a steep hill overlooking the La Cienega incline, the Artists' Tower Of Protest was completed in March 1966 with a groovy, surfink-style sign that read 'Artists Protest Vietnam War.' Susan Sontag spoke, and Judy Collins was there to sing. As one of the earliest examples of public resistance to the war in Vietnam, the instillation of the Artists' Tower Of Protest had far-reaching ramifications in terms of encouraging political thought in the music scene. But in these pre-*West* times, the news media largely ignored the work. John Wilcock of *The Los Angeles Free Press* gave the Tower its only press coverage, taking note of individual pieces such as a "Roy Lichtenstein mushroom cloud," nuclear disarmament logos, and "that symbol that obsessed the right-wingers, a giant dollar bill" on which the face of George Washington had been replaced by "that of Ho Chi Minh." Other panels, according to Wilcock, included stenciled slogans such as 'Body count,' 'War is very bad for children,' and 'I hate war, I love life, let me live.'

Somewhat ironically, the US State Department's Art in Embassies program, begun in 1963, had previously commissioned Walter Hopps to select works for high-level international exposure. In an interview with the art historian Francis Frascina, Hopps notes that government officials felt that the United States ought to have a pronounced, highly visible presence in the cultural world. Hopps calls the United States Information Agency, which was at the forefront of this policy, "a major propaganda arm," but adds: "The state department was tolerant of artists' radical statements—as long as they could be contextualized by ... 'American' art."

Frascina continues: "The Johnson administration was concerned with its public image at home" during the summer of 1965, having realized that "the escalation of the war [in Vietnam] led to a substantial increase in organized protests." President Johnson asked his Secretary Of Defense, Robert McNamara, to use the RAND Corporation (military planning committee) to research the Artistic Protest Committee's critique of US foreign policy. "A public relations agenda," says Frascina, "was becoming urgent for the government."[3]

When Hopps assembled this same group of artists for a display of solidarity against the Vietnam War, the impact was directly addressed by the oval office. After an Artists' Protest Committee-led, anti-RAND protest at the Santa Monica

Pier Carousel, a pair of debates were held between the two organizations. The first, closed session on July 7th 1965 was followed on August 3rd by a public debate at the Warner Playhouse on La Cienega. Admission to 'Dialog On Vietnam' was free; 800 people showed up to the 400-seat theater, so many had to listen to the discussion from speakers set up in the parking lot. Artists' Protest Committee member Irving Petlin (then a teacher at UCLA) had received inside information from a RAND informant, Roman Kolkowicz, on policies of technological warfare and population cleansing, and confronted the military organization with these. Dissatisfied with RAND's response, the committee decided to organize and promote the Tower.

As influential as it might have been on other artists and musicians, however, the direct impact of the Tower was perhaps not as widespread as the artists involved might have hoped. "The Artists' Tower Of Protest was a pivotal moment when the nature of protest was changing," notes art critic Richard Cándida Smith. "The transformations were due, in part, to the expansion of the mass media and the power that reporters and editors had to publicize or silence. The dilemma facing intellectuals engaged in protest in the 1960s sprang from the changing nature of celebrity and distinction. Those who understood this change successfully injected themselves into public discussion and changed public consciousness." Those who didn't "found their efforts failing to ignite public attention."[4]

The spirit of intellectual art and protest did not begin to have an impact on mass consciousness until essential help came from the aligned Sunset Strip teen scene. The anti-war movement was able to consolidate with a general audience only once it had been absorbed, applied, and transmitted by those who had also embraced the flippant attitude of Rocky & Bullwinke, modernist beat clubs, and the music created therein. Broadcast music filtered pop art and protest into something more digestible, which was then assimilated by the denizens of the Strip and twinned with a sense of natural, rebellious energy. LA rock'n'roll, through its media-center expanse, was the Trojan horse that brought these socially conscious artistic concepts into the discourse of everyday public awareness.

CHAPTER SEVEN

Far out

❝ *The message in the lyrics of most of these songs is delivered by implication. This is one of our teenagers' strongest weapons: it amounts almost to a private language. Many of the lyrics, in their oblique illusions and way out metaphors, are beginning to sound like real poems. And protected by this armor of poetry, our young lyricists can say just about anything they care to, and they do care.* **❞** LEONARD BERNSTEIN, *INSIDE POP*

By 1965, the Sunset Strip had become a weathervane of social change. With the musical landscape shifting from folk-rock to the wild abandon of garage-punk, keeping on top of the latest pop culture reality became quite a task for the LA media. There was always someone or something quite literally just around the corner ready to completely change the world's perception. The element of surprise kept people interested; the drama of the moment could be summed up in two words: "What's next?" Even in this environment, however, few would have expected much of a guy from Cucamonga, an Inland Empire city most resonant for its part in a running joke by Jack Benny.

As a teenager, Frank Zappa's musical interests developed in two seemingly polarized directions: hardcore rhythm & blues and the dadaist classical stylings of Varèse and Stravinsky. He had been driven toward a deep appreciation for music at a young age, in part because of a sense of isolation at school, which stemmed from the fact that he his family moved around a lot, and from the fact that he was of French-Italian heritage. (He recalled: "Being associated with someone of foreign parentage made it tough for me in school. There was that whole aspect of American life, and I never did understand it."[1])

In 1953, at the age of 12, Zappa moved with his family from Baltimore, Maryland, to California. He instantly gravitated toward the Chicano rhythm &

blues community, and within in a few years found himself drumming in a San Diego combo called The Ramblers. When the Zappa family then moved to the Southern Californian desert town of Lancaster in 1957, he joined an interracial rhythm & blues group called The Black Outs. More importantly, Lancaster introduced Zappa to a kindred spirit by the name of Don Van Vliet (better known, later on, as Captain Beefheart).

By 1958 Zappa had quit The Black Outs, switched from drums to guitar, and started collaborating with his new friend in The Omens (some of whom later joined The Mothers). Some of Zappa's musical passions of the time were revealed in a shortlived R&B/comedy show he briefly hosted on KSPC (Pomona College radio) that year. Zappa was kicked off the air after a few weeks when somebody noticed that he wasn't actually a student at the private college, but not before he had spun records by acts such as Big Jay McNeely, Howlin' Wolf, and Clarence 'Gatemouth' Brown. He and Van Vliet also shared an affinity for 1950s sci-fi and horror movies, as well as music by Varèse, Stravinsky, Richard Berry, and Guitar Slim.

After graduating high school Zappa began a loose partnership with Paul Buff, the engineer at PAL Studio in Cucamonga. PAL gave birth to records such as The Surfaris' 'Wipe Out' and the Chicano slow dance classic 'Queen Of My Heart' by Rene & Ray, not to mention numerous cash-in surf instrumentals (which, in Zappa's hands, often evoked the sound of Johnny 'Guitar' Watson's 'Three Hours Past Midnight'). After making his first recorded appearance on 'Break Time' by The Masters in 1962, Zappa produced Conrad & The Hurricane Strings' buzzing 'Hurricane' for Daytone Records and contributed incidental music to the horror television show *Jeepers Creepers*. (Zappa also produced 'Dear Jeepers' for Bob Guy, the show's host.)

The Cucamonga connection also yielded several minor successes for Original Sound Records. The Hollywood Persuaders' 'Tijuana Surf'—which featured Zappa's guitar-playing on the B-side, 'Grunion Run'—spent 17 weeks in the Mexican Top 10, while a Zappa co-write for the label, 'Memories Of El Monte' by The Penguins, was a hit in LA and remains a favorite among low-rider cruisers in East Los Angeles. While Zappa did have a genuine love for the 1950s rhythm & blues vocal group sound, 'Memories Of El Monte' is tinged with sarcasm, foreshadowing Zappa's 1968 parody of/tribute to doo-wop, *Cruising With Ruben & The Jets* (parts of which originate from Zappa's PAL period).

Perhaps the most notorious recording made during the PAL Studio days was the soundtrack to one of the greatest independent movies ever, *The World's Greatest Sinner* (1962). The movie was written, directed, and produced by Timothy Carey, who had previously acted in *The Wild One* (1953), *East Of Eden* (1955), and two movies directed by Stanley Kubrick, *The Killing* (1956) and *Paths Of Glory* (1957). Despite being made very cheaply—much of the action was shot in Carey's garage in El Monte—*The World's Greatest Sinner* was certainly ahead of its time. Carey plays a messianic rock'n'roll singer who invokes riots, while the ensuing political takeover predates by several years movies such as *Riot On Sunset Strip* and *Wild In The Streets*. The score was produced in November and December 1961, with Zappa recording a 20-piece chamber ensemble and a 55-piece orchestra at the Chaffey College auditorium, as well as an eight-man rock'n'roll band at PAL. (Zappa later made an off-color remark about the movie on *The Steve Allen Show*—on which he also 'played' a bicycle—effectively ending his relationship with Carey.)

In 1963 Frank Zappa and Don Van Vliet made a record at PAL as The Soots and submitted it to Dot Records in Hollywood. According to Zappa, the material included: "A cover version of the Little Richard song 'Slippin' And Slidin,' as if sung by Howlin' Wolf." Although Dot turned The Soots down, their rejection letter gave Zappa his famous epithet: "No commercial potential."[2]

By 1964 Paul Buff was spending an increasing amount of his time working at the Original Sound studio in Hollywood, leaving PAL empty for large stretches. It made a lot of sense, then, for Zappa to use the money he'd earned from providing the soundtrack to another movie, *Run Home Slow* (which was written by his high school English teacher, Don Cerveris), to buy the Cucamonga studio from Buff on August 1st. Zappa rechristened the place Studio Z, decorating it with bits of old sci-fi movie sets he had picked up while working on an idea for a movie called *Captain Beefheart vs. The Grunt People*. Buff, who continued to work with Zappa in an engineering capacity, recalls Zappa "asking for any junk electronics I had" and covering them in "DayGlo" paint. "He had turned the whole studio into his vision of a B-movie spaceship," says Buff. "The last time I was [there], to go to the bathroom you had to go out of the cockpit of this ship and crawl down tunnels underneath."[3]

In early 1965, Studio Z provided Zappa with an unplanned ticket out of Cucamonga. In an attempt to raise funds for and interest in *Captain Beefheart vs.*

The Grunt People, he gave an interview to a local newspaper, the *Progress Bulletin*. When the San Bernardino Vice Squad heard about the movie's title, they began to spy on Zappa, suspecting him of producing indecent material, and eventually framed him by commissioning Studio Z to produce an audiotape of a simulated sex act. Despite being no more risqué than later Mothers Of Invention material such as 'Suzy Creamcheese,' the recording led to a court case and a 10-day jail spell for Zappa, a significantly negative experience to encourage him to leave town.

Zappa had formed an association earlier in the 1960s with Ray Collins, with whom he co-wrote The Penguins' 'Memories Of El Monte,' recorded 'How's Your Bird' (1963) as Baby Ray & The Ferns, backed The Heartbreakers on 'Every Time I See You,' and collaborated with East LA band The Romancers. In 1964 Collins started playing in a Pomona-area covers band known as The Soul Giants with a Native American, Jimmy Carl Black, on drums, a Chicano, Roy Estrada, on bass, and surf music pioneer Ray Hunt on lead guitar. After Hunt was offered a job in a show group in Vegas, Zappa took over, and The Soul Giants started playing original material. With the addition of another surf guitarist, Elliot Ingber (who had played rhythm on 'Moon Dawg' by The Gamblers), the nucleus of a Frank Zappa band was in place—and just in time.

This new group, temporarily dubbed Captain Glasspack & His Magic Mufflers, rehearsed briefly at Studio Z before Zappa's Vice Squad bust convinced all five members to move to Echo Park. There Zappa got a job at the music store Wallich's Music City, which he used to work angles in Hollywood for his new band, now called The Mothers. (Zappa had previously played, sporadically, in a trio called The Muthers based at the Saints & Sinners in Ontario.) By this stage the LA discotheque scene had spun out of control. In the wake of The Byrds' groundbreaking performances at Ciro's in early 1965, The Mothers' wild ideas would be welcomed with open arms on Sunset Strip.

Shortly thereafter Zappa was introduced, through *Run Home Slow* screenwriter Don Cerveris, to a New York-based pop artist, Mark Cheka, who in turn brought The Mothers to the attention of Herb Cohen. Cohen had been a key figure on the Hollywood folk scene for some time. He lived with Odetta and booked folk acts at the Purple Onion during the late 1950s before opening the Unicorn coffeehouse on the Strip. He also ran Cosmo Alley, a dank beatnik cave behind the Ivar Theatre on Cosmo Street and forerunner to Bido Lito's.

Cohen introduced The Mothers to the beat and folk underground via the *Los*

Angeles Free Press, which led to the group's first booking, at the Action on Santa Monica Boulevard. Zappa memorably described the Action as somewhere "where actors and television personalities went to hang out with hookers."[4] Fittingly, John Wayne—Hollywood's most visible conservative—was in the audience on the night the man who would become the town's chief freak gave his debut performance. Zappa responded to Wayne's heckles—"I saw you in Egypt and you were great ... and then you blew me!"—by announcing at the start of The Mothers' second set that, although they couldn't get George Lincoln Rockwell, the leader of the American Nazi Party, they were pleased to be able to invite John Wayne up onto the stage. The inebriated Wayne started to slur an "if I'm elected" speech before being pulled from the stage by his bodyguards.

The success of The Mothers' four-week stint at the Action led to a series of gigs at Brave New World, the Trip, and the Whisky A Go Go. Herb Cohen brought MGM Records' Tom Wilson to one of the performances at the Whisky, strategically timing his arrival to coincide with the beginning of a big guitar rave-up, 'The Watts Riot Song.' The intention was to surprise Wilson (who had produced Bob Dylan for Columbia) with a more powerful song than anything on the demo he would have heard previously, which, according to Zappa, "was not particularly strange or outrageous in any way." It worked, and The Mothers started recording their debut LP for MGM's jazz subsidiary, Verve.

Because of the lengthy, unusual nature of a lot of The Mothers' material, the recordings ending up being released as a two-record set. "[MGM] had already spent $21,000 on this album," said Zappa, "so they had this bulk of material, more than they could stick on a single album. I suggested that I would take a cut rate on the publishing and they would release a double album [by an] unknown group, which was definitely a first in the biz."[5] The only compromise requested by the label was a name change, as they feared The Mothers might offend radio programmers. From then on, the group became known as The Mothers Of Invention.

The resulting *Freak Out*, recorded at TTG Studios on McCadden and Sunset, was—and is—near impossible to categorize. The album drags together disparate musical elements, rips the stuffing out of them, and reassembles the sounds with a wedge of echo and wry social commentary. 'Any Way The Wind Blows' is the only track that comes close to being commercially palatable; more typical is 'The Return Of The Son Of Monster Magnet,' a side-long rhythmic piece about dada, sci-fi, and *The Chipmunks*, or 'Trouble Every Day' (formerly 'The Watts

Riot Song'), on which The Mothers Of Invention prove themselves to be as punk as The Chocolate Watchband, as wyld on guitar as The Yardbirds, and as lyrically cunning as Bob Dylan.

Zappa wrote most of the songs while living in Echo Park, and described them as being about LA in 1965 and taking in both the teen scene where "they were seeing God in colors and flaking out all over the place," and "all that racial tension building up in Watts."[6] Another major theme is sexual inhibition, a subject on which Zappa shared an unconscious camaraderie with former Moulin Rouge headliner Louis Prima. (Both performers stayed sober in inebriated settings, while casually promoting the virtues of healthy intercourse.)

Shortly after the release of *Freak Out*, The Mothers Of Invention played on July 23rd 1966 at a benefit for *The Los Angeles Free Press* at the Aerospace Hall on Beverly Boulevard called GUAMBO (Great Underground Arts Masked Ball & Orgy). Around 1,250 people were in attendance, while another 2,000 were turned away.

Frank Zappa understood the importance of humor in social criticism. *Freak Out* loosened the political chains that surrounded the internal struggles of the 1960s, and took a vivid swipe at conformity. Henceforth, Zappa's albums serve as a running commentary on the times they were created in. Roger McGuinn once noted in a songbook that he perceived The Byrds' albums to be like "electronic magazines." By that measure, Frank Zappa was rock'n'roll's most gifted publisher.

While his lyrics were often acidic and humorous, Zappa's music could be emotionally rich, in part because of his talent for orchestration, but in a more primordial sense simply because he was such a gifted guitar player. His six-string prowess is at its finest on 'Invocation & Ritual Dance Of The Young Pumpkin' from 1967's *Absolutely Free*, while his facetious sensibilities were never more finely honed, at least in a pop context, than on 'Son Of Suzy Creamcheese.' *We're Only In It For The Money* (1968) tears into the San Francisco hippie movement and all the bands that had jumped on the *Sgt Pepper* bandwagon. In an echo of his pop-trash PAL studio material, Zappa produced the single 'Boy Wonder, I Love You' for Burt Ward, who had starred as Robin in the television series *Batman*. The B-side, 'Orange Colored Sky,' is a stunning spoof of psychedelic naivety.

With few places left to play in the wake of the Sunset Strip riot, The Mothers Of Invention opted to move to New York City in 1967, where they took up residency at the Garrick Theater. But it was the Hollywood club scene of 1965–66, where artistic compromise was never an issue, that jump-started Zappa's career.

That's not to say that there weren't detractors in LA, however. Stan Bernstein of *The Los Angeles Times* wrote a damning review of the group's legendary show at the Shrine Exposition Hall in September 1966. In a piece entitled 'Mothers Of Invention Find A Way To Bore Nearly Everyone,' Bernstein decries the volume of the performance—"so high that one wondered whether or not an air raid siren system had gone berserk," the "ridiculous" costumes, and "poor" singing by Ray Collins. He concludes: "A guard warned at the exit that re-admittance was not possible. It was the most welcome news of the night." *The Times'* more progressive insert magazine, *West*, took a rather different view: according to critic Tom Nolan, the performance was "remarkable."

* * *

In a measure of the speed at which things were changing, Nolan's article, headed 'The Frenzied Frontier Of Rock,' also refers to Brian Wilson as the rock'n'roll "establishment." Wilson's group, The Beach Boys, had in fact only been an LA phenomenon for four years. Wilson might have been less flamboyant than Frank Zappa in 1966 but he was equally far out. As chief songwriter, producer, and falsetto vocalist, Wilson was The Beach Boys' central plexus. It was his songs, his vocal arrangements, and his *sound* that made the group stand out. Having quit touring with the group in December 1964 to concentrate on songwriting and production, this boy-wonder hit-maker found himself in an enviable position on the verge of LA's mid-1960s renaissance.

Wilson knocked off a few more hits in the band's signature style, but by 1965 the Beach Boys sound had gravitated to one of dense intimacy, as heard on the second side of *The Beach Boys Today!* and, in particular, 'Let Him Run Wild' and 'California Girls' from *Summer Days (And Summer Nights!!!)*. Wilson bridged the gap between these two phases of the group's career with the rambunctious late-1965 single 'The Little Girl I Once Knew,' which sets the finely wielded symmetry of the imminent *Pet Sounds* LP against the pulse of their early hits.

'The Little Girl I Once Knew' was an experiment that worked better musically than commercially—radio deejays were wary of the record because of its odd time signatures, which left crucial moments of dead air. This element of musical surprise coupled with a mixed reaction from US radio outlets foreshadowed Wilson's most intensely creative period, from late 1965 to early 1967, during which time he created the music for *Pet Sounds* and *Smile*. *Pet Sounds* initially sold poorly until its success was buoyed by that of the double A-side single drawn from it, 'Wouldn't It Be Nice'/'God Only Knows.' His groundbreaking pre-*Smile* 45 'Good Vibrations' then hit the Number 1 spot in both the USA and the UK toward the end of 1966.

The romantic feel of *Pet Sounds* immediately engaged the melodic sensibilities of Paul McCartney (whose 'Yesterday' remains the most covered ballad of all time). McCartney had already copped some Beach Boys-like vocal tricks for The Beatles' 'Paperback Writer,' recorded in April 1966; when *Pet Sounds* was released a month later, he declared 'God Only Knows' to be the greatest song ever written. The conceptual sonic heartbreak that ran right through *Pet Sounds*—from the opening 'Wouldn't It Be Nice' through to the melancholic, closing refrain of 'Caroline No'—was the key, and the defining influence on The Beatles' decision to construct their subsequent *Sgt Pepper* LP as a unified whole. Individual tracks on *Pet Sounds* had a clear impact on The Beatles' psychedelic masterwork, too, notably the forceful backing track for 'Here Today' and the gentle reservation of 'You Still Believe In Me.'

Brian Wilson's primary inspirations for the music of *Pet Sounds* were Johan Sebastian Bach, Phil Spector's Wall Of Sound, and the subtle folk-rock of The Beatles' own *Rubber Soul* (itself influenced by The Byrds). The lyrics were by Wilson's songwriting partner Tony Asher. On songs such as 'I Know There's An Answer' and 'I Just Wasn't Made For These Times' the words are complex, introspective, and demanding on the listener; they ache with a sincerity still rare in the pop marketplace.

Shortly after the release of *Pet Sounds*, however, Wilson found a new lyrical foil after a chance meeting at a party hosted by Terry Melcher. Van Dyke Parks had assisted The Byrds in their psychedelic explorations on '5D (Fifth Dimension),' and recently signed a solo deal with MGM, for whom he released the ornate pop-masterpiece 'Come To The Sunshine' and a tripped-out 45rpm arrangement of Beethoven's *Ninth Symphony* called 'Number Nine.' Wilson immediately picked up on the young Parks's profundity and vast knowledge of American literary and musical folklore and brought him on board for his next project.

Even with *Pet Sounds* in the bag, Wilson's best was still to come. During the head-spinning summer and fall of 1966, he spent a full six months perfecting the next Beach Boys single. As well as topping the charts in Britain and America, the resulting 'Good Vibrations' set a new precedent for recording technique with its complex, modular construction. Wilson's goal was to make pictorial music that could conjure up visions in both the stoned and the sober. With this in mind, he set about collaborating with Parks on a suite of songs based in the imagery of the great western expansion of the 1800s combined with a musical representation of the four basic elements: earth, air, fire, and water.

Like Frank Zappa, Brian Wilson understood the importance of applying a sense of humor to his smooth tapestry webs, hence the original title of *Smile, Dumb Angel*. Although *Smile* was eventually 'scrapped' in the spring of 1967, roughly 50 minutes of finished songs from the project exist on tape, still awaiting an official release in a cohesive form. Despite Wilson's reticence to talk about the original *Smile* in the years after its non-release in 1967, it would prove difficult to argue upon hearing the music that a suite of songs including 'Our Prayer,' 'Heroes And Villains,' 'Wonderful,' 'Cabinessence,' 'Good Vibrations,' 'Mrs O'Leary's Cow,' and 'Surf's Up' would not have added up to one hell of an album. (Wilson and Parks did return to 'finish' *Smile* in 2004, both on stage and on record, but chose to re-record the songs entirely rather than return to the vastly superior original tapes.)

The tragedy of this lost record is twofold. On a personal level, Brian Wilson retreated from the happiness that his art helped him sustain; in a wider sense, we will never benefit from hearing the music other artists would have been inspired to make had *Smile* been released to the world at large during the 1960s. Once *Smile* session tapes did begin to appear in the public domain—first on bootlegs, and then on the officially released *Good Vibrations: 30 Years Of The Beach Boys* boxed set in 1993—the heights that Wilson soared to musically began to color the work of young bands thrice removed from his own generation. In this sense, the Brian Wilson of 1966 became an Icarus-like, mythical figure in rock'n'roll.

Van Dyke Parks took the energy from this project into his own *Song Cycle*, released on Warner Brothers Records in 1968, applying American Western imagery to a celebration of vintage Hollywood. Wilson, meanwhile, chilled out on the acoustic *Smiley Smile* and the rehearsal-like *Wild Honey* before delivering the marvelous, blissful, *Friends*. With tracks such as 'Busy Doin' Nothin'' and 'Diamond Head,' the eldest Wilson brother—still only 26—said goodbye to his leadership of The Beach Boys with a musical representation of a bright orange and purple Los Angeles sunset.

* * *

In 1966, the intermingling of pop and psychedelia was most prevalent in London and Los Angeles. While in San Francisco 'psychedelic' often meant little more than an extended guitar solo, musicians in London and LA were making ethereal sonic landscapes. The music produced by The Beach Boys, The Beatles, Love, The Rolling Stones, The Pink Floyd, and The Electric Prunes during 1966–67 was textured and multidimensional. In the course of three-and-a-half minutes—or less—a 45 could send the listener on a fantastic journey of circuitous enrichment and bring with it the sense of floating in a bubble of sound. Whereas boogie-laden jamming could bring with it feelings of mind-numbing detachment, the records coming out of the Carnaby Street and Sunset Strip scenes had a direct intensity. The best of them crystallize their ideas into the compact form of a song rather than a 'jam'—there was no time to space too far out, or you might miss something.

The Electric Prunes were fortunate to be based so close to the musical hub of Los Angeles. Recorded at Leon Russell's Skyhill Studio in November 1966, their 'I Had Too Much To Dream Last Night' was given its sonic sheen by Dave Hassinger, the pioneering engineer who had given The Rolling Stones' 'Paint It Black' its sonic depth and helped introduce the world to psychedelia with The Byrds' 'Eight Miles High.'

Hassinger's sonic experiments at RCA's Music Center Of The World also included 'Satisfaction,' which set The Rolling Stones off in a completely different direction. He added to the raw nerve of the Stones' earlier recordings, emphasizing the sense of danger in the rocking numbers, and eloquently complementing the diversity of the band's original repertoire. According to Hassinger: "With standard singers like Wayne Newton, it's not too complicated. When you get into rock'n'roll, though, that's when the work begins. Rock groups have to be creative and different to sell records."[7] For The Rolling Stones, however, this kind of experimentation resulted in inconsistency, as the group seemed to hit on great ideas at random. As such, once the *Aftermath* sessions were completed, Dave Hassinger went looking for a new band with which to continue his creative momentum. This being Los Angeles in 1966, he would not have to look very far.

The Electric Prunes started out as high school bands called The Sanctions and Jim & The Lords in Woodland Hills and Chatsworth on the western edge of the San Fernando Valley. They specialized in standard party fare, from rhythm & blues ('What'd I Say') to surf ('Moon Dawg') and from the Stones ('I'm Free') to The Beatles ('I'm Down'). One day, while the formative Prunes were rehearsing in a garage, a friend of the band stopped by and told them that she knew Dave Hassinger. They didn't believe her until they ran into him at a local party, and subsequently found themselves recording at Skyhill with Hassinger at the desk.

Released on Reprise, the first Electric Prunes single, 'Ain't It Hard,' is a rare example of folk-punk. The song was written by Roger and Terrye Tillison of the Gypsy Trips, a folk-rock duo in the Sonny & Cher mould who had been recording at Skyhill with Leon Russell and J.J. Cale. The follow-up came from an equally obscure source. 'I Had Too Much To Dream Last Night' was written by Annette Tucker and Nancie Mantz, who had also composed The Brogues' 'I Ain't No Miracle Worker.' The Electric Prunes first heard 'Too Much To Dream' on a demo record complete with full orchestration, a 'Be My Baby'-like beat, and a crooning lead vocal by Jerry Vale. Like The Rolling Stones in their formative years, The Electric Prunes' main strength lay in rearrangement. Taking heed of the key sensibilities of rock'n'roll, the Prunes' version of psychedelia clocked in at three minutes. Condensation was the key.

According to vocalist Jim Lowe, the oscillating noise that kicks off 'Too Much To Dream' came from an earlier recording session. "To save money," Lowe says, "we flipped the tape over so we could record going the other way. We could hear the tail end of this other song we'd recorded, playing backwards, since it was turned up so loud. It sounded like an airplane landing. We all said: 'Wow! What was that? Cut that piece off and save it!'" Bassist and keyboardist Mark Tulin adds: "It was just [guitarist] Ken Williams screwing around, hitting one fuzz-tone note and grabbing the tremolo." The hard part, says Tulin, was re-recording the sound, backwards, in time with the rest of the song.[8]

'Too Much To Dream' was followed by two absolutely chilling albums, *The Electric Prunes* and *Underground*, both of which were released in 1967. Each is, in part, a showcase for the effects created by Ken Williams's assortment of homemade fuzz-boxes, which he would connect together and use simultaneously. Among the highlights of the first album are 'Are You Lovin' Me More (But Enjoying It Less),' which recalls The Pink Floyd's 'Lucifer Sam,' and 'Sold To The Highest Bidder,' a natural successor to The Standells' raga-inflected 'Why Pick On Me.' On *Underground*, 'I Happen To Love You' goes from hushed panting to disturbed anguish, 'Hideaway' and 'Dr Do Good' veer into Gregorian chant/haunted house territory, and the single 'You Never Had It Better' gets as close to hard rock as is possible without giving way to bombastic self-indulgence.

The Electric Prunes had developed their sound at local high schools and parties during the latter part of 1966 and, like The Leaves, gained a huge following in the San Fernando Valley. Fortunately for them, 'Too Much To Dream' took off nationally, leading to instant invitations to tour, which meant the group could avoid the hassle of trying to break through on the fading LA club scene.

Sunset Strip venues were by now being forced to change from the psychedelic format or closed altogether during the anti-curfew demonstrations that took place between November 1966 and February 1967. (The group played what was billed as their "first and only LA engagement" at a shortlived teen club called Mod Street West on W Jefferson near the San Diego Freeway in March 1967.)

The group's first national tour, during 1967, came as part of a stunning package of bands, including The Beach Boys, hot on the heels of *Pet Sounds* and 'Good Vibrations,' ? & The Mysterians, who had recently topped the charts with '96 Tears,' and The Left Banke. An appearance on *American Bandstand* helped break 'I Had Too Much To Dream Last Night,' while the even greater success of 'Get Me To The World On Time' led to a spot on *The Smothers Brothers Comedy Hour*. The Prunes toured Europe in late 1967, where they found that their music fitted right in with post-Who, pop art/freak-beat groups such as The Move, John's Children and The Creation. During a live performance in Sweden, which was broadcast on the radio, the group apologized, as Americans, for the fiasco that had enveloped Vietnam.

By the time of the third Electric Prunes album, *Mass In F Minor*, however, management issues had set in. Only the first two tracks—'Kyrie Eleison' and 'Gloria' (a hymn, not the song by Them)—feature the whole band: the rest were fleshed out by a group of session musicians led by keyboardist Don Randi, a member of Phil Spector's Wall Of Sound Orchestra who had recently scored a Jack Nitzsche-arranged solo hit, 'Mexican Pearls.' Somehow David Axelrod, a record producer best known for his work with Art Tatum, Gerry Mulligan, and Lou Rawls, had been able to seize on The Electric Prunes' name to record his own concept album.

Mass in F Minor is psychedelic backdrop music at its finest, but in the course of its production The Electric Prunes had been left out of their own recording sessions, with no apparent legal recourse. There seemed to be little option for the group but to disband. In the meantime, another David Axelrod-produced album, *Release Of An Oath: The Kol Nidre* (1968), came out under The Electric Prunes' name despite featuring no involvement from the band whatsoever.

Fittingly, one of the few authentic Electric Prunes songs from this period, 'Kyrie Eleison,' was chosen to soundtrack the acid trip sequence toward the end of *Easy Rider* (1969), long after Axelrod's faux Prunes had taken over. By this stage Axelrod had started to make further records in a similar vein under his own name, such as *Songs Of Innocence* (1968) and *Songs Of Experience* (1969), while original Electric Prunes Mark Tulin and James Lowe appeared on an eponymous raga-rock album by Ananda Shankar (son of Ravi) in 1970.

* * *

Just as interesting as The Electric Prunes were a group of UCLA film students from Venice Beach who in 1965 started playing parties and cutting demos as Rick & The Ravens. One of these demos, 'Henrietta,' featured backing vocals by The Byrds, who, like Rick & The Ravens, had been recording at World Pacific.

Rick & The Ravens started out as a frat/surf band before developing a sound that took influence from both the campus beat-jazz and poetry scene and the sound of Them's 'Gloria.' The original line-up of the group, featuring Ray Manzarek and his brothers, Rick and Jim, made three mostly forgotten singles for World Pacific subsidiary Aura Records before disbanding. As the Manzareks sought new members, the band was given time to develop at World Pacific by its easy-going president, Richard Bock (an important catalyst in the Sunset Strip explosion who also nurtured The Byrds during his studio's off-hours). It was around this time that the group took a different name from the pages of Aldous Huxley's *The Doors Of Perception*—the title itself taken from William Blake's *The Marriage Of Heaven And Hell*—("If the doors of perception were cleansed, everything would appear to man as it is ... infinite"). The intellectual surroundings of UCLA and the Venice Beach area gave the group a mysterious, highfalutin appeal.

These early Doors recordings are rough and aggressive: Rick Manzarek's guitar dominates, while lead vocalist Jim Morrison's delivery has more scats and screams than it would later on. Initially, however, there was little label interest, except from Columbia, to whom the group briefly signed but didn't make any records for. Rick and Jim Manzarek (the latter a harmonica player) departed, as did the bassist for the session Barbara 'Bobi' Jackson. The classic Doors line-up was completed when drummer John Densmore brought in Robbie Krieger—who he'd found in a transcendental meditation class—on lead guitar.

Through late 1965 and early 1966 The Doors gradually began to pick up gigs in more central locations, including an opening slot for Love at Brave New World on Melrose. They finally hit the Strip in February 1966 when they took up residency at a cool little club between Clark and Hilldale known as the London Fog, which they used to tighten and formulate a sound of their own.

The London Fog was situated next door to the Galaxy. Its façade represented the epitome of the art style that had developed out of the work of Ed 'Big Daddy' Roth and Rick Griffin: a red and purple paint job picked out by silhouettes of go-go dancers and wicked, raunchy lettering. As striking as it might have looked, however, the club was overshadowed by the presence of the Whisky A Go Go a few doors down. Significantly, the Whisky's booking agent, Ronnie Haran, plucked The Doors from the London Fog to be her club's new house band.

At the Whisky A Go Go The Doors opened for Love, The Turtles, Captain Beefheart & His Magic Band, Buffalo Springfield, Johnny Rivers, and, most crucially, Them (who, in May 1966, were riding high on the success of 'Mystic Eyes,' 'Here Comes The Night,' and the double-sided killer 'Baby Please Don't Go'/'Gloria'). The Doors eventually lost their spot at the Whisky because of the club's management's fears about the incest-themed climax of the band's mesmeric epic, 'The End.' But the group carried on, and seemed to play just about everywhere else in LA during the remainder of 1966, from politically motivated benefit shows to stints at the Sea Witch, Gazzarri's, Bido Lito's, the Hullabaloo, and many others. At most of these venues The Doors' lyrical bent found welcome ears, while the band's reputation on the street grew when rumors began to spread about Jim Morrison's wild on-stage antics.

Initially, The Doors hoped simply to be as big as Love, whose frontman, Arthur Lee, suggested them to Elektra Records chief Jac Holzman. Holzman and Elektra producer Paul Rothchild (then in the midst of working on Love's second album, *Da Capo*) flew into Los Angeles from New York to assess the group and were suitably impressed. Rothchild started recording sessions with the group soon after Labor Day, 1966.

The Doors and its follow-up, *Strange Days* (both 1967), were specifically intended to sound as if the band was playing within the confines of a Sunset Strip nightclub. By 1969, however, Rothchild would be grafting the jazzy arrangements of Love's Da Capo onto The Doors' *The Soft Parade*. Jim Morrison would go through an image change during that time, his initial art student bravado replaced by that of a hedonistic, leather-clad satyr.

Keyboardist Ray Manzarek was The Doors' orchestrator and arranger, and gave the group its focus with his pulsating, fluid playing. Songwriting duties were mainly split between Morrison and Robbie Krieger, who wrote 'Light My Fire,' the April 1967 single that overwhelmed radio and sped up the growth of underground FM stations. This was the first record to receive an over-abundance of requests to be played in its full-length album version, leading radio station managers to begin to consider the possibility of playing songs longer than the standard three minutes.

Whatever the relative merits of the extended song—a phenomenon that gradually began to consume full sides of albums—The Doors' 'Light My Fire' managed to enthrall listeners for each of its six minutes and 50 seconds. In 1965, Bob Dylan's six-minute 'Like A Rolling Stone' had been split into two halves for radio. Heard this way, it was difficult to tell whether the first or second half was playing.

Taking note of what had been done to Dylan's song, Brian Wilson anticipated problems with The Beach Boys' 'Heroes And Villains,' so turned it into two distinct sections for a planned two-sided single (the 'cantina' section remained unreleased for many years). This would not have been possible with the extended organ and guitar section of 'Light My Fire.' Nonetheless, radio stations started to play the song in its entirety, and it became a hit in Los Angeles. The Doors then asked KBLA's Dave Diamond (the first disc jockey to play the full version) to create a 45rpm edit of the single for use in less-enlightened radio markets.

Social historians have correctly identified the contraceptive pill as the 1960s' great liberator, but 'Light My Fire' helped throw the sexual revolution into overdrive. Collectively, youth culture had already been throwing off the puritanical shackles of the past, with mod fashion intent on destroying the inhibitions of the conservative, cloudy 1950s and its gray, flannel suits. The key line in 'Light My Fire,' "The time to hesitate is through," was taken as a signal to spring into action by kids who knew that their moment of cultural influence had arrived. The Doors' breakthrough hit was to 1967 what 'Gloria' was to 1965 and 'Hey Joe' was to 1966. "I was trying to come up with something reminiscent of 'Hey Joe,'" said guitarist Robbie Krieger, on writing the song. "The version by The Leaves."

This time, the message was not buried in vague implication: it was immediate. The Doors were the harbingers of something brand new (even if their jazzy arrangements recalled the British group The Zombies at times). It seemed appropriate, therefore, that their first single was 'Break On Through.' The Doors were tailor-made to smash boundaries like plate glass windows amid rising tensions caused by the escalation of the Vietnam War (which was being waged against the will of many Americans). They were not the leaders of any particular movement, but Jim Morrison's reckless abandon challenged established ideas and had the power to lure in millions. The group's confidence grew with the size of their audience: defiance became The Doors' MO, first on the Strip, then across the United States and Europe. Their songs reflected and then fed the confrontational impedance that had exploded on the LA scene. The riots and arrests that took place at Doors concerts were reminiscent of events at early Rolling Stones shows. The difference was that The Doors channeled that hysteria into a sense of purpose.

Much has been made of Jim Morrison's poetic intuition, but his most inspired lines seemed to come out in bursts, in the form of calls to action. Something ominous lurks in 'Roadhouse Blues,' on which he proclaims the future to be "uncertain" and the end "always near," while an offhand line in 'The End' itself pinpoints the source of the new revolution: "The west is best/Get here and we'll do the rest." On 'Five To One,' from *Waiting For The Sun* (1968), Morrison announces: "They've got the guns but we got the numbers," before sneering at the type of drop-out hippie who would trade in activism to "walk across the floor with a flower in your hand/Trying to tell me no one understands/Trading your hours for a handful of dimes."

The music of The Doors is a match for Morrison's lyrical trips throughout, drawing its sounds from right across the LA spectrum. There are hints of the bossa nova cafe sound, a raga flavor no doubt picked up at World Pacific (or perhaps at a meditation class), beatnik bongos, and a general air of darkness and despair that reflects the fading architectural aura of Venice Beach, in a manner reminiscent of Charles Bukowski. Part of the group's sound, too, bears a resemblance to the cinematic jazz-noir of the 1950s, reinterpreted here with garage band instrumentation. *Waiting For The Sun*'s 'Not To Touch The Earth' is pure haunted house rave-up, building and building in frantic madness and exploding in the manner of Love's 'Seven And Seven Is.' 'When The Music's Over' from *Strange Days* stands as the group's definitive statement, with which their destiny and contribution can be measured.

The Doors' earliest albums are commonly considered to be their strongest, perhaps because of the sociological climate in which they were created. But the list of great records the group made seems endless. 'LA Woman' breaks loose with the speed of the freeway; '20th Century Fox' is imbued with the walking groove of the Strip; 'Touch Me' offers up a provocative slant on Tom Jones-style lounge music; and the moody 'Riders On The Storm' brought the group's oeuvre to a fitting close. Like the records cut by Phil Spector at Gold Star Studios, The Doors' collected output captures the very feel of Hollywood; neon signs, hills, winding roads, art deco, and all.

* * *

Another important group of the time, Kaleidoscope (not to be confused with the British band of the same name), spelt out their attitude on their debut single, 'Please': "Don't tell me about how I'm doin' right or wrong ... I've got to find my own way, and do my own thing." The group's use of bowed instruments backed by stark, beautiful, acoustic guitar figures has been cited by Jimmy Page as an influence on his work in The Yardbirds and Led Zeppelin. The similarity ends there, however; the string combinations used by Kaleidoscope have no other parallel in rock'n'roll.

Like The Rising Sons, Kaleidoscope came out of the traditionalist folk scene at the Ash Grove. According to Kaleidoscope's Chris Darrow, both groups were inspired by Mike Seeger of The New Lost City Ramblers: "He played fiddle, banjo, guitar; we *all* liked him. So when people started forming bands, we would take all these acoustic instruments, and apply them to electric bands. That's where this weird, multi-instrumentation thing came from." (Kaleidoscope's Chester Crill also had the same harmonica teacher as The Rising Son's Taj Mahal and Canned Heat's Al Wilson.) Starting out as The Baghdad Blues Band, the group was discovered by manager Barry Friedman, who had just left the Buffalo Springfield team.

Kaleidoscope started out in a democratic fashion: every band-member had strong points, and whoever introduced a song would take the lead while they worked on it. Darrow excelled on guitar, bass, banjo, and mandolin; David Lindley played fiddle, fingered and harp guitars, bowed violin, banjo, and guitar; Solomon Feldthouse played a Middle Eastern instrument known as the caz, as well as guitar; John Vidican was on drums and percussion; and Chester Crill played violin, viola, harmonica, and various keyboard instruments. The five band-members switched instruments on stage, taking it in turns to play the bass.

Right: Terry Melcher and David Crosby at Columbia Studios on Sunset, 1965. *Below:* The 'Byrds Ball' one block away at the Hollywood Palladium, 1965.

Clockwise from top left: The Rising Sons on the Venice Boardwalk tram, 1966; Love guitarist Johnny Echols jams with dancers at the Hullabaloo, 1966; Byrds followers outside the Trip during the band's residency there in 1965–66; P.F. Sloan watches the Grass Roots at the Trip, 1966; Jackie DeShannon and The Hollies at Imperial Records, 1966.

Clockwise from top left: The Standells on *The Hollywood Palace*, 1967; The Doors at the London Fog, May 1966, at a show due for release on CD in 2016; an exterior view of the same venue; The Chocolate Watchband on the set of *Riot On Sunset Strip*; The Merry-Go-Round on the set of *Boss City*; Bobby Fuller and friends, 1966.

Above: Captain Beefheart and his Magic Band, 1966.
Right: The Beach Boys at Pacific Ocean Park, 1966.
Opposite: The Mothers Of Invention in front of the Whisky A Go Go, October 1965; Frank Zappa at the Action that same night; The Electric Prunes, 1966.

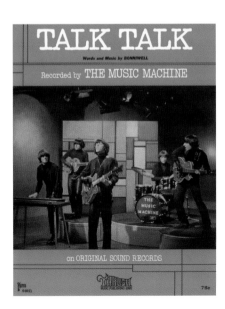

Top: Kaleidoscope with guests Larry Williams (standing) and Johnny 'Guitar' Watson (sitting) at Columbia Studios, Sunset Boulevard, 1967. *Above:* The Seeds so-called 'live' album, 'recorded' at Merlin's Music Box. *Left:* The Music Machine on *Boss City*, 1966.

Kaleidoscope's apparent lack of direction ended up benefiting the group. Their Epic Records debut, *Side Trips*, takes in a kind of skewed garage-punk, albeit played with unconventional instruments, snotty raga romps, crunchy fuzz-tone, and the unusual sound of the celeste. The group performed the single drawn from the album, 'Please,' on *Groovy*, but its combination of cracked, growling vocal and subtle chimes was perhaps too pure and fragile to have been a hit. Another album track, 'Keep Your Mind Open,' a biting criticism of the Vietnam War, was later included among the Rock'n'Roll Hall Of Fame's Top 50 psychedelic tracks of all time. (The accompanying book and exhibition *I Want To Take You Higher*, erroneously claims that the group came from Berkeley, when in fact they hailed from the San Gabriel Valley.) *Side Trips* also includes David Lindley's tough, fuzz-toned 'Why Try,' recorded with Feldthouse before the rest of the band had assembled. The dismissive chorus vocal is the most direct moment on a masterful, diverse album.

The title of Kaleidoscope's second album, *Beacon From Mars*, is a clear indication of where the group was headed next. Here the songs incorporate country, ragtime, and a fuzzy, harmonica-laden take on Don & Dewey-style rhythm & blues, 'You Don't Love Me.' The albums highlights are its extended pieces: 'Beacon From Mars' features organ-driven improvisation and spooky feedback, while the instrumental tones of the roots-raga 'Taxim' pre-empt Led Zeppelin's explorations of Middle Eastern styles.

The group's interest in rhythm & blues led unexpectedly to an invitation to record with Larry Williams and Johnny 'Guitar' Watson in 1967. Darrow explains: "They really liked our records, and were basically trying to figure out how to incorporate this psychedelic sound into the R&B mentality." For Kaleidoscope, this was a once-in-a-lifetime opportunity. Darrow retains vivid memories of the session, which resulted in a song, 'Nobody,' that was later recorded as the debut single by Three Dog Night. "[Williams and Watson] showed up at the session with matching cars and matching suits," he says. "One had a burgundy Cadillac and a burgundy suit, and the other had both in chocolate brown." The group was subsequently asked to play on *The Songs Of Leonard Cohen*.

* * *

As subtle as The Doors were abrasive, The West Coast Pop Art Experimental Band had a melodic sense best exemplified by their 'I Won't Hurt You,' which manages to be dreamy and atmospheric but also full of weird, surprising changes. The group's ace in the hole was Michael Lloyd, a supreme melodist who kept himself busy with various projects outside the band, notably writing music for cartoon shows such as *Cattanooga Cats* and *Hot Wheels*. Their earliest recordings, made in 1966, are akin to what a meeting between Bob Dylan and Buddy Holly in an echoing cave might have sounded like, or like The Left Banke with added throbs of feedback. The group showed early on that they didn't feel the need to play loud, but could be as uninhibited as the rest, as demonstrated on a wild cover of 'You Really Got Me.'

The West Coast Pop Art Experimental Band had close links to two other, less-recorded bands, The Sound Of The Seventh Son and The East Side Kids. All three groups rose from the ashes of The New Dimensions, Beverly Hills' finest surf act. Michael Lloyd began his songwriting partnership with keyboardist Jimmy Greenspoon in The New Dimensions, and carried it over into their new group. As The Rogues they cut a blatant 'Hey Joe' rip off, 'Wanted Dead Or Alive,' before being introduced by record producer Kim Fowley to an independently wealthy 30-year-old, Bob Markley, who wanted some help writing songs. At this point Fowley was in charge of promoting The Yardbirds in the USA, and booked them to play at a party at Markley's house. Noting how passionately teenyboppers responded to the music, Markley decided instantly to invest in The West Coast Pop Art Experimental Band—on the condition that he could be in the group.

Jimmy Greenspoon was, at the time, playing a house band engagement at Stratford On Sunset—sometimes known as the Castle On The Strip—with The Sound Of The Seventh Son. (Greenspoon later used this connection to get The West Coast Pop Art Experimental Band gigs there too.) The Sound Of The Seventh Son backed local rhythm & blues acts such as The Olympics, The Coasters, and Brenda Holloway, as well as visiting soul stars including Mary Wells and Martha & The Vandellas. The group released only one 45, 1965's 'I'll Be On My Way,' although a one-sided, folk-rock acetate of 'She Lost Me' was discovered years later in a La Mirada thrift store. Greenspoon also wrote the bouncy, ambient 'Hello Mr Sun' for Boystown—produced by Michael Lloyd and Kim Fowley—in 1967.

Situated on the hillside directly across from It's Boss and outfitted in a Tudor style, Stratford On Sunset was the perfect setting for a British Invasion-era dance club. Like many of their peers, The Sounds Of The Seventh Son kept themselves busy scooping up every new British import they could find at Lewin's Record Paradise on Hollywood Boulevard, which would then go straight into their sets at Stratford. Run by a British expatriate, Lou Lewin, who had new records shipped in as soon as they were released in the UK, the store was so hip that Jeff Beck briefly worked there after leaving The Yardbirds and relocating to Los Angeles. The Rolling Stones, too, would visit Lewin's when they were in town, while another regular patron was local boy-genius William Stout, who later designed the iconic covers to classic bootlegs such as The Yardbirds' *Golden Eggs* and *Who's Zoo* by The Who.

Lewin's provided a direct pipeline of new British records, which in turn allowed Greenspoon to blow LA kids' minds by playing songs such as the Stones' 'Get Off Of My Cloud' months before its US release. He was at the front of the line outside the store to buy The Beatles' *Rubber Soul* on its UK release date—Friday December 3rd 1965—and promptly scooted back to Beverly Hills to listen to it in the company of the rest of his band and some LSD-25. The Sounds Of The Seventh Son were never quite the same afterward. Stratford closed that same month, leading Greenspoon to quit its house band and form The East Side Kids, who put out a pair of singles in 1966, 'Listen To The Wise Man' and 'Close Your Mind.' The group took up a residency at a club called Wild Thing near Hollywood and Vine before moving on to the Hullabaloo, leaving their original house band spot to The West Coast Pop Art Experimental Band.

The West Coast Pop Art Experimental Band had a very eclectic palette. It's often difficult to tell that you're listening to the same group from song to song. A guy named Buddy Walters backed them with a continuous light show, which made use of every psychedelic toy money could buy at the time. Most notable, according to Jimmy Greenspoon, was "a clear glass dish of colored water and cooking oil positioned on an overhead projector" that produced an image that resembled "a swirling, colored amoeba."[9] Walters further developed this idea when he was hired to create light shows for The Animals and The Jimi Hendrix Experience in 1967. From there, his ideas went global.

The first West Coast Pop Art Experimental Band record was a self-titled album released in 1966 on the group's own Fifo label. The album captures the group in all its original frightening, echo-laden glory; this being a self-released work, they could get away with as much reverb, vibrato, and tremolo as they wanted. What is most striking about the group's best work is the freedom they allowed themselves, and the various combinations of sounds in their arrangements. They seem to arrive at something completely new on each track. The group subsequently signed to Reprise, for whom they cut three albums during 1967 and '68—*Part One, Volume Two,* and *Volume Three: A Child's Guide To Good And Evil*—that take in flower-power ballads, floating keyboards, moody surf guitar, charming folk-rock, vibraphone-laden ambience, fuzz-toned guitars, Association-like harmonic changes, and beatnik grooves. (Michael Lloyd kept his most direct, pop material for his work on Hanna-Barbera cartoons, although some of these originated from West Coast Pop Art Experimental Band material.)

The group's best known song, 'Smell Of Incense,' quickly became a hit for the Texan combo Southwest FOB. Other highlights of their concise career include 'In The Arena,' which addresses the Sunset Strip riots, and 'Suppose They Gave A War And Nobody Came,' a track worthy of The Mothers Of Invention's *Freak Out* LP. They made one final album, *Where's My Daddy*, for Amos Records in 1968 before folding, in part because of a sense of disillusionment and their failure to break through commercially. Nonetheless, The West Coast Pop Art Experimental Band left behind a number of great, varied recordings and played on some of the grooviest bills of the time.

* * *

As a recording artist, Kim Fowley seemed like a walking billboard, tuned into everything that was going on around him. He would travel—by bus, as he never drove—to wherever the music took him, from East LA to Bakersfield, drawing in everyone from Chicanos to suburban garage-punks, girl groups to street kids along the way. Encapsulating the simple beauty of the Sunset Strip aesthetic, he notes: "Everybody who wanted to could make a record for $100, and could be Number 1 in the world—and why not? You just showed up and you did it and there was always a label who would put it out. And everybody was waiting up and down the street." Fowley was the first point of contact in LA for many hit acts, although many tended then to take off without him. Soon after The Mamas & The Papas arrived from New York, for instance, he discovered the group and found them a deal with GNP-Crescendo, but they ended up signing with Dunhill.

Fowley first started producing records in 1959, and had his first hit with Skip & Flip's 'Cherry Pie.' In 1960 he started working as a runner for Alan

Freed at KFWB, who had moved to LA from New York to lay low after the payola scandal. Freed did, however, manage to break Fowley's most fantastic hit record, 'Alley Oop,' a 1960 chart-topper that will go down in history alongside the cartoon cavemen it portrays. Credited to The Hollywood Argyles, it was actually recorded by vocalist Gary Paxton, pianist Gaynell Hodge, bassist Harper Cosby, and drummer Ronnie Silico—all part of Fowley's roving team of outlaw, non-union players. ('Alley Oop' subsequently provided David Bowie with the pivotal line "Look at that caveman go," as used in his 'Life On Mars.')

Fowley hit pay dirt again in 1962 when he wrote and published the instrumental hit 'Nut Rocker' for B. Bumble & The Stingers (another loose aggregation of session players) which has, in recent years, been used at Olympic figure skating events. The guy was everywhere at once, turning The Players' 'Memories Of A High School Bride' into a mock radio drama and recording East LA cruisers such as 'Watch Your Step' by Larry Green & The Rhythmaires. Both of these directions echoed what Frank Zappa was doing at the time, a link that was made solid when Fowley later sang on 'Help I'm A Rock' on The Mothers Of Inventions' *Freak Out*. A chance meeting with David Gates (who picked up a hitchhiking Fowley), meanwhile, resulted in a number of songwriter-producer collaborations, most notably The Murmaids' 'Popsicles And Icicles,' a big hit on Chattahoochee Records.

In the mid 1960s Fowley 'dropped out' completely to absorb the new scene. "I had five years of being the responsible adult," he recalls. "[Then] I got to be a kid." It was around this time that he started to release solo 45s. 'The American Dream' on Mira Records was a tongue-in-cheek response to 'I Got You Babe' that begins with bells and a Sonny Bono-style spoken-word vocal but ends with the declaration: "Death and taxes and shovels and axes are all we've got to think about." 'Mr Responsibility,' released on his own Living Legend imprint, covers similar themes but in a style more reminiscent of The Kinks' Ray Davies.

Kim Fowley made a few more stops on his hit and miss recording odyssey in 1965 and 1966, the final years of the single's dominance in the rock'n'roll market. His recollection of the recording of the most famous of these 45s, 'The Trip'— "just an afternoon with friends"—speaks for them all. A completely improvised vocal set to music by Thee Midniters, 'The Trip' (1966) is perhaps the ultimate encapsulation of the sights, sounds, and feelings that abounded when the Strip was truly 'happening.' It was also, according to Fowley, a defining influence on

'Soul Kitchen' from *The Doors*. "During the time it was on the jukebox [at the London Fog], The Doors were the house band," he says. "'Soul Kitchen' [sounds] like the exact music of 'The Trip.'" Fowley's single cropped up in Peter Clifton's 1967 music clip hodgepodge *Popcorn* (1969) as well.

Another key Fowley production from 1966 is the self-titled single by Vito & The Hands, who were fronted by noted scenester and dance troupe leader Vito Paulekas. Fowley then made his own 'Underground Lady,' a Yardbirds-style rave-up with a mixture of rhythm & blues vocals and facetious spoken-word. The B-side, 'Pop Art '66,' is reminiscent of the innovative British producer Joe Meek, best known for The Tornados' 'Telstar' (1962).

As well as making hit records, Fowley was an important catalyst on the LA scene. When The Yardbirds found themselves unable to gig in September 1965 due to visa problems, Fowley set up a performance in front of the Sunset Strip in-crowd at the home of Bob Markley, who he then helped put together The West Coast Pop Art Experimental Band. When The Yardbirds returned for a four-night stint at the Hullabaloo the following January, so many people turned up that many—including Marlon Brando and Natalie Wood—had to listen from the curb outside.

Fowley took advantage of the buzz from this and his appearance on *Freak Out* and headed for Britain, where he produced an early incarnation of Soft Machine, The N'Betweens (who later became Slade), and a post-Van Morrison line-up of Them whom Fowley dubbed The Belfast Gypsies. He had a UK hit with his production of Napoleon XIV's novelty song 'They're Coming To Take Me Away, Ha-Haaa!,' co-wrote an early Cat Stevens B-side ('Portobello Road'), and hung out with The Beatles on the set of their 'A Day In The Life' promo film.

Returning to Los Angeles by early 1967, Fowley pursued production projects with Michael Lloyd of The West Coast Pop Art Experimental Band, with whom he wrote most of an album of efficient psychedelic wallpaper by a group called The Smoke. Members of Lloyd's band backed Fowley on a memorable solo album, *Love Is Alive And Well*, which was released on the Tower label in 1967 and includes a remarkable Seeds-esque track called 'Reincarnation.'

Fowley's next release of note was 'Music Is The Magic'/'Gypsy Canyon,' a doubled-sided single on which he describes the new scene that had sprung up among people who had migrated to Topanga Canyon after the destruction of the Sunset Strip scene. (He could also be heard talking about the 'canyon people' movement on a KNX news item that has since cropped up on various compilation albums.) He and Michael Lloyd subsequently co-produced a 1968 album by Topanga Canyon group St John Green that combines The Doors' darker moments with the twisted humor of much of Fowley's solo work. Tormented invocations such as 'Message From The Dead' and 'One Room Cemetery' are set against wacky send-ups ('Do You Believe,' 'Shivers Of Pleasure'), and a fistful of garage-psych tracks. Other highlights by this defiantly pre-hippie group include the snaking, sex-mad 'Canyon Woman' and the stop-start rhythm & blues grooves of 'Devil And The Sea.' The Fowley-penned theme song, 'St John Green,' opens with the unforgettable lines: "Just because we're so young and deadly/Did we have to lose our minds?"

In Kim Fowley's words, St John Green were "dripping with darkness," a mood that resonated with many in the immediate aftermath of the Sunset Strip riots. Fowley was there to broadcast it. His whole trip was a canny blend of the unashamedly exploitative and the thoroughly entertaining.

* * *

The most unusual group to emerge from the 1965–66 Sunset Strip scene was almost certainly Captain Beefheart & His Magic Band, led by a true outsider, Don Van Vliet. Chicago blues might have been hip among new groups such as The Rolling Stones and The Yardbirds on the early-1960s art school scene in London, England, but only one other soul shared Van Vliet's passion for it in the Inland Empire: Frank Zappa. For Van Vliet, there was no hardcore blues scene to speak of, no ready-made pool of musicians, no intellectual crowd to scrutinize his musical developments. Instead, his interpretation of the blues came from within a bizarre, tortured, and highly personal universe. This is challenging music, which perhaps explains why Captain Beefheart & His Magic Band had only one brief flirtation with popularity, 1966's debut single 'Diddy Wah Diddy.' By the time *Safe As Milk* emerged in 1967, its aggressive rhythms and scary, howling vocals couldn't possibly gibe with the airy sounds of the Summer Of Love, nor the endless guitar boogies of post-Monterey rock. John Lennon was a fan, however, and proudly displayed a pair of *Safe As Milk* bumper stickers—included in the earliest pressings of the album—on a cabinet in his home.

Born in Glendale in 1941, Don Van Vliet was a prodigiously talented artist. His parents would often take him to the nearby Los Angeles Zoo, where he would sketch some of the animals. A Portuguese sculptor by the name of Augustino Rodriguez noticed Van Vliet at the age of five, took the boy under his wing, and eventually invited him to appear on an educational television program. Although he made a number of appearances on the show, Van Vliet didn't enjoy the experience, describing it as "television patting me on the head and pinching my bottom and calling me a prodigy."[10] At 13 Van Vliet was awarded an scholarship to study sculpture in Europe, but his parents declined it on his behalf, deciding that all artists were "queers," and instead moving their child into the distant Mojave Desert suburb of Lancaster, far away from the arts scene.

It was in Lancaster that Van Vliet turned to the blues as an extension of his art. His abstract lyrics reflected beat poets such as Allen Ginsberg, while his unconventional arrangements embraced the free-jazz concepts of Ornette Coleman. His words are often rendered for effect, not consonance; tracks such as 'Abba Zabba,' 'Zig Zag Wanderer,' and 'Electricity' are not standard blues workouts by any stretch of the imagination. His music and lyrics twist and contort in unexpected directions, dizzying and dazzling the listener. Van Vliet was inspired by the Dutch painter Willem de Kooning, whose work is filled with unfamiliar patterns and textures that have been filtered through the artist's highly individualized sensibilities. Many listeners, of course, were baffled. But for those who could tune in to Van Vliet's strange frequency, the confusion made a perfectly wonderful sense.

As Captain Beefheart, Don Van Vliet took an abstract art approach to words and music. As far back as 1959, a coarse, home-recorded collaboration with Zappa called 'Lost In A Whirlpool' used the word "motherfucker" just for impact. There was no chance such vulgarity could reach the marketplace. While most of the white blues-singers of the 1960s would dance around in an attempt to get girls riled up, Captain Beefheart would throw himself into his own musical world, wringing out emotion with his eyes closed. (Some girls did appreciate the Captain, however: groupie-in-chief Pamela Des Barres refers to his early shows as being "earth-shaking events" in her autobiography, *I'm With The Band: Confessions Of A Groupie*.)

A true modern primitive, Van Vliet couldn't tell a B-flat from an A-sharp. Instead he would communicate to his musicians in visual terms, or by whistling, humming, growling, or grabbing a guitar neck and exclaiming: "Like this!" He made all of his recordings up until 1963 with Frank Zappa, before putting together his first Magic Band the following year. Two of the first three demos the group recorded at Gold Star Studios had a straight-up Howlin' Wolf sound, while a third ('Call On Me') was a folk-punk ballad. Things would only get stranger from here on.

Following Frank Zappa to Hollywood, Captain Beefheart & His Magic Band became a formidable live outfit, even winning, somewhat incongruously, the 1965 Teen-Age Fair's Battle Of The Bands. First prize was the opportunity to cut demos at Disney Studios. More important for the group, however, was that the win attracted the attention of A&M Records, who immediately offered them a two-single deal. David Gates brought them into Sunset Studio, where they cut the first of these, a storming rendition of Bo Diddley's 'Diddy Wah Diddy,' which, after a few months of heavy promotional pushing, hit big in Los Angeles.

Captain Beefheart & His Magic Band soon appeared on *Where The Action Is*, lip-synching their local hit at beachside. The single broke into several other markets but was eclipsed nationally by a version by the Boston area's most prominent group, The Remains. Beefheart's follow-up 45, a David Gates composition called 'Moonchild,' also failed to make an impact on *Billboard*. A&M didn't know what to do with the group, so dropped them, despite a groundswell of excitement about Van Vliet's crew on the Strip, which peaked with a support slot for Them at the Whisky A Go Go. Van Morrison was impressed by Van Vliet's harmonica playing and asked him for lessons. (In typically eccentric fashion, the desert bluesman told Them's frontman to try a fast drive on the highway, holding the harp out of the window.)

The Magic Band performed a number of times at San Francisco's Avalon Ballroom in 1966, and were on the bill for The Beach Boys' Summer Spectacular at the Hollywood Bowl in August (as were Love, The Leaves, and The Byrds). Derek Taylor recalls having difficulty trying to promote Captain Beefheart outside California: "I liked him very much … the issue in the beginning was how to get Captain Beefheart's ugly mug in *Sixteen* magazine." Taylor made several attempts to give the group a more palatable appearance, even dressing them "in big-collared shirts and ties and jackets and boots" and getting their hair cut, but his efforts were ultimately in vain.[11]

Fortunately, there were people in Hollywood then who believed in the unusual, involving sound of Captain Beefheart & His Magic Band. Record producer Bob Krasnow felt strongest about the group's potential, and eventually landed them a deal with fledgling New York label Buddah, who put out *Safe As Milk* in 1967. When the group came to record the album, blues guitarist Doug Moon had trouble with the complex material. Ry Cooder, formerly of The Rising Sons, was called in to stop the project being shelved. His contributions on bottleneck guitar pushed the choppy, rudimentary music of tracks such as 'Sure 'Nuff Yes I Do' and 'Autumn's Child' over the edge. 'Where There's Woman' is embellished with cabana-style bongos, 'Abba Zabba' features tribal vocals and percussion, and 'Electricity' is at once cynical and sinuous. The chords and fuzz-tone of 'Dropout Boogie' recall The Kinks, but the evil, snarling vocal is like nothing ever heard in the UK—or anywhere else on the planet. Elsewhere, Van Vliet's vocals range from slow and soulful on 'I'm Glad' to raging and climactic on 'Call On Me,' while 'Plastic Factory' is a fine example of the wild harmonica playing—which ranges from guttural to squealing—that so impressed Van Morrison.

Released in September 1967, *Safe As Milk* is unlike anything heard before or since. The following year's *Strictly Personal*, however, has more of a psychedelic feel alongside titles such as 'Ah Feel Like Ahcid' and 'Beatle Bones And Smokin Stones.' (Van Vliet later complained that Bob Krasnow's production had ruined the album.) Live recordings from this period, released in 1971 as *Mirror Man*, find the band in more of an improvisational blues mood. Next came the uncompromising double disc set *Trout Mask Replica*, issued on Frank Zappa's Straight Records label in 1969 and in many ways the ultimate realization of Don Van Vliet's avant-blues vision. A daring experiment in choreographed cacophony, it remains a landmark release, while later, less avant garde albums such as *Lick My Decals Off Baby* and *Clear Spot* maintained a high standard of work into the 1970s. All in all, the string of LPs recorded by Captain Beefheart & His Magic Band between 1967 and 1982 remain some of the purest expressions of the freedom that was encouraged on the LA music scene of 1965–66.

CHAPTER EIGHT

A giant amoeba

❝ *To try to pin down Los Angeles, to declare that it is indelibly this or irrevocably that, is to risk being made a fool of by the very nature of Los Angeles, which is at once all-encompassing and ever-changing, like a giant amoeba that constantly alters its structure, size, and shape. It's simply too big and too varied to take in at once.* **❞** ROBERT LANDAU AND JOHN PASHDAG, *OUTRAGEOUS LA*

The Greater Los Angeles area is one of the largest local broadcast markets on the planet. It covers parallel counties such as Ventura, San Bernardino, Riverside, and Orange, although local information and culture tends to lean on the city of LA by virtue of access and proximity. This is perhaps best defined by the nightly sign-on used by famed local newscaster Jerry Dunphy, who worked for various broadcast networks from 1953 until his death in 2002: "From the desert to the sea, to all of Southern California." During the 1960s, Sunset Strip remained the creative center of the LA area, but was immeasurably colored by artists from Orange County.

The youth of Los Angeles shook to the sound of Dick Dale & His Del-Tones from 1961–63, while LA County surf groups such as The Surfaris from Glendora, Palos Verdes's Eddie & The Showmen, and The Pyramids of Long Beach clustered around venues such as the Rendezvous Ballroom in Balboa, the Harmony Park Ballroom in Anaheim, and the Retail Clerks Hall in Buena Park. These Orange County venues outdrew and overshadowed the two main surf music locales in the LA region (A Teen Canteen in Azusa and the Revelaire in Redondo Beach).

There was much more of a surf scene in Orange County. The corner of Main Street and the Pacific Coast Highway, near the Huntington Beach Pier, was one of the focal points. The Golden Bear was on a par with the Ash Grove or the

Troubadour in Hollywood: Jimmy Reed and John Lee Hooker were regulars, and The Paul Butterfield Blues Band did their first LA-area gig there. (The venue's staff also booked one of Bob Dylan's earliest Californian gigs, at the Wilson High School in Long Beach on December 5 1964.)

Directly across the street, on the Pier itself, the Pavalon Ballroom was a haven for surf bands. Dick Dale & His Del-Tones and Eddie & The Showmen both headlined the venue, where they were supported by upcoming local acts. Beneath the Buzz Burger hamburger stand next door was another music hangout called the Salty Cellar. Next to that, a closed-down auto-supply store briefly became a rock'n'roll venue.

Melodyland—just across from Disneyland in Anaheim—became one of Orange County's most crucial venues when it opened in 1965. This 3,000-seat theater-in-the-round played host to touring groups such as The Animals, The Dave Clark Five, and Jefferson Airplane, and made it possible for Hollywood groups such as Buffalo Springfield, The Seeds, and The Mamas & The Papas to reach kids who found it difficult to get to the Strip.

Other inland Orange County hotspots included the Anaheim Bowl (a bowling alley), the Band Box, the Abrams Town and Country Hall, and the Tustin Youth Center, where a huge Battle Of The Bands took place every year. Among the groups to get their start here were leather-clad punks The Mods Incorporated, Santa Ana garage band Jamie & The Jury (who appeared in *The Angry Breed* and cut two singles for Columbia), and The Gents, who had a folk-pop sound similar to that of The Association.

Hailing from the Tustin and Westminster areas, The Human Expression were the minor-chord geniuses behind 'Love At Psychedelic Velocity,' an Accent Records punker in the same vein as Love's 'Seven And Seven Is.' Other great tracks such as 'Reading Your Will' and the expansive 'Follow Me' existed only as demos at the time. 'Calm Me Down' is quintessential garage, its moody verses and moaning backing vocals rising to a chorus that seems like a retaliation against the abuse described in the lyrics, while 'Optical Sound' is a chilling fusion of surf and psychedelia. The Human Expression made it to Gazzarri's on the Strip, and were offered two songs by a Canadian guy named Mars Bonfire. They recorded one of these, 'Sweet Child Of Nothingness,' but perhaps unwisely turned down the second, 'Born To Be Wild.'

Aside from being home to the Fender Guitar Plant, Fullerton's main claims to fame were The Fabs and The Satans. The Fabs cut the garage-punk staple 'That's The Bag I'm In'/'Dinah Wants Religion' for Cotton Ball Records in 1966, and played at venues such as the Salty Cellar, the Anaheim Bowl, and the Airport Club/Marina Palace in Seal Beach. They were also on the same bill as The Seeds, The West Coast Pop Art Experimental Band, and others for a Halloween show at the Great Western Exhibition Center. The Fabs later became The Stack, and moved toward a Who-like sound; their privately pressed 1969 album *Above All* is now highly collectable. The Satans, meanwhile, cut 'Makin' Deals' for Manhattan Records in 1965, a song notable both for opening an early *Pebbles* compilation and for its lyric, which predates The Rolling Stones' 'Sympathy For The Devil' with its sneer of: "Can you guess my name?"

The Syndicate's band-members hailed from Whittier and Long Beach, a pair of LA County townships that border Orange County. The group played a lot of local gigs, including the Long Beach Cinnamon Cinder, and featured on bills at It's Boss and the Sea Witch on the Strip. After cutting 'My Baby's Barefoot' (1965) for Dore Records, the group signed to the Dot label for 'The Egyptian Thing'—a harmonica-laden punk-raver with a guitar tone so over-modulated that it sounds like it could destroy the listener's speaker cones, and lyrics that reflect the Liz Taylor-in-*Cleopatra* look American girls of the time were copying. The song was intended for an album, *Five The Hard Way*, that ended up not being released and is still gathering dust in the vaults at MCA. The Syndicate appeared on the teen dance show *Bash!* in January 1966, but had split by the middle of the year in a fog of disappointment and frustration.

On a similar theme to The Syndicate's second single was 'Egyptian Surf' by a seven-piece group from Garden Grove that started out as The Temptations but then became The Spats when a certain group from Detroit hit big with the same name. Taking their cue from Dick Dale's 'Mr Peppermint Man,' The Spats recorded a song by Orange County's overlooked rhythm & blues songsmith, Alonzo B. Willis. 'Gator Tails And Monkey Ribs' earned the group a spot on *American Bandstand*, during which they alternated songs with Jerry Lee Lewis, who was promoting his 1965 hit 'High Heel Sneakers.' The group then cut an LP for ABC-Paramount, *Cookin' With The Spats*, which includes several more Willis compositions, notably his most famous song, 'The Roach.' The group maintained a neatly suited, slicked-back image throughout, but did veer into garage-punk on later cuts such as 'Tell Ya All About It Baby' and the buzz-saw fuzz of 'She Done Moved.' (Doug Rhodes briefly played in the group at this late stage before joining The Music Machine.)

Hollywood became a second home for Limey & The Yanks, who were constantly trekking out from their homes in Santa Ana to play shows at Bido Lito's or on any of the three stages at Gazzarri's. The group came within a whisker of fame with the release of the throbbing 'Guaranteed Love' (on Starburst) and a cover of The Marauders' 'Out Of Sight, Out Of Mind' (on Loma). They were capable, too, of a smooth, Zombies-like sound, as heard on 'Gather My Things And Go,' which is notable for its effective use of feedback. Perhaps the finest example of the brilliance of naïve, messy playing came by way of The Monacles, who ranged in age from 11 to 16. The group cut four singles for Variety Films Records in 1966, including 'I Can't Win,' which conveys the unadulterated desperation felt by so many teenagers in a way that could never have been achieved by a polished, 'grown-up' band.

The best-known artists to break out of Orange County during the mid 1960s were The Righteous Brothers. The duo of Bill Medley (from Santa Ana) and Bobby Hatfield (from Anaheim) were ushered in at the Rendezvous Ballroom in Balboa, where Medley's dad worked as a lighting engineer during the Dick Dale era. (Prior to that, Medley and Hatfield had sung at a teen hangout called the Bayou in Seal Beach.) Upon signing to Moonglow Records the duo had a string of hits including 'Little Latin Lupe Lu,' 'Koko Joe,' 'Justine,' and 'My Babe,' which was covered by numerous frat bands and later became a British hit for The Spencer Davis Group.

The Righteous Brothers began to move beyond their original Don & Dewey-style blue-eyed-soul sound after picking up a steady gig on *Shindig!*, which brought them under the wing of Phil Spector. The duo's debut for Spector's Phillies label, 'You've Lost That Lovin' Feelin',' shot both them and the song into international prominence. 'Lovin' Feelin',' written by Barry Mann and Cynthia Weil, is now generally considered to be the most broadcast record of all time. The Righteous Brothers continued to split their performances on *Shindig!* between their early, rockin' material and new Spector productions, such as 'Just Once In My Life,' 'Ebb Tide,' and 'Unchained Melody.' Spector also produced '(You're My) Soul And Inspiration' for the duo, but they jumped ship, finished the vocals without him, and released it on Verve. The record reached Number 1 on *Billboard*, but the move ultimately proved to be unwise, as, without Spector by their side, the hits stopped coming.

One of the stalwarts of the Orange County scene was Paul Floodman, who led a consummate house band called The Magnificent Seven and appeared in a number of ads for Fender. The Magnificent Seven landed a lucrative gig at the architecturally brilliant Tomorrowland Terrace in Disneyland, which had a stage that rose up from beneath the ground from what seemed like a futuristic planter braced by *Jetsons*-style stalactites. Several other groups, including The Rising Sons and The Dovers, were denied the opportunity to play there because of their long, Rolling Stones-like hair, as were greasy rock'n'rollers The Spats. Disneyland had no so such problem, however, with neater-looking local hit-makers such as Gary Lewis & The Playboys, The Grass Roots, or The Association, all of who graced the Tomorrowland stage. (During the folk craze, Disneyland also hosted a huge, annual Hootenanny in which many aspiring LA musicians took part. Chris Hillman's first folk-bluegrass group, The Scottsville Squirrel Barkers, are also said to have graced a stage at the theme park.)

Folk music was hugely popular in Orange County. The Golden Bear was the area's most diverse venue, but the Mecca in Buena Park was of similar interest. Located in an industrial building, the venue had a pseudo-Egyptian theme (in black light paint). Bob Dylan is rumored to have played there; The Dillards, The Pair Extraordinaire, and Joe & Eddie definitely did, as all three cut live albums at the venue. Local artists would bounce between here, the Golden Bear, and smaller places such as the Prison Of Socrates in Balboa, the Rouge et Noir in Seal Beach, the Rainbow Sign in Long Beach, the Paradox in Orange, Cafe Frankenstein in Laguna Beach, and Sid's Blue Beet, a beatnik-style nook in a brick-walled alley at Newport Beach. These nests of teenage bohemia would also play host to flamenco guitar players from Mexico, Central America, and South America (who taught a thing or two to the local surf musicians). The most notable of them was José Feliciano, who launched an internationally successful career in 1968 with a brilliant cover of The Doors' 'Light My Fire.'

Steve Gillette was an Orange County folkie who got his break playing at Cafe Frankenstein. He was exposed to the national folk music world at a young age when he toured in support of Bud & Travis and Judy Henske, which led to covers of his songs by Ian & Sylvia, Carolyn Hester, and Glen Yarborough. A record deal came from the prestigious New York label Vanguard. Back in Orange County, Gillette collaborated and swapped songs with some of the LA folk scene's most interesting songwriters, Tom Campbell, Pamela Polland, and Linda

Albertano (who, at the time, worked with Campbell at Disneyland). All three contributed to Gillette's eponymous solo debut, which became an influential album among insiders on the LA music scene soon after its release in 1967.

Among the album's highlights, Gillette's own 'Back On The Street Again' was later a hit for The Sunshine Company—who started out at the Mecca—and sung by Linda Ronstadt on The Stone Poneys' *Evergreen Vol 2*, while '2:10 Train,' an ethereal Campbell/Albertano co-write, was also recorded by The Rising Sons and The Stone Poneys. Pamela Polland contributed 'Goin' Home Song' just prior to forming her own group, The Gentle Soul, who would sign to Columbia and work with producer Terry Melcher—just as did The Rising Sons, demonstrating, yet again, the extent to which cross-pollination in the Greater Los Angeles area knew no borders.

* * *

Tim Buckley grew up in Anaheim and found plenty of opportunities to play locally in his teens before the release of his eponymous debut for Elektra in 1966 made him Sunset Strip's chief folk icon. *Tim Buckley*'s LA sound was heightened by the presence during its recording of arranger Jack Nitzsche and pianist Van Dyke Parks. It features some of Buckley's finest songs, including 'Song Slowly Song,' 'I Can't See You,' 'Valentine Melody,' and 'Morning Glory,' later recorded by The Stone Poneys as 'Hobo.' According to Linda Ronstadt, the song was written about a "groovy little beach house" that first she and then Buckley lived in. (It was also covered by Blood Sweat & Tears on their *Child Is Father To The Man* LP.) The highlight of Buckley's second LP, *Goodbye And Hello* (1967), was the melancholic 'Hallucinations.' He performed the album's anti-Vietnam War song 'No Man Can Find The War' on *Inside Pop: The Rock Revolution* and sang 'Song Of The Siren' on the final episode of *The Monkees*.

On the Orange County folk circuit, Buckley struck up a friendship with Jackson Browne, who was briefly a member of The Nitty Gritty Dirt Band—"He played the first two gigs, then went on a solo career," according to the group's John McKuen. Browne was introduced to the East Coast folk scene by Buckley, which led him to co-write several songs and play guitar on *Chelsea Girls* by former Velvet Underground vocalist Nico on the way to becoming a highly successful solo performer. (A series of pre-fame shots of Browne were taken at around this time by Linda Eastman—later McCartney—and included in her book *Linda's Pictures*.)

The Nitty Gritty Dirt Band hailed from Long Beach and were led by banjo, guitar, and mandolin player McKuen, who had previously worked as a magician at Disneyland, sometimes as a double act with comedian Steve Martin. The group crossed novelty songs with excellent folk-rock, and recorded a number of Browne's songs on their first three albums, including 'These Days,' 'Melissa,' 'It's Raining Here In Long Beach,' 'Holding,' and 'Shadow Dream.' The group played the Topanga Canyon Banjo & Fiddle Contest before making their LA debut in support of Merle Travis at the Ash Grove, building up a following over time in Buena Park and Newport Beach, Orange and Pasadena, Glendale and Hollywood. "We played everywhere from storefront parking lots to the Hullabaloo After Hours," says McKuen of the group's various gigs all around the Greater Los Angeles area, which he describes as: "Truly the Greenwich Village of the West Coast."

The group inked a deal with Liberty Records in 1966 and recorded the ebullient Top 40 hit 'Buy For Me The Rain' with producer Dallas Smith. This led to appearances on "all the TV shows that were shot locally," says McKuen, and a stint at the Troubadour on the post-Strip scene, during which time they began to add 1920s and 1930s-style jazz to their repertoire. At one point the band's ever-changing membership included Chris Darrow of Kaleidoscope on mandolin and fiddle. Darrow and the group's Jeff Hanna formed a separate group called The Corvettes, which backed Linda Ronstadt live and on television shows such as *Playboy After Dark*. Bernie Leadon, formerly of Hearts & Flowers, and Randy Meisner later joined The Corvettes, with the group's revolving line-up eventually coalescing into the Eagles. Ronstadt noted "a spirit of kinship," adding: "We were all trying to make headway in the same musical area—even though most people in the business thought we were crazy."[1]

Dave Myers & The Surftones were a red-hot surf group from Laguna Beach that continued to play right through the mid 1960s at the Harmony Park Ballroom—the very room in which Richard Berry had written 'Louie Louie' a decade earlier. In 1963 Myers's group alternated weekend bills with Dick Dale & His Del-Tones, while the renamed Dave Myers Effect cut a garage-punk single in 1965 called 'Come On Love.' Then came an album, *The Great Racing Themes*, that flits between surf, jazz, fuzz, percussive instrumentals, and more.

A December 1967 taping of *American Bandstand* hints at the reality of rock'n'roll dancing in Southern California at the time, years after the surf scene had, supposedly, faded. Dick Clark asks the audience who they think *Billboard* has rated as the year's top group. After initial, muted suggestions of Jefferson Airplane and The Doors, someone in the back row yells out "Dave Myers!" Incredibly, two others return the call, and several more whoop, hoot, and holler. After calming his audience down, Clark announces the actual winners, The Monkees, to a round of boos.

This must, however, have been the dying breath of the rock'n'roll scene. As Orange County scenester Gordon McLelland notes, with the arrival of the bombastic rock sound of the late 1960s: "Dancing became less important." The clubs that had played host to the early/mid-1960s music scene, such as the Harmony Park Ballroom, now struggled to survive, in part because, according to McLelland: "The bigger groups started to ask for more money than any nightclub or youth center could afford." And with those clubs went the daring and adventurous spirit of rock'n'roll.

* * *

Many musicians on the periphery of the Sunset Strip scene chose to settle in LA permanently. When Harry Nilsson moved in from New York City in 1962, he took a job at a computer center for a bank in Van Nuys. Pretty soon after that, however, he found himself commissioned to sing on demos of sweet, Buddy Holly-styled material by Tommy Sands's guitarist Scott Turner. By 1964 Nilsson had signed a publishing deal with Rock Music Inc and taken the plunge into the hustle of the LA music biz.

Nilsson made recordings with John Marascalco—who wrote 'Good Golly Miss Molly' for Little Richard—at Gold Star and cut 'Donna (I Understand)' for Mercury Records as Johnny Niles. He made Marascalco's 'Groovy Little Susie' as Bo-Pete and recorded a novelty song, 'Stand Up And Holler,' which was then synched up to 8mm footage of The Beatles (with whom he would become more formally involved later in the decade) and sold in the back of teen mags.

In 1965 Nilsson auditioned for a role in *The Monkees*, but was passed by. He was, however, beginning to make inroads as a songwriter. After two of his songs were recorded—but not released—by The Ronettes, he was commissioned by Phil Spector to write the theme to *The Big TNT Show*, which was then performed by The Modern Folk Quartet. This was not released on record either, but did lead him to sing on Spector's demo for 'Let Me Go,' a would-be Righteous Brothers song later recorded by Pat & Andre.

In 1966 Nilsson signed a recording contract with Tower Records, a subsidiary of Capitol for whom he cut a number of demos, which were later released as *Spotlight On Nilsson*. 'The Path That Leads To Trouble' in particular leads the listener to wonder what might have happened had Spector produced Nilsson in the jangly, folk-rock vein of the MFQ sessions. Nobody at Tower seemed interested in Nilsson as a performer, however, so it was time to move on again. In early 1967 he submitted several songs to *The Monkees*; they performed 'Cuddly Toy' in a spoof ragtime segment on their show, and would later record 'Daddy's Song' for the *Head* soundtrack. A publishing demo, *New Nilsson Songs*, contained 'Without Her.'

All the while, Nilsson was still working in his old job at the bank. He finally began to achieve success in his own right after signing a deal with RCA Records, for whom he cut 1967's *Pandemonium Shadow Show*. The Beatles were said to enjoy the album's wacky sense of humor, sound-collage ideas, and twisted medleys that parodied their own songs. John Lennon, it is claimed, once listened to the album for 36 hours straight while being chauffeured around London in his psychedelic Rolls Royce under the influence of LSD. Another admirer was British record producer Mickie Most, who quickly cut a version of Nilsson's 'Ten Little Indians' with The Yardbirds, while Hearts & Flowers took on 'She Sings Hymns Out Of Tune' back in LA.

In 1968 Nilsson recorded the soundtrack to the absurd Otto Preminger movie *Skidoo*, for which he also sang the credits. His famous song 'One' was first recorded by producer Gary Zekley with The Fun And Games, but it was Three Dog Night who turned the song into a big hit. Nilsson then made his second RCA album, *Ariel Ballet*, for which he recorded, at the suggestion of producer Nick Venet, a Fred Neil song: 'Everybody's Talkin'.' It was subsequently included in the 1969 movie *Midnight Cowboy*, and won Nilsson a Grammy. He was then chosen to sing the theme to the situation comedy *The Courtship Of Eddie's Father* before being given a television special of his own, *The Point*, in 1970.

Another emigrant to Los Angeles was Ian Whitcomb, who arrived in the early 1960s from the UK (by way of Seattle) and liked what he saw. As the British Invasion picked up steam, he rented an apartment and played regularly in town. Like Nilsson, Whitcomb signed a deal with Tower Records but had rather more immediate success, scoring a KRLA Top 10 hit in 1965 with 'This Sporting Life.' The record was later cited by producer Tom Wilson as being a key influence on the arrangement of Bob Dylan's 'Like A Rolling Stone.'

Whitcomb first came to the USA in 1963. Splitting his time between the UK and the Pacific Northwest, he encountered a scene that produced The Sonics, The Wailers, Paul Revere & The Raiders, and The Kingsmen. Between resident-status stints back home, he set his sights on a permanent move to Hollywood. Whitcomb's background in ragtime piano and traditional string music helped him to become the first rock'n'roll act to headline at the Troubadour. Backed by garage-punk combo Somebody's Chyldren, he worked his wide knowledge of pre-rock'n'roll records into hot cover-versions of songs such as 'High Blood Pressure' by Huey 'Piano' Smith & The Clowns and his biggest hit, the sweaty, panting 'You Turn Me On.'

Whitcomb's recordings for Tower are a mixed bag, spanning novelty hits ('Where Did Robinson Crusoe Go With Friday On Saturday Night'), rhythm & blues ('That Is Rock'N'Roll'), garage punk ('Dance Again'), pop ('Sally Sails The Sky'), and ragtime instrumentals with a rock'n'roll beat ('Soho'). Throughout, his songs invoke a sense of fun grounded in his knowledge of the comic traditions in music. He has since become a noted music historian, releasing themed albums in long-forgotten musical genres (including an album of songs played on the Titanic that came out a year before the blockbuster movie) and writing the acclaimed music books *After The Ball* and *Rock Odyssey*.

* * *

Given the number of record labels and studios operating in Los Angeles during the 1960s, it seems logical to assume that there was also a preponderance of notable sound designers. And indeed there were: Gary Usher wrote songs with Brian Wilson, collaborated with Curt Boettcher on the sunshine pop sound, and produced three classic albums by The Byrds. Snuff Garrett was responsible for the hit sound of Gary Lewis & The Playboys, and helped nurture the talents of studio-arranger Leon Russell. Jimmy Webb wrote, arranged, conducted, and played on numerous records by The Fifth Dimension, Richard Harris, and Glen Campbell. Mike Curb created soundtracks for a number of Sunset Strip teen exploitation movies of the time. Shel Talmy learned his trade in LA before moving to England in 1963 and producing The Who, The Kinks, and The Creation.

RCA engineer Dave Hassinger was a primary catalyst in putting psychedelia on record, and the link between 'Eight Miles High,' 'Satisfaction,' 'I Had Too Much To Dream Last Night,' and Jefferson Airplane's *Surrealistic Pillow*.

Four local producers stand out above the rest. Phil Spector is, without a doubt, the most celebrated record producer of the 20th century. Between 1958 and 1966, Spector made maximum use of the studio as an instrument in itself. He hit Number 1 at the first attempt with his own group The Teddy Bears' 'To Know Him Is To Love Him' before moving to New York City to work under the noted songwriting team of Jerry Leiber and Mike Stoller. (By sheer coincidence, Spector, Leiber, and Stoller were all born in New York, had all moved to Los Angeles's Fairfax district with their families at a young age, and by 1960 were now all back in NYC working together.)

As an apprentice to Leiber & Stoller, Spector played lead guitar on The Drifters' 'On Broadway,' co-wrote 'Spanish Harlem' for Ben E. King, and gained valuable production experience on 'Every Little Breath I Take' by Gene Pitney, 'Corrina Corrina' by Ray Peterson, and 'Pretty Little Angel Eyes' by Curtis Lee. In late 1961, while still in Manhattan, he discovered The Crystals and founded the Philles label with Lester Sill—the 'Les' to Spector's 'Phil.'

After The Crystal's debut, 'There's No Other (Like My Baby),' hit the *Billboard* Top 20, Spector returned to Los Angeles to produce the follow-up. There he began to develop his Wall Of Sound production style on 'Uptown' and on sessions with The Ronettes, a group of former backing vocalists for Joey Dee who quickly became Philles' second success story with 'Be My Baby' (1963). Two further Crystals hits, 'He's A Rebel' (1962) and 'He's Sure The Boy I Love' (1963), featured vocals by Darlene Love, who subsequently had Philles hits in her own right such as 'Today I Met The Boy I'm Gonna Marry.'

As The Ronettes, The Crystals, Darlene Love, and Bob B. Soxx & The Blue Jeans continued to have hits, it became evident that the label's real star was its producer. The singer on a Phil Spector record was, in most cases, merely the *talent*. Also key to the Philles successes, however, were the arrangement skills of Jack Nitzsche and a largely New York-based pool of songwriters led by Jeff Barry and Ellie Greenwich.

In creating the Wall Of Sound, Spector was influenced by producer Frank Guida, who had lent an air of ecstatic aural chaos to Gary US Bonds' 'Quarter To Three,' which sounded like it had been recorded in the middle of a crowded rock'n'roll party. Spector built on this 'crowded sound' concept, using LA's best session musicians to create a more controlled, multilayered cacophony that always built up to a sweet release. Philles Records' completely immodest but totally accurate billing for these advancements in technique was "Tomorrow's Sound Today."

Philles brought The Ronettes a string of hits that made them, alongside The Shangri-Las, the toughest, coolest act of the girl-group era. The group had four Top 40 hits in 1964: 'Baby I Love You,' 'The Best Part Of Breaking Up,' 'Do I Love You,' and 'Walking In The Rain,' which earned Spector a Grammy Award for 'Best Use Of Sound Effects' of all things. Some of Spector's best work with the group was never released during the 1960s, notably the majestic 'I Wish I Never Saw The Sunshine.' Ronettes sessions became major art projects for Spector; the group's Veronica Bennett would later become Mrs Spector.

Phil Spector kept close tabs on the mid-1960s scene on Sunset Strip. Philles released *Lenny Bruce Is Out Again*, while Spector himself did everything he could to support Bruce during his many brushes with the law. He produced several major hits for The Righteous Brothers, worked with The Modern Folk Quartet, and was an early champion of Harry Nilsson's songwriting talent. He then scored *The Big TNT Show* and created what he considered to be his masterwork, Ike & Tina Turner's 'River Deep Mountain High' (1966).

By this stage, however, Spector's cavalier attitude had provoked a jealous backlash within the music industry. Although it did well in the UK, 'River Deep Mountain High' was blackballed on US radio, and stalled at a lowly Number 88 on *Billboard*. That, coupled with The Righteous Brothers' defection to Verve, led Spector to phase out Philles (which was now completely under his control). He retreated from the public eye for several years, only returning in 1969 when invited to co-produce The Beatles by John Lennon and George Harrison (both of whom he later worked with as solo artists). That year also marked the release of his fitting farewell to the 1960s, 'Black Pearl' by The Checkmates.

Philles Records made 'one-sided' singles—that is, the A-side was meticulously crafted, while the B-side tended to be a throwaway instrumental, named for the shoeshine man outside the studio ('Brother Julius') or the musicians that played on it ('Nino And Sonny—Big Trouble'). The neatly crafted A-sides were anticipated like jewels by fans and deejays alike. As a result the label had an unprecedented hit rate: of the 36 singles released by Philles, 21 made the

Billboard Top 20. Making records as monumental as cinemascope movies, Phil Spector brought the studio and the producer to the fore. In the wake of his groundbreaking experiments came The Beach Boys' ambitious *Pet Sounds* and The Beatles' elaborate *Sgt Pepper's Lonely Hearts Club Band*.

The arranger behind the Philles hits, Jack Nitzsche, has his own legacy of superb hits and misses for a wide variety of labels. Whereas Spector's heavily compressed Wall Of Sound aimed for a direct intensity, Nitzsche's orchestration was more spacious and fantastical. Nitzsche took the grandiose sweep of Spector's records and spread the sound out to envelop the listener in a swarm of profound mood elevation. The effect was closer to Mozart's chamber music than the concentrated, Wagner-esque command of Spector.

Nitzsche had his first hit in 1959 with 'Bongo Rock' by Pandora's Box mainstay Preston Epps before going on to produce great girl-group sides for Yolanda & The Charmaines ('There Oughta Be A Law'), Yolanda & The Castanets ('Meet Me After School') in 1962, and the original, Merry Clayton version of 'It's In His Kiss' a year later. By 1964 he had really hit his stride, arranging a rock'n'roll ballad, 'Move Over Darling,' for Doris Day plus The Marketts' noisy hit 'Out Of Limits,' Karen Verros's echo-laden freak-out, 'You Just Gotta Know My Mind,' and Jackie DeShannon's masterful *Breakin' It Up On The Beatles Tour*.

Nitzsche also made instrumental singles under his own name. 'The Lonely Surfer' was a hit in 1963, while a follow-up, 'The Last Race,' became part of his soundtrack to the 1965 garage-punk movie *Village Of The Giants*. (This led, eventually, to further, memorable movie score work, notably 1970's *Performance* and 1975's *One Flew Over The Cuckoo's Nest*.) All the while he continued to make rock'n'roll records, maintaining a pretty high batting average on records such as Donna Loren's orchestrated take on 'Call Me,' Lou Christie's magnetic 'If My Car Could Only Talk,' and Bob Lind's 'Elusive Butterfly,' which pre-empted the hit sound of Glen Campbell.

Taken as a whole, Jack Nitzsche's combined output comes close to what Brian Wilson achieved on *Pet Sounds*—a lofty claim, and one no other producer could make; but one also that it is hard to deny of a body of work that includes 'Jill' by Gary Lewis, 'What Am I Gonna Do With You' by Lesley Gore, 'Daddy You Just Gotta Let Him In' by The Satisfactions, 'My Good Friend' by The Paris Sisters, 'I Miss My Surfer Boy Too' by The Westwoods (actually The Honeys in disguise),

'Expecting To Fly' by Buffalo Springfield, 'The Porpoise Song' by The Monkees, and Jackie DeShannon's great 'Baby That's Me,' as recorded by The Cake.

The only reason that Jack Nitzsche is not widely held in the same regard as Phil Spector or Brian Wilson is that his work has never been compiled, definitively, in any long-playing format. His 45s came out on an endless stream of labels, making it difficult now for them to be compiled together. Nitzsche was not one for the album-rock, one-label mindset—for which we can be glad, as it resulted in a wonderfully diverse (if rather disorganized) catalog.

Brian Wilson has finally received his due as a record producer, thanks largely to the belated international appreciation for *Pet Sounds*—which was always considered as a benchmark release in the UK, but took time to reach that level of opinion in the USA—and his recent return to his *Smile*-era material. At the core of all of Wilson's work is a fascinating talent for arrangement. His application of the notation of 1950s' abstract-jazz vocals to instrumental arrangements saw him create a web of complex sound topped off with imaginative singing.

Like Nitzsche, Wilson took Spector's Wall Of Sound and gave it breathing room. In between recording The Beach Boys' early material he cut girl-group records for The Honeys (one of whose vocalists, Marilyn Rovell, he later married) and Sharon Marie, and then applied the same ideas to a male vocal group on The Castells' 'I Do.' Wilson took on a mature, country & western groove for Gary Usher's 'Sacramento' (1964), while his production of Glen Campbell's 'Guess I'm Dumb' a year later inspired the singer's later work with Jimmy Webb.

By 1965 Brian Wilson's work with The Beach Boys had begun to reach a level of Spectorian glory on records such as *The Beach Boys Today* and 'California Girls.' He stopped undertaking outside productions soon after that to concentrate on *Pet Sounds*, before reaching his peak as a producer on 'Good Vibrations' and the *Smile* project. Sessions for that album broke down before it could be completed, but led Wilson to discover the charms of minimalism on the oft-overlooked *Friends* (1968). Years after Wilson's mid-1960s purple period, he is now recognized as the patron saint of the neo-sincerity movement.

Although he is rarely discussed in the same light, Lee Hazlewood was no less spectacular a producer. This is confirmed by a quick listen to his duet with Nancy Sinatra, 'Some Velvet Morning' (1966), which becomes all the more striking when you consider that the song was cut live, without any tape splicing (for proof, just listen to the way the ride cymbal carries through the changes).

Hazlewood kicked off his career a decade earlier in Arizona, producing Duane Eddy and Sanford Clark. Eddy was rock'n'roll's single most important instrumental performer. Alongside Link Wray, he set the tone of the genre—a tone that he developed with Hazlewood on 1958's 'Rebel Rouser.' It was on rockabilly sides for Sanford Clark, such as 'The Fool' (1956), that the roots of what Hazlewood later brought to Nancy Sinatra's records can be heard. Somewhere in that rockabilly depth lies the comfort zone for a second great Sinatra voice.

Hazlewood's music is much more western than country. He and Duane Eddy came out to Los Angeles from Arizona during the late 1950s to make use of the echo chamber at Gold Star Studios. There he met a young Phil Spector, who was using the same studio to develop an entire sound-world of his own. Spector subsequently made a trip to Hazlewood's studio in Arizona, and then cut a Duane Eddy-esque guitar instrumental 45 of his own, 'Bumbershoot,' as Phil Harvey on Imperial Records. He also poached saxophonist Steve Douglas, a key player on the Duane Eddy records, and formed Philles with Lester Sill, a business partner of Hazlewood's.

In 1963 Hazlewood started working for RCA, which enabled him to take advantage of the most elaborate studio in Hollywood and bring his warm sound to its logical peak. He gave a few of his songs at this point to a group called The Astronauts, who turned them into some of the most important surf records ever made: 'Baja,' 'Movin',' and 'Surf Party.' Hazlewood kept his ear to the ground, signing Texas Garage group The Kitchen Cinq to his own LHI label for an album called *Everything But …* . LHI also issued psychedelic LPs by Aggregation (*Mind Odyssey*) and The Surprise Package (*Free Up*), as well as the first album to feature Gram Parsons, *Safe At Home* by The International Submarine Band (which was, in fact, essentially a Parsons solo album).

Around the same time, Hazlewood began an association with the vocal trio of Dino, Desi & Billy. His collaboration with Jack Nitzsche, 'I'm A Fool,' gave the group a hit during the summer of 1965, which was followed into the charts by two Hazlewood solo compositions, 'The Rebel Kind' and 'Not The Lovin' Kind.' These drew the attention of Reprise Records' chief Frank Sinatra—his fellow Rat Packer, Dean Martin, was the father of the group's Dino—whose idea it was for Hazlewood to work with his daughter, Nancy.

Nancy Sinatra had been making 45s for several years but wasn't able to step out of her father's shadow until she started working with Lee Hazlewood. Nancy

& Lee produced a string of hits that only ended when they stopped working together after three years. Hazlewood's 'These Boots Are Made For Walkin'' as recorded by Nancy Sinatra is without doubt one of the most iconic singles of the 1960s, and defines the overriding female fashions on the Strip at the time—a West Coast take on the mod look. Hazlewood had written the song with the intention of singing it himself, but Sinatra made it her own.

The chart-topping 'Boots' was followed by a run of Hazlewood-produced solo albums by Nancy Sinatra and duets by Nancy & Lee. Highlights of this period include the acid-laced 'Sugar Town' and 'Some Velvet Morning,' as well as 'Sand,' 'Summer Wine,' 'Jackson,' and 'This Town.' In the midst of this, Hazlewood put together the soundtrack to *The Cool Ones*, a strange but affectionate take on the go-go moment. Between this and his work with Sanford Clark, Duane Eddy, The Astronauts, The Kitchen Cinq, Gram Parsons, and Nancy Sinatra, a full reassessment of Hazlewood's talent and overall contribution to popular music is definitely in order.

CHAPTER NINE

Folk rock is a beautiful thing

" *Bruce and I came to Los Angeles in an old hearse to, uh, we were gonna be stars. [We] were just about to leave, and I saw [Stephen Stills] in a van going the other way on Sunset, and he stopped me, and we stopped, and we all stopped, and then we started.* **"** NEIL YOUNG, *AMERICAN BANDSTAND*

Every day after school in 1965–66, kids would turn on the television set at 3:30pm to catch Dick Clark's ambitious ABC television show, *Where the Action Is*. The concept of the show was that, wherever you were in America, there were fun things to do, cool places to do them in, and cool bands to keep you entertained. You'd see The Four Seasons singing 'Rag Doll' to a girl in Central Park, The Four Tops hosting a patio party with 'Reach Out (I'll Be There)' at the Roostertail club on Lake Michigan, and The Knickerbockers rolling around in the pool at the entrance to Pacific Ocean Park, singing The Beatles' 'Help!'

The main theme to *Where The Action Is*—'Action,' sung by Freddy Cannon— was a huge hit on AM radio in 1965. Its most rousing stanza left no doubt as to "where the action is," declaring: "Let's go to the place on the Sunset Strip!" Sunset Strip had become the nerve center for teenage America, not just the Greater Los Angeles Area. Dick Clark's offices were right across the street from Phil Spector's, and both were just a few doors down from GNP-Crescendo Records and the 9000 Building, a hub of music publishers and small labels, as well as The Byrds' fan club and rehearsal room. World Pacific and A&M were just down the road.

The story of how Buffalo Springfield formed right on the street itself, passing in cars after separate 3,000-mile treks across the continent, is emblematic of the Strip's magic at this time. The excitement of any out-of-town kid taking their first cruise through the hub of mid-1960s American rock'n'roll must have been palpable—but exponentially more so when those kids are musicians serendipitously encountering lost friends from Ontario, Canada and New York

City. That is exactly how Buffalo Springfield formed, after stumbling upon each other on Sunset Strip.

Stephen Stills and Richie Furay were both late arrivals to the Greenwich Village folk scene. Furay recalls arriving in New York in 1964, disappointed to find that the folk scene was, in fact, "over." He did, however, form a nine-member group—"seven guys and two girls"—named The Au Go-Go Singers for a cafe situated across the street from the Bitter End, called Cafe Au Go Go. "That's basically where I met and got to know Stephen," says Furay. "We were pretending all the way that folk music was still happening."[1]

After recording one album, *They Call Us Au Go-Go Singers* (Roulette Records, 1964), the group split, and Stills took some of the band-members on a tour of Canada, where he met Neil Young. "He told Neil: 'Go on down to New York, Richie's down there,'" Furay continues. Stills was already on his way to Los Angeles by this stage, but Young did meet Furay in New York, where the pair worked on an embryonic version of Young's tune 'Nowadays Clancy Can't Even Sing.' Furay also traded songs around this time with Gram Parsons (about whom he later wrote 'Crazy Eyes'), who was then on a similar search for the end of the vanished folk rainbow—as were musicians such as John Phillips and Peter Tork. Some of them would soon head west to follow the clarion call of The Byrds at Ciro's. They would not be disappointed.

Neil Young came from more of a rock'n'roll background. He'd previously made records with a surf band called The Squires and, after cutting folk demos for Elektra Records in New York, returned to Ontario to play with a hard-edged, interracial rhythm & blues group, The Mynah Birds. The group signed to Motown in early 1966 and had cut nearly a dozen tracks for the Detroit label before frontman Ricky James Matthews—who later became famous as funk singer Rick James—was busted during a recording session for draft evasion (which is why he'd been in Canada).

Neil Young had become involved with The Mynah Birds after a chance meeting with their ace bass player, Bruce Palmer. The group fell apart after Matthews's arrest, at which point Palmer and Young decided to head for Los Angeles, partly in the hope of finding Stephen Stills. "By 1966, I knew I had to leave Canada," notes Young, "and the sounds I was hearing and the sounds I liked were coming from California."[2] Richie Furay was still in New York at this point, but was soon invited in a letter from Stills to join a new band in California.

When he got there, however, Furay recalls: "It was just me and him. I looked around and said: 'Oh brother, here I go, what have I done now?'"[3]

It was around the time that Furay, Young, and Stills were drifting in and out of New York that The Lovin' Spoonful were rising to a prominence with a new brand of folk-rock in the city. As such, it's no stretch to hear the group's influence on the sound of Buffalo Springfield, particularly in terms of their guitar tone. After their chance encounter on the Strip, Stephen Stills and Neil Young would refine their sublime guitar-interplay at Gold Star Studios in Hollywood on a finished version of 'Nowadays Clancy Can't Even Sing' (which Young had first taught to Furay in New York, and Stills had subsequently learnt from Furay before Young's arrival in Los Angeles).

Richie Furay recalls his and Stills's meeting with Young in LA with enthusiasm. "We got caught in the old Sunset traffic, and this hearse with Ontario license plates pulled up beside us. Stephen knew that Neil had a hearse, and we both knew he was from Ontario. We maneuvered our way through traffic and pulled up beside, and, unmistakably, there was Neil behind the wheel."[4] After three separate westbound journeys, these drifting minstrels had fused together right at the center of Sunset Strip, in the parking lot outside Ben Frank's– the very place where Love had formed—flanked by the Trip, the Playboy Club, the Sea Witch, and Dino's Lodge.

Stills and Furay immediately invited Young and Palmer to form a band; an accomplished, professional drummer, Dewey Martin, joined a few weeks later. Martin had previously played with country singer Faron Young, and with rockabilly acts Roy Orbison, Carl Perkins, and The Everly Brothers. He had also cut singles as a vocalist with Sir Raleigh & The Coupons, and had recently worked on electric sessions with The Dillards. His love of rhythm & blues, meanwhile, would later provide the drum hook on 'For What's It Worth,' which Martin copped from Lee Dorsey's 'Get Out Of My Life, Woman.'

After a mere week of rehearsals, Buffalo Springfield played their first gig at the Troubadour's Folk Den on April 11th 1966. Chris Hillman was in attendance, and booked the group to open for The Byrds four days later at the Swing Auditorium's Orange Showgrounds in San Bernardino. Hillman also helped the group secure a six-week residency at the Whisky A Go Go, where they immediately became LA's hottest new band. By all accounts, the group's live act was more powerful and upbeat than their records (a view supported by early demos such as 'Baby Don't Scold Me,' 'Neighbor Don't You Worry,' and 'We'll See,' all included on the 2001 *Buffalo Springfield* boxed set).

Richie Furay has fond memories of the Whisky A Go Go engagement. "When we started, nobody knew who we were," he says, "and when we finished … they were lined around the block, literally."[5] Stephen Stills agrees: "I wish someone had been recording those concerts live. Because by the fourth or fifth concert we were so good it was absolutely astounding, and the first week at Whisky a Go Go was absolutely incredible. We were just incredible, man, that's when we peaked. After then, it was downhill."[6]

It's imperative to understand the contrast between the raucous, three-guitar attack of Buffalo Springfield's live shows and the gorgeous interplay of those same guitars on record. The group was as adept at multilayered noise as delicate, ornamental sounds. Their hastily produced debut, *Buffalo Springfield*, emphasizes the latter, delivering soulful songs that evoke The Beatles' *Rubber Soul*.

The *Buffalo Springfield* sessions at Gold Star Studios in 1966 were like an attempt to capture lightning in a jar. Neil Young and Stephen Stills had more than enough great songs to fill out the debut album, at the expense of an excellent Richie Furay number, 'My Kind Of Love,' which features a guitar solo so muted that it could well be a loosely tuned banjo swathed in echo. The mystery in Buffalo Springfield's music came from counter-melodies that seemed to flow through the listener. Stills and Young were as melodic in their playing as they were in their songwriting; as dreamy and romantic as flamenco guitar from Spain or the mandolin sounds emanating from Italy.

Among the highlights of *Buffalo Springfield* is the way Richie Furay's echo-drenched, angelic voice fits around Neil Young's melodies on 'Flying On The Ground Is Wrong' and 'Do I Have To Come Right Out And Say It.' Stills's 'Sit Down I Think I Love You' became a hit for The Mojo Men the following year, complete with a Van Dyke Parks keyboard part, while 'Everybody's Wrong' delights in the relaxed atmosphere of the West Coast in 1966: "Those of us who run to catch a moment in the sun/Find out when it's done that we weren't supposed to run."

When the Sunset Strip riots shook the LA rock'n'roll scene in late November, Atco Records quickly released Buffalo Springfield's 'For What It's Worth' as a single. The song's commentary on police violence and the abuse of teenagers struck a nerve, and sent it to Number 7 on the *Billboard* chart. It was then tacked onto the moderate-selling *Buffalo Springfield* and gave the album a significant sales boost.

A wealth of similarly superb tracks were left in the can during Buffalo Springfield's initial creative burst in mid 1966 but are important signifiers of the group's identity at the time. These include the flowing country jazz of Stills's 'Pretty Girl Why' and Young's 'Down To The Wire,' which he later used to open his *Decade* anthology. 'So You Got A Lover' offers an early glimpse of Stills's fine solo acoustic guitar work, while other tracks, such as 'Buffalo Stomp (Raga),' 'There Goes My Babe,' and 'Sell Out,' are rumored to have been intended for a quick second album, dubbed *Stampede*, that was ultimately never released. (As with the group's early demos, many of these *Stampede* tracks feature on the 2001 boxed set.)

In June 1967 Buffalo Springfield followed 'For What It's Worth' with the double A-side 'Bluebird'/'Mr Soul,' which hit Number 2 in LA but stalled at 58 nationally. By this stage, however, the group was in disarray. This unraveling had begun during the political unrest of late 1966, during which time Bruce Palmer was arrested for marijuana possession (under circumstances that suggested he'd been framed). In trying to defend Palmer, Neil Young was arrested, incarcerated, and, allegedly, physically abused. According to Buffalo Springfield's road manager, Dickie Davis, Young had to be taken to hospital after his release from jail. "That's when the wars against the police began," says Davis. "That's when they became pigs."[7] After this, Palmer fell into a cycle of deportations and illegal returns to Los Angeles. Young, meanwhile, began to be hampered by epileptic seizures, which abated only after Buffalo Springfield disbanded.

Young first left Buffalo Springfield in May 1967, but rejoined the group in August, only after the group had performed at the Monterey Pop Festival with a replacement guitarist, Doug Hastings of The Daily Flash, and David Crosby filling in the vocal harmonies. During his break from the band, Young arranged 'The Daily Planet' for Love's *Forever Changes*, and made his first steps toward a solo career in sessions with Jack Nitzsche, with whom he cut 'Whisky Boot Hill,' 'Slowly Burning,' 'Falcon Lake (Ashes On The Floor),' and 'Expecting To Fly.' While only the last of these four songs was released on vinyl, it is an apt indication of what could be achieved when Young's songwriting and guitar textures met Nitzsche's chamber-pop Wall Of Sound.

Jack Nitzsche and Neil Young's ethereal recording has an interesting parallel in The Monkees' movie *Head*. Nitzsche produced the music for the opening sequence, which serves as a logical artistic follow-up to 'Expecting To Fly.' After jumping from the Vincent Thomas Bridge between Long Beach and San Pedro,

Mickey Dolenz is enveloped in a psychedelic underwater world to the sound of Nitzsche's production of Goffin & King's siren-like 'The Porpoise Song.' Later in the movie, Dolenz's voice on 'As We Go Along' is draped in a web of Springfield-esque guitar (played by Neil Young, Ry Cooder, Carole King, Ken Bloom of the Lewis & Clarke Expedition, and Danny Kortchmar). The accompanying imagery is similar to that used later in Easy Rider to the sounds of The Byrds' 'Wasn't Born To Follow' (another Goffin & King number).

These musical landscapes became fully realized when Neil Young rejoined Stills, Furay, and co to make *Buffalo Springfield Again*. Furay contributes the reflective 'Sad Memory,' on which his acoustic guitar and vocal are set against Young's subtle electric guitar, which hovers beneath the song like flowing tears. Young's previously released 'Mr Soul' evokes the rambling confusion of Sunset Strip nightlife with a guitar line lifted from The Rolling Stones' 'Satisfaction.' 'Bluebird' is positively overflowing with guitar overdubs—"11,386 of 'em," according to the liner notes. Stephen Stills finds the missing link between jazz and fuzz on 'Everydays,' and evokes the dreamy tempo changes of The Mamas & The Papas on 'Hung Upside Down.' His 'Rock'n'Roll Woman,' a tribute to Grace Slick, was inspired by David Crosby, who scat-sang a hookline similar to the ones he lent to The Byrds' 'Renaissance Fair' and CSN's 'Guinnevere.' The closing note of 'Rock'n'Roll Woman' echoes like a spinning silver spur. (Young achieved this effect by loading his guitar with vibrato sustain, accented by a tremolo bar, and turning down the frequency rate on his amplifier as the tone began to fade.)

Taken as a whole, *Buffalo Springfield Again* amounts to a full realization of the group's potential. Released a year before The Beatles' diverse *White Album*, it feels like more than just a collection of solo tracks by the various songwriters (even if that, ultimately, is what it is). A telling hint of the band's imminent demise lies in the liner notes, however—Bruce Palmer, whose immigration problems were mounting, plays bass on only half of the songs. Palmer's role within the group was crucial, and not just in terms of his basslines, which were often as complementary to the music as the layered guitars of Young and Stills. When the songwriters in the group began to butt heads, Palmer cooled the quarrels. But his continuous deportations made it impossible for him to remain in Buffalo Springfield. He was replaced, briefly, by engineer and surf instrumental whiz Jim Messina, but the end was nigh.

In a general sense, 1967 was so filled with ups, downs, drop-ins, fade-outs, and changes of direction that the momentum of 1966 seemed like a distant memory. Buffalo Springfield managed to hold it together until March 1968, but a marijuana bust in Topanga Canyon—which snared Furay, Young, and Eric Clapton—was the final straw. Tired of the many obstacles in their way, Buffalo Springfield threw in the towel.

Buffalo Springfield were only active for two years, from April 1966 to May 1968. (Richie Furay considers it to have been even less time, making the distinction that they were "only a *group* for the first seven, eight months.") By the time they folded, says Furay, "folk music was now gone. But we were [basically] folk singers with a backbeat." The group did, however, leave an important legacy, not least on their own future endeavors. The debut albums by Crosby, Stills & Nash, Poco, and Neil Young are essentially extensions of *Buffalo Springfield Again*. David Crosby revised the scat-singing of 'Rock'n'Roll Woman' on CSN's hit 'Suite: Judy Blue Eyes," and Furay continued in a Springfield style with Poco (members of whom also play on Young's Jack Nitzsche-produced solo debut).

After the split came *Last Time Around*, a collection of leftover singles and out-takes. Somewhat ironically, *Rolling Stone* magazine found this to be Buffalo Springfield's finest album, citing Jim Messina's 'Carefree Country Day' as the best track. A more fitting testament to *Last Time Around*, however, is that in an era beginning to be dominated by extended jams and other excesses, this was an album of good, short songs—such as Young and Furay's jazzy 'It's So Hard To Wait,' Stills's Latin jazz-styled 'Pretty Girl Why,' Furay's carnival-esque 'Merry Go Round,' and Young's wry 'I Am A Child.' The album is bookended by its strongest tracks. The opener, Young's 'On The Way Home,' was a Number 5 radio hit in LA, but again failed to make an impression nationally—perhaps surprisingly, given its full-blown pop production, complete with vibraphone, strings, and horns. The closing 'Kind Woman,' Richie Furay's best known song, sets honky-tonk piano against a lonesome pedal-steel part played by Rusty Young of the Colorado group Boenzee Cryque, who had been introduced to the group by Randy Meisner of The Poor.

Like Buffalo Springfield, The Poor found a subtle beauty in minimalist guitar work. They released four singles, cropped up on the soundtrack to *Hell's Angels On Wheels*, and appeared in the television detective show *Ironside*. Laced through their records is that same chiming, tremolo guitar sound that brought such a stunning close to Buffalo Springfield's 'Rock'N'Roll Woman.' What set The Poor apart were their complex harmonies, which were dominated by bassist Randy Meisner, whose vocal range was similar to that of The Hollies' Graham Nash.

The Poor were discovered by talent scout Barry Friedman, who also brought Buffalo Springfield and Kaleidoscope to prominence in Los Angeles. Originally from Denver, the group was briefly known as The Soul Survivors, but changed their name as a result of the conditions they lived in upon their arrival in California. "There were five people living in a one-bedroom place, sleeping on the floor," says Meisner. "We used to sell *The Los Angeles Free Press* on corners so that we could eat."[8] All six band-members contributed to the group's pioneering vocal sound—Meisner, guitarists Allen Kemp and John Day, guitarist/pianist Randy Naylor, keyboardist Veeder Van Doren, and drummer Pat Shanahan.

The Poor's October 1966 debut single, 'Once Again'/'How Many Tears' captures the group in a smooth, upbeat groove. The better-known follow-up, 'She's Got The Time (She's Got The Changes),' was a local hit, and was later covered in the pop art style by a British group called The Afex. The original is driven by Meisner's throbbing bassline and the powerful momentum of the vocal. Next came the slow, pounding 'My Mind Goes High,' while a year passed before Decca issued 'Feelin' Down,' a more intense take on the psychedelic bounce of The Turtles' 'Happy Together.'

Shortly after 'Feelin' Down' came out, Buffalo Springfield's Richie Furay and Jim Messina asked Meisner to join their new group, Poco. Alongside Dillard & Clark, Linda Ronstadt & The Corvettes, and The Flying Burrito Brothers, Poco were at the forefront of a whole new folk-rock scene that was focused around The Troubadour in the aftermath of the Sunset Strip era.

* * *

Way back in 1964, and long before all of this, a new duo by the name of Caesar & Cleo put together a stage act at the Purple Onion, backed by regular house band Pat & Lolly Vegas. This was a long time coming for the man then dubbed Caesar, but better known today as Sonny Bono. Bono worked at Specialty Records during the 1950s, which afforded him the opportunity to absorb rock'n'roll at its source. Then, in the early 1960s, he worked as a runner for Phil Spector, from whom he picked up two things: the various production techniques of the Wall Of Sound and an ear for talent, notably that of a certain Cherilyn Sarkisian LaPiere, a wallflower backing vocalist on The Ronettes' 'Be My Baby.'

At the time, numerous one-shot 45s aped the sound of Spector's landmark recordings, such as The Orchids' 'Ooh Chang A Lang' and The Girlfriends' 'My One And Only Jimmy Boy.' Bono had the benefit of being an insider, so was able to give an authentic Wall Of Sound paint-job to 'Dream Baby,' the debut single by Cherilyn, which came out just prior to Bono's collaboration with Jack Nitzsche on Jackie DeShannon's proto-folk-rocker, 'Needles And Pins.'

In early 1965 Sonny & Cher—as they were now known—broke out of from the Purple Onion with a medium-sized hit, 'Baby Don't Go.' They continued the role of poor, downtrodden lovers on the follow-up, which became their most important record together: 'I Got You Babe,' which, with its unbreakable human spirit, touched the same nerves as had songs such as 'Side By Side' and 'Yes, We Have No Bananas' in the 1930s.

Sonny & Cher have taken numerous critical knocks over the years. As Sonny Bono became a force to be reckoned with in the pop world, his sincerity came into question. That his own vocalizations were lifted from Bob Dylan became apparent in his solo records of the time, such as 'Laugh At Me' and 'The Revolution Kind,' but just as influential to this were the 1950s stylings of Louis Prima and Keely Smith. Sonny played the hammy, goofball Italian, while Cher became the pretty, torch-singing 'Indian Girl.' The genius of Bono's presentation was the way he mixed Louis & Keely with Spector and Dylan. His mastery of folk-rock was clear on the backing track for Cher's first solo hit, a 1965 cover of Bob Dylan's 'All I Really Want To Do' that builds from calliope-like 12-string guitar into a hypnotic river of sound, complete with incessant bassline and rapturous, mantra-like beat. The following year's 'Bang Bang (My Baby Shot Me Down)' was an even bigger hit that peaked at Number 2 on the *Billboard* Hot 100.

What made Sonny & Cher seem insubstantial was the combination of their over-the-top embrace and exaggeration of the latest Carnaby Street fashions and an apparent lack of commitment to the folk-rock movement at large. Cher even dismissed the poetry of the age in *Teen* magazine, claiming: "Politics and pop music don't mix. Does Barry McGuire have the qualifications to talk about politics? … I think there has been just too much protesting. Maybe there are a lot of problems in the world, but it seems like an OK place to me." (Cher's attitude must have changed fairly soon after that, as she would take part in the sit-in protests at Pandora's Box that evolved into the Sunset Strip riot.)

Sonny & Cher records did, however, inspire an internal thoughtfulness, and caused their huge radio audience to consider previously overlooked issues. 'The Beat Goes On' (1967) illuminates societal contrasts in a similar way as would The Temptations' 'Ball Of Confusion.' Cher's 1967 solo single, 'You Better Sit Down Kids,' addresses the hardships brought on by love, divorce, and responsibility, while her expressive vocal on Burt Bacharach's movie theme of the previous year, 'Alfie,' questions the brave new world of free love and discovery. The aspirations on these records might not be as lofty or direct as those expressed by The Byrds or The Mothers, but they helped bend the general public's ear to the concerns of youth culture.

Sonny Bono made a point of meeting and greeting The Rolling Stones on one of their 1965 visits to Los Angeles. The group took a dim view of Bono to begin with, believing Sonny & Cher to be something of a joke. Their condescension was unfounded, however, and diminished when Bono revealed that they had covered one of his songs, 'She Said Yeah,' on the UK version of their recent *Out Of Our Heads* LP. (Bono had written the song under the pseudonym Sonny Christy while working at Specialty.)

Sonny & Cher might have draped themselves in kooky outfits, but by posing as honeydew lovebirds they were able to win over those for whom The Mothers and their ilk were far too outrageous. Sonny & Cher were harmless; their songs couldn't and wouldn't stop any wars, but by expressing love as a matter of trans-generational importance, they in fact set the stage for subsequent arty endeavors by John & Yoko. "It's the little things that mean a lot," sang Cher in the duo's movie, *Good Times*, surrounded by a montage of pop art paintings on the walls of It's Boss.

What Sonny & Cher had to offer rings true with the soul of the 20th century like a glockenspiel on top of the Wall Of Sound; the implicit message being that love will overcome. This was at a time when the youth rebellion had begun to oppose the negativity of war with Ghandi-like, non-violent innocence. Just as when protesters put flowers into the barrels of militia rifles, breezy records by The Association and The Mamas & The Papas seemed to offer positive alternatives.

The Mamas & The Papas took traditional folk harmonics and added pop orchestration, a rock'n'roll beat, and early hippie overtones (not to mention some serious LSD-25). By bringing in elements of bossa nova, lounge-jazz, fuzz-toned guitars, and parlor music arrangements, The Mamas & The Papas—like Sonny & Cher—managed to win over a cross-generational audience. This came as more and more people were beginning to understand for the first time the objective necessity of opposing elected officials tied in with corporate lobbyists and the Military Industrial Complex. The drums of Spector's main man, Hal Blaine, had already powered Simon & Garfunkel's leap beyond mainstream folk. Now the West Coast seemed ripe for a similar crossover.

The Mamas & The Papas of 1965 added a fourth voice and rock'n'roll instrumentation to the three-part harmony style of Peter, Paul & Mary. Their dense, folk-rock-meets-Tin Pan Alley recipe gave birth to the entire flower-power sound. The songs and arrangements of John Phillips filled the airwaves with earnest ideals and pretty voices that beckoned a sympathetic ear to the timeless idealism of youth.

Like The Beach Boys' early hits, 'California Dreamin'' felt to Los Angeles teenagers like an anthem when it was released in early 1966. It spoke for a lot of people who saw LA as the escape hatch from an ancient world and its ancient values. 'Go Where You Wanna Go,' meanwhile, epitomized the subconscious freedom that The Mamas & The Papas seemed to evoke. There was a boldness in the way Michelle Phillips (John's wife) sang of how people "don't understand that a girl like me can't love just one man." These were strong words, but she meant them. Michelle Phillips was a genuine free spirit, and when she wasn't helping her husband write songs, she was certainly inspiring them.

The graceful male tenor on The Mamas & Papas came courtesy of Denny Doherty, while Cass Elliot provided bolting strength and feminine dignity. Her voice wasn't far, at times, from the torch singers of the 1940s, which was useful to the group's cross-generational appeal. She sang The Beatles' 'I Call Your Name' in full ragtime mode, giving the song a context that couldn't be dismissed by doubting traditionalists, and repeated the trick (in reverse) with folk-rock adaptations of songs by Rodgers & Hart. She gave John Phillips's 'Words Of Love' a similarly vintage twist, before reaching the apex of her Broadway vocal appeal on a beautiful rendition of 'Dream A Little Dream Of Me.' This clearly signaled an oncoming solo career, which brought Cass widespread popularity during the final days of vaudeville-like television variety shows in the late 1960s and early 70s. Cass Elliot became a network TV regular, and a Las Vegas headliner.

The Mamas & The Papas' knack for surprising arrangements was not limited to old-school appeal. They were also adept at quizzically stoned takes on great rhythm & blues songs, notably their Michelle Phillips-sung take on The Shirelles' 'Dedicated To The One I Love.' The group's albums are loaded with interesting John Phillips material such as the hazy, dream-like 'Look Through My Window,' the straight-ahead 'Somebody Groovy,' the acid-drenched 'Strange Young Girls,' a pacifist reaction to the Sunset Strip Riots ('Safe In My Garden'), and an homage to the natural utopia the group then found in Laurel Canyon, 'Twelve Thirty (Young Girls Are Coming To The Canyon).'

Some of these songs formed part of a string of massively popular hits, including 'Monday Monday,' 'I Saw Her Again,' and the autobiographical 'Creque Alley,' which tells the story of the group's interaction with members of The Lovin' Spoonful and others back in New York City and their subsequent shift to Los Angeles. (Cass Elliot, for example, brought with her Jim Hendricks, with whom she sang in The Big Three. Upon arriving in LA, Hendricks formed Lamp Of Childhood, with whom he recorded the sweeping, orchestral 'First Time, Last Time' and the Kinks-like, tack piano-driven 'Two O'Clock In The Morning.')

The Mamas & The Papas' musical bed was made by Hollywood's best studio musicians under the direction of producer-impresario Lou Adler. Their gentle, graceful vocal arrangements were often complemented by Larry Knetchel's harpsichord and piano playing, Peter Palafain's electric violin, or the flute and woodwind flourishes of Jim Horn or Bud Shank.

The group used their fame and wealth to become pied pipers of a new, self-aware generation. John and Michelle Phillips bought a glamorous mansion in Laurel Canyon that had once been owned by the actress Jeanette MacDonald and turned it into a Xanadu for pop stars passing through (and partying in) Hollywood. (Laurel Canyon became home to numerous stars of the time, including Jim Morrison, Frank Zappa, and The Turtles' Mark Volman, who recalls: "My neighbors became the history of rock'n'roll, and each one of their names is also the foundation of stories that fill me with endless memories. ... We knew these creative people as 'family.'")

It was here too that the Phillipses helped instigate and arrange the 1967 Monterey Pop Festival, an event that will forever stand as a demarcation point in 20th century music. With police harassment systematically crimping LA's music scene, they and Lou Adler wisely focused their energies elsewhere. They understood all too well the strengths of their opponents, so shifted the Summer Of Love north.

As heavily as The Mamas & The Papas involved themselves in the freedom movement of the time, they were still happy to play songs such as 'Got A Feelin''—described in the liner notes of their own debut LP as "feathery"—at Monterey. One positive offshoot of their unashamedly sweet, flower-power pop sound was the subsequent emergence of The Fifth Dimension, who hit big with 'Up, Up, And Away,' 'Go Where You Wanna Go,' 'Aquarius/Let The Sunshine In,' and a host of others.

As The Fifth Dimension shot up the charts, band-members Billy Davis Jr, Florence LaRue, Lamonte McLemore, Marilyn McCoo, and Ron Townson were often criticized for sounding too "white." In the context of the rest of the group's history, however, their adoption of a breezy, pop sound was far from surprising. This was a group that had previously failed to chart with singles produced by Barry White at Bronco Records (back when they were known as The Versatiles) or with hard soul cuts issued by Johnny Rivers' Soul City Records. 'Train Keep On Moving' and 'Too Poor To Die' were big, Motown-style productions—they sounded great, but went nowhere.

When The Fifth Dimension heard a demo of 'Up, Up, And Away' by Jimmy Webb (who had previously been hawking his songs to Tamla Motown's Jobete publishing company), they immediately picked up on the song's infectiousness. But when they lent their harmonic strength to this undeniably 'pop' song, some members of the black community were not best pleased; Gil Scott Heron even deigned to note that the revolution "will not be written by Jimmy Webb" in his seminal 1970 record/poem 'The Revolution Will Not Be Televised.' What The Fifth Dimension's critics failed to realize was that, whereas Motown operated under strict parameters, black music in 1960s Los Angeles reflected a far more diverse palette, which took in everything from Richard Berry and The Olympics to Sam Cooke, Love, The Rising Sons, Brenda Holloway, Billy Preston, The Afro Blues Quintet Plus 1, Señor Soul, The Watts Prophets, and many more. Color had little to with The Fifth Dimension's music, or to groovy records such as 'Stoned Soul Picnic.'

For all their counter-cultural trappings, The Mamas & The Papas were not dissimilar, musically speaking, from The Association. This unassuming group was integral in pioneering the airy, sunshine pop sound unique to Los Angeles with a consistent stream of hits. While The Byrds had previously drawn on traditional folk harmonies and The Beach Boys had taken influence from vocal jazz, The Association were distinct in that they grafted both of these elements—and Stan Kenton's progressive jazz arrangements—onto their rock'n'roll sound.

The Association's hybrid sound was further developed by Curt Boettcher, who produced their debut album, *And Then … Along Comes The Association* (1966).

Boettcher had already attempted a similar blend of folk and Brian Wilson-style vocal experiments with his own group, The GoldeBriars, but his productions of The Association's 'Along Comes Mary' and 'Cherish' were the defining influence on sunshine pop.

The Association rose to prominence in Pasadena, one of the oldest and most traditional townships of the Los Angeles area. (In his book, *Los Angeles: The Architecture Of Four Ecologies*, Reyner Banham notes: "The stand-offish independence of Pasadena has become almost proverbial.") The group first settled, locally, at The Ice House, a straight-laced folk/comedy club located just off Colorado Boulevard that also played host to Bob Lind, Hearts & Flowers, and The Deep Six. Various members of The Association had originally made the trek out to Troubadour in 1964, where they formed part of The Men, dubbed "the first folk-rock chorus and orchestra" by the club's proprietor, Doug Weston. The Men—13-strong to begin with, according to bandleader Terry Kirkman— played in the main room of the club while The Beefeaters (who subsequently became The Byrds) performed in the front room, then known as the Folk Den.

From this large aggregation came the original line-up of The Association: multi-instrumentalists Terry Kirkman and Jim Yester, guitarists Gary Alexander and Russ Giguere, bassist Brian Cole, and drummer Ted Bluechel. The sextet released the stirring, garage-folk-rock single 'Babe I'm Gonna Leave You' in the fall of 1965 before signing to Valiant Records for the Dylan cover 'One Too Many Mornings,' which they performed on *Hollywood A Go Go*.

Valiant Records then suggested The Association work with Curt Boettcher who, post-GoldeBriars, had been playing in a shortlived folk-rock duo, Summer's Children, and a group called The Ballroom. All three were the beneficiaries of his unusual experiments in vocal arrangement, which seemed to combine earthy, oceanic, and outer-space sounds. Boettcher is also said to have unintentionally influenced Brian Wilson during the spring of 1966. Wilson was finishing up *Pet Sounds* when he heard a voice cutting through the walls of the studio, draped in echo and oscillator effects; a sound like that which he should be aiming for (and would, on *Smile*). The voice was Boettcher's, and featured on his production of Lee Mallory's 'That's The Way It's Gonna Be,' which was being recorded in the same building.

Boettcher already knew the group, as they were all part of the same scene at the Ice House. Boettcher had also sung the original demo of 'Along Comes Mary,' which The Association's Gary Alexander played on. It was included on one of two albums of demo songs written by Tandyn Almer for the Davon Music publishing company. The first of these, *Davon Music Catalog*, focused on folk material, and features the vocal talents of Linda Ronstadt. The second, *New Songs Of Tandyn Almer*, has more of a straight-ahead folk-rock feel. Curiously, given the quality of the material, most of these songs were not picked up, although Mr Lucky & The Gamblers cut 'Alice Designs' (which was essentially an LSD-themed follow-up to the marijuana-laced 'Along Comes Mary'), and both The Garden Club and the British group Peter & The Wolves recorded versions of 'Little Girl Lost And Found.' According to Terry Kirkman, Davon Music introduced lots of "valuable things: Mason Williams, Ed Ruscha, The Smothers Brothers, Tandyn … All of these people were part of this *community*."

'Along Comes Mary' provided The Association with the perfect debut hit in 1966. It was catchy, but also had the requisite underground credentials. The Stan Kenton-meets-folk vocal sound of The Association was the perfect match for Boettcher's playful talents. The immediate success of this and 'Cherish,' a Terry Kirkman composition to which Boettcher added his own ethereal vocals, afforded the group the opportunity to appear a number of times on *The Smothers Brothers Comedy Hour* and at the Monterey Pop Festival.

There were many other Association songs of note, including 'Pandora's Golden Heebie Jeebies,' a poetic farewell to Pandora's Box from their early 1967 album, *Renaissance*. The same year's *Insight Out* features the massive hits 'Windy' and 'Never My Love,' while the anti-Vietnam War song 'Requiem For The Masses' set Mozart-inspired singing against a military beat. The hit single 'Everything That Touches You' followed in 1968, and is included on the glorious psychedelic LP *Birthday*. After recording the soundtrack to *Goodbye Columbus* in 1969, the group returned to their folk roots on *The Association*, which seemed to court the growing country-rock movement. It's worth taking the time to discover each of these records and their dynamic blend of sophisticated naiveté.

After helping to establish The Association's sound on their early hits, Curt Boettcher moved on to other projects with a newfound reputation as one of LA's hottest producers. He gave Tommy Roe's era-defining smash hit 'Sweet Pea' its blend of innocence and warped garage organ, and ghost-produced the excellent self-titled LP by Eternity's Children. In late 1966 he began to work with Gary Usher in a studio group called Sagittarius. They had already cut the excellent

45 'My World Fell Down' (which features vocals by Glen Campbell and Bruce Johnston) before Boettcher joined and lent his talents to the rest of the superb *Present Tense*. Sagittarius evolved into The Millennium, whose band-members included three-fifths of The Music Machine.

Boettcher's various harmony-driven projects highlight what David Crosby would later refer to as the penchant for "cross-pollination" in Los Angeles (which, in Crosby's case, included collaborations with Buffalo Springfield and Jefferson Airplane, as well as the formation of Crosby, Stills & Nash). This sense of musicians helping each other to achieve visibility was, at times, the most enriching aspect of the LA scene. The very nature of The Association was emblematic of this, as band-member Jim Yester once told Dick Clark on *Where The Action Is*. The group's name, according to Yester, came from thumbing through the dictionary until they found "something that said exactly what we were, and that was 'a group of individuals united toward a common goal.'"

This unselfish attitude first became apparent when, before The Beach Boys had hit Number 1 on their own, Brian Wilson gave 'Surf City' to Jan Berry. Wilson even sung the crucial falsetto lines on the Jan & Dean chart-topper himself, thereby flouting all sorts of record company policies and music industry 'morals.' Despite the angry response from both his label and his overbearing father, Wilson pulled this stunt again and again, as his 'Drag City,' 'Dead Man's Curve,' 'New Girl In School,' and 'Ride The Wild Surf' all became hits for Jan & Dean. What Wilson realized, even if those around him didn't, was that, by getting his ideas out on more than one front, he was feeding the public's interest and keeping his sound alive. This same idea reached its pinnacle within the various interconnected circles of folk-rock, most notably in the game of musical chairs played by The Byrds and Buffalo Springfield.

The environment in which this music was made resulted in a lot of it focusing on the good feeling generated between people. These ideas reverberated throughout the listening public, who enjoyed records such as 'Good Vibrations' in a spirit that best represented the 1960s as a whole. There was nothing wrong with feeling good about The Association's 'Windy' when you could feel the purity of the time and mood in which it was created. Another Association song, 'Never My Love,' written for the group by Dick and Don Addrisi, was recently certified as the second most-played BMI song of all time—behind The Beatles' 'Yesterday'—and has been covered over 300 times.

The Addrisi Brothers had recorded for Del-Fi Records in 1959, hitting and then missing in the LA area with 'Cherrystone' and the brilliant 'It's Love.' One of their most important (albeit lesser-known) songs from 1965 is 'That's When Happiness Began,' which was recorded, brilliantly, by LA's The Grains Of Sand and the UK group The Montanas. The Addrisi Brothers also wrote the excellent theme to the television dance show *Malibu U* for Harpers Bizarre, while their 1969 theme to *Nanny And The Professor* epitomized sunshine pop. Terry Kirkman notes: "Don [Addrisi] was one of the best melody writers, and had an incredible gift for voicing harmonies to the music that he wrote. He didn't just write a song—he wrote a whole sound."

In the wake of The Association's success, the Ice House connection had an immediate effect on the fortunes of The Deep Six. They cut an album for Liberty that overlapped with The Association's penchant for quirky arrangement, harpsichord, and harmony. 'What Would You Wish From The Golden Fish' and the hit 'Rising Sun' are driven by neat, fuzzy guitar and keyboards by session player Mike Rubini, a forgotten hero of many of LA's flower-power records. The Deep Six's first steady engagement was at a San Diego coffeehouse called Land Of Oden, at which folk-rock had just begun to transcend traditionalist stylings.

The same spirit of cross-pollination drove The Palace Guard, The Gene Clark Group, and The Merry-Go-Round. As house band at the Hullabaloo, The Palace Guard played hot cover versions of *Rubber Soul*-era Beatles nuggets such as 'Paperback Writer' and 'Nowhere Man,' and, like Paul Revere & The Raiders, wore uniforms that made them seem like folk-rock redcoats. The group was fronted by 14-year-old David Beaudoin with his brothers, John on harmony vocals and tambourine, and Don on guitar. A 15-year-old Emitt Rhodes played drums, with the line-up rounded out by lead guitarist Chuck McClung and bassist Rick Moser. The group backed singer and actor Don Grady on his 1965 single 'Little People' before striking out on their own (Grady was later backed on 'The Children Of St Monica' and 'Impressions With Syvonne' by The Greefs, and was an incognito member of The Yellow Balloon).

The Palace Guard then cut several great, jangly sides for Orange Empire and Parkway Records. 'All Night Long' was a local hit, featuring a stripped-bare production by Jack Nitzsche and fun, lightweight lyrics. The follow-up, 'Like Falling Sugar,' swept the listener away with a raw, yearning lead vocal complemented by fading, cascading harmonies. It made enough local noise to be picked up by Verve for national release. This was something of a problem for the Hullabaloo, however, which—despite featuring such groups as The Byrds, The Yardbirds, The Everly Brothers, and Jan & Dean—had no replacement house band to draw in the teenybopper audience. An engagement by Neil Diamond was met with two nights of empty seats. The Palace Guard were important to the club in the sense that they sustained a consistent audience; like The Knickerbockers at the Red Velvet, they were locked into a contract at the Hullabaloo that made it difficult for them to promote their hits outside Hollywood.

Hot singles by the group did continue to appear including an early version of David Gates's 'Saturday's Child'—which later featured on *The Monkees*—as well as 'A Girl You Can Depend On,' the raga-stomper 'Greed,' and a cool, Bob Marcucci-produced version of Claudine Clark's 'Party Lights.' But rather than being compiled as an album, these singles were primarily sold at the Hullabaloo memorabilia booth—which also offered Palace Guard sweaters, jackets, windbreakers, T-shirts, mugs, and glossy photos—further stifling any possibility of widespread success. The group did have one unforgettable moment in the spotlight, however, when they performed in front of what seemed like the entire pop world—including Bob Dylan, Mick Jagger, James Brown, Herb Alpert, The Byrds, The Beach Boys, Ike & Tina Turner—as the opening act at the KRLA Beat Awards (held at the Hullabaloo). Lead vocalist David Beaudoin recalls performing Buddy Holly's 'True Love Ways' from a small, raised stage at the event: "I was dressed in my crisp, red, tailored Palace Guard uniform. A spotlight hit me. With Don's one strummed guitar chord, I immediately started singing … in a deep tone of voice, a-cappella style. … I felt like I was the president or something."[9] Not bad for a 14-year-old kid in a garage band.

Few could claim to have mingled with as many other musicians as Gene Clark in the late 1960s. Leaving The Byrds in early 1966 gave him the perfect opportunity to establish himself as the first major group star to go solo in the 1960s, and to collaborate with whoever he chose. (Of the split, he says: "In cases like The Beatles and The Rolling Stones, they had more of a direction. They'd been together longer [and had] already [been] through their hard knocks and come up the ladder slowly. [The Byrds] were only together eight months when we were on top of the heap, and I don't think we were ready to handle it as well." All subsequent attempts at a reunion, according to Clark, have failed because of there being "too may chiefs and no Indians.")

Clark began his solo career with a series of gigs at the Whisky A Go Go, for which he was joined by various local folk-rock players: Chip Douglas of The Modern Folk Quartet on bass, The Leaves' Bill Rinehart on guitar, and Joel Larson of The Grass Roots—who would later play in The Merry-Go-Round—on drums. For his debut solo album, Clark called in the cream of the scene: Doug Dillard, Clarence White, Vern and Rex Gosdin, Bill Rinehart, Van Dyke Parks, Glen Campbell, Earl Palmer, Leon Russell, Jerry Cole, and his old rhythm section, Chris Hillman and Michael Clarke. The Gary Usher-produced single 'Echoes' received a fair amount of airplay in LA, but its dark, poetic stylings passed over the head of the mainstream audience.

Released in early 1967, *Gene Clark With The Gosdin Brothers* stands alone in its successful embrace of country & western within the dynamic and rhythmic setting of folk-rock. 'Needing Someone,' 'Think I'm Gonna Feel Better,' and 'So You Say You Lost Your Baby' in particular have a great energy and bounce to them. The Gosdin Brothers went on from these sessions to cut singles of their own with various Clark alumni, including Rinehart, Hillman, Clarke, and White. Their 'One Hundred Years From Now,' 'Hangin' On,' 'No Matter Where You Go (There You Are)' (all 1967) and *Sound Of Goodbye* (1968) are all valuable early examples of proto-country-rock.

Gene Clark went back into the studio in early 1967 with the intention of cutting a quick second album, but this never saw the light of day. 'The French Girl,' 'Only Colombe,' 'Los Angeles,' 'That's Alright By Me,' and a cover of Dylan's 'I Pity The Poor Immigrant' took over 30 years to come out of hiding; eight further tracks, including the excellent '7:30 Mode' and 'Past Once,' have emerged in more recent years. During the 1960s, these songs were only heard as performed by other artists: West Virginia (by way of Los Angeles) group The Rose Garden (who had a *Billboard* Top 20 hit with 'Next Plane To London') recorded a couple, as did Blow Up star David Hemmings.

* * *

For a time, the blending of folk-rock and Beach Boys-style harmonies seemed to color everything in pop culture. The Turtles were particularly guilty of this on their theme tune for a Pepsi ad, 'Pepsi Pours It On,' while Don Knotts's hilarious movie *The Love God?*—apparently based on *Playboy* chief Hugh Hefner—includes a scene featuring Darlene Love & The Blossoms backed by a nameless, Association-style band. The theme tune to the long-running game show *To Tell The Truth* was another example of how completely sunshine pop had permeated the era.

Two of the most dedicated sunshine pop acts, The Yellow Balloon and The Parade, were studio concoctions more than they were proper nightclub groups. Songwriter-producer Gary Zekley was behind the success of The Yellow Balloon. His song 'Yellow Balloon' was first recorded by Dean Torrence—who was still at this point recording as Jan & Dean after a serious car accident had left Jan Berry incapacitated—but Zekley wasn't happy with the results, so recorded another version with studio stars The Ron Hicklin Singers, who had sung on countless 45s by everyone from The Monkees and Frank Sinatra to Elvis Presley and The Chipmunks. The Ron Hicklin Singers were, in fact, to pop and rock'n'roll what The Randy Van Horne Singers were to Esquivel, Martin Denny, and *The Flintstones'* theme tune. Both groups sang on numerous television ads produced in Hollywood during the 1950s and 60s.

Like The Grass Roots, The Yellow Balloon were formed to fill the shoes of a hit record that had been made under an assumed name. To his surprise, however, Zekley happened to unearth Don Grady, a talented songsmith who would write the next two Yellow Balloon singles, the sunny 'Good Feelin' Time' and the Left Banke-esque 'Stained Glass Window.' The group's lone, self-titled album is full of classic Zekley material such as 'How Can I Be Down' and 'Can't Get Enough Of Your Love,' which brought the sound of The Beach Boys' transitional 1965 single 'The Little Girl I Once Knew' into the environment of 1967.

The Parade, on the other hand, were the brainchild of singer, songwriter, and record producer Jerry Riopelle, a former Phil Spector understudy responsible for the brilliant Bonnie & The Treasures single 'Home Of The Brave' (1965). Riopelle and Gary Zekley collaborated on an unreleased Ronettes song, 'Close Your Eyes,' which they then re-recorded with Bonnie (of The Treasures). Riopelle and Zekley then produced the magical 'Baby Baby It's You' for The Group, who had earlier performed 'The Fun We Had' as The Ragamuffins and 'Summertime Summertime' as Our Gang. (The name 'The Group' came from a contemporary play, which was advertised by a go-go girl announcing: "They called me little Lolita."

In 1966 Riopelle recorded a demo of 'Sunshine Girl' with a couple of friends. The song was released under the name The Parade by A&M, who financed a series of additional 45s when it became a hit in March 1967. 'This Old Melody' is space-age, Beach Boys-meets-rustic folk, 'She's Got The Magic' a pulsating romp, and 'Kinda Wasted Without You' has a perfect Turtles bounce. The only repeat hit for The Parade, however, was the sweetly insistent 'She Sleeps Alone' (1968). Riopelle subsequently became a staff producer at A&M; his short, sharp, Chicano-style arrangement of 'Suzie Q' for Shango was a cool if somewhat opportunistic AM radio hit in 1969 (Creedence Clearwater Revival's extended version already had FM radio covered).

The intermingling of folk-rock and Beach Boys harmonies eventually became a genre unto itself: psychedelic surf pastiche washout. The surf boom was clearly over, but its lingering imagery and sound informed and brightened the folk-rock era. This spawned some oddball singles, such as The Giant Jellybean Copout's 'Awake In A Dream,' which pits Hendrix fuzz against a Brian Wilson-like falsetto, and The Full Treatment's 'Just Can't Wait.'

Just as The Beatles and The Byrds exchanged ideas, several groups in Europe—where *Pet Sounds* and 'Good Vibrations' were worshiped much more reverently than in the USA—contributed similar sounds. British groups such as The Fenmen, the amusingly named Californians UK, The Robb Storme Group, Orange Bicycle, and Tony Rivers & The Castaways all took off from this psych-surf pastiche. Swedish group The Tages, meanwhile, were an effective integration of The Who and Brian Wilson. In the USA, the sound was virtually defined by The Cowsills' 1967 hit 'The Rain, The Park, And Other Things' and its follow-up, 'We Can Fly' (1968). Produced by Artie Kornfeld (who was also responsible for the 1969 Woodstock festival), the Newport, Rhode Island group was the real-life inspiration for *The Partridge Family*.

The work of these non-Californian artists amounted to perhaps the best exploration of what Brian Wilson started with *Pet Sounds* and *Smile*. These are records of unparalleled splendor that can be considered among the most joyous outpourings of the 20th century. They are imbued with a shimmer and sunny disposition that came from Los Angeles's reflection of light, which itself had been most evident in the wake of the surfing craze. Pop artist David Hockney moved to LA from England in order to infuse his work with that light, while countless television commercials of the time exploited the same feel in both sound and vision.

From right within the House Of Beach Boy, Jan & Dean were veering in this direction when writer/producer Jan Berry suffered a near-fatal car crash in early 1966 near Dead Man's Curve, just west of the Strip on Sunset Boulevard. In a cruel twist, Jan & Dean had hit the charts two years earlier with 'Dead

Man's Curve,' a song written about a drag race through Sunset Strip. The hit version changed the word "Strip" to "street," but the original recording—which featured Brian Wilson on falsetto backing vocals—is full of Sunset Strip flavor and includes lines such as "I flew past La Brea, Schwab's, and Crescent Heights/ And all that they could see was my French taillights/They passed me at Doheny and I started to swerve." The same sentiments were echoed by The Beach Boys' 'I Get Around.'

Jan & Dean's transition into the groovy sounds of the mid 1960s wasn't exactly smooth. Their first attempt, *Folk & Roll* (1965), was extremely shaky and tinged with inappropriately right-wing values. Although his girlfriend and collaborator, songwriter and model Jill Gibson (who briefly replaced Michelle Phillips in The Mamas & The Papas during Phillips's affair with Gene Clark), was thoroughly liberal, Berry maintained a Republican perspective. Of his 'The Universal Coward,' a response to Donovan's 'Universal Soldier,' Gibson notes: "I almost died when he wrote that. It was so reactionary. That song embarrassed the hell out of me."

Jan & Dean's association with the masterful P.F. Sloan served them better. Their versions of his 'I Found A Girl' and 'Where Were You When I Needed You' helped rebuild their stricken credibility. After making the comedy album *Jan & Dean Meet Batman* the duo threw themselves headlong into psych-surf. Berry produced backing tracks for flower-power pop songs such as 'Fan Tan,' 'Girl You're Blowing My Mind,' 'Love And Hate,' and 'Hawaii,' which was colored by the sound of a sitar. With this new type of material, and a planned pre-*Monkees* TV show, *Jan & Dean On The Run*, the duo hoped to return to their 1963–64 level of popularity.

Before they could put this plan into action, however, disaster struck. On his way back from a military recruitment office on April 12th 1966—having been called up by the draft board—Jan Berry "lost control of his sports car and crashed into a parked truck," according to *The Los Angeles Times*. The *Times* report notes that Berry, who as well as being half of a rock'n'roll hit-machine was also a UCLA medical student, had suffered a fractured leg a few months earlier during the shooting of a movie, *Easy Come, Easy Go*. The movie, like *Jan & Dean On The Run*, was never completed.

With Berry in a coma, Dean Torrence took it upon himself to try to keep Jan & Dean alive. *Save For A Rainy Day* was, essentially, a solo album. Gary Zekley provided the two key tracks, 'Like A Summer Rain' and 'Yellow Balloon;'

Torrence also reworked and added new vocals to a recording he'd made with Zekley in 1965, 'Summertime Summertime.' When Jan Berry began to regain some of his health one year after his accident, an array of sympathetic session men pitched in to help Berry finish the songs he had started in 1966, among them Hal Blaine and Glen Campbell, who by now was a hit artist in his own right. The resulting songs, such as 'Mulholland' and 'Carnival Of Sound,' show that Jan & Dean were on the right track before having to take an unfortunate, forced hiatus. (*Carnival Of Sound* was finally issued in 2010.)

Another group of the time, The Sunrays, had a similarly direct connection to the originators of the surf vocal sound. They began as a rock'n'roll dance band, Gary & The Cardigans, with Gary Zekley as the lead singer. They recorded surf instrumentals, hot-rod songs, and garage cuts under various names before being taken under the wing of Murry Wilson—who had recently been fired as manager of his sons' band—to give The Beach Boys some 'competition.' The group's summer 1965 hit 'I Live For The Sun' summed up and bade farewell to the genre encapsulated by The Beach Boys' *All Summer Long*. Several other hot hits and cool misses followed, including 'Andrea,' 'Don't Take Yourself Too Seriously' (both from 1966), and 1967's 'Time (A Special Thing).' After The Sunrays demise, frontman Rick Henn teamed up with Brian Wilson to record the long-unreleased Beach Boys cut 'Soulful Old Man Sunshine' (1969).

Like Gary Lewis & The Playboys, Dino, Desi & Billy were given a huge head start by their familial connections. The band-members were, respectively, the son of Dean Martin, the offspring of Hollywood stars Lucille Ball and Desi Arnaz, and a talented neighbor, Billy Hinsche, whose father was a successful real-estate developer. After being 'discovered' at a 'jam session' at the home of Dino Sr, the trio were signed to Frank Sinatra's Reprise label. With production by Lee Hazlewood and Jack Nitzsche and an enormous promotional budget, their 1965 single 'I'm A Fool' was a sure-fire hit. Where similar groups such as The Bantams and TJ & The Fourmations had to make do with a spot in rock'n'roll movies such as *The Cool Ones* (which Hazlewood scored), Dino, Desi & Billy made use of their music industry contacts to land an appearance on *The Ed Sullivan Show* (and a gig at It's Boss).

Despite their rather nepotistic route to fame, Dino, Desi & Billy did end up with a few great tracks to their name, such as the Spector-meets-fuzz-punk of 'The Rebel Kind' (1965) and a version of Baker Knight's analysis of the Sunset Strip scene, 'She's So Far Out, She's In' (1966). Both are hilarious—and successful—

takes on the folk-punk idiom, complete with 12-string Rickenbacker and a wash of teen angst. With session players such as guitar men Barney Kessel and Billy Strange and drummer Hal Blaine in tow, records such as 'Please Don't Fight It' were guaranteed to sound good, while the backing vocals on the Turtles-like 'I Hope She's There Tonight' are a dead ringer for those of Brian and Carl Wilson.

Dino, Desi & Billy's appearance at the Beach Boys Summer Spectacular at the Hollywood Bowl in 1965 held a lot of meaning for the group, who worshiped their hometown heroes much more than they did The Beatles. It also began a highly beneficial association with The Beach Boys, which became even closer when Carl Wilson fell in love with, and eventually married, Billy Hinsche's older sister, Annie. (He later married Dino's sister, Gina Martin, too, but never found time to embark on a relationship with Desi's sister, Luci.) Brian Wilson was involved in the production of Dino, Desi & Billy's *Friends*-like 1968 single 'Tell Someone You Love Them,' and wrote their 'Lady Love' (1970). While many groups of the time simply stole The Beach Boys' harmony arrangements, Dino, Desi & Billy were occasionally given them first-hand, and clearly benefited from this, peaking on later works such as 1969's ethereal 'Spray Colored Glasses.' Hinsche later became part of the touring Beach Boys group around the time of their *Holland* album.

There were numerous other, less successful exponents of the psychedelic surf sound in the Los Angeles area. Unknown elsewhere, Joey Paige became a Beatles-esque teen idol in LA with his Spector-meets-folk sound. 'That Don't Mean That I Don't Love You' and 'Goodnight My Love' were both local favorites in 1965–66. Paige also holds the distinction of being the guy who first showed The Rolling Stones around Los Angeles, having met the group in the UK while playing bass in The Everly Brothers' touring group. The Hard Times, meanwhile, moved from San Diego to Laurel Canyon in 1966 after landing a slot on *Where The Action Is*, and promptly cut an LP for World Pacific, 1967's *Blew Mind*, that ranges from beachside ballads and bubblegum to dark, garagey mood pieces and the US hit 'Fortune Teller.' The group's psychedelic flavor came from the interaction on their records of keyboards, vibes, and mandolin.

Folk-based pop groups continued to come out of the woodwork, among them The Peppermint Trolley Company, best known for recording the theme song for the first season of *The Brady Bunch* in 1969. Described by rock'n'roll historian Ken Barnes as being "kinda folk, kinda rock, kinda soul," the group originated from Redlands and played on the Strip in 1965–66, but had their greatest success in 1968 with 'Baby You Come Rolling Across My Mind,' which hit Number 59 on the *Billboard* Hot 100. A defining influence for the group was P.F. Sloan's 'Lollipop Train,' which they covered and released as a single.

* * *

Flower-power pop records might sound incredibly dated to some, and it would be hard to justify a group such as The Sunshine Company in a modern context. But their 'Happy' remains an unparalleled encapsulation of the positive outlook of the 1960s. The Sunshine Company got their start at the Mecca, an Orange County folk club, before becoming the main pop project of producer Joe Saraceno. The group's albums are loaded with jumpy, jangly excursions such as 'Love Is A Happy Thing' and 'Back On The Street Again.' (By contrast, Saraceno's other projects of the time took in garage rock, psychedelia, and the brilliant 'No Matter What Shape Your Stomach's In,' a surfy instrumental credited to The T-Bones and based on a television ad for Alka-Seltzer.)

The Ashes were a band in constant transition during 1966 and 1967. They began with a heartfelt, folk-roots take on the flower-pop sound on songs such as 'Dark On You Now,' which subsequently became a hit, in a more upbeat arrangement, for The Love Exchange, who renamed it 'Swallow The Sun.' The major talent in The Ashes was vocalist Sandi Robison, the wife of Brain Train/ Clear Light's Robbie Robison. The group's minimalist jangle was the perfect foil for her clear vocal style, which was best exemplified by a version of Jackie DeShannon's 'Is There Anything I Can Do?'

Robison subsequently took six months of maternity leave from the group, during which time drummer Spencer Dryden left to join Jefferson Airplane. On her return, Robison led a reconfigured group, which included members of Sea Witch house band The Crossing Guard and was given a new name, The Peanut Butter Conspiracy. This new group recorded the dynamic raga-folk-punk single 'Time Is After You' before signing to Columbia Records for the buoyant, Gary Usher-produced hit 'It's A Happening Thing' in early 1967.

'It's A Happening Thing' was swiftly followed by an album (marketed with bumper stickers) called *The Peanut Butter Conspiracy Is Spreading*. Gary Usher seemed at this time to be somewhat overstretched, however—he was simultaneously involved in records with The Byrds and Sagittarius. The Peanut Butter Conspiracy were never satisfied by this album or its successor, *The Great*

Conspiracy, but others were: Mike Stax, the compiler of the *Nuggets* boxed set, describes the "melodic pop sheen" Usher provided as being "undeniably effective" in the way it gave a textured backdrop of "inventive guitar melodies and vibrant percussion" to the group's "rich, folk-based harmonies."

Another group in this vein, with similarly high aspirations, were The Gentle Soul, formed by singer-songwriters Pamela Polland and Rick Stanley in 1966. Their songs were recorded by The Rising Sons and The Byrds ('Tulsa Country' on *Ballad Of Easy Rider*), but the group's own warm, melodic records were perhaps too subtle for radio. Neither of their 1967 singles for Columbia Records, 'You And Me' and 'Our National Anthem,' were hits. The group then moved to Epic—a subsidiary of Columbia—and recorded the little-heard but unquestionably beautiful *The Gentle Soul* (1968). The album is full of spacious acoustic guitars, tabla, harp, cello, and close male/female harmonies. It features Van Dyke Parks on harpsichord and Larry Knechtel on organ, with sonically diverse guitar interplay provided by Ry Cooder and Mike Deasy and improvisational flute by bebop-jazzman Paul Horn. There is nothing remotely commercial on the album, just great, flowing folk-pop.

Similarly warm-sounding on record were The Stone Poneys, whose name came, according to vocalist Linda Ronstadt, from "leafing through an old blues record catalog"[10] in about 1964. She and guitarists Bobby Kimmel and Kenny Edwards eventually settled on the name of a Charley Patton record, 'Stone Poney Blues.' It took some time for the group to catch a break, but when they did, it was somewhat fortuitous: their singing was heard by a couple of guys "who were having lunch across the street … and immediately wanted to become our managers," says Ronstadt.

The Stone Poneys' cut a Mike Curb-produced, folk-rock single for Mercury Records, 'So Fine'/'Everybody Has His Own Ideas,' in 1966, that remained unreleased while the group was still active. They then signed to Capitol, who wanted to turn the trio into a West Coast Peter, Paul & Mary. The soft-focus cover of *The Stone Poneys* (1967) shows Ronstadt, Edwards, and Kimmel in a stained-wood, antique living room decked out with tiffany lamps; the sporadic highlights of the record itself include versions of Fred Neil's 'Just A Little Bit Of Rain' and Linda Albertano's '2:10 Train.'

The group eventually worked their way up, through stints at various smaller venues, to playing at the Troubadour, although, Ronstadt notes, "Kenny [Edwards] was always an Ash Grove hanger-outer, [and] there was always a sort of bubbling rivalry between the more ethnic Ash Grovers and the rather more commercial Troubadour set."[11] For their first performances at the Troubadour, the group was erroneously listed in *The Los Angeles Times*, somewhat amusingly, as The Stoned Ponies.

A second album followed before the end of 1967. *Evergreen Vol II* was a marked improvement on *The Stone Poneys*, with producer Nick Venet taking a leaf out of the *Pet Sounds* guide to record production. The album jacket was rendered, fittingly, in a similar green to those used on the covers of recent landmark LPs *Mr Tambourine Man*, *Rubber Soul*, *Sounds Of Silence*, and *Pet Sounds*.

Evergreen Vol II is informed both by light-hearted, optimistic pop and serious, indignant folk. The title track is a wavering, lilting dream sequence that leads into a sitar-laden space-out, while a reading of Pamela Polland's 'I'd Like To Know' stands out as a pop masterpiece, and sheds a different light on the songwriter's work with The Gentle Soul. Ronstadt notes that her group sought out "the most interesting songwriters of the period," citing Steve Gillette, Tom Campbell, and Jackson Browne among others. The group hit their stride on a song by Mike Nesmith, 'Different Drum,' which gave the group their first hit and helped Nesmith in his pursuit of artistic credibility. Ronstadt had first heard the song on a record by The Greenbriar Boys, who, says Ronstadt, "made three albums for Vanguard [that] really influenced The Stone Poneys. I used to listen to their singer, John Herald, a lot … I was really impressed by his vocal delivery and phrasing."[12]

The Stone Poneys were part of a superb bill at the Santa Monica Civic Auditorium on September 29th 1967 that also starred Love, The Strawberry Alarm Clock, and Spirit, and toured the northeast briefly with The Doors. By 1968 Capitol Records had begun to focus their attentions almost exclusively on Ronstadt, leading Kenny Edwards to quit the group and form a new band of his own, Bryndle. *Stone Poneys & Friends Vol III*—and a version of Laura Nyro's 'Stoney End' in particular—foreshadows Ronstadt's imminent solo career, but is kept interesting by the inclusion of Mike Nesmith's 'Some Of Shelly's Blues' and three Tim Buckley Songs. Kimmel and Edwards contribute some material, but this was clearly the Linda Ronstadt show. She is alone on the front cover, while the back features a great shot by Henry Diltz of a gathering of post-Sunset Strip friends—Bruce Palmer, Tim Buckley, Bernie Leadon, and others, all sat on Ronstadt's porch—that predates his iconic photograph on the cover of *Crosby, Stills & Nash* (1969).

Capitol Records had thrown themselves heavily into the folk-rock game by this stage. Marketed in conjunction with The Stone Poneys were Hearts & Flowers, another group that focused on a warm acoustic guitar sound. The key figure in the group was Larry Murray, who was originally part of Chris Hillman's San Diego-based bluegrass group, The Scottsville Squirrel Barkers. A joint Capitol Records advertising campaign for Hearts & Flowers and The Stone Poneys called them "flower children gently bringing songs of love and happiness" and offered free posters of either or both groups to anyone who wrote in.

The validity of the music was never in question. The first Hearts & Flowers album is in the same vein as *Evergreen Vol II*, right down to the Nick Venet production and green album cover. Larry Murray duets with Linda Ronstadt on a version of Carole King's 'Road To Nowhere,' while on Hoyt Axton's '10,000 Sunsets' he makes the grandiose statement that he'd trade in his whole life if he could be like Jesus for one single day. Another highlight is an intriguing, off-time reading of Marty Cooper's 'View From Ward Three.' According to Ronstadt, "nobody was doing country-rock" at the time, apart from these two groups. "I was sure it could cross over and take off," she says. "But like I say, nobody believed it."[13]

That would, of course soon change, but not in Hearts & Flowers' lifetime. The group's lone hit was a rendition of 'Rock'N'Roll Gypsies' by Roger Tillison of the folk-rock duo Gypsy Trips. The song became an immediate anthem for Sunset Strip kids during that uncertain, post-riot moment when people were trying to keep the scene alive. The second Hearts & Flowers album, *Of Horses, Kids, And Forgotten Women*, has a more light-hearted feel, and features the vocal and instrumental talents of Bernie Leadon, who played with Murray and Chris Hillman in The Scottsville Squirrel Barkers and would later co-found the Eagles. The album includes the carnival-like pop of 'Color Your Daytime,' which evokes Buffalo Springfield's 'Merry Go Round,' the swirling psychedelia of 'Ode To A Tin Angel,' and a reading of Arlo Guthrie's 'Highway In The Wind' that seems to predict the oncoming culture of the road (which would soon consume the flower-power scene). There are sad overtones throughout Hearts & Flowers' music, which perhaps explains why 'Rock'N'Roll Gypsies' appears on both of their LPs, declaring: "The rock'n'roll gypsies are ridin' tonight / On the carnival strip they play / for tomorrow will soon be yesterday."

CHAPTER TEN

Some other
kinds of bands

" *[The] scene was so intense, nobody could take their eyes off it for long; it was like a magical kaleidoscope that kept changing, each knock of the chips more fantastic and amazing.* **"** EVE BABITZ, *EVE'S HOLLYWOOD*

The youth of Los Angeles were brought together by an absurdist, camp sense of humor during the 1950s and 60s that blew away any conceits of pomposity, erudite elitism, and smug self-righteousness. LA teens flipped the bird to pretension, giving the city's scene a unique flavor unavailable in other cosmopolitan centers. "If New York punk was about art, and London punk about politics, LA punk was about pop culture, TV, and absurdity," notes journalist Greg Shaw. "But then again, LA has always been phony and self-deprecating and goofy and cartoonish and pop culture-obsessive. The combination is an authentic expression of the real intrinsic spirit of Hollywood." A symbolic vestige of this sensibility remains in the form of the rotating Rocky & Bullwinkle statue near the Chateau Marmont, which was unveiled on September 18th 1961 directly across the street from a statue of a twirling Las Vegas showgirl atop a long-running billboard for the Sahara Casino.

The statue's creator, Jay Ward—who also gave the world Boris Badenov, George Of The Jungle, and a host of other understated characters—helped pioneer the idea of beat-flavored, 'adult' cartoons in the 1950s. His Rocky & Bullwinkle statue, located outside his Jay Ward Animation Studios and adjacent to the Strip's political epicenter, the Fifth Estate, embodied the facetious mood of Los Angeles at the time. The youth and the media were becoming integrated, but in a subversive way that kept squares at bay. A fine example of this was an episode of *Get Smart* starring Larry Storch of the comedy series *F Troop* as the Groovy Guru, backed by a mock band called The Sacred Cows. The Groovy Guru turns out to be an agent of KAOS with the aim of brainwashing American teens with The Sacred Cows' sloppy sounds and hypnotic, psychedelic effects.

This plot might sound implausible now, but with Nikita Khrushchev threatening to take over the USA through its own young in the real world, many parents saw rock'n'roll as some kind of communist plot. This sort of thinking caused a lot of discomfort during the mid 1960s. Both the HUAC (the Special House Committee On Un-American Activities) and the Kefauver Committee had investigated rock'n'roll during the 1950s. Senator Kefauver's Senate Subcommittee On Organized Crime spent a lot of time looking into the links between rock'n'roll and organized crime, as well as any possible links to communists. They didn't find very much, as the revolution being proposed by the youth of America had more to do with civil liberties and hip consumerism than classless society and collective farming.

The aforementioned episode of *Get Smart* was a brilliant parody of conservative paranoia, but also exemplified what was actually happening in a different way. Rock'n'roll *was* delivering a message to the youth through television and radio. As Roger McGuinn put it on the April 1967 CBS News documentary *Inside Pop: The Rock Revolution:* "I think we're out to break down those barriers that we see to be arbitrary. … I feel like there's some sort of guerrilla warfare, psychological warfare going on, and I feel like a guerrilla. I feel good."

Kids in Los Angeles understood that the ideas that permeated their own scene were now gaining ground in intellectual circles. The sense of accomplishment that came with these social changes resonated in the excitement of the moment as a shared identity. The iconography of the Strip, in cartoon form, inspired the television sensation of 1966, *Batman*, with its DayGlo décor and rock'n'roll cameos. Paul Revere & The Raiders appeared on the show, providing a complete coalescence of art and pop, while Lesley Gore made a cameo as an accomplice to Catwoman. Julie Newmar's Catwoman character frequents a discotheque called the Sandbox in another episode, which features a faux house band called Benedict Arnold & The Traitors and a go-go dancing Toni Basil. Meanwhile, Burt Ward, who played Robin, recorded a parodic 45 with Frank Zappa. These televised 'happenings' were beginning to blur with reality.

At the center of the action on Sunset Strip was a neon Neverland that the mod set called home. Following Jay Ward's lead, animators began to recognize the intergalactic potential in the Strip's architecture and nightlife. The futurist design of Ben Frank's and restaurants such as Googie's and Ships began to color the palates of imagination in the local animation industry.

The unheralded genius behind Hanna-Barbera's adaptation of mid-1960s LA teen-culture was animator Iwao Takamoto, who drew landscapes and exotic special effects. A September 1962 episode of *The Jetsons* entitled 'A Date With Jet Screamer' features a nightclub suspended in outer space that closely resembles Tiny Naylors', the drive-in on the northwest corner of Sunset and La Brea than Dustin Hoffman and Katherine Ross go to in *The Graduate*. (Mike Nichols' 1967 movie is something of a Sunset Strip travelogue—Hoffman and Ross also take in burlesque at the Largo, and are later seen outside the Whisky A Go Go.)

'A Date With Jet Screamer' was a sign of things to come in the animation world. Jet Screamer was voiced by Howard Morris, who played bungling hillbilly Ernest T. Bass on *The Andy Griffith Show*. This anti-authoritarian bumpkin paralleled the way kids of the time aimed to overwhelm uptight conformity and repression with an absurdist take on conservative hypocrisy. This might well have been coincidental, but the adaptation of Sunset Strip motifs by animators was not. While *The Flintstones* offered a prehistoric take on pop culture, *The Jetsons* reflected the aesthetic balance between primitive and modern ideas in a futuristic society.

An outer-space teen idol with slicked-back hair and a house band look, Jet Screamer is suspiciously reminiscent of P.J. Proby's early incarnation as Jett Powers. He performs a song called 'Eep Op Ork' that was carefully fashioned in-house at Hanna-Barbera in a Phil Spector/Monkees vein. The song was then issued as a single by Little Golden Records, complete with a *Jetsons* picture sleeve. On vinyl, the vocal is by Janet Waldo (better known as Judy Jetson), who transforms 'Eep Op Ork' into a strident girl-group record.

Even as they cropped up in *The Jetsons* or *The Graduate*, places such as Tiny Naylors' continued to be regular hangouts for LA teens. Tony Pascuzzo of Pandora's Box group The Banned recalls how these eateries blended in with the Strip's music venues and the whole psychedelic experience, noting: "Everyone from A to Z was there … you'd have Stephen Stills in there buying a little pie and sitting at the counter."

Then there was Sunset Boulevard itself, which winds romantically through the Hollywood Hills in curves that seem to bend with the texture of the architecture. After passing the majestic Ciro's on a modest, regal incline, subtle changes begin to draw attention, such as the left curve at the Trousdale Apartments, sweeping downhill through the area where the Sea Witch, Dino's Lodge, Fred C. Dobbs', the Playboy Club, the Trip, and Ben Frank's melded into the 1920s colonial structures of the Sunset Plaza. The panorama from the corner of Sunset and La Cienega faces southwest over the incline, creating a mystical turn of the wheel as it overlooks the most angular vista in the region.

What spread out before you were endless streams of twinkling lights, from homes designed by Richard Neutra and Pierre Koenig in the hills above to the far-reaching residential horizon below. This highway veranda funneled into neon club marquees ahead, with the ocean peeking through in the distance. Sky-reaching movie premiere lights somewhere off in the distance often accentuated this view. The combined effect looked from a distance like the pixie dust from Tinkerbell's wand.

Much like the club in *The Jetsons*, a trip to the Sunset Strip in the mid 1960s felt to many visitors like a journey into outer space. Stepping out onto the street into this atmosphere—following an intimate performance by The Byrds, Love, Them, or any of the bands playing regularly on the Strip—brought on a sense of shared euphoria. While LSD-25 was, until October 6th 1966, legal and readily available, and accompanied many of these trips into the unknown, the prevailing mood of unprecedented surrealism on the Strip meant that drugs often weren't needed to feel sky high.

Sunset Strip in the mid 1960s represented one of the most successful applications of space-age pop motifs onto 20th Century curvilinear street-layout. The survey, engineering, and road layout dramatically complements the contour of the hills and their scenic merit. Like the panoramic break in the middle of The Beach Boys' 'Good Vibrations,' this futuristic utopia reached its peak with a jangling fusion of space-age design and the culmination of dada, surrealism, cubism, Bauhaus, and modernism. These diverse elements encompass all the loose ends of science and physics in a manner reminiscent of Einstein's unified field theory.

Pop art brought the future to the present. The ethereal, otherworldly, outer-space experiences on the Strip made real the dreams first presented at the 1939 New York World's Fair. That vision of the future, which seemed all-important during the depression, had come to life: the future was *now*.

On a drive to the Strip's central plexus at La Cienega, one building was impossible to ignore: Dino's Lodge. It sat right in the middle of the Sea Witch, Fred C. Dobbs', the Playboy Club, the Trip, and Ben Frank's. Nothing made you feel that you were in the center of a dream more than catching sight of Dean Martin's lackadaisical mug flashing in alternating red-and-white neon in the middle of the most crowded area of Sunset Strip. It gave the feel of some elusive, illicit thrill; if any place was swingin', this was it. The façade of Dino's Lodge had been foretold as the holy grail since its use in *77 Sunset Strip*, and its impact would only intensify as the mid-1960s music scene blossomed around it. *Crawdaddy!* journalist Sandy Pearlman summed up the importance of Dino's Lodge with the declaration: "Your roots are there. My roots are there."

* * *

The word 'psychedelic' has over the years been misconstrued as describing a tie-dyed, washed-out stereotype. In fact, few things were more psychedelic than comic book art of the 1950s. The images of vintage DC comics crossbred in young minds with the satirical wildness of Harvey Kurtzman, Basil Wolverton, and Wally Wood in early EC titles *Mad* and *Panic*, giving definition to the term 'warped.'

Terry Gilliam came out of LA's Birmingham High and Occidental College, and worked briefly with Kurtzman on his post-*Mad* project, *Help!*, in New York. After a brief sojourn to Europe, Gilliam returned to Los Angeles, where he worked between 1965 and 1967 at Carson Roberts' advertising agency. There he often worked with Tony Asher (Brian Wilson's collaborator on *Pet Sounds*) on campaigns for products such as Mattel's Creepy Crawlers, Incredible Edibles, and Creeple People. He also turned his hand to television and print advertising, which led his images to pop up at random during the creative whirlwind of the LA teen scene.

Gilliam recognized the transformations that were taking place both in him and Los Angeles at the time. With just the adoption of a Beatles-style haircut, he says, "the world totally changed." He found himself attacked by "old women … in drug stores" and followed by police cars "at least once a week." He then took part in "the first real demonstration in America," a protest against Lyndon B. Johnson on the occasion of a presidential visit to Los Angeles. The protest was attended by "a total mixture of people," Gilliam says, including "lawyers, doctors, academics, middle-aged, young, hippies, all anti-Vietnam War." Reflecting on the resulting heavy-handed tactics used by the police, he recalls: "At that point I felt either I become a full-time activist or I get out of here and go back to Europe." He chose the latter option, and went on to add his cartoon and assemblage techniques to a trans-continental rock'n'roll show called *Go Go Scope* before joining the Monty Python comedy troupe.[1]

The Los Angeles Free Press gave a generous amount of space during the mid

1960s to Ron Cobb, who was perhaps the most crucial transitional figure between the halcyon days of EC and DC comics and the underground era of Crumb, S. Clay Wilson, former Ed Roth employee Robert Williams, and others. Cobb's densely packed political cartoons were unparalleled in their condensation of harsh, sardonic whimsy. He operated at a time when no one came close to what would come to be called the 'underground' style, while also maintaining a day job as a B-movie special effects artist. (In later years he created the famous bar scene in *Star Wars*, worked on *Alien*, and sketched the title character in Steven Spielberg's *E.T.*, for which he was granted one per cent of the movie's future profits.)

The surrealism of the movies and comics these artists worked on from the 1950s through to the mid 1960s was also present in the seaside carnivals, amusement parks, and fun houses of the time. With their wacky mirrors and colored lights, these too were designed to alter reality, while the organ sound used by garage bands—and even The Doors—can be traced back to carnival music.

LA's approach to this all-American reverie was epitomized by Pacific Ocean Park, which was coincidentally located alongside Venice, where The Doors first learned their craft. POP, as it was known, opened in 1958 as the ultimate confluence of space-age modernism and the oddity of 19th century sideshows. The entrance echoed the spires and arches of the LA Airport Theme Building, which here were flanked by floating orbs, seahorses, and cheese-cut walkways that passed through a nautically themed fountain.

The main attractions at POP were variations of familiar themes, such as The Sea Serpent roller-coaster, Davy Jones's Locker, Neptune's Kingdom, and the Ocean's Skyway ride, a spherical bubble over the ocean. Most exquisite was the South Sea Island train ride, which Museum Of The Odd curator Mickey McGowan recalls went through "a spinning underground lava tube that simulated a volcanic flow with exotica music, jungle birdcalls, and speakers booming out eruptive sounds." As frightening as this might sound, McGowan calls it "more of a relaxing thing, a last outpost escape from Los Angeles ... it was at the proverbial end of the pier, the last point of demarcation."

At the entrance to POP sat the Aragon Ballroom, which hosted dance bands such as Harry Owens & His Royal Hawaiians and The Lawrence Welk Orchestra in the 1940s and 50s, before opening its doors to Dick Dale & His Del-Tones and The Dovers during the 60s. Pacific Ocean Park became the main teen outpost of LA's amusement park trend, eclipsing even Disneyland for a short time. The first Teen-Age Fair and Battle Of The Bands were held there in 1962, while the Park's very logo spelt out its direct link to the POP scene.

"There was so much happening, you couldn't swing a slingshot without hitting something cool," recalls garage-punk musician Shelly Ganz. "Because everyone was into The Beatles, The Rolling Stones, The Strawberry Alarm Clock … there was a *commonalty*, there was no factionalism. You were all a member of the same club and were either going to POP, the Teen-Age Fair, the Sunset Strip, or one of a dozen other teenage hangouts."

The trusting, laissez faire harmony enjoyed by teens in these early rock'n'roll days would be nigh on impossible to find today. "Hitchhiking was very common," notes scene regular Pam DeLacy. "You could meet people at any of these places on the Strip, or on Hollywood Boulevard, and spend the rest of the day and night with a gang of people you had never met before, drive down Sunset to the beach or Pacific Ocean Park and have one of the best days of your life. You knew that you may never see them again, but it was cool anyway." "People were open with each other," adds dancer Carl Franzoni. "You could just walk up and talk to somebody and they wanted to know you. Especially in Hollywood, everyone was interested in show business or a part of it and they wanted your attention, they wanted to meet you."[2]

On one such occasion, Neil Young hitched a lift with Ruthann Friedman, who occasionally sang folk songs at the Fifth Estate. Upon learning that they were both songwriters, they went back to her place to play guitars. Soon after that, Young was making records with Buffalo Springfield, and Friedman began to hear a version of her song, 'Windy' (as performed by The Association), all over the radio. Another young girl interviewed on the 1965 ABC television documentary *Teenage Revolution* summed up the feelings of her peers: "All of a sudden, we have a feeling of being a generation, and having some sort of bond with every other teenager on the street. Maybe I feel it's different because, you know, I've never experienced another generation. But I do feel we'll have something to say; we'll make a gigantic splash in the world to come."

The egotistical megalomania of the 'rock star' had not yet polluted the attitudes of popular musicians or their audiences. The person standing next to you could be a musical sage, a cutting-edge thespian, or just a regular Joe out for kicks: it wouldn't make a difference. So much creativity abounded on Sunset Strip that mutual respect was an unspoken given. There was no separation between audience and artist. "The band was a part of the audience, and vice versa," says The Byrds' Roger McGuinn. "We consciously felt that we shouldn't be aloof, and so there was a lot more interaction."[3] Or, as Sherry's house band leader Don Randi put it in the liner notes of his *Live On The Sunset Strip* LP: "Sit down—on your right will be a TV star; on your left, a garage mechanic."

Before the sterile, 'rock' establishment took hold, the spontaneity and raunch of garage kept rock'n'roll fresh. The fact that mistakes were allowed gave things more character: spontaneously recovering from a flaw with an instant, inspired reaction or a gritty comeback made for much more exciting records than those full of re-takes, careful separation, and the 'perfection' of punched-in, edited sound. The stone-age motif of *The Flintstones* offered an interesting parallel to the semi-conscious 'caveman' aspect of 1960s garage. (Gary Paxton and Kim Fowley pre-empted that idea with 'Alley Oop,' a 1960 hit for The Hollywood Argyles that was based on the caveman comic strip of the same name.)

Such primitive delivery gave rock'n'roll its sexuality. Sophistication is fine, but it's nothing without the raw deal. On *The TAMI Show*, Jan & Dean introduced The Barbarians—one of the USA's first long-haired garage combos—with the words: "And now, from their caves in old Cape Cod, here are The Barbarians!" This was soon followed by brilliant records such as 'Be A Cave Man' by The Avengers and 'I Want My Woman' by The Emperors, on which vocalist Bill Hughes howls: "Cave woman! I want my WOMAWWWN!"

These primitive ideas were apparently popular in girls' fashion magazines such as *Teen*, too. The August 1966 issue of *Teen* includes articles whose titles declare 'I Dreamt I Was A Cavegirl' and 'I Was A Teenage Go Go Dancer,' as well as fashion spreads featuring members of The Leaves, The Byrds, The Bobby Fuller Four, and other voguish groups of the time surrounded by teen models. It's no real surprise, then, that teenage girls on Sunset Strip could at times be seen wearing *Flintstones*-style leopard-print. As early as 1962, on her Number 7 hit 'Johnny Get Angry,' Joanie Sommers had sung: "I want a brave man/I want a caveman/Johnny show me that you care."

The caveman aesthetic cropped up all over the mid-1960s music scene: Paul Revere & The Raiders aped it in their live shows, while The Robbs and Sonny Bono took their prehistoric fashions to preposterous extremes. In 1965 Bono was denied entry into the swish, industry watering-hole Martoni's for wearing a fur vest, an incident he subsequently related in his solo hit 'Laugh At Me.'

Bono then cut 'The Revolution Kind,' which was both a defense of his First Amendment right and a lampooning of conservative suppression of the youth. The Robbs, meanwhile, had the audacity to wear fur vests with no shirts and long, Brian Jones-style hair. The Rolling Stones' guitarist became the model on which most garage band musicians based their look, and was no stranger to caveman chic himself: When the Stones made their first appearance on *The Ed Sullivan Show*, they played in front of huge, Neolithic boulders. Cavemen (and women) cropped up on the silver screen, too, in movies such as Roger Corman's *Teenage Caveman* (1958) and *One Million Years B.C.* (1966), which introduced the world to Raquel Welch (whose big break came after she appeared on billboards for *The Hollywood Palace*).

* * *

Today's world of toned-down expectations and monotony will most likely never witness the wild, rock'n'roll showmanship of radio deejays such as KHJ's 'The Real' Don Steele. (The same could be said of many other cities around the USA in days gone by, notably Cleveland, Ohio, which was once home to Alan Freed, Mad Daddy, and Ghoulardi.) Their screaming excitement and wild sense of humor enlightened and entertained listeners in the same way as did the revolutionary records of the time.

"Despite hardships—in fact, because of them—successful black deejays enjoyed astonishingly strong, direct communication with a mass audience, a feeling of solidarity that was unprecedented in commercial broadcasting," notes former KGFJ disc jockey The Magnificent Montague in his autobiography, *Burn, Baby! Burn!* "We were the equivalent of movie stars, the sole link between listeners and the music." Now, he says, radio is governed by demographic studies, with no room for the personalities—like himself—who filled the airwaves in the 1960s. These characters actually enhanced the potency of rock'n'roll. Music on the radio then wasn't 'scientifically' selected in a Midwestern marketing office—these disc jockeys had to go out and find the records themselves. Their livelihoods depended on finding something cool—something that would solidify their credibility with their audience.

This level of insight allowed Top 40 AM radio stations to guide their sponsors, who would then tailor their advertisements for a more socially aware audience. As there weren't so many stations available—FM was still strictly classical for most of the 1960s—stations could select their sponsors carefully, and adjust the timbre of their corporate image for their own benefit. (Product design, in turn, began to embrace modernism and ecological concerns through consumer demand.)

With this kind of leverage and direct connection to listeners, the most successful early rock'n'roll disc jockeys were able to protect their increasingly savvy audience from bogus music and uncool promotions. These deejays were able to hold out and keep their noses to the street for much of the decade, until, says Gene Sculatti of *Billboard* magazine, their control was usurped by "program directors," which led to "generic, less localized playlists."

What helped these disc jockeys maintain their position, says Sculatti, was an "ego-driven desire to connect with their young audiences." In a 1965 *Los Angeles Herald Examiner* piece, Richard Baxter notes than Al Burton, producer of rock'n'roll television for KHJ and a key figure behind the Teen-Age Fair, "likes to feel that he is sophisticating teens as well as giving them what they want." In the same article, Burton himself adds: "I say you should meet teens with respect and you will get respect back."

The Byrds were in agreement. According to David Crosby: "The kids are hipper than anybody thinks … On [a] basic musical level, they know whether it's right or wrong."[4] The key here is that disc jockeys, club owners, musicians, and producers did not underestimate their audience in the way that is so common today. They assumed that, by virtue of being in school, kids were *thinking*. They also realized that these kids' 'dumb' sensibilities were in fact a form of ridicule; the subtle puns in, for example, Jay Ward's cartoons allowed the audience to be in on private jokes; to 'dig.'

Jay Ward used television to invade and then overturn the conservative bias of mainstream culture. Cartoons devised in his Sunset Strip studio, such as *Rocky & His Friends* (ABC, 1959) and *The Bullwinkle Show* (NBC, 1961), were subversive in the same way that *The Simpsons* has been in more recent times. Between 1959 and 1964, Ward was able to infiltrate prime-time network television with ultra-hip, grown-up satire.

"*Rocky & Bullwinkle* was a cartoon that rewarded you for paying attention," says Simpsons creator Matt Groening in Louis Chunovic's *The Rocky And Bullwinkle Book*. "If you're watching carefully, there's lots of extra jokes in there." Groening was heavily influenced by the way Ward was able to slip sociological puns into an otherwise censorial medium. "I was fascinated by the minimal animation, and the sloppiness," he tells Chunovic, and by extension realized that "good writing, good voices, [and] good music" were more important than visual slickness.[5] (Like Ron Cobb, Matt Groening's work was first exposed to the world at large in a local, alterative periodical, *LA Weekly*.)

Groening was similarly inspired by *The Flintstones'* use of animated guest appearances by celebrities from other areas of popular culture. The brass at Hanna-Barbera were quite to pick up on the freewheeling success of *Rocky And His Friends*, which became the first prime-time cartoon series in 1959. Hanna-Barbera had previously lagged far behind Disney and Warner Brothers in the animation industry, but *The Flintstones* helped bridge the gap. While the idea of the show was rooted in *The Honeymooners*, starring Jackie Gleason, its fictional setting of Bedrock bore a striking resemblance to Los Angeles with its palm trees, stacked freeways, drive-in movie theaters, and restaurants.

One *Flintstones* guest star was Ann-Margret, here dubbed Ann-Margrock and featured as a performer at the Hollyrock Bowl, while the opening episode of the show's 1965–66 season, 'No Biz Like Show Biz,' reflects an early flower-power vibe. Pebbles and Bamm-Bamm form a band and perform a song called 'Open Up Your Heart' that features the repeating phrase "Let the sun shine in." They are taken under the wing of Eppy Brianstone—a spoof of Beatles manager Brian Epstein—and become teen idols after a performance on *The Hollyrock Palace*. But all of this, it turns out, has taken place in a dream: in a neat, ironic comment on the times, Fred Flintstone had fallen asleep in front of the television, annoyed at how teenage go-go shows have taken over the traditional schedule.

The clip of Pebbles and Bamm-Bamm performing 'Open Up Your Heart' was so popular that it aired on *Shindig!*, *Hullabaloo*, *Hollywood A Go Go*, and *The Jimmy Dean Show*. A year later, the phrase "Let the sun shine in" was used during the climax of the Broadway musical *Hair*. It was then repeated and chanted by rained-on fans at Woodstock. Ironically, 'Open Up Your Heart' was originally a 1952 hit for Stuart Hamblin, an LA-based country & western radio preacher.

Hanna-Barbera would do more than simply invent pseudo-bands for the rock'n'roll content of *The Flintstones* or *The Jetsons*. One episode of The Flintstones features Johnny Rivers as a Strip-style 'stone-age idol,' while another is based entirely on the rock'n'roll television show *Shindig!*, complete with host Jimmy O'Neilstone (played by former KFWB deejay and Pandora's Box emcee Jimmy O'Neil) and a musical performance by San Francisco folk-rock combo The Beau

Brummels. At this point it became difficult to tell if art was imitating life, or life imitating art. In *The Flintstones*, The Beau Brummelstones perform their debut hit, 'Laugh Laugh,' in an unnamed nightclub that clearly resembles the interior of a Chinese restaurant on the Strip, Ah Fongs, with its dark walls and colored orbs suspended from the ceiling.

In another dream sequence in the same episode, Fred invents a new dance craze that is subsequently learnt in the White House *and* The Kremlin; famed New York dance instructor Arthur Murray(rock) asks for lessons as well. The scene is soundtracked by a trippy, improvised folk/surf instrumental full of echo, tremolo, and wild, untraceable bass patterns. This sonic trip/dream sequence predated the release of psychedelic records such as The Byrds' pioneering 'Eight Miles High' by almost six months. Because the animators of shows such as *The Flintstones* frequented Sunset Strip nightclubs in 1965, they were able to pick up on psychedelia at source and spread it on network television before it appeared on radio or in print media.

Other 'bands' that appeared on *The Flintstones* during the 1965–66 season were The Beasties, The Way Outs ('That's Where the Fun Is'), and The Bugs, who performed at the New York World's Fair. In fact the cross-pollination went back all the way to the 1960–61 season, during which, in one episode, Fred Flintstone disguises himself as an Elvis-style rocker called Hi-Fye; Wilma and Betty put him in his place by etching a square in the air with their fingers. Two years later, in a parody of the twist craze, Fred sings a song called 'The Twitch,' while in an episode from the 1964–65 season, the Flintstones go surfing and listen to two uncredited tracks by The Fantastic Baggys, who were in real life the brainchild of P.F. Sloan and Steve Barri. Sloan & Barri then recorded a Fantastic Baggys LP, *Tell 'Em I'm Surfin'*, for Imperial Records, before ghost-recording the folk-rock album *Where Were You When I Needed You* for The Grass Roots.

These episodes of *The Flintstones* embody an innocent vitality that would soon disappear. When the 'rock music' industry fell into place after the Monterey Pop Festival in 1967, attitudes became much more somber and serious. While pop artists in bona fide media centers such as London, New York, and Los Angeles appreciated how animation could bring subversive social parodies to the mainstream, the tastemakers at *Rolling Stone* and its ilk failed to understand a correlation that sometimes exists: that 'cool' and 'ridiculous' are not necessarily independent of each other.

Many cartoon programs produced by Hanna-Barbera were accompanied by full-length storyline records on the HBR label, complete with dialog by voiceover artists and featuring some great buried rock'n'roll treasure that never made it onto the television shows. These include releases by The Hillbilly Bears, The Gruesomes, and an entire *Monster Shindig* album featuring Danny Hutton, whose HBR single 'Roses And Rainbows' reached Number 73 on the *Billboard* charts after being given a subtle plug in a 1965 episode of *The Flintstones.*

HBR also released a whole load of hardcore garage-punk records between 1965 and '67, including 'Hey You' by The Guilloteens, 'Loose Lip Sync Ships' by The Hogs—actually The Chocolate Watchband using a pseudonym—and 'Story Of My Life' by The Unrelated Segments. Most notably, the label picked up 'You're Gonna Miss Me' by The Thirteenth Floor Elevators for national distribution during the summer of 1966. This limited pressing came as a result of a verbal agreement between HBR producer Tom Ayers and International Artists, which put the disc out originally.

The same spirit of cross-fertilization spread into movie and television appearances for cutting-edge bands, resulting in some entertaining and hilarious match-ups. Few sights could be more incongruous than that of The Seeds cavorting with Eve Arden and Kaye Ballard before miming a frenetic 'Pushin' Too Hard' on *The Mothers In Law*—one of the few surviving pieces of footage of lead singer Sky Saxon's dynamic dancing in a Nehru outfit. The sight of a performance such as this in the confines of a fake living room is simultaneously transparent and eerie … not to mention highly entertaining.

Musically themed episodes of TV shows, complete with guest appearances by bands of the time, were rife during the mid 1960s, while the incidental music in many of these shows was right in tune with the teen scene. One episode of *Gomer Pyle U.S.M.C.* shows Pyle (played by Jim Nabors) dancing to a couple of uninterrupted minutes of an earth-shattering, guitar-and-organ-based instrumental garage-punk. Psych-pop garage group The Factory pop up during another episode, in which Pyle is asked by an uptight General to escort his daughter to the movies. On the date, she ditches her dad's strict plans and has Gomer take her to "one of those go-go clubs." On arrival, she strips off her prim and proper clothes to reveal a wild, mod outfit; The Factory—whose lead singer, Lowell George, would later front Little Feat—play 'Lost' and 'Candy Cane Madness' in the background. The extras rounded up for this fake nightclub scene were a mixture of thespians and

Sunset Strip denizens. The idea of kids saying goodnight to their parents and then sneaking off to wild nights on the Strip rang true with the times—as did the very character of Gomer Pyle who, in each episode, would unintentionally subvert his Sergeant in his naïve search for 'the truth.'

The Standells were among the major beneficiaries of the intermingling of television and music. The group popped up in an episode of *The Munsters* in 1964, and quickly followed it with an appearance on a shortlived situation comedy called *The Bing Crosby Show* in which, prompted by an invasion of Beatlemania in the Crosby household, Bing joins The Standells for a rousing rendition of 'Kansas City.' They subsequently cropped up in the medical drama *Ben Casey* before graduating to movies such as *Get Yourself A College Girl and Where The Boys Meet The Girls*. The group also cut the theme to a children's movie, *Zebra In The Kitchen*, which ran over a suitably primitive animated sequence.

Other bands of the time made more fleeting forays into the world of television. The Enemys, one of many Whisky A Go Go house bands—and, alongside The Standells and The Chocolate Watchband, a crucial component of the movie *Riot On Sunset Strip*—appear in episodes of *The Beverly Hillbillies* and *Burke's Law*. The pilot episode of *The Mod Squad* features a performance by The Other Half at the Cheetah. The Poor turned up in an episode of *Ironside*, while the similar-sounding Buffalo Springfield showed up on *Mannix* (as did The Peppermint Trolley Company). The Strawberry Alarm Clock did *The Danny Thomas Show* and *Laugh In*, and The Righteous Brothers did a turn on *Please Don't Eat The Daisies*. Boyce & Hart made appearances on two of the era's finest sitcoms. They teamed up with Phil Spector in a music-biz-themed episode of *I Dream Of Jeanie*, and sang in a witches' nightclub on *Bewitched*. The duo of Tommy Boyce and Bobby Hart also contributed the title song to the 1968 movie *Where Angels Go, Trouble Follows*, which is heard during a highly stylized mod dance scene and lip-synched by The "In" Group.

Television shows would, on occasion, concoct offbeat bands and songs that were just as wild as anything on the scene itself. The most psychotic of these is The Tomahawk 3, who perform a wicked instrumental called 'Tomahawk' at 'the Playbrave Club' on an episode of *F Troop*. Meanwhile, eschewing political correctness and historical accuracy, the entire cast of the show gets worked up over an "Indian go-go chick." Another episode of *F Troop* features a band called The Bed Bugs, who in reality were The Factory.

The instrumental madness continues on a color episode of *The Andy Griffith Show*, in which Opie (played by Ron Howard) joins a band called The Sound Committee. A later episode takes Opie, Sheriff Taylor (Andy Griffith), and Aunt Bee (Frances Bavier) on a drive down Sunset Strip past Dino's Lodge, the Whisky A Go Go, and several other hotspots. In an episode of *The Addams Family*, meanwhile, the Frankenstein-like butler, Lurch (played by Ted Cassidy), becomes a teen idol. 'Lurch' then cut a single, 'The Lurch,' for Capitol Records, which features haunting organ playing and groaning vocals similar to the sound that The Doors would later mine to great success.

* * *

As well as recording as a solo artist for Canterbury Records and being a background member of The Yellow Balloon, Don Grady played the eldest of three siblings, Robbie Douglas, on *My Three Sons*. One episode from 1966 features Grady and his band The Greefs performing at a Pandora's Box-like club, while another concerns the fallout after Robbie's younger brother Chip grows his hair and joins a garage band. Grady also wrote a mock-Motown number for the show called 'Ugga Bugga,' and might have been more than a little surprised when, less than a year later, Brenton Wood released the similar sounding 'The Oogum Boogum Song.'

On an episode of *Gidget* called 'All The Best Diseases Are Taken,' the title character, played by Sally Field, hires beatnik folk singer Billy Roy Soames (a take on P.F. Sloan) to sing at a protest rally. Soames later gets into a deep discussion about social change with Gidget's dad (Don Porter). In a subsequent episode, Gidget forms a garage band called Gidget & The Gories, all of whom dress like Morticia Adams. (Sally Field went on to star in another sitcom, *The Flying Nun*, which once featured a psychedelic appearance by The Sundowners.) Elsewhere, an episode of *Gilligan's Island* featured a battle of the bands between The Mosquitoes (fronted by the show's star, Bob Denver) and a girl group called The HoneyBees (made up of Ginger, Mary Ann, and Mrs Howell).

The connection between LSD and the rock'n'roll scene cropped up on television shows too. The positive side was examined on an episode of *Gumby*, in which a boy drinks a magic potion and instantly grows a Beatles hairdo. There were all sorts of other strange happenings on this supposed kids' show, including a 'Mirrorland' episode where Gumby explores various parallel universes. The downside of the LSD craze was well handled in two episodes of *Dragnet*. In the first, a spaced-out kid "known locally on the Sunset Strip scene [as] Blue Boy" becomes a problem to Sergeant Friday (Jack Webb) and later overdoses; in the second, Friday visits a 'priest'—clearly based on Timothy Leary and Richard Alpert—who uses LSD as sacrament. Friday can't arrest him—LSD had not yet been criminalized—but does provoke an interesting debate about the drug. This was the epitome of the camp, knowing television of the 1960s.

While some garage bands' appearances in situation comedies have achieved an extended life through syndication, most have since faded from memory. A more lasting impression was made by the overflow of concocted bands that appear in various cartoons. Just as in reality, the most influential band in the animation world was The Beatles. When King Features' syndicated Beatles cartoon became 1965's top-rated children's television show, characters in other Saturday morning cartoons decided that they, too, could form rock'n'roll bands. Although they were dismissed at the time amid the emergence of the San Francisco hippie mentality, many of these animated bands and their songs are now rather more fondly recalled. There is even a 1995 tribute album, *Saturday Morning: Cartoons' Greatest Hits*, which features covers of cartoon theme tunes by acts such as The Ramones and The Violent Femmes.

The steady flow of cartoon bands from 1965–75 includes *The Archies*, *The Banana Splits*, *The Cattanooga Cats*, *The Jackson 5*, *Josie & The Pussycats*, *Fat Albert & The Cosby Kids*, *The Impossibles*, *The Beagles*, and many more. The characters in *Scooby Doo* had their own band during the show's first season, while the subsequent *New Scooby Doo Movies* used mid-1960s LA icons Sonny & Cher, Davy Jones, and Mama Cass as animated rock'n'roll stars years after their prime. No matter what year these cartoons came out, the sounds and fashions seemed always to be backdated to Sunset Strip circa 1965–66. So complete was the realization of sound that 'Hangin' On A String' by 1966 garage-punk icons ? & The Mysterians could easily be mistaken for a 1969 Archies track. The bubblegum ambiance allowed Boyce & Hart to make a return to the action on an episode of *Sigmund & The Sea Monsters*, while The Monkees' Mickey Dolenz surfaced on the shortlived *Butch Cassidy & The Sundance Kids*. A Davy Jones cameo in *The Brady Bunch* is another moment that no one seems able to forget.

These nuggets are impossible to separate from the garage-punk idiom. Not only did these cartoon combos introduce a lot of people to the garage band sound, but much of the music they played was on a par with the best efforts of many of the 'real' bands of the mid-to-late 1960s. The animators of the time made sure they were working with top-rate songwriters, musicians, and producers. One need look no further than the best-selling record of 1969, 'Sugar Sugar' by The Archies, which was written by Jeff Barry, whose other songwriting credits include 'Leader Of The Pack' and 'River Deep Mountain High.' *The Archies* and *The Monkees* provided a welcome outlet for artists such as Barry after the demise of the girl-group genre.

Cartoons bands have, in a way, kept an important element of the 1966 garage scene alive through their continuous syndication, which has led to them being enjoyed and absorbed by successive generations of kids. Their perky tunes, effervescent echo-delays, and infectious, candy-coated vocals added a Warhol-like fakery to the LA garage sound, and brought the music to a higher level of impact on popular culture. While somewhat removed from the sociological subversion of The Byrds, The Seeds, or The Mothers Of Invention, the psychedelic sequences in *The Banana Splits* or the crunching Farfisa organ on 'Feelin' So Good (Scooby Do)' by The Archies, serve as an instant evocation of the Sunset Strip era.

CHAPTER ELEVEN

TV a go go and the battle of the bands

> **"** *From Santa Monica, California, it's Groovy!,*
> *the new show from the sunshine, surf, and bikini*
> *country! Turn on to the happening and the pop*
> *sounds, scenes, and people of today! And now,*
> *here's your Groovy host, Michael Blodgett!* **"**

Perhaps the strongest but, ironically, least demonstrable element of the mid-1960s LA scene was the very excitement in the air. It was palpable: when you walked out of your house, you could touch it, and it rose in intensity the closer you got to the Strip. The only physical evidence of this, however, is that which has been captured on rotting, two-inch videotape reels of rock'n'roll television shows that were broadcast locally in Los Angeles, and on air-checks of screaming disc jockeys who put together inventive radio programs filled with cool records.

The radio newspaper *KRLA Beat* offered brilliant coverage of the mid-1960s LA rock'n'roll scene. *KRLA* deejay Bob Eubanks is quick to point out *KRLA Beat's* importance, referring to it as "the first newspaper format for rock'n'roll" (in the USA, at least) and "the predecessor of *Rolling Stone*." Created by the radio station's John Barrett and Cecil Tuck, *KRLA Beat* was distributed in Los Angeles, San Francisco (as *KYA Beat*), and Minneapolis/St Paul (as *KDWB Beat*). Each included an insert covering local acts, as well as the latest news on which rock'n'roll bands would be in town, where they were playing, and what was really going on in their creative lives. (Another LA station, KGFJ, spawned a similar paper for rhythm & blues enthusiasts called *The Soul*, published by deejay-turned-newscaster Ken Jones and his wife Regina.)

In December 1965 the first annual *KRLA Beat Awards* were staged to coincide with the opening of the Hullabaloo, and were broadcast live on KCOP Channel 13. 'Satisfaction' by The Rolling Stones was named Best Vocal Record, The Beatles' *Help!* won Best LP, and Bob Dylan was voted Best Male Vocalist.

'A Taste Of Honey' by Herb Alpert & The Tijuana Brass nabbed the award for Best Instrumental 45, *The In Crowd* by The Ramsey Lewis Trio claimed the corresponding Album award, Brian Wilson was crowned Best Producer, Sonny & Cher were named as the Best Duo, and The Beau Brummels triumphed in the Best New Vocal Group category. "Teen-agers Take Over Moulin Rouge," announced *The Los Angeles Times*, which noted (with a certain sneer) that the Hullabaloo was just one of several upstart rock'n'roll nightclubs to have usurped the grand, old venues of the Sunset Strip's past, following the trend set earlier by Ciro's and the Crescendo (now It's Boss and the Trip).

It was primarily through rock'n'roll that alternative publications began to reach the ever-widening audience ignored by the conservative, mainstream press. *KRLA Beat* covered the full spectrum of music of the time, but anything specifically political, sexually provocative, or about the art scene and its various happenings was more likely to be reported on by *The Los Angeles Free Press*. Published and edited by Art Kunkin, who also owned several Free Press Bookstores in the Greater Los Angeles area, *The Los Angeles Free Press* was the second alternative weekly to emerge in the USA, following *The Village Voice*, from New York City. It started out as a bastion of jazz and folk, and was just as condescending toward rock'n'roll—albeit in a different way—as the *Times*. But once Bob Dylan crossed over into rock'n'roll territory, expanded club listings and groovy ads and artwork started to appear in the *Free Press*. The defining beacon of change was an exclusive, three-part interview with Dylan by Paul Jay Robbins.

The Los Angeles Times, meanwhile, continued to ignore creative people who were not well-established entities already, thereby missing out on the real action of the moment. But between them, *KRLA Beat* and *The Los Angeles Free Press*—both of which emerged in mid 1964—provided a true forum for the intermingling of the allied arts in the city of Los Angeles.

* * *

This community wasn't entirely self-starting. There were master showmen at work behind the scenes who pitched in and helped the whole operation run smoothly. Al Burton was the producer of several important rock'n'roll television shows, including *Hollywood A Go Go*, *POP Dance Party*, *9th Street West*, and *Malibu U*, and introduced the idea of the Battle Of The Bands to 1960s teen culture at the annual Teen-Age Fair. Refreshingly, Burton—and some of the other independent entrepreneurs of the rock'n'roll era, such as Art Laboe, Billy Cardenas, and Johnny Otis—had a genuine interest in and enthusiasm for the next generation. Unlike those who merely cashed in, cynically, on modern trends (ignoring teen frustration), Burton and his peers made it their business to help out those who were not yet 'of age.'

Burton was first turned on to rock'n'roll in 1964, while working on a show called *Teleteen Reporter*, when a 12-year-old model told him to check out the late-night radio deejay Huggy Boy. "I didn't know who he was then," recalls Burton. "I listened to it, and I was very pleased to report to her that I that I got it. It was a revolutionary sound, and he was a revolutionary disc jockey."

Similarly pioneering was Gene Norman of the Crescendo who, right back in 1950, brought integrated music to television screens in Los Angeles with *Snader Telescriptions*, for which he teamed up with Lou Snader to show performances by Nat King Cole, Peggy Lee, Count Basie, and Stan Kenton. This NBC show was followed, during the mid 1950s, by *Gene Norman's Campus* on KHJ Channel 9 and the shortlived *Gene Norman's Music Room*. More typical were shows such as *Peter Potter's Jukebox Jury*, on KCOP Channel 13, which would take seemingly random stabs at 1950s teen energy. (A 12-year-old Sonny Bono cropped up on one of Potter's talent segments.)

Rock'n'roll television in the LA area began to hit its stride in 1955. Hunter Hancock hosted a show during 1955–66 called *Rhythm & Bluesville* on the local CBS channel, KNXT, while *The Johnny Otis Show* on KTLA Channel 5 was one of the earliest television showcases for pure rhythm & blues. In 1957 KCOP ran a half-hour program on weeknights at 10:30pm called *The Jimmie Maddin Show*, episodes of which focused on different genres: jazz, country & western, rock'n'roll, comedy, and even a folk night presented by Doug Weston with acts from the Troubadour on La Cienega.

KTTV Channel 11 threw its hat into the ring in 1956 with *Rock'N'Roll Rhythm Ball*, hosted by Jack Slattery. KTTV had already been filming a country & western show, *Town Hall Party*, at Compton Town Hall, which, in LA's broad definition of the genre, extended to sets by Eddie Cochran & The Kelly Four and Gene Vincent & The Blue Caps. A syndicated spin-off show, *Ranch Party*, soon followed. LA rockabilly duo The Collins Kids were regulars, as were Joe Maphis, Billy Mize, and Dick Glasser, while visiting stars such as Carl Perkins, Wanda Jackson, and Johnny Cash would all appear on the show when passing through town in the 1950s.

Saturday nights were dominated by country & western. The hours between 7:00–10:00pm were filled by KCOP's *Country Barn Dance*, shot live in Baldwin Park and presented by Les 'Carrot Top' Anderson, *The Spade Cooley Show*, filmed at the Santa Monica Ballroom for KTLA, and *Hometown Jamboree*, hosted by Cliffie Stone and Tennessee Ernie Ford at El Monte Legion Stadium. All of that was then followed by three hours of *Town Hall Party*. Then, on Sunday afternoons from 1957 until the end of the decade, came three more hours of hillbilly music courtesy of Cal's Corral on KTTV, which was beamed live from Cal Worthington's car lot in Huntington Park.

Rock'n'roll featured occasionally on the long-running *Make Believe Ballroom*, hosted by Al Jarvis first for KLAC (which later became KCOP) and then for KABC Channel 7. Each show ended with a wacky dance segment, 'The Bunny Hop.' Jarvis, who lived at the Garden Of Allah, also made a local spin-off, *Let's Dance*, between 1953–56. It was re-titled *Hollywood Rock'N'Roll Record Hop* as the new genre rose to prominence.

KABC's eight-month run of *The Vampira Show*, starring Maila Nurmi, gave another clue as to the new direction of the LA teen scene in 1954, while Lenny Bruce, Dennis Hopper, and Jett Powers all made appearances on KCOP's wild, amateur-hour show, *Rocket To Stardom*. Like *Make Believe Ballroom*, *Rocket To Stardom* offered 1950s teens both the requisite camp cool and a chance to catch aspiring rock'n'roll stars. *The Art Laboe Show*, meanwhile, transposed the success of its host's radio broadcasts to television during its run between 1958 and 1960 on KTLA, during which time it showcased both national and local—Bobby Day, Ritchie Valens, Preston Epps—rock'n'roll acts. Larry Finley did much the same on his KTLA Channel 5 variety program *The Larry Finley Show*, which was telecast nightly direct from his Sunset Strip supper club above the Mocambo. "It was one of the rare late-night shows that you could get black artists on," says Jimmie Maddin. "There was a lot of prejudice in those times, but that didn't make any difference to Larry."

In the early 1960s two programs emerged from the local black and Chicano scenes. Long-serving disc jockey and newscaster Larry McCormick hosted a soul show for several months of 1963 that featured The Mixtures on a regular basis. "It was called *Kiixville*," said McCormick, "because it was on station KIIX Channel 22 [now KWHY] at the time." The Mixtures had previously been the house band on KCOP's *Parade Of Hits*, which aired on at 6pm on

Saturdays during 1962. Rampart Records president Eddie Davis was the talent coordinator on the show.

Despite the pioneering spirit of television in LA, it was still very difficult to bring rock'n'roll into any kind of public arena during the 1950s. Radio outlets playing rhythm & blues all carried a weak signal right at the end of the dial. This changed in 1958, when KFWB adopted a rock'n'roll format. That same year, NBC in Burbank, looking to cash in on ABC's success with *American Bandstand* in Philadelphia, introduced *Buddy Bregman's Music Shop in color. For 13 episodes, L.A.'s first national rock 'n' roll television show featurured local artists* such as The Teddy Bears and Ritchie Valens long before the music industry pendulum swung west.

During this rise in broadcast visibility, Al Burton, a veteran of both teen and arts programming, was called in to produce rock'n'roll television for the local RKO subsidiary, KHJ-TV. In 1958, Burton was asked by KHJ to meet with Wink Martindale, a radio deejay who had previously worked in Memphis. "I was really fascinated with him," Burton recalls, "because he knew Elvis." The two of them ended up making *Wink Martindale's Dance Party*, which ran for three years before the production moved to Pacific Ocean Park in 1961 and evolved into *POP Dance Party*. "That," says Burton, "led into the Teen-Age Fair."

Burton was also the producer of the sophisticated *Oscar Levant Show* for KCOP, which he continued to work on throughout his rock'n'roll endeavors. His next moment of innovation came with his decision to combine teenage rock'n'roll culture with the idea of a World's Fair (such as the one held in New York in 1939). It was an instant success that drew enthusiastic community involvement. Burton came up with the idea while making *POP Dance Party*, watching kids enjoying themselves at Pacific Ocean Park. These kids could "fill the place" during Easter week, he thought, which would offer a worthwhile alternative to what Southern Californian teens would traditionally do during their spring vacation: maraud the beaches at Balboa, which often resulted in large-scale disorder. So, in 1962, the first of 11 annual Teen-Age Fairs opened. It was attended by 300,000 kids, but gave rise to "not a bit of trouble," according to Burton. "We had national advertisers," he adds, "but nobody could exhibit without supplying a game or some form of entertainment. So it was just built-in fun."

These teenagers' intense involvement with rock'n'roll was of virtually no interest to the elders of Los Angeles, who cared little for the personal interests of the youth. Burton, however, sought more widespread community involvement, and used his skills at gathering talent for television to bring together rock'n'roll acts from all around to play at what became known as the Battle Of The Bands. Very few groups rejected the opportunity, according to Burton, resulting in an event that was "overloaded" with musical performers. "This was not some slick, professional operation," he says. "There were five stages with each band playing 20 minutes, and this is going on all day long."

This first Fair was so well received that a larger venue was required for the next one. The 1963 Teen-Age Fair was held at the Pickwick Recreation Center in Burbank, and was a defining event in the history of surf music, featuring performances by Dick Dale & His Del-Tones, The Beach Boys, The Centurions, The New Dimensions, and many other raunchy instrumental acts. Another year passed and an even bigger venue was needed: this time, Burton chose the parking lot outside the Hollywood Palladium. The event—described by the *Los Angeles Herald Examiner*'s Bob Hull as a "mobile explosion of merchandise and music for the moderns"—was given widespread coverage by KHJ-TV. Its popularity led to Teen-Age Fairs being held throughout America and playing host to countless great acts on multiple stages across the nation.

Al Burton and his team were quick to recognize that diverse interests were a part of the discovery process in a youth experience. Exhibitors at the fair were carefully chosen to further the concept of the event, and to reflect the rock'n'roll aesthetic. A quick overview of the 1965–67 Teen-Age Fair programs shows which companies were leaning in this direction: Yardley Of London, Clairol, Hollywood Sporting Goods, Suzuki, Roll Eez Hair Rollers, Ludwig, Vox, Fender, Milani Pizza, and Records A Go Go, are just a handful of those involved. The Royal Crown, Coca Cola, and Pepsi soda companies were all on board, as were various community and charity organizations, such as the American Cancer Society, the Department Of Public Health, and the YMCA. Surf moviemaker Walt Phillips screened his movies, while The Challengers had their own booth, as did KHJ-TV and KRLA radio. Attendees could take home proto-psychedelic souvenirs in the form of 'spin art'—gloopy paint dripped onto five-by-seven inch cards rotated at varying speeds.

Two hot-rod exhibitors—George Barris and Ed 'Big Daddy' Roth—helped forge a link between high and lowbrow art. According to Burton, it was a display of their cars that inspired a piece Tom Wolfe wrote for *Esquire* magazine called 'The Kandy-Kolored Tangerine-Flake Streamline Baby.' The story was later included in Wolfe's first book, to which it lent a title, and which vividly illuminates what made Los Angeles such a unique entity during the early to mid 1960s.

Several acts achieved their first real break by performing at the Teen-Age Fair, where even the most radical groups were more than welcome. In 1965, one of LA's most esoteric and artistic homegrown acts gained notoriety in this environment: Captain Beefheart & His Magic Band. "[Beefheart] wasn't a superstar," says Burton, "but we put him on the center stage of the Hollywood Palladium." The audience was so impressed by the group's performance of Bo Diddley's 'Diddy Wah Diddy' that it became a huge LA hit the following year— even as The Remains' version of the song hit the charts elsewhere. 'Diddy' and the Teen-Age Fair provided the momentum for the rest of Beefheart's career.

It's clear from Burton's recollections that, had other establishment figures of the 1960s shared his attitude, the generation gap might not have proved such a problem. "We were so popular, the musicians hung around us," he says. "I didn't recognize [all of] them, but I did know that into our little administration tent walked Jimi Hendrix, on a Friday evening. He said, 'Hey, I'll get up there and play, but I don't have my axe.' He was very sweet … high, but sweet. So I sent my mother to get a guitar out of the Fender exhibit." Burton's mother brought Hendrix a right-handed Fender, which the left-handed guitarist needed to restring—which he did as the instrument sat across Mrs Burton's knees. "That's one the funniest sights I ever saw," says Al Burton. "And then he got up and jammed. He [did] a long solo turn. He went wild, and of course his riffs were fabulous."

A band called The Way were performing on another stage at the same time as Hendrix's unscheduled appearance. The teenage group felt like abandoning their set in the face of such striking competition, but decided they ought to carry on for fear of letting down their guitar-manufacturing sponsors. The Way's members included David and Dan Kessel, the sons of noted session player Barney Kessel, whose work ranged from playing with Charlie Parker in the late 1940s to arranging Julie London's 'Cry Me A River' in the 1950s and playing 12-string electric guitar on 'Then He Kissed Me' by The Crystals in the early 1960s. He also played on The Beach Boys' 'Good Vibrations,' and introduced Brian Wilson to the sound of the theremin at a jazz gig. The Spector connection drew John Lennon and George Harrison to Barney Kessel's Music World on Vine Street and Yucca, opposite the Capitol Tower. "People like Eric Clapton would go in there and buy strings and hang out," recalls David Kessel. "I think if we'd have served alcohol, it would have stayed in business longer."

Places such as Barney Kessel's Music World formed part of a character in Hollywood that has since completely disappeared. The southeast corner of Crescent Heights and Sunset, just across the street from Pandora's Box, was a cool daytime hangout. Schwab's was there, as was Gee Gee's, 31 Flavors Ice Cream, and Sherry's coffeeshop, which doubled as a jazz club at night. (House band The Don Randi Trio cut a *"Live" On The Sunset Strip!* set there.) For records you had the Groove Company and Tape City, one of the first car audio stores. The small shopping district was rounded out by a hip clothing store, Zeidler & Zeidler. Lenny Bruce did radio ads on KBCA for Zeidler & Zeidler, while the store proudly noted in advertisements in *The Los Angeles Free Press* that it had provided outfits for Love and The Seeds. (The same ads also subtitled the store with the tag 'Mothers Of Alteration.')

There were plenty of mod boutiques, too, in the vicinity of Sunset Strip. At the tip of Sunset Plaza, a few doors away from Ben Frank's, the Trip, Dino's Lodge, and the rest, was deVoss, which carried high-end mod gear from Europe and served as the location for a promotional film by The Mamas & The Papas. (The Rolling Stones, in town to film *Hullabaloo*, paid deVoss a visit in 1965 and, having picked out a selection of clothes, asked the store to send the bill to the William Morris Agency. The management company actually had nothing to do with the group, however, so deVoss never saw the money.)

The Look, featuring fashions by Arlan Flaum, had a store less than a block from the Whisky A Go Go, while Belinda, which sat alongside Jay Ward Studios on Sunset, sold the first Hollywood miniskirts. The Byrds and Love had their Indian 'ribbon shirts' custom-made at The Bestiary on Santa Monica Boulevard, just down the street from Sidereal Time, where Neil Young picked up his collection of fringed jackets and military shirts.

Right in the middle of it all on La Cienega was Hole In The Wall, which provided outfits for *Hollywood A Go Go*, *Shindig!*, *Where The Action Is*, and *The Dating Game*. The Beau Gentry boutique on Vine Street looked like a British pub, while Hell Bent For Leather on Hollywood Boulevard was another of Neil Young's favorite outfitters. Nancy Sinatra bought clothes at Jax in Beverly Hills, while Sy Devore carried great Carnaby Street shirts out in the valley.

Another prime locale for the youth of Los Angeles was Fairfax Avenue, which boasted a *Free Press* bookstore, a hip pool-hall called Mother's Billiards, an Old Time Movies theater, a pizza joint, an antique store, several art galleries, and three record stores-cum-head shops, Infinite Mind, the Righteous Source, and Hieronymus, which doubled up as a coffeehouse. Norty's, the record shop in which Jerry Leiber had worked during the 1950s, remained open for business, surrounded by hip boutiques with outlandish names such as Granny Takes A Trip/West and I'm A Hog For You Baby. The less strangely named Rubicon and Pleasure Dome also sold the latest fashions, while prime hangouts included folk coffeehouses the Garret and the Blue Grotto, a diner called the Coffee Cup, Dome's Drugstore, and the ever-present Canter's Delicatessen. Fairfax High, meanwhile, hosted a show by The Byrds in October 1965, and performances by The Bobby Fuller Four and Herb Alpert & The Tijuana Brass in 1966. Also on Fairfax was the headquarters for a local version of *The Oracle*, a San Francisco-based underground newspaper.

One coffeehouse in central Hollywood, Bizarre Bazaar, is best remembered for the time they made good on a special advertisement running in *The Los Angeles Free Press* for a weekend of 'LSD Coffee.' It was served alongside house regulars 'Love Punch' and 'Bizarre Banana,' which promised a "new improved formula" so that customers could "get high legally." "Coffeehouses were a big deal," recalls Tomata DuPlenty of 1970s punk act The Screamers, who cites: "Mother Neptune's near Heliotrope [Avenue] on Melrose, where old beatniks mixed with hippies; the Blue Grotto on Fairfax, [which] seemed to always be playing Donovan in the background; a groovy little hideaway [called] 8727 on Melrose; and the Fifth Estate on Sunset Strip, where they showed Andy Warhol and Luis Buñuel films on a sheet."

* * *

Even with all that Sunset Strip had to offer, however, straying too far from a television set between 3:30 and 6:00pm would not have been wise. Los Angeles easily outstripped any other local area in terms of rock'n'roll television. Dick Clark had moved *American Bandstand* to Los Angeles from Philadelphia in March 1964 and soon set up the offices of his production company one block west of Gazzarri's at 9121 Sunset Boulevard. "By late 1963 I realized how rapidly times were changing," Clark later wrote. "I knew *Bandstand* would be out of date unless I did something about it. Teen stars were moving to Los Angeles in the hope of getting into the movies. The Philadelphia music scene was fading, while in Southern California Jan & Dean and The Beach Boys were making fresh, new sounds."[1]

In 1965, Clark produced a beach-based, teen-orientated soap opera called *Never Too Young*, starring Tony Dow from *Leave It To Beaver* alongside Cindy Carol, Robin Grace, Pat Connolly, Tommy Rettig, and Michael Blodgett. Rock'n'roll stars such as The Castaways or Johnny Rivers would make appearances at a fictitious club called Alfy's High Dive, located by the Santa Monica Pier. Later the same year, Clark took on the most ambitious rock'n'roll program of his career: *Where The Action Is*, telecast nationwide at 3:30pm on ABC during 1965–66, and featuring location shoots filmed right across America and in London. The Knickerbockers were regulars, but the group most synonymous with *Where The Action Is* is Paul Revere & The Raiders.

Kim Fowley had met The Raiders in Portland, Oregon, while trekking up and down the West Coast promoting The Wailers' 'Tall Cool One' in 1960. Fowley encouraged the group to move to Los Angeles after their 1961 instrumental 'Like Long Hair' became a hit for Gardena Records. After local deejay Roger Hart became their manager the group signed to Columbia, and began to rise to prominence just as Dick Clark realized that, with the craze for Fabian and Frankie Avalon-style teen idols having been obliterated by The Beatles, he needed a real rock'n'roll band for his new show.

Clark rolled with the sea change in music tastes and began to present the most exciting new bands of 1965–67 on his television shows. *Where The Action Is* and *American Bandstand* are great sources of rare clips of bands such as Count Five, The 13th Floor Elevators, Them, The Lefte Banke, ? & The Msyterians, The Leaves, and Love. Right in among them were Paul Revere & The Raiders, performing 'Steppin' Out,' 'Just Like Me,' 'Kicks' (an anti-drugs song hated by David Crosby at the time), 'Hungry,' 'Good Thing' (which featured Ry Cooder on guitar), and 'Him Or Me—What's It Gonna Be?'

Paul Revere & The Raiders formed in 1960, and were among the best of many fantastic bands operating in the Pacific Northwest, such as The Wailers, The Kingsmen, Don & The Goodtimes, and The Sonics. As soon as The Beatles came along, these struggling bands—previously considered too raunchy for radio—suddenly had an outlet beyond that of the local high school dance. The only difference between Paul Revere & The Raiders in 1963 and 1965 was that the band-members stopped slicking back their hair and combed it over their faces instead; their music retained the same charge it had carried with it when the group had rockabilly hair. They would get a jolt of fresh energy from the organ-led sound of The Animals and by The Kinks, who inspired both original material and a cover of The Wilde Knights' 'Just Like Me.' (The Wilde Knights, best known for 'Beaver Patrol,' were also from the Pacific Northwest, but played regularly on the Strip. They recorded the original 'Just Like Me' amid the Watts Riots at the same South Central studio that had produced The Penguins' 'Earth Angel' and *Wipe Out* by The Impacts.)

Paul Revere & The Raiders' crunchy guitar, thick, cheesy organ, and gritty vocals were made for the rock'n'roll culture of the mid 1960s. Lead singer Mark Lindsay seemed like an American Mick Jagger: he could sing and dance the crowd into a frenzy, and turned the heat on with the girls in the audience. Their penchant for colonial uniforms and wacky nicknames—Lindsay and keyboardist Paul Revere were joined by Harpo, Smitty, Fang, and The Kid—led to them being tagged, initially, as a gimmick band, but they were able to back up their image with solid music and performance. Like The Byrds, The Raiders were produced by Terry Melcher, and received heavy coverage in the rock'n'roll magazines of the day. Alongside The Standells, they are among the most obvious examples of the archetypal 1960s punk group.

The daily half-hour burst of *Where The Action Is* was followed all over the country by local rock'n'roll programming at 4:00pm. A deejay from a Top 40 radio station in each city would take over emcee chores on a local television channel, presenting bands that passed through town and new 45s that kids would dance to for the viewers at home. Los Angeles had many more rock'n'roll radio stations and independent television stations than, say, Baltimore. ABC's *Shindig!*, *Shivaree*, *American Bandstand*, and *Where The Action Is* were all based in town, and there were more rock'n'roll nightclubs than, well, anywhere else. As such, the overload of talent in LA was more than sufficient to keep the abundance of locally produced rock'n'roll television programming sizzling.

Shindig!, shot in Hollywood, was actually an extension of the brilliant programming being produced in the UK by Jack Good. His early shows *6.5 Special* and *Oh Boy!* were exciting to watch, despite the rock'n'roll talent on show in 1950s Britain being mediocre at best. When Good arrived in America, he immediately booked Bo Diddley, Jerry Lee Lewis, and Chuck Berry for *Shindig!*, and then brought over new performers from Britain such as The Kinks, The Who,

The Pretty Things, The Yardbirds, The Zombies, and The Rolling Stones. The Beatles gave *Shindig!* an exclusive in late 1964, performing their as-yet unreleased 'I'm A Loser' and 'Kansas City.' This followed a special Good had just produced in the UK called *Around The Beatles*, which celebrated the group's arrival back home after their invasion of America. Trust in Good served *Shindig!* well.

The half-hour *Shindig!* was so successful that ABC expanded its format to a full hour, then split that hour off into two half-hours during the week. Many of Phil Spector's Wall Of Sound musicians worked steadily on *Shindig!*, with long-time Spector session bassist Ray Pohlman serving as music coordinator. Among the regular performers on the show were The Everly Brothers, The Righteous Brothers, teen-belter Donna Loren, and rhythm & blues girl group The Blossoms (featuring a certain Darlene Love on lead vocals).

The slick Bobby Sherman served as the resident teen idol, but the show's rockin' essence was provided by The Shindogs, a made-up beat-garage combo featuring James Burton on lead guitar, Delaney Bramlett on guitar and vocals, Joey Cooper on bass and vocals, and Chuck Blackwell on drums. Glen D. Hardin was an auxiliary Shindog, playing electric piano on about half of the group's *Shindig!* appearances, and serving as their musical arranger. Various other hot session players floated in and out of televised jams with The Shindogs, including Billy Preston, Leon Russell, and Glen Campbell. The group scored a national hit in 1966 with the garage-punk 45 'Who Do You Think You Are,' which was produced by Russell for the Viva label, and made an appearance on *The Patty Duke Show*.

As the hottest network television outlet for rock'n'roll, almost all of the crucial performers of both the 1950s and 60s appeared on *Shindig!* (the only notable exceptions were Elvis Presley and Bob Dylan). The show was hosted by KFWB disc jockey Jimmy O'Neil, who had brought rock'n'roll—in the form of The Beach Boys, Jackie DeShannon, and others—to Pandora's Box on Sunset Strip in 1962. O'Neil brought a Hollywood-style zip to proceedings that threw Jack Good's thrilling sense of presentation into overdrive. The go-go dancers on *Shindig!*, led by Toni Basil, were often lit with dramatic, film noir-style shadows, giving their rock'n'roll dancing a pronounced sense of the ominous. British journalists Philip Jenkinson and Alan Warner rightly praise Good's pioneering style, taking note of his "incredible sense of spontaneity," his use of "spotlights [that would] dazzle the camera lenses" and "direct (as opposed to playback) sound," and his keenness on keeping "the cameras, audience, and artists *moving*."

"Rock'n'roll suited his visual style perfectly," they write. "It gave him a beat to cut his camera shots on, a garish array of clothes, make-ups, and instruments, and, above all, it gave his cameras a constantly changing, sexy kaleidoscope of exotic visuals. He and he alone truly linked the sound with the visual experience."[2]

Like *Shindig!*, the nationally syndicated Shivaree was shot at the ABC studios in the Los Feliz/Silver Lake district. Jerry Hopkins of *The Los Angeles Free Press* worked on *Shivaree* as a talent coordinator, and enduring actress Teri Garr was the choreographer. The show's set design instilled a sense of excitement from the get-go: behind the stage were minimalist rafters just about sturdy enough to hold a shaking pillar of mods and go-go dancers; in front of that was a huge dance floor. KFWB's Gene Weed was the host, with 'Diamond Head' by The Ventures serving as a regular theme song. The Rolling Stones, The Bobby Fuller Four, The Crystals, Jackie Wilson, and The Byrds were among the guests, with the overall effect resembling a rock'n'roll Tower Of Babel.

The lower-budget *Lloyd Thaxton Show*, which aired on KCOP Channel 13, was unlike any other rock'n'roll program on the air. Thaxton, the creator of the original *Tiger Beat* magazine, fronted a wacky, unique show that garnished cool bands and dance segments with surreal lip-synch parodies. As with most rock'n'roll deejays of the time, Thaxton was eager to pick up on new records the second they came out, but was equally comfortable to present them in a goofy style on television.

Thaxton had an excellent sense of rhythm and timing, and his parodies were often very funny. The introduction to his show shot the audience through the window of a miniature, cardboard malt shop, outside of which stood Dawk, an eerie, Cousin Itt-style rubber doll. Once Thaxton had welcomed viewers inside and introduced himself, the running gag was for his dancers to shout back "So what?!," mocking the pomposity of other television hosts. He would then stand on a circular riser amid the dancers and pretend to sing in a strained, hammy style. That was Lloyd Thaxton: happy to make fun of himself, the people who made records he played, the show's sponsors, and even its audience, but never in an offensive manner.

Thaxton would pretend to play instruments, too, and got kids in his audience to lip-synch—or trumpet-synch—to records such as 'Hello Dolly' by Louis Armstrong. "Our show was more personal," says Thaxton. "We purposely didn't allow the voiceover announcer to yell 'From Hollywood!' during the intro. We never gussied it up to be a network show, and when we syndicated it nationally, people thought it was coming from their own town." 1970s punk singer Tomata DuPlenty recalls how attending a taping of the show as a teenager—with a "fire-dancer [from] San Gabriel" as his date—provided a huge boost to his credibility. "We won the 'stop dance' contest, and then I got to talk to Bobby Fuller ... After that I was no longer considered a geek at school."

Thaxton would make use of strange sound effects on the show and don bizarre outfits to become characters based on the novelty or hook of a record. Danny Hutton had a particularly surreal experience on the show. "The first time I'd ever taken LSD happened to be the night before a scheduled appearance on *The Lloyd Thaxton Show*," he recalls. "Without any idea the feeling would last into the next morning, there I was at the taping, and out comes Lloyd Thaxton dressed in a costume like something out of the Arabian Knights, playing it to the hilt. Obviously, there was no way that I could contain the laughter, and I couldn't help breaking up during the interview." Thaxton himself adds: "The Sunset Strip at that time was something that was very close to the way television handled things during 1961–68. There was a complete change in the air. With some of the negative things that had happened politically, we were trying to offer a different outlook on life."

Of all the Los Angeles programs that were syndicated outside the area, KHJ-TV's *Hollywood A Go Go* stands out as the most intense. Its production stemmed from the genius of the Teen-Age Fair's Al Burton. His *POP Dance Party* had mutated into something called *Pickwick Dance Party*, with Bob Eubanks replacing Wink Martindale—who had moved on to quiz shows—as host. Then, in 1964, Burton moved the *Dance Party* back into the TV studio, having previously shot it outside, and installed Sam Riddle as host. "Once Sam started, he owned the place," says Burton. "He just had a great touch with the kids." *9th Street West* aired on weekdays at 6.00pm, and was popular enough that by the end of the year it spawned a more extravagant, Saturday night program, *9th Street A Go Go*, which was quickly renamed *Hollywood A Go Go* to reflect its content: "A lot of frills, many more stars, [and] a line of dancers, the Gazzarri Dancers," according to Burton.

What set *Hollywood A Go Go* apart from the rest was the sense that it was being transmitted from directly within the spinning cataclysm of Sunset Strip nightlife. Burton recalls intending it to look "dark and foreboding," the kind of place where, under normal circumstances, teenagers "weren't allowed in." His pioneering production techniques provoked constant conflict with the show's engineers until Burton explained his ideas to them more fully. "They were hip guys," he says, "but they had learned what the rules are, and they stuck by the rules. I didn't want to do that, because by seeing mistakes everywhere, I'd learned what the mistakes were that looked good." Burton used "motion picture-type lights, as opposed to television floodlights," which he could shoot directly into, creating impressive flare effects, while blaring the music out "way beyond the red line." The overall effect, he says, "was half-amateurish, because professionals would not have allowed us to be that primitive. But your set came on louder on our show than anyplace else."

Hollywood A Go Go was capped off by a group of non-professional dancers—actual rock'n'roll chicks who would go-go out of a passion for the records. Burton would scour Sunset Strip nightclubs for the best dancers and pay them to appear on the show. Being on *Hollywood A Go Go* was an unexpected thrill for these girls; they were not actresses, and it showed in the expressions on their faces. Burton would send the dancers out to Hole In The Wall to choose clothes for the show, and would duplicate the best outfit of the ones picked out for all the girls to wear. The overall effect was wholesome, but with an underlying sexuality that was both obvious but elusive. "We wanted them to be the girl-next-door, but doin' great moves," Burton says. "They wore enough clothes, but they were underdressed: almost always jeans and striped shirts cut away at the shoulders, and we made them dance barefoot. They never wore shoes. The dark, hippie stage didn't hit us at all. The girls would wear bangs, straight long hair, or ponytails." The show was a huge success, eventually airing in "114 different countries," according to Burton, who notes: "We even did a special in Hawaii called *Aloha A Go Go*."

Shebang was more typical in format, with several round risers circling the back of the studio in an arc fronted by a huge dance floor loaded with LA teens. It was shot in color, and utilized chromakey effects, preceding Germany's excellent *Beat Club*, which developed the blue screen idea further several years later. Hosted by Casey Kasem, *Shebang* ran on KTLA Channel 5 for an hour daily at 5:00pm—opposite Lloyd Thaxton (who had also begun to shoot in color). In these days before home video recorders, Tivo, and YouTube, viewers would have to flick back and forth between the two shows. Fortunately, Kasem would often replay performances, and often reused them again as the host of *America's Top 10* during the 1980s. His *Shebang* clips seemed to jump right out of the screen when juxtaposed against glossy, soulless promos by contemporary artists.

Kasem kept many irons in the fire during the mid 1960s, hosting Friday night dances at the Hawthorne Recreation Center called the Drop In. Los Angeles design historian Jim Heimann describes the Drop In, and similar venues such as Harmony Park in Anaheim and Darby Park in Inglewood, as "places outside of the clubs and TV shows that anybody could go to, [which] were hugely popular because there wasn't enough room for all the kids who wanted to dance, even with the massive amount of clubs in Hollywood." The Drop In's house act was Band Without A Name, featuring vocalist Eddie Haddad (soon to front The American Revolution) and former Beach Boys guitarist David Marks. "Casey Kasem booked us around town," recalls Marks, "backing Sonny & Cher, Dick & Dee Dee, Freddy Cannon, people like that. The Bobby Fuller Four would be on the bills too. Kasem had all these different artists working, and it would be like a free gig for publicity." (Band Without A Name recorded a folk-rock cover of Glenn Yarbrough's 'Baby The Rain Must Fall' for the movie of the same name, says Marks, but their live show also took in songs by Ike & Tina Turner, Fats Domino, and James Brown.)

"The Standells played at the Drop In on one of the nights I went to," Heimann adds, noting that these sorts of venues were big enough to take in fans who couldn't get in to nightclub shows, but not so large as to be overwhelming. Sadly, he notes, "[the scene] dispersed pretty quickly once the forum for dance shows ended and serious rock became the order of the day."

* * *

As 1966 gave way to 1967, *Hollywood A Go Go* vanished from the airwaves, as did *Shindig!* and *Hullabaloo* (which was shot mostly in New York, and aired on NBC). These shows had made it on to television amid the initial rush of Beatlemania, which was now over. KHJ Channel 9 in Los Angeles, however, held a tight grip on a huge share of the local market with this type of programming, so introduced two new shows to take place of *9th Street West* and *Hollywood A Go Go: Boss City* and *Groovy*. By 1967, 'Color TV' had become the industry standard, so *Boss City* and *Groovy* came complete with proto-psychedelic graphics. *Boss City* was similar in look to *Shebang*, but aired on Saturday nights only, and had the wildest of hosts. The Real Don Steele was hard of hearing, so screamed even louder than he had to, giving him a devil-may-care attitude that was accentuated by the fact that he often seemed unsure as to what was going on around him.

Steele's gags were wild and irreverent. The best was a solo dance sequence, during which Mitch Ryder & The Detroit Wheels' recording of 'Devil With A Blue Dress On/Good Golly Miss Molly' was cranked to full volume each week. Heedless of lawyers or insurance, Steele would pull kids out of the audience at random and force them to freak out or go-go dance atop a circular riser. If Steele was not pleased with the performance, he would push the poor sap off the cylinder and drag someone else up out of the crowd. In this inverted predecessor to stage diving, kids were propelled by a mixture of fear and excitement, not cocky decadence. Those who were not being pushed off the riser by Steele would be busy laughing—partly out of relief at not having been chosen.

Steele also injected political humor into *Boss City*, screaming 'news' reports at the top of his lungs during one wonderfully acidic, opinionated weekly segment. In September 1969 *Boss City* became *The Real Don Steele Show*, which ran until 1975. Neither Steele nor the show mellowed over the years, despite the changing times, which left him with far fewer garage-punk style records to draw from than had previously been at his disposal. With the Top 40 awash with soft rock and FM radio dominated by bands that were too heavy for rock'n'roll-style dancing, Steele turned instead to such records as The Sweet's 'Little Willy,' Daddy Dewdrop's 'Chic A Boom,' and blaxploitation-era soul 45s—the kind of thing that was also favored by Lester Bangs. Even after his television show came to an end, Steele continued to work on radio. He and KHJ attempted to break tracks from *The Ramones* on its release in 1976, which led to his appearance as Screamin' Steve in the group's 1979 movie *Rock'n'Roll High School*. (Steele had been calling bands such as The Sweet "punk rock" since 1972.) The Real Don Steele's star can be seen on the Hollywood Walk Of Fame today on the southeast corner of Hollywood Boulevard and La Brea Avenue.

The last and most far-out show of the go-go era to air on KHJ Channel 9 was *Groovy*, hosted by another screamer, Michael Blodgett, who became the reverend of 1960s punk in Los Angeles. *Groovy* summed up the previous three years of rock'n'roll television in one daily program. It had the best name since *Hollywood A Go Go*, showed off the cream of LA's early psychedelic graphics, and was broadcast from the beach—usually near Santa Monica Pier—every day at 4:00pm. After the show, the cast and crew could be found at Chez Jay's, a nautically themed pub across the street from the beach that remains open to this day.

The '66 look still ruled on *Groovy*, on which kids danced in their beachwear on the sand to records such as 'A Thousand Shadows' by The Seeds. On occasion, Blodgett would mock the overt silliness of psychedelic dress in 1967 by looking knowingly ridiculous in Donovan-style rags on the sand. Each program featured a bikini contest, which would be judged by guests such as The Merry-Go-Round at the end of the hour. The contestants—and the bikinis themselves—showed off that wonderful mix of surf, pop, and psychedelia that could only have come from mid-1960s Los Angeles.

Groovy would broadcast sand crab races, sack races, and pie fights on the beach, while Blodgett's 'Question Of The Day' gave kids much more leeway than the similar segment on *American Bandstand*—discussions ranged from frank political and sexual issues to whether or not a new trend in car customization was cool. Being outdoors seemed advantageous during this segment in that it allowed the youth to speak out while taking a breather from all the fun, rather than being packed into a cavernous television studio. Another segment had gravestones set up in the sand, during which Blodgett announced—or rather screamed—"Today, we are burying prejudice on *Groovy!* Can ya dig it?"

Groovy later moved indoors and was hosted first by Sam Riddle and then by Robert W. Morgan, who had previously been on shortlived *Morgan's Alley*. The popularity of Blodgett's version of *Groovy* led to Riddle presenting a new show called *The Groovy Game*, which was an LA spin on the British game show *Juke Box Jury*. *The Groovy Game* also introduced Kam Nelson, an LA version of Cathy McGowan, co-host of *Ready Steady Go*. "We needed a young lady to introduce all the contestants," recalled Riddle. "We asked her to come on, and within two or three months she became sort of a 17-year-old phenomenon in Los Angeles. And then when *The Groovy Game* became *The Groovy Show*, [in] about July of 1968, we had what we called Kam's Corner, where you sent letters asking Kam for her 'advice.'"

The various permutations of *Groovy* and *Boss City* were like the heartbeat of 1966 refusing to die out. Michael Blodgett's popularity led to a self-titled, Sunday night show on KTTV Channel 11 in 1968. He continued to work as a writer and actor, appearing in *The Trip* and playing a key role in Russ Meyer's cult hit *Beyond The Valley Of The Dolls* (1970). Sam Riddle, meanwhile, carried on some of the *Groovy* vibe when he hosted *Get It Together* for ABC in 1970.

LA's gritty, self-deprecating, and facetious sense of rock'n'roll humor carried over into other programs on KHJ Channel 9 and beyond during the mid 1960s.

The channel's amazing art and prop staff, led by beatnik surfer and cartoonist Mike Dormer, designed a creepy set for *Shrimpenstein!*—"A cross between *Soupy Sales* and *Shindig!*," according to its press kit. There were also suggestions of *The Addams Family*, *Boss City*, pioneering television comic Ernie Kovacs, and *Time For Beany*, a late-1940s puppet show that was really an adult satire in disguise, and which evolved into a cartoon show, *Beany & Cecil*, in the early 1960s. (One of the voices of *Beany*, Stan Freberg, later became a major comedy album artist, and did a series of wild ads for KRLA in 1966.)

Shrimpenstein! had a hip appeal that went beyond its intended age group. Frank Sinatra and Sammy Davis Jr were fans and, legend has it, once called in at KHJ-TV to show their appreciation. As noted earlier, Kaleidoscope made a point of ending their rehearsals in time to get home, get high, and catch the show at 5:00pm; Rod Sterling of *The Twilight Zone* also tuned in regularly. The show's host, Gene Moss, and puppeteer Jim Thurman later picked up jobs writing comedy bits for Dean Martin, Carol Burnett, and Bob Hope. The duo had written for the animated series *Roger Ramjet*, which was loaded with Hollywood in-jokes and pop culture references, before establishing themselves as masters of psych-pop improvisation on *Shrimpenstein!* It remains something of a surprise that the censors let this one slip by: there'd be sly references to booze and LSD, jokes about a ventriloquist's dummy being "a little impotent," seemingly inexplicable snickering and guffawing off-camera, sped-up parodies of Herb Alpert by a group called The Tijuana Bats—television like this would not reappear until *Pee Wee's Playhouse* came along in the 1980s, and even then was never quite the same.

The spirit of the Strip was so abundant in 1966 as to leak onto LA's most popular television show for kids, *Cartoon Express With Engineer Bill* (which had a vaguely rockabilly-esque theme song). The show's host, Bill Stulla, then made *Bill Stulla's Shake Shop* for KHJ Channel 9, on which pre-teen tikes would dance to the latest rock'n'roll sounds. (*Kiddie A Go Go* followed in Chicago, while *Wonderama* from New York City followed suit with a tots-gone-go-go segment.)

Elsewhere, the gap left by the departure of *The Vampira Show* in the mid 1950s was belatedly filled, in 1962, by KCOP Channel 13's *Jeepers Creepers*. The title character was initially played by deejay Bob Guy, and then by Jim Sullivan, who carried the role into the mid 1960s; in between times, KCOP introduced Lietta Harvey in *Ghoulita*. KTLA Channel 5 cashed in on the camp horror resurgence with *Shock Theater*, while KHJ made *Creature Feature* and *Fright*

Night, which tipped a sly nod to Alfred Hitchcock's distaste for commercials by segueing into ad breaks with the sound of a toilet flushing. KHJ's low-budget, offhand approach continued into the 1970s and 80s, during which time *Fright Night* became *Movie Macabre* and introduced Elvira—a combination of *The Vampira Show* and Frank Zappa's 'Valley Girl'—to the world.

The Dating Game, which debuted in 1965, carried the LA rock'n'roll-show vibe in both its logo and its sense of humor. The whole affair was livened up by incidental music by Herb Alpert & The Tijuana Brass, while there were occasional performances by Sunset Strip groups such as The Grass Roots, Iron Butterfly, It's Boss house band The Regents, and The Strawberry Alarm Clock, whose members would also sit in as surprise contestants.

Without exception, no other time or place has produced so many television programs catering to a vital music scene. These shows, from *Shindig!* and *Hollywood A Go Go* straight through to *Groovy*, provided not just a direct link to who and what was happening on Sunset Strip to both local and national audiences, but also a unique sense of humor that made for some great rock'n'roll coverage—and some of the most entertaining moments in television history.

* * *

American International Pictures' teen flicks were based on the same premise as the dance shows of the time: doing things from the kids' point of view. These are not movies that should be judged on the preconceived, traditional values of critical response and mainstream box office appeal. It would be ignorant to denounce *Faster, Pussycat! Kill! Kill!* or *Muscle Beach Party* as 'bad' movies, or to attempt to compare their unadulterated wit to the works of Orson Welles. What matters is that movies such as *Rat Pfink And Boo Boo* or *Hot Rods To Hell* spoke in a completely different language, and poked fun at the very standards by which they are judged.

"These movies don't really need a plot or a decent story line," says garage-punk musician Shelly Ganz, "because in a sense, they are docudramas of Americana that typify the idealized youth or psychedelic experience, which in and of itself is fascinating. At the root of it, it all goes back to Archie comics creating an environment that every teenager really wanted to be in. Jan & Dean and The Beach Boys did the same thing. So did Charles Schulz with his comic strip *Peanuts*, [which] was like *Archie* on a smaller scale. [American International

Pictures] was at the forefront of shaping that imagery in the 1950s and 60s, so even the most rudimentary plot is sufficient."

Kids were smart enough to discount highbrow artistic approval ratings and simply enjoy these fun movies for what they were. As far back as 1956, American International Pictures (AIP) released *Shake Rattle And Rock*—on which *Rock'n'Roll High School* is based—featuring Big Joe Turner and Fats Domino. Then, in 1958, AIP made the stunning *Hot Rod Gang*, which gave starring roles to Gene Vincent & His Blue Caps. A year later, *The Ghost Of Dragstrip Hollow* perfectly encapsulated the oncoming rush of LA garage. In it, The Renegades throw a monster ball in a haunted mansion; their producer, Kim Fowley, joins in, miming along with the group in full monster garb. (The movie's musical director Jimmy Maddin, with whom Fowley would later work at the KRLA Teen Club, also makes an onscreen appearance.)

The beat carried on through the early 1960s with the Frankie & Annette *Beach Party* series, which features the music of Dick Dale & His Del-Tones, Brian Wilson & Gary Usher, The Pyramids, and The Kingsmen. When AIP made *The TAMI Show* and *The Big TNT Show* during the mid 1960s it was very clear that Sunset Strip was now at the center of the teenage universe. Without hesitation, AIP then delved into the most erratic element of this new world and emerged with a whole new moviemaking genre: the biker movie.

The first of these was *The Wild Angels*, which stars Peter Fonda and Nancy Sinatra in a series of formless, improvised, decadent scenes. The key themes of these movies—gratuitous sex, getting wasted, and living outside the law—did not, however, preclude an appreciation for social interaction. In 1965, a notice went up outside the Plush Pup requesting that bikers refrained from revving their engines in the nearby residential area of the Strip, where they tended to park, as it was close to the prime biker-hangout Stripcombers (as seen in *The Trip*). Another hotspot for LA bikers was Handy Andy's on La Cienega and Santa Monica Boulevard.

Although there was an essence of violence in the biker trip, it did not overwhelm Sunset Strip in the way that it would at Altamont. The peace-loving Mamas & The Papas even took their name from the biker vernacular. An element of danger did lurk in the biker aesthetic, but most chose to absorb it vicariously through the movies rather than dismiss the world at large in the manner of the onscreen bikers.

One positive aspect of these biker movies was the soundtrack music, which was produced by Mike Curb and played by Davie Allen & The Arrows. Allan first took off with a version of The Shadows' biggest hit, which he renamed 'Apache '65.' His next project was the soundtrack to an art movie called *Skaterdater*, which won an award in the Short Subjects category at the 1966 Cannes Film Festival. *Skaterdater* introduced both Allan and Curb to the world of biker movies. They were quickly hired for *The Wild Angels* (1966), *Devil's Angels*, *Born Losers*, *The Glory Stompers* (all 1967), and *The Hellcats* (1968), which includes a cameo by Somebody's Chyldren.

The soundtracks to all of these movies came out on vinyl, as did a couple of other LPs by Allen and Curb in the same vein, *Freakout USA* and *Astrology For Young Lovers* (both 1967). The duo also produced soundtracks for documentaries (*Mondo Teeno: Teenage Rebellion* and *Mondo Hollywood*, both from 1967), a surfing movie (1968's *The Golden Breed*), and more standard AIP fare, such as *Dr Goldfoot & The Girl Bombs* (1966), *Thunder Alley* (1967), and *The Wild Racers* (1968). Their work appears on the soundtracks to the super-cool *Riot On Sunset Strip* (1967), *Maryjane*, and *Wild In The Streets* (both 1968). Less impressively, they also churned out music for forgettable exploitation fare such as *Killers Three* and *Jennie, Wife/Child*.

Davie Allan, Mike Curb, and their studio accomplice Bob Summers left behind a treasure trove of incidental music in teen flicks: the opening sequence of *It's A Bikini World* (1966), for instance, or the bar-fight scene of *Hell's Angels On Wheels* (1967). Who could top their non-vinyl themes to *The Love Ins* (1968) or *The Angry Breed* (1969)? The musical climax of *Maryjane* provides a definitive moment of wafting organ and erotic, fuzz-toned guitar. 'Blues Theme' (from *The Wild Angels*) and 'Devil's Angels' both become hit records for Davie Allen & The Arrows, who shared bills with The Music Machine, The Standells, The Turtles, and The Seeds.

Allan's fuzz-laced instrumental style could be heard everywhere in mid-1960s Los Angeles: on television sets, radios on the beach, in passing cars, on commercials, in cartoons, or blasting out of record stores and clubs. But not all of these records were actually his: another rarely discussed session-player, Mike Deasy, once of Eddie Cochran's band The Kelly Four, was similarly prolific in bombarding the media with fuzz-tone. "He was Mr psychedelic/fuzz-tone guitar," says studio historian Russ Wapensky. "You hear him on all of the Hollywood studio records of the second half of the 60s. The reason his name hasn't come up previously is that most discussion about the LA Wrecking Crew centers around the first of half of the60s and Phil Spector's Wall Of Sound era."

Davie Allan's music spread into AIP's 1967 foray into the acid experience, *The Trip*. Peter Fonda took the starring role, with Dennis Hopper and Bruce Dern as supporting acid-gurus. It was one of many movies produced by Roger Corman who, says Fonda, "gave young people movies they could relate to, not films they had to fish for. He gave a whole new generation of moviegoers films that weren't products of their parents. No way *The Wild Angels* or *The Trip* was made by anybody's parents!"

Whether or not *The Trip* is like a real LSD experience is of no real consequence: the movie is interesting simply because somebody tried to make it. Fonda managed to get one of his favorite groups, The International Submarine Band, into two sequences, but the music they 'play' in the club segment was actually by The Electric Flag. The ISB do perform an instrumental version of 'Hang On Sloopy' near the beginning of the film, however; the group—which featured Gram Parsons—is seen rehearsing the song. Bruce Dern's character, meanwhile, lives in a psychedelic pad that was in fact the real-life home of Arthur Lee.

In direct contrast to the risqué subject matter of movies such as *The Trip*, Warner Brothers' *The Cool Ones* (1967) focuses on the clean-cut flipside of the Sunset Strip reality. Debbie Watson and Gil Peterson star in a pop star success story loosely based on that of Sonny & Cher; Watson starts out as a go-go dancer on a *Hullabaloo*-like television show called *Whizbam*, which is choreographed by Toni Basil. After being fired from *Whizbam*, she is dragged off by her friends to see The Leaves performing 'Dr Stone' in a bohemian nightclub in Palm Springs. She then meets Peterson, and the duo eventually rise to success under the direction of a Phil Spector-like music industry Svengali played by Roddy McDowall. *The Cool Ones* features scenes shot along Sunset Plaza and at the Whisky A Go Go, and brief cameos by Vito Paulekas and Sheryl Carson. The excellent soundtrack is the work of Lee Hazlewood; one song, 'The Tantrum,' is reminiscent of later material by The Cramps, while another, 'This Town' (sung by Watson in the movie), was later recorded on 45 by both Frank and Nancy Sinatra.

Roddy McDowall also appeared in another key black-and-white document of this LA moment: the criminally overlooked *Lord Love A Duck* (1966), essentially *The Cool Ones* in a more intellectual setting. Tuesday Weld plays a starry-eyed teen-vamp in a college classroom full of punk guys in sunglasses. After she and McDowall draw attention to several scenes of Southern Californian hypocrisy, Weld ends up starring in a spoof beach movie called *Bikini Widow*. The soundtrack to *Lord Love A Duck* is by Neil Hefti, predating his work on *Batman*, and includes some great 1966-vintage garage by The Wild Ones (who had, a year earlier, recorded the first version of 'Wild Thing').

Sonny & Cher made a movie of their own in 1967 called *Good Times*. Sonny Bono was given complete control of what ended up being a messy excursion, but is worth sitting through for Cher's solo turns, which include her singing 'It's The Little Things' in front of the pop art paintings on the walls of It's Boss. More enjoyable is the earlier *Village Of The Giants* (1965), which features The Beau Brummels playing at the Whisky A Go Go, with Toni Basil dancing in a cage and a thunderous soundtrack by Jack Nitzsche. Ed 'Big Daddy' Roth's The Surfite also makes an appearance, while the dialog reads like a dictionary of 1960s punk. The following year's *The Pad (And How To Use It)* features more great footage of go-go dancing at the Whisky and a brief appearance by The Knickerbockers, who also donated the title song for *They Ran For Their Lives* in 1968.

Countless bands of the era made cameo appearances in these movies. The Sons Of Adam show up in *The Slender Thread* (1965), which also features Whisky A Go Go dancer Daryle Ann Lindley; The Grass Roots perform 'Feelings' in the Doris Day movie *With Six You Get Eggroll* (1968); and a vivid, color segment of The T-Bones playing at Gazzarri's can be seen in the deranged classic *Nightmare In Wax*, which came out in 1969 but was shot several years earlier. There's another color segment shot at Gazzarri's, featuring Blue Boy & The Artists, in the wacky Tommy Kirk comedy *Mother Goose A Go Go* (1966), while The Don Randi Trio, a house band at Sherry's, show up in the same year's *Fireball 500*. *Mondo Bizarro*, meanwhile, features an incredible overhead shot of the area between Clark and Hilldale, in which you can see The Doors' name on the marquee at the tiny London Fog and Love listed as headliners outside the Whisky. Most of *The Hallucination Generation* was shot in Spain, but there is a cool LA party scene at one point, while both *The Hippie Revolt* and *Acid Dreams* (both 1967) feature a slew of naked ladies, painted by Sheryl Carson and dancing the night away at Vito's Studio, with Vito Paulekas and Carl Franzoni in tow. There's more slapdash genius in *It's a Bikini World* (1967), which features a cameo by Bobby 'Boris' Picket of 'Monster Mash' fame and appearances by Pat & Lolly Vegas,

The Toys, The Castaways, and The Animals, all of whom appear on the Haunted House stage. *Girl In Gold Boots* (1968) was based entirely around the same venue, and features extensive footage of the club's go-go dancers and a beautifully shot night-drive down the Strip from Sunset and Doheny to Vine Street. Pandora's Box bongo player Preston Epps also makes an appearance.

Three documentaries from 1967 in the *Mondo Cane* vein offer an indispensable look at the Sunset Strip of the mid 1960s. The most realistic of these is *Mondo Mod* (1967), which takes the viewer on a cruise through various teenage activities of the time; there's a noisy segment on dirt bikes, a bird's eye view of an acid trip, an interview with the glazed-over owner of Mod boutique Belinda, plus surfing, dancing, and a karate class. Al Mitchell of the Fifth Estate coffeehouse talks about the generation gap over footage of the Sunset Strip riots, while the movie ends at a bongo-blastin' pot party, at which the 'mods' strip down to their skivvies.

Mondo Teeno: The Teenage Rebellion also includes riot footage, set to an organ-and-fuzz-driven title song by The Glass Family. Other riots, such as the famous battle between mods and rockers in Brighton, England, in 1965, also feature. Sheryl Carson, Vito Paulekas, celebrity hairdresser Jay Sebring, LSD guru Richard Alpert, health food freak Gypsy Boots, exotic dancer Jennie Lee, surf filmmaker Dale Davis, sculptor Valerie Porter, an early incarnation of The Mothers, and The Great God Pan all make appearances in Robert Carl Cohen's *Mondo Hollywood*, which also includes a lengthy interview with disgruntled singer Bobby Jameson, who had written 'Girl From The East' for The Leaves, released a Love-styled LP called *Songs Of Protest And Anti-Protest* as Chris Lucey, and made the Curt Boettcher-produced *Color Him In* under his own name. (Frank Zappa wrote and played on his 'Gotta Find My Roogalator.') In the movie, Jameson performs a Bo Diddley-like raver in which he repeatedly, angrily howls "Vietnam." The Executive Present of the Hollywood Chamber Of Commerce, Clark E. Grimes, also pops up, and praises the "unusual talents" and "creative genius" among LA folk. "They are the ones," he adds, "who spark a way of life that has changed the habits of the entire world."

Mondo Hollywood also profiles Louis Beech Marvin III (previously seen in Andy Warhol's *Tarzan And Jane Regained … Sort Of*), who had recently put together an event dubbed the Moonfire Happening. *The Los Angeles Free Press* of June 24th 1966 called the event, held at the Santa Monica Civic Auditorium, "one of the strangest attempts at a happening" ever staged in Los Angeles. There

Left: Lee Hazlewood and Nancy Sinatra, Gold Star Studios. *Above:* Jack Nitzsche at the Griffith Park Love-In, 1967. *Below:* Phil Spector with The Ronettes, Gold Star Studios, 1963.

Above: Buffalo Springfield at the Whisky A Go Go, 1966. *Left:* The Stone Poneys, featuring Linda Ronstadt. *Opposite:* John and Michelle Phillips at deVoss boutique, 1966; Cass Elliott and Denny Doherty at Western Studio, 1966; *Hey Joe* by The Leaves.

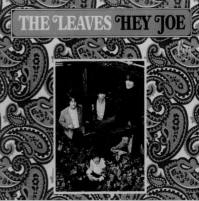

THE LEAVES · HEY JOE

Above: The Rolling Stones at RCA Music Center Of The World, recording 'Satisfaction', Sunset Boulevard, 1965. *Left:* Bob Dylan in Los Feliz, 1966. *Opposite:* Teri Garr (*top*) and Toni Basil (*bottom*) at the Action, 1965; The Turtles in front of the Hullabaloo for the KRLA Beat Awards, 1965.

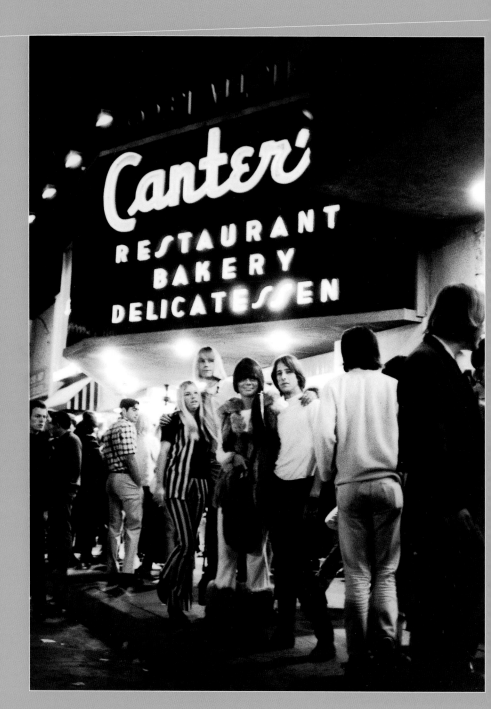

Top: The Sea Witch, 1965. Left: Paul McCartney, John Lennon, and Ringo Starr at a press conference for *Revolver*, 1966. *Above:* Paul signs autographs at Capitol. *Opposite:* Canter's deli on Fairfax, summer 1966.

Above: Riot on Sunset Strip, Saturday November 12 1966. *Right:* What began as a nonviolent demonstration to save Pandora's Box turned into a police riot. *Below:* The neon sign above Dino's Lodge was a beacon to teens.

was an abundance of "fantastically costumed dancers" and light machines, as well as "huge masked figures," projections, body painting, and a wide range of music that took in everything from "a jug band" to "Indian sitar playing" alongside the obligatory rock'n'roll. "All 2,700 seats" of the Civic were taken, according to the *Free Press*, which also noted Marvin's difficulties in trying to bring the party to a close by its scheduled end.

Elsewhere in the movie, both Vito Paulekas and Dale Davis express—somewhat unexpectedly—their disapproval of the LSD phenomenon. Paulekas declares the notions of drug-taking being "something fresh and new" or a gateway to a broadened or expanded consciousness to be "nonsense." "I'm particularly disturbed [by] the rationalizations that are taking place," he says, "because in some of the so-called best intellectual circles, there are discussions about taking LSD in order to make a special kind of person out of you. This is the great threat." The interview is juxtaposed with footage of a teach-in by acid guru Richard Alpert.

The musical highlight of *Mondo Hollywood* comes in the form of three outstanding camp horror rock'n'roll tunes by Teddy & Darrel, which are used to soundtrack scenes of a Beverly Hills pool party (complete with dancing 'ghouls' who eerily predate the David Johansen look), Sheryl Carson's body painting, and a group of 'monsters' on their way to the Teen-Age Fair. (Around the same time, Teddy & Darrel cut a notorious, Mike Curb-produced album, *These Are The Hits You Silly Savage*, of homoerotic parodies of 1966 hits such as 'Wild Thing' and 'Hold On I'm Comin'.')

Near the end of *Mondo Hollywood*, teen idol Jerry Naylor sings a hammy, crooning rendition of 'The Magic Night' over an excellent montage of Hollywood freeways and streets crowding toward the nightlife rush. The twirling Sahara-billboard showgirl and the Rocky & Bullwinkle statue are juxtaposed in tongue-in-cheek fashion, while a mock-paparazzi montage shows everyone from Brigitte Bardot to an absurd-looking Ronald Reagan, who is captured giving an extreme right-wing speech. The Lawrence Welk billboard next to the Hollywood Palladium is made to look similarly ridiculous, with Welk's baton moving in time with visual and musical cues. Naylor then belts out the line "Freaking my mind to sensation" in a wonderfully oblivious, inappropriate manner. The movie closes with spliced-together footage of 1965/66 dance floor action from various Sunset Strip nightclubs, culminating in a clip of The Mugwump Establishment performing their garage-punk 'Mondo Hollywood Freakout.'

Equally detached from the adult world was Barry Feinstein's *You Are What You Eat* (1968), which spawned a Columbia Records soundtrack. Feinstein's involvement with the underground culture on the Strip began in the mid 1950s, when he poured espresso at Chez Paulette. He later married Mary Travers of Peter, Paul & Mary, and shot the famous fisheye photograph for the cover of The Byrds' *Mr Tambourine Man*. The movie has no narration, only music and a series of great Teen-Age Fair advertisements read by KBLA deejay Rosko over footage of go-go girls dancing in front of sports cars and kids in plastic Germany army helmets. Rodney Bingenheimer is shown observing the madness, while David Crosby makes a weird cameo, looking as if he'd walked right off the cover of The Byrds' *Younger Than Yesterday*. Hot-rods rumble; Tiny Tim sings 'I Got You Babe' with Nico-like chanteuse Eleanor Baruchian over footage of screaming fans at The Beatles' final concert at San Francisco's Candlestick Park; Barry McGuire runs through a field of flowers to the sound of Van Dyke Parks's 'Come To The Sunshine,' as recorded by Harpers Bizarre; bodies are painted at Vito's Studio in preparation for a freak out. The movie ends with footage of Carl Franzoni and others in Vito's troupe dancing at The Mothers Of Invention's Freak Out at the Shrine Exposition Hall on September 17th 1966. (Strangely, as with the International Submarine Band segment in *The Trip*, the sound heard is an overdubbed recording by The Electric Flag.)

Barry McGuire was also involved in *The President's Analyst* (1967), a twisted sequel to *Our Man Flint* and *In Like Flint*. James Coburn plays a shrink who, on the run from international spies, opts to hide out as a hippie in McGuire's band. Predating the businessman-to-bohemian role reversal of James Fox and Mick Jagger in *Performance* by a year, *The President's Analyst* features music by Clear Light, who back McGuire on their excellent 'She's Ready To Be Free,' and a McGuire solo turn on 'Inner Manipulations.' (Beware cheap, video versions of the movie, for which some of the original music has been replaced by terrible prog rock instrumentals to avoid the cost of licensing Clear Light and McGuire's songs. They were restored for the 2004 DVD edition.)

AIP's *Psych-Out* (1968) is set in San Francisco but features two Los Angeles bands, The Seeds and The Strawberry Alarm Clock (who are shown playing not in Frisco, but at the Cheetah at Pacific Ocean Park). The Chocolate Watchband also crop up in the same year's *The Love Ins*, which spawned their stunning '(Are You Gonna Be There) At The Love In' 45. The movie's hilarious *Alice In*

Wonderland-style hallucination scene should not be missed. It also features the obscure all-girl band The UFO, who moved to LA from Boston, and can be seen belting out 'I'm A Woman'—as The Unidentified Flying Objects—in Andrew Meyer's 1966 short *An Early Clue To A New Direction*.

The Love Ins was produced by Sam Katzman, who can almost certainly lay claim to have documented more rock'n'roll acts on film than anyone else. His work includes the Bill Haley movies *Rock Around The Clock* (1956) and *Don't Knock The Rock* (1957); a whole series of Alan Freed Movies featuring Chuck Berry, Frankie Lymon & The Teenagers, The Johnny Burnette Trio and many others; and two twist movies with Chubby Checker (one of which also has a cameo by Dion). Even more impressive, however, is *Get Yourself A College Girl* (1964), which includes early clips of The Animals, Jimmy Smith, The Standells, The Dave Clark Five, and Astrud Gilberto singing 'The Girl From Ipanema' with Stan Getz. Katzman didn't wait around for the mainstream to catch up with these acts; he struck while the iron was hot.

As soon as the real-life demonstrations on Sunset Strip cooled off, Katzman made *Riot On Sunset Strip* (1967). The movie's rediscovery in the early 1980s inspired the first wave of post-punk garage in much the same way that The Who's big-screen version of *Quadrophenia* shifted the post-punk mod revival into high gear. A 1983 screening of *Riot On Sunset Strip* and *Mondo Mod* at the Nuart Theater in Santa Monica, hosted by *Riot* star Tim Rooney, was akin to a summit meeting for Los Angeles artists and musicians, who proceeded to spread the legacy of Sunset Strip '66 around the world.

Riot on Sunset Strip is not without fault. It doesn't accurately reflect the indignant behavior of the LA County Sheriffs or County Supervisor Ernest E. Debs, while the alarmist reactionaries of the Sunset Plaza Merchant Association are merely represented by a group of left out, conservative businessmen. But any faults are more than offset by the appearance of three bands in a mocked-up Pandora's Box, which, according to Dave Aguilar of The Chocolate Watchband, was "a spot on depicting, right down to the spider webs." The Watchband give a genuinely scary performance, while Whisky A Go Go house band The Enemys provide another shrill battle cry with their rendition of 'Jolene. And The Standells are up to the challenge of kicking the movie off with the title track, which is, in its own way, as riveting as 'A Hard Day's Night' in The Beatles' movie of the same name. The brazen nerve of Mimsy Famer and Laurie Mock (who had previously starred together in *Hot Rods To Hell*), meanwhile, perfectly encapsulates the mood of time: a moment of innocence becoming a wild ride. (Mock had previously played a Whisky A Go Go waitress in John Cassavetes's *Faces*, in a scene that summed up the club's watusi-frug-jerk era of 1964–65. The Stu Gardner Trio perform a wild, soul version of 'Skate-A-Ling' in the background.)

Wild In The Streets is the clincher in the AIP series; released in 1968, it turns around the false idealism of drug culture as a means to political action. (Los Angeles's Artists' Protest Committee shared this view, perceiving Ken Kesey's Merry Pranksters to be a hindrance to truly confrontational activism.) Christopher Jones plays Max Frost, a young singer/politician—based, perhaps, on Jim Morrison—who takes over the government on the strength of the under-30 vote, which in the movie amounts to 52 per cent of the population. Richard Pryor pops up in a supporting role.

One of the buzz phrases of the time was "Never trust anyone under 30." *Wild In The Streets* carries this theory to the extreme by having everyone over 30 detained in concentration camps and force-fed LSD. According to a *Playboy* review of the time: "The comedy may sound excessive, but it is mounted with an irreverent improvisational air that blows in right off the pop protest scene." The movie's soundtrack was put together by a team of musical heavies: Les Baxter provided the incidental music, Mike Curb the rock'n'roll tracks, and Davie Allan played lead guitar, while many of the songs were written by Barry Mann and Cynthia Weil. It also spawned a hit single, '(Nothing Can Change) The Shape Of Things To Come' by Max Frost & The Troopers. Frost's singing voice was provided by Michael Bishop, who played in a band called The Second Time. Explaining how he ended up being involved with *Wild In The Streets*, Bishop says: "We won the Pepsi Boss Battle in early 1966 at the Teen-Age Fair. Through that, Mike Curb saw us on TV and contacted our manager, Robert Fitzpatrick, who [worked] two floors away from Curb in the 9000 Building."

The absurdity level of *Wild In The Streets* peaks with the use of Paul Frees, a key voiceover artist for Jay Ward's cartoons, as a post-apocalyptic narrator. Frees had previously voiced Boris Badenov in *The Bullwinkle Show* and George Harrison and John Lennon in the Beatles cartoon, as well as several rides at Disneyland, such as *The Haunted Mansion* and *Monsanto's Adventures Through Inner Space*. That hammy, Disneyland style is recognizable at the close of the movie, in which he describes a psychedelic 'new world' created by teenagers.

* * *

The mainstream movie industry's attempts to integrate with rock'n'roll culture were somewhat uneasy. Whisky A Go Go cage-dancer Daryle Anne Lindley recalled the strange scenes when Elizabeth Taylor and Richard Burton put on a private party at the venue. "Everyone who was there was a star," she told *Teen* magazine. "And you wouldn't have believed the strange concoctions of clothes we saw. From the glass cage you can see the whole dance floor. I think that many of the stars are dressed so often by wardrobe people that they have little taste when it comes to choosing their own clothes."

The movie world had several exclusive rock'n'roll-clubs of its own, notably the Daisy Club, which, according to Michael Bishop, who played there with The Second Time, was a chic hangout for "all the rich people"—mostly movie stars and record producers. "[They] were trying to get 'hip' to what the kids were doin' on the Strip," he says. "So it was kind of a weird hybrid of people who didn't know what was going on, but dressed like it." Michael Lloyd of The West Coast Pop Art Experimental Band has similar recollections of the club and another Beverly Hills venue in the same vein, the Other Place. "It was the Hollywood movie crowd in a private club," he says. "It was not a big place, but it was like one of those London kind of clubs, with billiards and other diversions … there was this giant movie theater screen put up around the wall, with an overhead projector [and] strobe lights." Phil Spector, The Monkees, and The Beatles all dropped by on occasion.

The author Harlan Ellison wrote a lengthy article entitled 'Nightmare At The Daisy' for *Los Angeles* magazine, describing the club and its attendees in great detail. The main bar room was decorated with "antique mirrors and antique ceiling fixtures," and "filled with tables that clog the center of the room and line the wall." In the main room one might have found "a dark, kaleidoscopic, and somehow vegetable movement of bodies in motion" and "a noise level of voices that runs sub-current to the aural slam of rock music blared through a PA system at full gain." "Mia Farrow and Adam West are dancing," he adds, and Paul Newman was playing pool—but not, apparently, to the standard of his performance in *The Hustler*.

"The Daisy was housed in the shell of the old Romanoff Restaurant [on Rodeo Drive]," according to LA historian Jim Heimann. "There were no neon signs," he says, "the idea was to be discreet." This was the kind of place that would be frequented by the "Rudi Gernreich, Viva, and Andy Warhol crowd." Heimann also draws attention to another venue that opened shortly after the Daisy, the Factory, which commanded a $400 membership fee: "They had faux Tiffany lamps above the pool tables, Tiffany windows, and stained glass windows. That was shabby chic—posh, pop art industrial."

If anyone in 1964 needed to hide from their fans, it was The Beatles, but in fact the group would hit the 'public' scene at the Whisky A Go Go as soon as they arrived in town. Things were different for self-important movie folk, who wanted to maintain the exclusivity of past venues such as the Trocadero and the Mocambo. "The idea of the Daisy, the Candy Store, the Other Place, and The Factory was to keep the riff-raff out," Heimann says. "They were bankrolled by celebrity people [who] had illusions of hipness, but didn't have a clue. [These clubs were] for a select crowd who were trying to mimic what was happening on the street. In their sterility, the big shots missed the real excitement of Hollywood during the 60s."

There was clearly a need for movies to plumb the depths of the emerging rock'n'roll scene—but this was something that could not be expected of the major Hollywood studios. Directors Russ Meyer and Ray Dennis Steckler both applied themselves to rock'n'roll in a manner that major studios—who had not had a success in this field since the one-off fluke *The Girl Can't Help It* in 1956— could not understand. They bucked the odds and ended up with something atypical even of AIP's scruffy approach.

By virtue of having been made outside of the usual parameters and pressures of the Hollywood industry, Meyer and Steckler's movies remain timeless, yet thoroughly enmeshed within the grit of the mid 1960s. On its release in 1966, Meyer's *Faster, Pussycat! Kill! Kill!* enjoyed a long engagement as a double bill with his earlier *Mudhoney* at the Cinema, which had catered to the beat and independent moviemaking scenes since the 1950s. *Faster, Pussycat! Kill! Kill!* tells the story of three go-go dancers who retreat to the desert and drag race each other in their sports cars. The superb dialog soars high above the cracked and arid landscape as rocket-breasted vixens Tura Satana, Lori Williams, and Haji overpower the movie's degenerate males with smart punchlines, karate chops, and go-go-boot kicks. The Bosstweeds, fronted by Rick Jerrard, offer up proto-Doors-style garage-punk on the soundtrack.

When given the chance to work with a major studio—20th Century Fox—a few years later, Meyer made *Beyond The Valley Of The Dolls* with screenwriter-turned-critic Roger Ebert. This 1970 movie features Sunset Strip favorites The Strawberry Alarm Clock and a fake band, The Carrie Nations, fronted by *Playboy* centerfolds Dolly Read and Cynthia Myers (most of whose vocals were handled by Lynn Carey of Mama Lion). *Beyond The Valley Of The Dolls* is a camp classic: one long party sequence overflowing with psychedelic orgies and Hollywood in-crowd hustle.

Ray Dennis Steckler was about as low budget as you could go in mining the riches of mid-1960s rock'n'roll culture. His magnificently titled *Incredibly Strange Creatures Who Stopped Living And Became Mixed-Up Zombies* (1963) exhibits a nothing-to-lose bravado and takes in a monster go-go dance sequence to a song called 'The Mixed Up Zombie Stomp.' (In its early theater runs, Steckler employed people to don zombie costumes and run through and freak out the crowd.)

Steckler's immersion in rock'n'roll began when he was the cinematographer for Timothy Carey's 1962 movie *The World's Greatest Sinner*, which features a soundtrack by Frank Zappa. His *Wild Guitar*, also from 1962, predates AIP's *Beach Party* by a full year in its use of dancers twisting in the sand and on the rocks of Malibu beach. Both ideas would become stereotypical of the genre, cropping up in over 40 movies and many more television shows between 1963 and 1967. *Wild Guitar* also seems to pre-empt the Sunset Strip garage-rock scene in the way that many of the songs on its soundtrack feature that characteristically chunky, cheesy organ sound.

In the movie, the endearing Arch Hall Jr rides into Hollywood on a motorcycle with a guitar case slung around his back, arriving at the Capitol Tower to gaze in awe at the structure that would soon shift rock'n'roll's center to the West Coast. He then all but bows at the shrine of Dino's Lodge, dreaming and backcombing his hair like Ed 'Kookie' Byrnes. He then meets a sympathetic go-go chick at a Schwab's-like diner, and the two of them appear on a local talent show based on KCOP's *Rocket To Stardom*. Steckler himself—using the pseudonym Cash Flagg—turns in a great performance as a sadistic bodyguard who question's Hall Jr's potential and calls him a "punk." All in all, *Wild Guitar* is a perfect, time capsule of a movie that somehow manages to anticipate just about everything cool that would happen in Los Angeles rock'n'roll over the next five years.

In 1964 Steckler made a cheapie called *Rat Pfink And Boo Boo* that, while not released for a further two years, has since become a cult favorite. (The Rat Pfink of the title was lifted directly—and rather mischievously—from Ed 'Big Daddy' Roth's copyrighted Rat Fink character.) The script was written by Ron Haydock, who had all the right rock'n'roll credentials, having previously fronted a rockabilly/ garage-punk group, Ron Haydock & The Boppers. Haydock also stars in the movie as Lonnie Lord, who greets fans and signs autographs in front of the Captiol Tower and, having tapped his foot on Gene Vincent's star on the Hollywood Walk Of Fame, performs the Vincent-esque 'Runnin' Wild' and '(You Is A) Rat Fink.'

When his girlfriend Cee Cee Beaumont (played by Carolyn Brandt) is abducted, Lord transforms into a superhero, complete with a goofy ski-mask, cape, and trunks. His gardener friend becomes Boo Boo, donning zebra-striped headgear with animal ears and blinking lights. This dynamic duo proceed to fight crime in a motorcycle and sidecar in a manner reminiscent of the Marx Brothers' *Duck Soup*. As soon as they put on their superhero outfits, the black-and-white movie turns red and Lord's rockabilly-wildman voice morphs into a Yogi Bear-style delivery. Garage-punk electric piano and fuzz guitar spurs their search for the kidnappers. (One scene on their quest, in which a fake-ransom suitcase is filled with comic books, is a sly nod to Haydock's parallel career as a writer and publisher of monster stories under the nom de plume Vin Saxon.)

Rat Pfink and Boo Boo do away with most of their adversaries with a swift biff to the head. When confronted by an ape, Pfink defeats the animal by … impersonating it, thereby displaying the kind of camp lunacy that would soon bring success to the *Batman* television show, The Beatles' *Help!*, and *The Monkees*. The movie ends with the entire cast (crooks aside) gathered at Will Rogers State Beach to read *Rat Pfink* comic books, fall off surfboards, and dance to Lonnie Lord's 'Big Boss Go Go Party'—even the ape joins in the fun. Ray Dennis Steckler once summed up the inspiration for his pioneering movies with the words: "If you don't have any money, use your imagination."

Working on a similar budget, Kenneth Anger and Bruce Conner made beat movies in LA during the same period. Perhaps best known for his book *Hollywood Babylon*, Anger was adept at blending Hollywood history with the avant-garde. His creative muse took him around the globe, but Los Angeles remains the focus of movies such as *Scorpio Rising* (1963) and *Kustom Kar Kommandos* (1965). *Scorpio Rising* pioneered the effective use of pure rock'n'roll on a movie soundtrack, its tough, girl-group sounds accompanying scenes of a leather-clad, gay-biker scenario. Anger's later *Lucifer Rising* (1968) inspired The Rolling Stones'

'Sympathy For The Devil,' which in turn gave its name to a movie the British group made with Jean-Luc Godard.

Bruce Conner's work was less auspicious, but every bit as powerful in its own way. He began in 1958 with a deconstruction of existing cinematic genres and cliches called *A MOVIE*, which brought assemblage art into the field of movie editing. In 1962 he made *COSMIC RAY*, an intensely thrilling series of clips—from atomic explosions to the twist—cut to the rhythm of Ray Charles's magnificent 'What'd I Say.' Of all Conner's movies, the one most affected by mid-1960s rock'n'roll is *BREAKAWAY*. This 1966 black-and-white short features super-fast cuts of Toni Basil go-go dancing to a song of the same name that she'd released that year as the B-side to her 'I'm Twenty Eight' 45. Her figure is forcefully edited and lit in a bare, black room above the carousel on the Santa Monica Pier, the same apartment used for Dennis Hopper's *Night Tide* in 1963. Basil's dancing, she says, has a "go-go spirit," but also incorporates "ballet leaps and jazz moves, a lot of different styles." Music writer Michael Hacker describes Conner as "the first [person] to unveil the mysterious and spectacular effect of combining image with a single piece of pop music."

* * *

Through movies, television, and marketing (at the Teen-Age Fair), the media's absorption of Sunset Strip counterculture had reached critical mass. Primarily shot on the LA scene, the CBS News documentary *Inside Pop: The Rock Revolution* aired on Tuesday April 25th 1967 and marked the first time that this new rock'n'roll culture and its accompanying quest for societal change, had been properly understood and acknowledged by the mainstream news-media. Paul Robbins of *The Los Angeles Free Press* was interviewed for the documentary, as were Frank Zappa, Roger McGuinn, Pamela Polland and Rick Stanley of The Gentle Soul, members of Canned Heat, The UFO, and angry kids filmed at the Sunset Strip riot. *Inside Pop* closes with Brian Wilson's solo performance of his finest collaboration with Van Dyke Parks, 'Surf's Up,' a song that ridicules the "blind class aristocracy" and suggests that the establishment listen to what the younger generation had to say about universal love.

The documentary's host, Leonard Bernstein, was able to break down the inventiveness of pop music in a way that 'the establishment' could understand, capping it all by presenting Janis Ian singing 'Society's Child,' a song about conservative parents' objections to interracial dating. Elsewhere, reporter David Oppenheim hits upon something rather obvious that has nonetheless been lost in Soviet-style, revisionist histories of 'rock' music. Over footage of first Tim Buckley and then over a Sunset Strip montage soundtracked by The Byrds' 'Captain Soul,' he notes: "Most of us have been raised on the tradition of Tin Pan Alley, where the songs, beautiful or not, were meant to amuse or beguile, but that's all. They were embellishments on life. What these young people seem to say is that their music isn't just decorative: it comes right out of their world. And whatever is working on today's youth is working out in their music. And the crucible is Los Angeles."

The most visible extension of the energy of the Sunset Strip, in the multimedia sense, was a phenomenon that could have only happened in Los Angeles during 1965–66. *The Monkees* touched so many young people on so many different levels that it continues to be misunderstood by detractors and overzealous fans alike.

Yet here lies the dichotomy. After introducing Buffalo Springfield at Monterey Pop, Peter Tork of The Monkees was later asked to calm a tide of gatecrashers by announcing from the stage that, despite rumors, The Beatles would *not* be making a surprise appearance. The call came during a performance by The Grateful Dead, and gave the group's bassist, Phil Lesh, the opportunity to cruelly deride Tork.

As the Monterey Pop Festival was organized in LA with a spirit of camaraderie, the vindictive opportunism of the steadfast San Francisco clique seems entirely misplaced. But Lesh's reaction exemplified the smug, territorial, self-righteous attitude that had begun to waft from San Francisco's hippie movement toward anything from Los Angeles.

This is an attitude that has prevailed through the years. In his 1992 book *Monterey Pop*, San Fran music scribe Joel Selvin says: "For some reason, the counterfeit Beatle, Peter Tork, was sent in to interrupt the Dead set and deny the rumors. It was more than Phil Lesh could take. The 29-year-old, classically trained bassist watched this plastic, square, contrived teen idol sent to be the mouthpiece of Lou Adler. Everything Lesh hated was standing right in front of him, interrupting his show." As if the Grateful Dead had something more to offer the world than The Monkees. (The Beatles did not share The Grateful Dead's snobbish aversion to The Monkees; Mike Nesmith even made an appearance in The Beatles' promotional film for 'A Day In The Life,' which documented an orchestral recording session for *Sgt Pepper.*)

The innocent scenario of *The Monkees* television show was simply a great idea. The concept was first mooted in 1963, with the theme set to be a traveling folk group, but by 1965 producers Bob Rafelson and Bert Schneider decided instead to capitalize on the popularity of The Beatles and the new folk-rock and fuzz-punk sounds that were taking over Sunset Strip. Rafelson and Schneider noticed this early, but between the airing of the pilot episode in September 1965 and the debut of the television show proper a year later, the national consciousness had grown to meet *The Monkees*, and the group was surprisingly voguish when they hit the tube.

When Rafelson and Schneider placed ads for "4 insane boys, age 17–21 … spirited Ben Frank's-types" in 1965, Sunset Strip was clearly ahead of the rest of America in terms of social provocation. Around the same time as *The Monkees* appeared, a similar amalgam of pop, art, and camp arrived in the form of the television version of *Batman*. These two shows stand as the best representation of Los Angeles's allied arts scene and the creative environment of Hollywood at the time. There is simply no current parallel, because these arts are no longer on the same plane. Today, Hollywood sees music as subservient to movies and television; during The Beatles' heyday, this was definitely not the case.

None of this condescension was evident during the creation of *The Monkees* in 1965. First, there was a logjam of unused Brill Building songwriting talent eager for an outlet that had been denied since The Beatles inspired kids in bands to write their own songs. Despite the prolific output of Lennon & McCartney, Jagger & Richards, Brian Wilson, and others, 'professional' songwriting teams such as Goffin & King, Barry & Greenwich, and Mann & Weil were equal contributors to the 1960s pantheon. The concept of *The Monkees* gave these teams a focus after the sad demise of the girl-group genre (which had preceded Beatlemania). Although The Beatles covered The Shirelles, The Cookies, and The Marvelettes, the British Invasion and its aftereffects overwhelmed even the best efforts by the songwriters associated with girl groups.

The Monkees, in absorbing the rock'n'roll *band* format, were able to put Goffin & King, Barry & Greenwich, and their ilk back on the radio in a near-seamless shift in fashion. Neil Diamond, for one, got a new lease on life as the Brill Building reveled in its final moment of vitality. Once The Monkees hit with his 'I'm A Believer,' deejays started to spin Diamond's own records, with 'Cherry Cherry' and 'Solitary Man' leading the pack.

With a wealth of great songs to pick from and the backing of LA's top-notch 'wrecking crew' of session musicians, it's no wonder that The Monkees' records hold up so well. The Sex Pistols would later taunt the hippie-dinosaur mindset by covering 'I'm Not Your Stepping Stone.' This was a logical extension of the punk tradition: early versions of the song, written by Tommy Boyce and Bobby Hart, had been recorded by Paul Revere & The Raiders and The W.C. Fields Memorial Electric String Band. It was one among several Boyce & Hart songs that had been recorded by other groups prior to The Monkees cutting their versions: The Leave's had recorded 'Words,' and both The Sons Of Adam and The Astronauts had cut 'Tomorrow's Gonna Be Another Day.' (Similarly, 'Saturday's Child,' written by David Gates, was first played by Hullabaloo house band The Palace Guard, and Goffin & King's 'Take A Giant Step' had been recorded but not released by The Rising Sons.) Boyce & Hart had previously struggled to find steady work; now, as the LA wing of the *Monkees* songwriting team, their reputation was enhanced. They subsequently made a wonderful, *Rubber Soul*-like pop album, *Test Patterns* (A&M, 1966), and had a 1967 hit with 'I Wonder What She's Doing Tonite.' They also lent their distinctive sound to Tommy James & The Shondells' 'I Think We're Alone Now,' a great song about the thrill of teenage sex.

A wide array of Sunset Strip hopefuls showed up for auditions to become one of The Monkees. Stephen Stills might have made it were it not for his bad teeth, while Harry Nilsson also just missed out, but would later contribute two songs to the group's repertoire. The original Monkees combination—two singing actors and two musicians 'off the street'—was very carefully planned. But in the end, the four "Ben Frank's-types" that made the cut wound up having far more influence on the show than their music coordinator Don Kirshner planned.

Mike Nesmith was a folkie running 'Hoot Nights' at the Troubadour, and had appeared on *The Lloyd Thaxton Show* as Michael Blessing. He also wrote songs, one of which, 'Different Drum,' became the first hit record for Linda Ronstadt (as a member of The Stone Poneys) in 1967. As time went on, Nesmith would contribute Gene Clark-style songs to The Monkees, as the four band-members agitated for more creative control. Peter Tork, meanwhile, was a true example of the Ben Frank's clientele: a struggling teenage musician with a look copped from Brian Jones of The Rolling Stones. Stephen Stills recommended Tork for the part, having met him during their shared Greenwich Village days.

Of the four, Davy Jones was the shoo-in: cute, young, and English, he had performed in the Broadway version of Oliver, and by chance appeared on the same February 9th 1964 episode of *The Ed Sullivan Show* that introduced the USA to The Beatles. Jones was not as interested in rock'n'roll as his fellow Monkees, being an actor and all, but was very impressed by the reaction of teenage girls to The Beatles—particularly as he was the same age as a lot of those girls. Jones had previously recorded for Columbia, and his out-of-touch managers were keen to find a television outlet for their teen idol protégé. In the wake of Beatlemania, 1950s-style teen idols were being passed by; luckily for Jones, he was British.

Of the actual band-members, Mickey Dolenz was the most integral to the personality of The Monkees. Alongside The Turtles' Howard Kaylan, he had a voice that came to define the effervescent spring of flower-power pop. Both singers possess great range even within the natural timbre of their speaking voices, a yearning sound that evokes and provokes youthful idealism. Another link between The Turtles and The Monkees was both groups' employment, behind the scenes, of The Modern Folk Quartet's Chip Douglas. Douglas played bass and arranged The Turtles 'Happy Together,' and then produced The Monkees' *Headquarters* and *Pisces, Aquarius, Capricorn & Jones Ltd*. He came up with the memorable guitar riff on 'Pleasant Valley Sunday' and arranged 'Daydream Believer' for *The Birds, The Bees, And The Monkees*.

Dolenz had starred in his own show called *Circus Boy* in the 1950s and appeared in some early Rod Serling television plays. He had also attended Valley Junior College and was friends with Bill Rinehart of The Leaves, Joel Larson of The Merry-Go-Round, Denny Bruce (who spent six months in the original Mothers), and Lowell George of The Factory. "Junior colleges in California are like high school with ashtrays," says music writer Harvey Kubernik. "They didn't even cost a hundred bucks a semester—with books—to attend. In the 60s, they were a good way to stay out of the draft and many of the creative people enrolled to do just that."

Although ostensibly an actor, Dolenz had played in a garage band called The Missing Links, and once worked at Wallich's Music City. (Frank Zappa worked at the same place, and later cemented this connection by appearing on an episode of *The Monkees* and in the group's subsequent movie, *Head*, in which he played a music critic.) "Mickey was accessible, and a friendly person," says Denny Bruce. "He was not some stuck-up child star."

The Monkees arrived at just the right time to fill an interesting void in teen magazines in late 1966. These publications had, for the past few years, been focused primarily on The Beatles and The Rolling Stones, but both had become less appealing in the wake of talk of LSD usage, cross-dressing (in the case of the Stones' advertisements for 'Have You Seen Your Mother Baby Standing In The Shadow'), and those dreaded mustaches of 1967. Parents would have been outraged had these magazines reported on the decadent lifestyles these bands now led. As such, The Monkees provided just the required antidote to keep this teenybopper pulp alive.

The beauty of *The Monkees* was that these guys were given great songs to sing from the get-go, and that kick-start helped inspire genuine creativity among the band-members. '(Theme From) *The Monkees*' was a hip steal from The Dave Clark Five's 'Catch Us If You Can' (as used in *Having A Wild Weekend*), which itself was a rollicking take on The Beatles' theme to *A Hard Day's Night*.

'(Theme From) *The Monkees*' also suggests that the producers were listening to The Who (well before the British group had become well known in America). The use of controlled feedback as a psychedelic effect seems modeled on the punk energy of The Who's 'Anyway Anyhow Anywhere,' while the super-fast staccato guitar at the close is an almost identical mirror of the pill-poppin' mod sound. This, remember, was for the intro to a television show targeted at little kids and young teenagers; the inclination was to go wild from the start.

Though not a 'real' rock'n'roll band to begin with, by the time of their third LP, *Headquarters,* The Monkees had become an authentic group of their own volition. After scoring back-to-back Number 1 hits with 'Last Train To Clarksville' (from *The Monkees*) and 'I'm A Believer' (from *More Of The Monkees)*, the group hatched a plan to wrest control from their musical coordinator, Don Kirshner—with the support of Bob Rafelson and Bert Schneider. (Kirshner subsequently went on to 'manage' the animated group The Archies, who would never be able to ask for creative control.)

The scheme began with Tork's anti-war comments in *The New York Times*, which were followed by complaints by Mike Nesmith in *The Saturday Evening Post* about things everybody on the LA music scene already knew: that The Monkees did not play on their own records, and were being stifled as songwriters. As such, from *Headquarters* onward, The Monkees began to exert creative control. Tork's 'For Pete's Sake,' a reverential paean to the flower-power movement, was added to the television show's end credits. Another track from the LP, Dolenz's 'Randy

Scouse Git,' was a perceptive but overlooked protest song. It offsets a ragtime motif with a classically tinged rock'n'roll chorus, and deploys timpani to pound out its message: that the illogical Vietnam War had been instigated by the same people who ridiculed 1960s youth culture.

The Monkees played on *Headquarters*, but eventually chose to use session men on their later records. Their success afforded them near limitless studio time (paid for by contractual obligations) to explore creative ideas. This was a rare luxury, and left behind numerous neat, fully realized pop experiments. A great example of this is 'Acapulco Sun' from the 1970 album *Changes*, which blends Small Faces-style vocals with Latin American rhythms. By this stage, any sense of a unified Monkees sound had gone out of the window in favor of artistic freedom, but the group continued to make great records until the end. The final Monkees single, 'Oh My My,' crosses fuzz-punk with Zombies-style vocals, and shows the group to still be a cut above the bubblegum pack at a time when animated bands seemed to be coming up with stronger material than most human groups.

Davy Jones had a clear niche: a teen dreamer prior to *The Monkees*, his music was carried on the billowy, white puffy clouds of what Frankie Avalon would have sung if he'd had a British accent (and then met The Turtles during their psychedelic phase). Jones made cheesy flower-pop for girls to gush over, from 'Daydream Believer' (late 1967) to 'Girl,' which Jones performed alone on *The Brady Bunch* in 1971.

Dolenz, meanwhile, hit his peak with the Jack Nitzsche-produced 'The Porpoise Song,' which soundtracks the opening segment of The Monkees' milestone 1968 movie, *Head*. While it was ignored outside Los Angeles upon its release, the movie has grown in stature and respect over the years. The posters made to advertise the movie don't even mention The Monkees by name, so keen were the band to shed the notion of being manufactured. This they address in a line at the beginning of *Head*—"The money's in, we're made of tin, we're here to give you more"—that becomes a recurring theme for much of what follows.

Luckily for the people of Los Angeles, *Head* shared a bill with The Beatles' *Yellow Submarine* in local movie theaters. The quality of The Monkees' movie was not lost on the audience, who caught the in-jokes after experiencing various highs in the parking lot beforehand. As the movie progresses, The Monkees are led into a factory wearing sanitized white uniforms. A series of accidents happens around them as they are led by a corporate 'tour guide' into a dark chamber, where they become trapped. The Monkees only realize where they are when the lights come on, and they are revealed to be living dandruff in a hair tonic commercial; the implication being that The Monkees had not been given proper recognition by either the establishment or the counterculture.

Bob Rafelson wrote the *Head* script with Jack Nicholson (fresh from penning *The Trip*) over an intense weekend of hash pipe smoking in Ojai. The script covers a wide range of topics, from an anti-war foxhole scene, which is juxtaposed with the All-American football mentality, to the insanity of screaming fans storming the stage and tearing body parts from the band-members' torsos. A moment of release comes during the 'Can You Dig It' segment, in which The Monkees become Arabian Sheiks, puffing on hookah pipes. Dolenz offers a 'hit' to the viewers with an inviting smirk while Toni Basil and Teri Garr lead a group of belly dancers in time with the spellbinding music.

The disapproval and misunderstanding of the Monkees phenomenon in both underground and intellectual circles obscured the brilliance of Bob Rafelson and Bert Schneider's concept. It would take some time for the pair to be given their dues as the prime generators of the subversive New Hollywood cinema movement (as outlined in Peter Biskind's *Easy Riders, Raging Bulls*).

Bay Area scribe Ralph Gleason best embodied the 'intellectuality' seeping into rock'n'roll at this time in the way that he shortsightedly felt that the San Francisco hippie mentality could offer the music a newfound "dignity." His agenda is clear in the subtitle of his 1967 public television special, *West Pole; An Essay Of The San Francisco Adult Rock Sound*. Al Burton notes that 'teen' "became a bad word" in 1968, to the extent that, a year later, he felt compelled to change the name of the Teen-Age Fair to Pop Expo.

By and large, Los Angeles didn't find it necessary to throw out the fun in order to take on political ideas. Burton clearly remained a strong force against the odds. Even as the scene began to disintegrate, he continued to make great rock'n'roll television, from a December 1966 special called *Go*—featuring Buffalo Springfield, Herman's Hermits, Bryan Hyland, and the omnipresent Toni Basil—to *Malibu U*, perhaps the sunniest summer replacement show of all time, hosted by Rick Nelson. Burton fondly recalls one particular episode of *Malibu U*, which was set to include a performance of 'Light My Fire' by The Doors. "Jim Morrison didn't show up," he says, "[So we] put a sweater on someone who looked like [him] from the back." (Burton added in footage of Morrison shot from the front a week later.)

By 1968, the rot had set in. The TET Offensive awakened the nation to the fact that the Vietnam War was far from over, a newly aggressive draft was installed, and the resultant unrest of youth—in and out of colleges—revealed how low morale had fallen in the USA since the murder of J.F.K. "The young people were inspired by Kennedy," says Burton. "They had a *vigor*; they were terrific." Then things began to change. "It started with the assassination of Martin Luther King. I saw a physical change, a palpable change in teenagers. The spirit was no longer what it had been."

Against all odds, Burton continued to carry his torch of optimism: the Teen-Age Fair, which continued to draw in fans by the hundred thousand until the start of the 1970s. "We never really failed to get the attendance," says Burton. "We just did not have the total success with business wanting to reach teenagers the same way they [had]. We were going downhill." The 1972 Fair proved to be the last one. "Our audience didn't leave us; they were there. But the spirit left our audience. … The hope and the vigor was failing. Those very years of my disillusion represented the disillusion of teenagers."

❝ *Thank you, everybody, and thank you Los Angeles! It's been Groovy.* **❞** **ROBERT W. MORGAN**

CHAPTER TWELVE

There's battle lines bein' drawn

❝ *Whatever it takes is going to be done. We're going to be tough. We're not going to surrender that area or any other area to beatniks or wild-eyed kids.* **❞**
ERNEST E. DEBS, LOS ANGELES COUNTY SUPERVISOR, 1966

Is history written by the winners? Perhaps, but their stories often have less to do with truth than with cover-up. In the case of the 1966 Sunset Strip riot, history has been clouded by myth. Many people in mid-1960s LA hated rock'n'roll, and longed to see it eradicated. There could be whole other books about—or at least a full investigations into—the events surrounding the 1959 Payola scandal, or the removal of Elvis Presley (military service), Chuck Berry (a Mann Act bust), Little Richard ("religion"), and Jerry Lee Lewis (slander) from the airwaves right around the time of the Buddy Holly/Ritchie Valens plane crash. In light of this, rock'n'roll, teenage curfews, and police harassment on Sunset Strip in 1966 could be seen as part of a larger plot. Here, at least, we are aware of the culprit: a bad civic plan that never got off the ground.

The reasoning is reminiscent of why General Motors, US Rubber, and City Hall killed off Pacific Electric Red Cars, leaving LA without an efficient form of public transportation. According to politician and activist Ralph Nader: "In the late 1930s and 40s, General Motors, with the help of a few oil and tire companies, purchases electric mass transit in 28 cities. It soon disabled these systems and began to lobby for new highways in the hopes of increasing its sales of vehicles, gasoline, and tires."[1] It is similar, too, to why nothing was ever really done by the city government to improve living conditions in South Central Los Angeles after the 1965 Watts Riots. Few realize how much was promised to the black community then, and how little was actually delivered; fewer still recall the Chicano Moratorium of 1970, when a peaceful human-rights demonstration turned into a police slaughter, culminating in the murder of *Los Angeles Times* journalist Ruben Salazar. The fact that there were further riots in South Central in 1992—which echoed across America—highlights continuing problems of cross-cultural neglect and prejudice.

Byrds manager Jim Dickson bore witness to the events that led to the Sunset Strip riot, which had been developing for some time. "We really upset the city fathers," he says. "They wanted Sunset Strip to become a huge financial district, and were trying to lure investors so that big skyscrapers could be built. They had already built the 9000 Building, and Continental Bank [which would soon become the Playboy Building] was one of the first to take the bait."

As illustrious as the jazz scene had become in Hollywood, it was of no concern to conservative investment bankers, who were dismayed by the racial integration at these clubs. They viewed the societal progress taking place on the Strip as something that was reducing glamour and, by extension, property values. Dickson saw the writing on the wall: "The County Supervisors were in the process of depressing the area. Jazz places like the Renaissance (which had been the Mocambo), and coffeehouses such as Chez Paulette could afford the rent there because of that depression."

It took about 10 years for this to rise to the surface. "Ernest E. Debs was the man behind it all," says Dickson. "He wanted to build a new freeway, coming from the Santa Monica Freeway to Sunset Strip. They'd already condemned houses and had torn a lot of them down on San Vicente, the very route they wanted to use."

Unfortunately for Debs, another element with even more money and power than his stepped in to block the progress of his master plan, the 14-mile Laurel Canyon Freeway. "Beverly Hills stopped them from building a freeway," Dickson laughs. "We sort of upset the apple cart for Ernest E. Debs [as] the Sunset Strip gradually became a creative center." Dickson noticed that Ciro's—a posh, exclusive venue in its heyday—was almost empty, and saw an opportunity for The Byrds to play there, which brought the Strip back to life. The Whisky A Go Go, too, began to book more interesting bands.

The relentless excitement that ensued proved unfathomable to Los Angeles' County planners. Like the chiefs of movie studios and major record labels today, these people turned a blind eye to grass roots developments. "When the kids started coming to Sunset Strip, it became clear to the city of Beverly Hills that the area was not suited to become a financial district," Dickson adds. "The density of the traffic was intensified [by] all these kids, who were really there for rock'n'roll, not to protest."

Even without the creative explosion on the Strip, Debs's plan was simply impractical. Dickson notes that, although the freeway would have brought traffic up from the south: "There was no northern outlet, as the Hollywood Hills stood in the way. The county had been used to putting freeways wherever they wanted, and were shocked when they found out that Beverly Hills had the power to nullify their plans."

There's an amusing parallel in *The Beverly Hillbillies*, in which Mr Drysdale struggles to appease the hillbillies while still having to play the role of banker. In an attempt to sate the investors who had bought into his awkward civic plan, Debs used the money raised to build the Pacific Design Center on Beverly Boulevard. Even in this, however, there was a final note of irony: the owners of a property that, at the time, housed Hugo's Plating, refused to sell their small plot of land.

Shrouded by trees for many years, 8661 Melrose Avenue stood as the ultimate defiance; the last bastion of anti-corporate feeling in Los Angeles. The awesome contrast between Hugo's and the big blue whale beside it became a metaphor for those who try to do their own thing in Hollywood: you can exist, but only without acknowledgement of your existence. This remains the plight of the most adventurous and interesting artists and musicians in town.

* * *

The us-against-them aspect of the Sunset Strip riots that began on November 12th 1966 becomes even clearer when juxtaposed with the election of right-wing extremist Ronald Regan as Governor Of California three days earlier. This is an indicator not only of a struggle over Hollywood's widespread cultural influence, but of the beginnings of a larger, physical resistance to conservative inertia, as reflected, too, in the Berkeley campus riots of 1965 and '69.

Filmmaker Robert Carl Cohen deploys footage of a particularly reactionary speech by Reagan in *Mondo Hollywood* to highlight the absurdity of this former actor becoming a Stalin-like political force. CARR—Californians Against Rightist Reaction (or just Ronald Reagan)—made clear this sentiment in an advertisement in *The Los Angeles Free Press*. "Reagan is the figurehead of the most reactionary individuals and groups in and out of the Republican Party in

California and the nation," the ad read. "The well organized and abundantly financed center of Reagan's support is the hardcore far-right."

The cleansing of longhairs and their non-conformist rock'n'roll scene from Sunset Strip was a parallel byproduct of Ernest E. Debs's plan. His main intention was to convince Beverly Hills that the area would be suitable for a financial district, and that it would not be crowded by a new freeway. Like General Jack Ripper in *Dr Strangelove*, Debs was a man obsessed. Working closely with County Sheriff Peter J. Pitchess, Debs suddenly and without warning enforced archaic and discriminatory statutes on patrons at teenage nightclubs, ignoring the fact that these kids weren't looking for trouble; they were simply going out to see their favorite bands (the same ones that appeared daily on television and radio) and hang out with their friends.

The Sunset Plaza was rife with crisscross foot traffic from the clubs just west of La Cienega, with Cyrano, Wil Wright's Ice Cream Parlor, and the deVoss boutique lodged inside the Plaza's center. Francis J. Montgomery and his brother, George, who owned a neighboring plot of land, took the role of defensive capitalists. As leaders of the Sunset Plaza Merchants Association, the Montgomerys were primed to deride youth culture in the press. Ten days before the riot, on November 3rd, both spoke to *The Los Angeles Times*, with George revealing that he has asked the West Hollywood Sheriff's Office (and Debs) to "enforce the curfew and loitering laws" in the wake of kids "all over the place causing commotion," and Francis complaining about the "unlimited licenses [granted] for entertainment such as topless places and underground films." Expressing an interest in Debs's plan for a new Sunset Strip financial district, George added: "The small buildings will have to be replaced by larger ones, for tax reasons."

Of particular concern to Debs, the Montgomery brothers, and others were Ben Frank's and the Trip, which bordered Sunset Plaza property. The famous La Rue Restaurant, a half-block away, had seen a raft of dinner cancellations by stuffy patrons scared off by the stream of garage and mod kids that had begun to stream in. A contemporary demo by Tandyn Almer, 'Sunset Strip Soliloquy,' describes how many of these upright citizens' complaints were no more than attempts to tarnish the reputation of teenagers. "The Playboy Club is retching," wrote Almer, "'cause someone gave them a tip/A bomb is going to explode next door inside the Trip/But the bomb turns out to be another Freudian slip/By the folks who'd thought it'd be better off without them."

The ethics of such scare tactics were never a consideration. (In fact, they continue today, as Homeowners Associations block plans to build public transportation through their LA County neighborhoods for fear that it might encourage ethnic mixing.) As Sunset Strip remained an unincorporated part of LA County—Mayor Frank L. Shaw hadn't wanted its seedy, gambling culture of the 1920s and 30s to fall under the jurisdiction of the city—both the LAPD and County Sheriffs were called in to enforce 10pm curfews for under-18s (or, rather, to harass patrons of rock'n'roll nightclubs and other teen venues). KTLA's conservative newscaster George Putnam reinforced the battle line nightly with the words: "It's 10pm in the southland. Do you know where your children are?"

The type of clientele sought by the Sunset Plaza Merchants Association did not include mods, beatniks, surfers, Chicanos, blacks, or anyone who could not afford to be carted around in a limousine. This, remember, was a time when most high schools did not allow boys to wear hair over their ears, let alone their collars, and it was primarily these kids who inhabited rock'n'roll nightclubs on Sunset Strip. Their general sentiment was aligned to that of the neo-beatnik/hippie movement, but with a sharper sense of fashion and style as culled from the British mod scene. Their connection to the movement was driven by a social consciousness: far from wishing to drop out, they wanted to help the culture around them grow.

Police harassment, however, began to seem like a redneck free-for-all. As black Strip veteran Paul Body recalls: "It was endless. I remember I got pulled over in front of Whisky A Go Go, just after making a 'purchase,' and man, I saw my life flash before my eyes; I thought it was over. It turned out [that] they'd pulled us over because I had a British Racing Green Austin Healy, and they'd thought I'd stolen it. They saw me as a young, vibrantly dressed black guy. It was a drag, because they'd see me and say, 'Oh, this guy, he's too young to have this car,' and they'd do the check."

"I could go around and do all sorts of horrible things and never have any trouble with the police," adds Johnny Legend, "but I would get rousted for absolutely no reason, at least 10 or 12 times during that period. I'd be with my mother driving along in a Dodge Dart, and they'd pull us over and harass us for an hour. The guy would be screaming at my mother, 'Male or female passenger?' in reference to me, due to my long hair. My friends and I were also pulled over by Valley State College once with rifles leveled at all our heads for like, 15 minutes, sure we were going to get blown away, and then a very slight mumbled apology and back in the squad cars and gone. That type of thing, all the time."

The LAPD logo, displayed on the side of all patrol cars, declares the force's intension: "To protect and serve." But in the case of Sunset Strip, it was not really the citizens of Los Angeles who were being 'served,' just greedy politicians such as Ernest E. Debs. An October 1966 article in *West* magazine noted how the West Hollywood Sheriff's Station on North San Vicente was "as much a center of Strip action as the Trip or Whisky A Go Go." The article described how the "Showup Room," usually intended for line-ups, became, on Friday and Saturday nights, somewhere for "holding juveniles [picked up on the Strip] until their parents come for them." The station would then fill up with "indignant parents retrieving teenage daughters who had been swinging along the Strip in hip-huggers when they were supposed to be at slumber parties in Tarzana"

Parents dragged downtown to pick up their kids were not pleased with the heavy-handed treatment of their children. "We feel that the 10:00pm curfew for children and young adults between the ages of 15 and 18 is unrealistic," said Mr and Mrs Ben J. Karras of Beverly Hills in a November 24th 1966 letter to LA Mayor Sam Yorty. "We feel the cities of Beverly Hills and Los Angeles have been woefully inadequate in providing activities for this age group, and the age group from 18 to 21. There is not a bowling alley in the confines of Beverly Hills. Nor is there a place where young people can dance and listen to their kind of music. I would much prefer that my son and daughter be in a supervised public place, with police officers or security guards around to avert trouble, than at a private party, where the supervision is sometimes lax, and unlocked liquor cabinets are on hand."

Another letter to the City Council, from a Mrs R.R. Green of San Pedro, noted that, even before the Sunset Strip scene sprung up, there were insufficient places for young people to enjoy themselves. "What can healthy, energetic teenagers do now?" she asked. "There are no big beach-dance places, the movies are very, very poor. The kids cannot dance in cocktail bars. House parties get too noisy with the music they like, and are closed by the Police, so what is there? ... Teenagers are here to stay and they need activity—not maybe what you and I want, but what they want and enjoy."

The City Council responded to letters such as these with out-of-touch lists of high-school events such as chess, archery, weight lifting, dramatics, ballet—

and the occasional school dance. Such 'solutions' completely missed the point: it was one thing to attend a once-a-month school dance in a basketball gym with a neighborhood band playing hit records of the day; it was quite another thing to see internationally renowned groups such as The Byrds, The Doors, The Velvet Underground, or The Mothers Of Invention in the space-age bohemia of a Hollywood nightclub. But such concerns were never considered by the City Council, who evidently had no idea whatsoever about the cultural renaissance shaking their city.

"I graduated from high school one month after my 17th birthday," wrote 21-year-old Mrs William Stepp in 1968, "and began attending classes at the California Institute Of The Arts one week later. I felt that if I were mature and intelligent enough to be attending an art college, I was surely old enough to dance in a public place. Not only did I miss the dancing, but also the entertainers I so longed to see. I would like to point out that the time I would have spent dancing was frequently passed in parked cars, and I wasn't alone. I think this is still the case for many 17-year-old girls. Public dancing is surely more healthy and moral than long periods of heavy necking for young unmarried people." Mrs Stepp also made the point that if a young man of 17 is deemed old enough to serve in the military, surely he should be considered able to "conduct himself reasonably on the dance floor."

* * *

The first real sign that the LA's conservative element wanted to put an end to the far-out happenings on Sunset came in May 1966, when The Velvet Underground's residency at the Trip was cut short by the authorities (with the venue shut down until further notice). More trouble surfaced at 10pm one evening in early July 1966, when officers began hauling anyone they suspected to be underage away from Gee Gee's restaurant. As Frank Zappa notes on his *Freak Out! Hot Spots* map, this former Googie's location would soon be "mysteriously forced out of business." Later the same month, police carted customers away from Canter's by force.

Kent Simpson of *The Los Angeles Free Press* spoke to one such arrested patron, Dana Sitner, who was "told that he was being arrested for blocking the sidewalk," despite the fact that he was merely trying to get from the restaurant (in which he and his girlfriend had just eaten) to their car, which was parked across the street. Simpson also stated: "Twice, the management at Canter's spoke to the police, asking them to stop blocking the entrance," but to no avail. The police were on a mission, even going so far as to employ long-haired, undercover agents wearing LSD and anti-authority buttons. In all, approximately 276 people were arrested at Gee Gee's and Canter's; there was a police van ready to cart kids away from these restaurants even before any 'trouble' started. According to a report in *Los Angeles* magazine, "three busloads of juveniles" were arrested at Ben Frank's restaurant (for which Francis Montgomery held the lease) at Halloween. The fact that this followed a meeting between the "Sunset Strip Chamber Of Commerce," which Montgomery headed, and "representatives of the Sheriff's Department" to discuss ways to "cope with teenagers" was in no way coincidental.

In an attempt to counter this kind of harassment, some prominent members of the music scene, led by Jim Dickson and Elektra Records' Billy James, put together a grass roots organization, CAFF, or Community Action For Facts And Freedom. According to Derek Taylor, one of CAFF's principle aims was "to subsidize, maybe pay for, the defense and (maybe) fines of kids framed by law enforcement agencies." CAFF was also, as *New Musical Express* reporter Tracy Thomas put it, keen to "emphasize, through the press, the good, creative side of the young people whom most of the establishment believe to be dirty, dishonest morons."

The Fifth Estate coffeehouse became a rallying point for those who were outraged at how 'curfew enforcement' was being handled. Its proprietor, Al Mitchell, started work on a movie about the police situation, *Blue Fascism*. One day, two 17-year-old kids came in with a flyer promoting a peaceful demonstration to be held in front of Pandora's Box. Mitchell felt the flyer had merit and pitched in $20 to print 2,000 more; after passing the hat around the Fifth Estate, another 3,000 were made.

Just before the demonstration, KBLA disc jockey Humble Harv made an announcement that there would be a rally at Pandora's Box that night, and cautioned people to tread carefully. This of course only succeeded in triggering more to turn up for a massive sit-in in front of the club, with celebrities such as Peter Fonda, Bob Denver, David Hockney, and Sonny & Cher joining the teenage demonstrators. Bono made audio recordings of the events, which he then used for a documentary 45, 'Sunset Symphony,' which was credited to People Of Sunset Strip and set on-the-scene interviews and other sound bites against throbbing bass and drums.

The riot that followed could have easily been avoided, had the demonstrators' issues been addressed. "If the police had displayed the calmness they exhibited on successive nights," said Art Kunkin in *The Los Angeles Free Press*, "it would have been possible for a few officers to keep the crowds on the sidewalks from the very beginning of the demonstration in conformance with ordinary traffic regulations, keep traffic moving, and thus prevent some or all of the incidents that later developed."

The same November 18th issue of the *Free Press* also gave Captain Crumly of the LAPD a say. Claiming his actions to be less premeditated than those of County Sheriff Pitchess, he noted that, initially, he had no reason to believe that the demonstration would be "anything less than lawful." He acknowledged a certain "time-lag" in assembling adequate forces to deal with the protestors after events began to get out of hand, but added that: "As soon as the police were able to move effectively, we did so."

Contemporary reports differ on the number of demonstrators present: *The Los Angeles Herald Examiner* figured it to be around 1,000, with the *Free Press* claiming around three times that amount. "We sat, cross-legged, in the street, Sunset Boulevard, holding hands and singing," says Pamela Des Barres of what was, originally, a distinctly pacifist demonstration. "Kids had guitars, thousands of kids, it stopped traffic for miles on either side of Sunset."

The first signs of trouble arrived when several off-duty Marines involved in a minor traffic accident got out of their car and struck the driver of the other vehicle involved, "threatening him with a cane," according to *The Los Angeles Times*. *The Free Press* put much of the blame for "a few fistfights between servicemen and Sunset Strip youth" on the Marines, one of whom, said the *Herald*, was "hit on the head with a [picket] sign" (whether or not this was intentional is unclear). The Marines were arrested for assaulting two policemen with a deadly weapon, but by now the torch paper had been lit.

Once the clock struck 10pm, the County Sheriffs and LAPD turned to militaristic tactics on cue. Both felt that the previous year's Watts Riots had been handled inefficiently, so called in bigger numbers to quell what, this time around, was a group of peaceful picketers. "Because of the police," said the *Free Press*, "it became unsafe to be in the area. The policemen would start running, poking people painfully in the backs with their clubs so they would move faster." *The Times* concurred, albeit in less colorful language: "At 10:35pm, the officers, many in helmets, began a sweep and clear operation. Advancing along the sidewalk in a column of about fours, they pushed bystanders out of the way, sometimes using nightsticks. The police, tempers visibly short, ordered everyone to leave the area."

"At the height of the conflict, things got nasty," Derek Taylor recalled. "I saw my first police 'flying wedge' on Sunset Boulevard, saw how professional cops can always crush amateur freedomniks if they had a mind to, saw a Sheriff's Deputy spit on a woman, saw Peter Fonda in handcuffs, saw how bad things could be before they got worse." Fonda was in fact taken into custody near the Fifth Estate. He was involved in documentary photography on the Sunset Strip and, with Brandon de Wilde, was preparing a presentation for a proposed film. He was subsequently released without charges.

Art Kunkin in the *Free Press* reported on how police stormed Pandora's Box with "drawn billy clubs, chasing the assembled youth out and, in several cases, throwing them over the high picket fence." (One unfortunate teenager apparently found himself impaled on the fence, before being pushed over by a police officer.) The *Herald*, meanwhile, noted: "Several teenagers were injured, and were taken to nearby hospitals. Youths quickly abandoned any thought of peaceful demonstration and moved into the street."

Faced with nightstick-wielding policemen in riot gear, the crowd ran amok. Pamela Des Barres recalls a group of "long-haired boys taking over a bus," an incident that was given prominent coverage in various newspapers. The *Free Press* described how demonstrators sprayed a fire extinguisher at and broke the windows of a bus that had got stuck in traffic, and then "began to rock the bus until the six passengers and driver got out." One youth, named by the *Times* as Allan W. Gordon, then tried to set light to the bus by dropping matches into the fuel tank. He was unsuccessful, but was still booked for attempted arson.

Police tried in vain to disperse the demonstrators, but it seemed that, as soon as one section of a block was cleared, the youths would reassemble elsewhere. Pandora's Box was shut down for an hour in the course of the action, after which protestors threw "a coke bottle and an unidentified missile" at police from the window of the Liquor Locker, according to the *Free Press*. The more hysterical *Herald*, which ran headlines such as 'Teenage Rampage,' 'Long Hair Nightmare,' and 'Bus Burns In Sunset Strip Riot,' claimed that youths were throwing "Molotov cocktails," but this seems unlikely when the most serious arrest at this point was for malicious mischief.

"The situation is aggravated by the presence of more than 1,000 youthful bums," said LAPD Captain Crumly in his statement to *the Free Press*, "living by their wits within and without the law in Hollywood. These transients commit unlawful and asocial acts which reflect on the whole youthful group." In response to accusations of police brutality and harassment he continued, somewhat dismissively, to invite anyone with a specific complaint to meet with him, promising to take action to "correct the situation" in the case of any wrongdoing.

LA County Sheriff Peter J. Pitchess was offered a similarly unedited space in the *Free Press* to air his views, but said only that he did "not feel that such interviews would be worthwhile." The newspaper subsequently wondered whether "more effective psychological testing could weed out some of the hostility toward non-conformists." In London's *New Musical Express*, self-declared 'Hollywood war correspondent' Tracy Thomas noted that, while events on Sunset Strip "may seem a bit trivial to the 'outside world,' they are assuming monumental proportions to those of us who make a living here."

"I came down Laurel Canyon Boulevard and was greeted by that riot," recalls Stephen Stills. "I sat down and wrote the song ['For What It's Worth'] in 15 minutes. The last time I had seen cops on one side of the street and a bunch of students on the other side was when I was living in Central America—the government changed three days later. The Sunset Strip riot [was] just a funeral for a bar. But then you had the immortal genius of the idiots that ran the LAPD, who put all of those troopers in full battle array, looking like the Macedonian army, up against a bunch of kids."

Inside Pandora's Box were 75 patrons out for what they had assumed would be a typical night of dancing—until, that is, officers began beating on the back door and ordering "Everyone Out!" The club's management yelled back that the police would have to break the door down before they would be allowed inside. The police withdrew just before 2am, perhaps realizing, as the *Free Press* opined, that it might appear somewhat ludicrous to wait outside a club for the chance to arrest a group of teenagers who were not breaking any laws.

Art Kunkin of *The Los Angeles Free Press* put the situation down to a conflict between "two groups of businessmen." He continued: "Because the traditional Strip nightclub was not making money, a few of them converted to licensed teenage clubs and found that they were making more profit than before. The other restaurant owners and the property owners began to suffer from traffic congestion. The police, in effect, have been cooperating with one very wealthy group of property owners on the Strip against a less powerful group of businessmen." According to Kunkin, police were also misinterpreting—no doubt willfully—the curfew law, which had been "designed only to prevent juveniles from loitering," but was being used as permission to take any youth seen out after 10pm into custody, "even if he is walking to a car or otherwise on his way home."

A November 15th *Los Angeles Times* editorial claimed there to be "no deep-rooted sociological or economic causes for the weekend rioting." But in the eyes of the *Free Press*, the rioting was the result of police getting "caught up in a power struggle" and "not acting in an impartial manner." An immediate musical response came in the form of the only single by Terry Randall, 'S.O.S.,' on which the singer asked, over descending piano chords, incessant organ, and a rolling drumbeat, whether the cause of all of this was "'coz they think we dress funny/ Or because we don't spend enough money?"

With a grim irony, Francis J. Montgomery makes that very same complaint three decades later. "They didn't spend any money," he says of the Sunset Strip youths and, when confronted about the vibrant, creative scene that was stamped out on the Strip, simply declares: "None of it was any good."

* * *

The demonstrations continued for another four nights. On Sunday November 13th, 300 demonstrators surrounded Pandora's Box, and were met by 200 officers pooled from the LAPD, County Sheriff, and California Highway Patrol. Art Kunkin found the officers to be "in a state of panic." They used "shocking language," said Kunkin, and continued to deploy their billy clubs despite the fact that the vast majority of protestors were "already obeying their instructions to move out of the area."

The area between Fairfax and Crescent Heights was sealed off and a tactical alert was issued; half of all police on duty throughout the city were on stand by for emergency assignment. Sgt Bill Houge of the Hollywood Division used a bullhorn to announce: "You are hereby ordered to leave this area—you have five minutes to disperse." Officers marched toward Sunset, and cleared the area in less than five minutes. "Some of the youths raced into Schwab's Pharmacy," reported the *Times*, "but officers locked the door and would not permit them to leave immediately." They were eventually let out at 11:45pm.

The following day, Fred Rosenberg, president of the Sunset Strip Association, called a meeting at the Marquis Restaurant on Sunset Boulevard to discuss ways of preventing further disturbances. Representatives from the West Hollywood and Sunset Strip Chambers Of Commerce, the Sunset Plaza Association, and the Hollywood Division of the LAPD all attended, as did West Hollywood Sheriff Peter J. Pitchess and LA County Supervisor Ernest E. Debs.

According to Sheriff Victor Riesau, the demonstration started out as "a kind of carnival, just a bunch of kids letting off steam." Captain Crumly of the LAPD felt the events had been accelerated by "left-wing groups and outside agitators," while Rosenberg stated simply that he felt it was time to rid Los Angeles of its image as "an attraction for teenagers and beatniks." Sunset Plaza Association president Allan Alder went a step further, declaring that "kid hangouts" were "where the trouble really begins," and that, as such, they should be shut down. After Rosenberg suggested that, if these establishments were to reopen, it should be in "a new form, aimed at adults," Debs asked whether "both the Board Of Supervisors and the City Council ought to explore the possibility of new legislation in this field." Police Chief Thad Brown seems to have been the lone moderate voice: "We can't put a kook in jail just because he walks down the street with a beard," he said, but Alan Alder was adamant, demanding that the teenage clubs he called "sanctuaries for anti-social, and now illegal behavior" be closed, forcibly, forthwith.

That night, 11 out of a group of 48 protestors were arrested while walking, shortly after 10pm, from Pandora's Box, via the Whisky A Go Go, to Doheny. Then, on Tuesday, 40 more demonstrators showed up, but showed little resistance to the 11 police officers they encountered when the curfew hit. Finally, on Wednesday November 16th, 500 demonstrators gathered in front of Pandora's Box between 8:30 and 10pm, where they were met by an assembly of 200 policemen. *The Herald Examiner* noted that 95 per cent of the crowd was made up of "spectators and newsmen," so little force was required on the part of the police. Sixty picketers marched for several blocks with placards bearing such slogans as 'We're Your Children, Don't Destroy Us,' 'Fark The Nucks,' and 'Ban The Billyclub'; several speeches were made. "We don't want to take over the Strip," one youth told the *Herald*. "We just want someplace to meet and talk. We want equal rights as human beings."

Shortly after 10pm, Los Angeles Mayor Sam Yorty appeared in the parking lot of Lytton Savings And Loan, on the grounds of the old Garden Of Allah, just to "see what was going on." He invited teenagers to come and speak to him at City Hall about the issues that had led to the protests of the past week. The demonstrations subsequently subsided, in anticipation of a just hearing that never came.

By Saturday November 19th, it seemed as though order had been restored. The flow of traffic and pedestrians on Sunset Strip was smooth. But Sheriff Pitchess held firm. At 10pm sharp, according to the *Free Press*, "a ludicrous standoff took place," as teenagers and the police simply stood and stared at each other. The crowd eventually grew bored and disbursed. Behind closed doors, however, Ernest E. Debs was working to make more permanent changes. On Monday November 21st, the County Board Of Supervisors rescinded the ordinance that had permitted teenagers to dance in Sunset Strip clubs licensed for that purpose. According to the author Art Fein, Debs's skewed argument was that the existence of these nightclubs on the Strip was the reason that kids hung around in the area at night, so by closing the clubs down, the loitering problem would disappear. The whole meeting, Fein says, was conducted in a jolly manner, with one member of the board, Supervisor Warren M. Dorn, interrupting proceedings twice to make jokes. Debs, meanwhile, kept on track, referring to the Sunset Strip youth as "misguided hoodlums" and suggesting that a crackdown on their parents ought to be considered, too.

At no point was any consideration given to the popularity of the venues themselves, or the dazzling array of recording artists they presented. In the eyes of these elected officials, brisk business for rock'n'roll-related ventures was not a good thing. The councilors reveled in the fact that they were about to "eliminate the so-called 'teen clubs'"—and not just on the Strip, but right across the county. Ernest E. Debs, says Fein, likened the motion being approved to King Herod receiving the head of John The Baptist on a silver platter. "I just want to say on behalf of my constituents out there," said Debs, "thank you for the action you have taken today."

Board Order No. 195, Urgency Ordinance No. 9228 went into immediate effect, declaring, essentially, that those under 21 not be allowed to "participate in any dancing" at such clubs "unless accompanied by [a] parent, guardian, or spouse over 21 years of age." (Those aged between 18 and 21 were given special dispensation to dance in clubs that did not serve alcohol.) The ordinance also noted that "extreme police problems" have been caused by minors in recent times, and that, were they to continue "for even an additional 30 days" there would be serious repercussions, which could "endanger the public health, safety and general welfare."

One immediate response came in the form of a *New Musical Express* article by Tracy Thomas, who noted: "This seems to please several Strip property owners, who wish to bring back the 'good old days' ... and do away with the long-haired element." Declaring that the youth of Los Angeles "don't intend to let our clubs die with outside a fight," Thomas was nonetheless already aware of the consequences of the new law: "Hollywood will certainly lose some importance as a rock'n'roll center next year."

Having already defeated a movement by Ernest E. Debs to have specific licenses revoked earlier in the year, the Galaxy, Gazzarri's, the Whisky A Go Go, and the venerable Sea Witch were, fortunately, exempt from a retrial, much to Debs's chagrin, and thus remained open. But by the end of the year, the Trip, the London Fog, It's Boss, Stratford On Sunset, the Action, and Pandora's Box were all closed down for good.

On Christmas day, Pandora's Box reopened for one night. Buffalo Springfield's Stephen Stills put on an acoustic show with Michael Clarke of The Byrds and several other musicians. It amounted, essentially, to a free party, because permits were not necessary at Christmas. Stills's performance of 'For What It's Worth' was an inevitably poignant highlight of the evening.

The whole issue of teen clubs on Sunset Strip fell into political neglect in early 1967, leading to a further protest at Pandora's Box on Saturday February 11th, which was attended by 3,000 people. This gathering was organized in solidarity with simultaneous demonstrations in the black Watts neighborhood, the Chicano areas of East LA and Pacoima, the Venice beat scene, and at gay nightclub the Black Cat in Silver Lake (which had been raided on New Year's Eve). These demonstrations were more peaceful than those of November 1966. Lawyers and speakers from the American Civil Liberties Union were present, while the police were conspicuous in their relative absence.

CAFF followed these demonstrations by hosting a benefit concert at the Valley Music Theatre on George Washington's birthday (February 22nd) to raise awareness, gather bail money for arrested demonstrators, and pay for damages incurred by businesses affected by the riot. A litany of contemporary stars played in front of a capacity crowd of 3,200, including The Doors, Hugh Masekela, The Byrds, and Buffalo Springfield. The headliners were Peter, Paul & Mary, of whom Tracy Thomas of the *NME* noted: "Songs that meant so much to them six years ago in Greenwich Village"—'The Times They Are A-Changin',' 'When The Ship Comes In'—"are just as meaningful today. Their harmony, humor, musical accompaniment, enthusiasm, in short, everything was perfect." The trio prefaced their set with a reminder that the teenagers of Sunset Strip "are not the first, nor the last, to have to fight to be individuals."

The success of the CAFF concert led its organizer, Alan Pariser, to plan a larger event. He and Ben Shapiro (who had managed the Renaissance, and Miles Davis) began to organize what became the Monterey Pop Festival with the help of various other LA scene-makers: former Beatles publicist Derek Taylor called up Paul McCartney, who suggested The Who and Jimi Hendrix play; Barry Feinstein brought along John Phillips, who in turn brought Dunhill's Lou Adler into the picture. The result was a landmark event that became the defining moment of the Summer Of Love. And with Los Angeles struggling amid the destruction of its creative nucleus, it was also the moment that turned San Francisco into the instant media-center of the 'psychedelic 60s.'

* * *

It has always been natural for people to congregate in the center of a city. Suburbs offer no cultural content, so the youth of post-war LA made the Sunset Strip their public epicenter. "You could sit, stand, walk, lay down, go from a clump of people to another clump of people and [know] that you were going to be welcome," says Pamela Des Barres of the Strip in 1965–66. "There was no intimidation; there was no separatism; there was no fear. It was all just this one big ball of unity." The gigantic Greater Los Angeles area, which extends from Santa Barbara to San Bernardino and as far South as San Clemente, had found a natural entertainment Mecca for the first time since the early 1930s demise of the now-dilapidated downtown LA, but shortsighted politicians began rushing to stop it almost as soon as it appeared.

The Sunset Strip was a place where Jim Morrison and Dean Martin could culturally co-exist. The swingers of the Rat Pack crowd had no issue with the new action on the Strip: how could they when Dean Martin's son was playing in a band at It's Boss, and Frank Sinatra's daughter reigned supreme as the West Coast queen of go-go boots and miniskirts, and made records that appealed to rockers and swingers alike. Ironically, The Stan Kenton Band was performing at the

Playboy Club when the riot kicked off. Members of his band had instigated the West Coast jazz scene, which in turn pushed the Sunset Strip toward becoming one of the world's hottest creative centers. (The Playboy Club's parent, Hugh Hefner, could also lay some claim to having fostered the progressive, sophisticated sexuality of the 1960s.)

The riot, brought on entirely by the conservative element, killed Sunset Strip as a center of nightlife for *everyone*. In response to the turmoil, Hugh Hefner moved his Playboy Club to the sterility of Century City. It would take another 25 years for the Strip to regain its earlier position of preeminence as the cross-cultural social center of Hollywood.

A symbolic moment of decline was captured on the local CBS affiliate KNXT during the October 29th 1967 episode of the hip, intelligent *Ralph Story's Los Angeles*. A group of teenagers from disparate backgrounds—rockers, surfers, black kids, Chicanos, middle class suburbanites, folk-rockers in turtlenecks and suede coats, mod girls with flower-power body painting—form a human wall in front of Pandora's Box, having painted a homemade sign to hold up against a Cleveland Wrecking Company bulldozer. Story tells of the destruction of Pandora's Box in a most sympathetic manner, noting that, to these youths, "the lavender nightclub had become as holy as St Peter's Basilica." A rockabilly kid with a pompadour claims that this demolition is akin to tearing down "our home," while a surfer with short, blonde hair declares: "They're trying to get rid of us, but it's not going to work!" "The actual flattening of Pandora's Box took about 20 minutes," concludes Story. "It was significant in the history of the Sunset Strip, I guess, but no great challenge professionally."

"The whole city was alight," says Jim Heimann of Hollywood's rock'n'roll heyday. "Traffic would be backed up from Fairfax through Doheny. It was like this for the last time in the summer of '67, but after that it was clear that Sunset Strip was no longer a center of attention."

In 1967, attempts were made to find an alternative center for the LA music scene away from the heavily patrolled Sunset Strip. Two years earlier, *Venture* magazine had already extolled the virtues of its near-namesake, Ventura Boulevard, "which is lined with restaurants and nightclubs ranging from such lavish enterprises as Sportsman's Lodge to such exotic ones as La Zomba, perhaps the oldest burlesque restaurant in the area." Several psychedelic nightclubs opened up in this stretch up in the Valley in 1967. The Magic Mushroom rose up in place of the Cinnamon Cinder, and played host to great, diverse bills such as one on August 17th that featured Spirit, Phil Ochs, Jackson Browne, The Peanut Butter Conspiracy, and the W.C. Fields Memorial Electric String Band. Comedy was an important part of the schedule, with the Firesign Theatre group getting its first major exposure at the Magic Mushroom. The group would broadcast their shows from the club live on KPPC, KPFK, and KRLA.

A club called the Third Eye—which bore no relation to the former Third i in Redondo Beach—sprung up on Ventura around the same time; this 'mini Strip' was flanked by two more psychedelic venues, the Wild Scene and Middle Earth. It's Camp on Vineland and the Cougar on De Soto clung on to the old Strip aesthetic. "There was a bona fide attempt to bring foot traffic to the Valley in '67," recalls the author Harvey Kubernik, "but it didn't have the lure or *lore* of Hollywood. For some reason it didn't seem quite right to say that you were going to take your date to Encino. People in Los Angeles feel the need to go to Hollywood to get their entertainment."

Suburban politicians reacted in a typically alarmist manner to these new developments. In Glendale, the Savoy Light House promoted its opening show with the phrase: "Where the Strip ended, this is where we begin." The Peanut Butter Conspiracy and Teddy & His Patches (a San Jose group who had just cut a flipped-out, garage-punk version of The Mothers' 'Suzy Creamcheese') were set to play a two-night stand on December 16th and 17th 1966. Acting on a tip from the LAPD Hollywood Division, however, local authorities worked to close the Savoy Light House down immediately. The second night—which was planned as no more than an innocent gathering of 250 people—had to be cancelled, or else the club's equipment would have been impounded.

It is important to note the matter-of-fact acknowledgement in the ads for this late-1966 venue that the Strip scene had already "ended." With the fires of creativity in danger of being extinguished everywhere, some looked to San Francisco, where there were a number of clubs and auditoriums to play in, as an alternative. But what these LA groups didn't realize is how provincial their Californian neighbors could be. The Doors' Ray Manzarek recalled The Grateful Dead having an enormous "support system," taking in everything from roadies to personal chefs, to the extent that "they had no need for normal human interaction or discourse." Any attempts to integrate with this "completely insulated" scene were entirely in vain.[2]

When the Cheetah opened up in the old Aragon Ballroom at Pacific Ocean Park in March 1967 it marked the first stage of the LA music scene taking its cues from San Francisco's ballrooms. A branch of the hip, mod discotheque in New York City, the Cheetah certainly caught the mood of the times: there was even a line of Cheetah clothes. An early bill twinned Love with The Chambers Brothers, while The Standells and The Leaves played together there later in the year. The Cheetah was soon followed by the Bank in Torrance, which played host to John Mayall, Bo Diddley, and Magic Sam, while the Shrine Exposition Hall opened its doors to performances by The Who, The Yardbirds, The Jimi Hendrix Experience, Procol Harum, and Fleetwood Mac.

The trouble with these venues, however, was that they lacked the intimacy and the residency aspect of a club, and gave little opportunity for garage bands to hone their sound, as they had been able to do on the nightclub scene of 1965–66. In downtown Hollywood, Bido Lito's remained true to this spirit, as did Gazzarri's and the Galaxy. The Whisky A Go Go, however, made a complete 180-degree turn, banning psychedelic groups and instead opting for an all-soul format (which seemed, coincidentally, to have been tailored to the showbiz direction the Motown label was headed in during the late 1960s). That's not to say that the early headliners weren't impressive—they included The Miracles, The Temptations, Little Anthony & The Imperials, Sam & Dave, The Four Tops, The Impressions, and Jimmy Smith.

Exclusive, highbrow venues such as the Daisy and the Candy Store carried on as normal, but were still no place for teenage fans or lowly garage-rock acts. The only major forum for emerging groups in the wake of the Sunset Strip riots was the Hullabaloo, which began an ambitious series of After Hours shows on January 14th 1967.

Thirteen groups were scheduled to play between 2:00 and 6:00am at the first After Hours event, including Love, The Seeds, and The Electric Prunes, but in the end only eight of them made the stage. The Monkees, The Mama & The Papas, and The Miracles were all in the audience. "[KBLA deejay] Humble Harv promoted it, and we split the profits," recalls club proprietor Gary Bookasta. "It was his idea, so he got all the other disc jockeys on KBLA to promote it … which was much better than running a regular commercial."

The club had a fire limit of 850 people, but let in 6,000 on the first night with, says Bookasta, "10,000 [more] trying to get in the door at 2:00 in the morning." Bookasta's claim is backed up by a contemporary report in *The New Yorker*, which described "the longhairs waiting outside … extending radially over the area" and a parking lot "full of cars, nearly all with their radios on, so a kind of concert of Donovan, The Beach Boys, Sonny & Cher, and Buffalo Springfield was rising from the asphalt."

Eventually, says Bookasta, "the fire marshal came, because you couldn't move in the place. He came up to my office and said 'Listen, it would be more safe for me not to do anything. If I try to close this place, there'll be a riot, so I'm gonna go home, try and go to sleep, and forget this ever happened. But if it ever happens again, I'll put you all in jail.'" After Hours was enormously popular for much of the next year, but became a victim, according to its proprietor, of its own success: "The city got so many applications for after-hours clubs that they changed the law, made it illegal to have live entertainment after 2:00am." Bookasta had a permit until mid 1968, but after that the After Hours nights had to stop.

In April 1967, having previously tried and failed to open up elsewhere, a roving club called the Kaleidoscope took on the lease of the Ciro's building, which had until recently been home to It's Boss. The Doors, The Peanut Butter Conspiracy, and The UFO were on the opening-night bill, but this club, too, was soon nudged off the Strip. The Kaleidoscope rose again, briefly, in the Grand Ballroom at the Ambassador Hotel, for shows headlined by Big Brother & The Holding Company and Buffalo Springfield.

Finally, with the Hullabaloo forced to bow out due to continually increasing rent, the Kaleidoscope took on the old Moulin Rouge building and opened, says departing proprietor Gary Bookasta, "with a big flourish." LA historian Marc Wanamaker was involved with this latest incarnation of the Kaleidoscope, which ran from March 1968 until early the following year. The end came rather suddenly, according to Wanamaker: "[We] found out that the backers were mobsters when they took the club away from us at gunpoint." The headliner, Janis Joplin, was forced to play on as normal that night, but "when people on the scene found out what happened, everyone stayed away in droves [from then on], and the mobsters gave up."

One interesting Kaleidoscope sideline was its inventive series of late-night movie parties called Kaleidoflicks, which were something of a prototype for the underground/revival movie house scene that followed. Eric Caidin, who later established the Hollywood Book And Poster store on Hollywood Boulevard, recalls how, after the night's bands had performed, a movie screen "would come down behind the revolving stage." Attendees would bring sleeping bags or blankets, and settle down to watch such cult favorites as *The Pit And The Pendulum*, *Comedy Of Terrors*, and *House Of Usher*.

* * *

When publicist Derek Taylor was asked to rejoin The Beatles in London around the time of the formation of Apple Records in 1968, he held a 'de-immigration' party in the Ciro's building that seemed to be not just a farewell to him, but also to LA's most vibrantly creative period. Captain Beefheart, The Byrds, and Tiny Tim all played at the party. "[It] was a fine, bold stroke," recalled Taylor, "but only in Hollywood; it didn't strike me till later, as I wondered how any of it happened, wondered if any of it had happened. So much living was crammed into the three years we spent in Hollywood. We flew out of Liverpool in 1965 and sailed back into Liverpool in 1968 totally changed, totally. We had learned so much from the young and from the music in America. From Beefheart, from The Byrds, from The Beach Boys, from the Southern California experience, which is like no other."[3]

Hope continued to linger in the air for a while, but the reserves were almost depleted. Eve Babitz recalls how quickly things changed after the last hurrah of Monterey Pop, noting that while some groups had "grown rich," others had "split up and fallen apart." Those who found success, she says, "decided that 'the city' was simply out of the question and they wanted to be ranchers like real men"; the rest went off to either Hawaii or Topanga Canyon, took drugs, and "waited for the next thing." (Whisky A Go Go owner Elmer Valentine would later note: "You could shoot a cannon down the middle of Sunset Boulevard and not worry about hitting anyone."[4])

Marshall Brevetz made one final attempt to open a psychedelic nightclub in Hollywood in 1969: Thee Experience, which was located on Sunset, three quarters of a mile east of the Strip. The same room had been known earlier in the 1960s as King Banjo's Pizza Parlor and Genesis IX; Brevitz had Jimi Hendrix's face painted over the front of the building, with the guitarist's mouth doubling as the front door. Thee Experience put on shows by Kaleidoscope, Captain Beefheart & His Magic Band, 'Frank Zappa & Friends,' and The Flying Burrito Brothers, as well as British acts such as Screaming Lord Sutch, Tyrannosaurus (later just T.) Rex, and Joe Cocker & The Grease Band. It was also here that former Animals frontman Eric Burdon hooked up with LA group War (formerly Señor Soul), with whom he would soon hit with 'Spill The Wine,' while Jimi Hendrix himself once dropped in to jam with The Bonzo Dog Doo-Dah Band. As impressive as all this might sound, however, the energy of 1965–66 had in truth all but dissipated. Moreover, says Harvey Kubernik: "Once you're past the Mason/Dixon line of Fairfax, it's a different kind of Sunset. The psychic and geographic lay of the Strip's bends and curves turn into a straight line."

By 1969, a veil had fallen over youth culture in LA, which just a few years earlier had been awash with good vibes and cool venues. During 1965–66, the main agent of intoxication at teen clubs was marijuana or, on special occasions, LSD, but, says Kim Fowley: "Then the drugs changed, from pot and acid in the mid 60s, to cocaine and heroin in the late 60s. That's when you get hippies killing people." On top of that, without venues such as It's Boss or the Trip in which to congregate, some kids ended up in places like Spahn Ranch, the infamous home of Charles Manson and his 'Family.' The rest is criminal history, or what Paul Body might call "bad juju."

Paul Johnson of The Everpresent Fullness concurs with Kim Fowley on the drug-related aspect of the scene's deterioration. While drugs such as LSD provided a "purely psychedelic experience," the fact that subsequent substances were "laced with methedrine turned it into an ugly situation. PCP became widespread in 1968," he says, "and that made people do *really* weird things. Everything started out idealistic and ended up hedonistic." Rodney Bingenheimer, meanwhile, notes that drugs were "never the main focus" on the Strip, but that they became more important on the Haight/Ashbury scene. "People started getting into downers and the dress got sloppy," he says. "People started not caring about themselves anymore."

In *Art, Politics, And Dissent*, Francis Frascina explains how many on the LA scene, particularly within the protest movement, considering the 'drug dropout' aesthetic promoted in San Francisco to be a major hindrance. "To the consternation of many," says Frascina, "the influence of the drug culture, advocated by [Ken] Kesey and [Dr Timothy] Leary, began to deflect radicals from campaigns for civil rights, workers' rights, and the withdrawal of the United States from Vietnam."

Frank Zappa, too, was of this view. "I was just never enthusiastic about drugs or drug culture," he told CNN reporter Sandi Freeman. "I saw what it had done to a lot of people, musicians that I had worked with, the ways that it had affected their lives." Zappa also noted that, because taking drugs is illegal, "[it] gives the government another different type of leverage over you. It puts your freedom in jeopardy, aside from what it does to your health, and what it does to your mind."

Francis Frascina notes "fundamental contradictions" between LA's proactive Artists' Protest Committee and the passive, non-participatory politics of Ken Kesey and his Merry Pranksters. "In the eyes of some theorists," says Frascina, "the activities and recommendations of the latter were of potential assistance to the state in its regulatory dissuasion of active and organized dissent."[5]

Frank Zappa agreed. "I believe the government likes to have drugs in the marketplace because it keeps the population in a very useable state," he told *CNN*. "Does it sound far-fetched to talk about using an entire American community for chemical and biological warfare testing? Well, you know that's been done. If the government can do *that* to their people, there's no reason to believe that they're above giving them drugs, and collecting money for those drugs being used, and having the benefit of the stupefaction of the population [as well]."

Hard drugs began to inhibit social interaction. The manic, joyful enthusiasm of rock'n'roll, c. 1955–66, was gone. To be lively, vibrant, perky, or upbeat was now 'suspect,' and as such no longer 'cool' in the eyes of the San Francisco hippies. It was as if these people were *ashamed* of the rock'n'roll that came before them. At the same time, such publications as *Crawdaddy!*, *Rolling Stone*, *The Village Voice*, and *The Los Angeles Free Press* all marked the passing of rock'n'roll and the birth of a new, more 'mature' genre: rock. (Underground deejays preferred the term progressive rock, which later gave rise to classic rock—or, to its naysayers, corporate rock.)

In 1967, the revolutionary torch was passed from the denizens of the Sunset Strip rock'n'roll scene to San Francisco through the organization of the Monterey Pop Festival. The city to the north took this as an opportunity to promote their Summer Of Love (while simultaneously ridiculing LA's scene-makers). The mainstream media soon turned its spotlight on San Francisco's hippie groups, whose elitist attitudes brought rock music to unheard-of levels of pretension, and fledgling publications such as *Rolling Stone*.

With the San Francisco psychedelic community toiling in a fog of unrestrained improvisation, The Beatles, Bob Dylan, The Rolling Stones, The Beach Boys,

The Byrds, and The Mothers Of Invention all cut 'back to basics' albums in 1968, but this proved to be too little too late. The social revolution ushered in by the Sunset Strip movement now stood for something entirely different by virtue of the Bay Area: self-absorbed, self-indulgent excess. With the ensuing blowout and burnout, rock'n'roll lost its original vigor and sense of purpose. When drugs because a primary factor, the early spirit of rock'n'roll disappeared.

The momentum that had been building in Los Angeles since the 1920s was derailed completely at the end of 1966. Once this creative center was systematically blown apart, the powers of the Hollywood movie industry—which also own the major labels—regained control of broadcast music, compartmentalizing the recording industry as a mercenary chore. Like scriptwriters at the bottom of the movie food chain, music in Hollywood resumed its pre-1950s subservience, de-emphasized and neglected in a mad dash toward creating the next big-screen blockbuster.

Studio moguls, hand in hand with ASCAP, had arranged the Payola scandal and the first decline of American rock'n'roll during the late 1950s in an attempt to derail the independent labels that had come to dominate radio (specifically Sun, Chess, and Specialty). The uninfected British scene accidentally gave rock'n'roll a second wind in the USA during 1964–66. But the organized resistance to rock'n'roll by the establishment in Hollywood, which led to the riot on Sunset Strip, put an end to the momentum of actual rock'n'roll for good.

CHAPTER THIRTEEN

Aftermath

❝ *The initial flash is over. The thing they call rock—
what used to be called rock'n'roll—it got decadent.
And then there was a rock revival sparked by the
English. That went very far. It was articulate. Then
it became self-conscious, which I think is the death
of any moment. It became self-conscious, involuted,
and kind of incestuous. The energy is gone. There is
no longer a belief.* **❞ JIM MORRISON TO *ROLLING STONE***

The 1960s were like the chase scene at the end of a movie. The sounds were vital, visceral, and completely in synch with a momentary cultural confluence borne out in the galactic glow of the futurist Sunset Strip. The rock'n'roll environment was young, fresh, and sparkling; an unspoken bond among kids of the time, who had been raised on the concept of 'progress,' was the desire to move forward and improve the world. When the Civil Rights Act was passed on December 14th 1964, it seemed as defining a moment as the defeat of fascism during World War II and the subsequent establishment of the United Nations—the epitome of social progress, couched in modernism.

Once the civil rights movement had begun to gain momentum during the 1950s, society overcame repression at a faster pace than at any previous time in American history. Both rock'n'roll and the Beat generation were fueled by the sense of breaking through social barriers. For one final, fleeting moment in mid-1960s Hollywood, they combined with the rest of the allied arts world in a moment of unheralded creativity and positive cultural solutions. When the establishment resisted, the movers and shakers of Sunset Strip organized the Monterey Pop Festival of 1967 from an office in Stratford On Sunset, the British Invasion-style club that had been shuttered in December 1965. (The same building had also housed the Renaissance jazz club during the 1950s.)

The Summer Of Love found its center at Monterey Pop and, from then on, San Francisco claimed ownership of this 'revolution.' The Woodstock Music And Arts Fair of 1969 was simply an East Coast imitation of Monterey Pop: Jimi Hendrix, The Who, and various aggregations of The Byrds and Buffalo Springfield headlined both. Woodstock was a New York media phenomenon that marked the end of an era. The idea that it 'defined a generation' is wishful and convenient, since the real moment of creative crystallization had long since passed. But even though the Monterey Pop Festival was simply an outgrowth of the Sunset Strip rebellion, the pre-burnout thrill of 1964–66 is now overlooked and obscured by the sound bite culture of the present day.

The only surviving Hollywood clubs from this period, the Troubadour and the Whisky, are in no sense now as they are depicted here. The rooms have been gutted of their original artistic character, while the club's booking policies, which are given over to different promoters nightly, have brought Los Angeles to the creative nadir of modern music (as evidenced by Penelope Spheeris's 1988 movie *The Decline Of Western Civilization Part II: The Metal Years*). The Whisky A Go Go even changed its neon marquee to 'the Whisky' when it abandoned its integrity and became a pay-to-play venue in 1984.

The credibility of the Whisky A Go Go lasted for its first 18 years. Moving with the times, the club featured proto-punk groups as early as 1976, which helped bring some excitement back to Sunset Strip for a brief while. The club still had tables and booths back then, and played host to fun shows by such groups as The Berlin Brats, The Quick, The Screamers, The Germs, The Dickies, and X. But, in an echo of times gone by, this did not go down too well with the Hollywood elite, who petitioned to have punk banned from the Whisky for being, according to Kim Fowley, "too intense."

The punk scene relocated to a club called the Masque on Hollywood Boulevard, run by Brendan Mullen. "Whisky A Go Go was always banning punk rock," he recalls, "but then they realized how much money there was. When a big name was coming through, all of a sudden the band would be listed. It was always about dollars." These big names included Elvis Costello (in 1978), The Specials (in 1979), and a host of other new wave acts who weren't quite as frightening as their punk peers.

One local group, Black Flag, was almost single-handedly responsible for bringing the LA punk rock scene to its knees. The group (and its PCP-loving audience) left a string of bans on punk at most of the venues they played. "Black Flag would not take any responsibility for what was going on in the crowd," notes Stan Ridgway of the group Wall Of Voodoo, "and they frequently went out of their way to stir things up."[1]

A show by Black Flag and D.O.A. at the Whisky A Go Go on October 8th 1980 resulted in a major police riot after the club's owners oversold tickets to double the legal capacity. "There were cop cars all over the place, the entire Strip was shut down, and traffic was bottlenecked," recalls Mullen. "It was quite clearly, totally Whisky A Go Go's fault … It's a sore point with club owners here because the Whisky and the Roxy [formerly the Largo] are in the county fire department jurisdiction, whereas if you're in the city, they'll shut your ass down. Somehow, they just carry on, always packing the places beyond the occupancy, all the time. Nothing ever happens to them, and a lot of people in clubland wonder why."

After a series of stops and starts with punk and new wave, the Whisky A Go Go closed its doors in 1982. "The Whisky takes this paternalistic 'we supported the local music scene for thirty years' attitude," says Mullen. "Yes, when it suited them. In fact, the local music scene has supported the Whisky." When the Whisky reopened in 1984, the cozy seating/tables/dance floor arrangement vanished in order to maximize the capacity. In the years since, the club has given up on booking cutting-edge bands, instead opting to rent space out to whoever could afford it. Punk, and the wide variety of styles that have emerged in its wake, have been completely shut out, their place taken by mid-1970s-style dinosaur rock. The dreaded pay-to-play philosophy, meanwhile, spread to other Los Angeles nightclubs, severely hampering the flow of grass roots creativity in town.

What many local residents failed to realize at the time was that pay-to-play would also dissuade interesting bands from other locales to completely bypass the Greater Los Angeles area. "There was a whole backlash against Los Angeles because of pay-to-play," says LA art dealer and chef David Weidman. "It was like a boycott … [that] spread around to all of the groups from other cities, who then would just skip LA on their itinerary. There's nobody willing to take a chance in that West Hollywood environment."

Detached from interaction with other music scenes, Hollywood musicians soon became internalized and stale. "You'd see this kind of strange attitude at places like the Viper Room," says Weidman. "[Occasionally] they'd have really exceptional acts, but the people who would go there couldn't care less. So the atmosphere in the audience was people looking at *you* when you walked in, not the band."

The true artists of Los Angeles began to congregate on the east side of Hollywood. As West LA grew more and more out of touch, such 1990s places as Spaceland in Silver Lake and the Derby in Los Feliz offered an alternative to what was going on to the west. This new scene had its roots just after the late-1970s mod revival in England; LA's answer was its early-1980s Paisley Underground. Then came a scene inspired by 1960s garage-punk (The Unclaimed) and new developments in rockabilly (Big Sandy & the Fly Rite Trio), swing (Royal Crown Revue), exotica (DJ Senor Amor), surf (The Boardwalkers, The Untamed Youth), pop (The Wondermints, Baby Lemonade), jazz (Black Note), and burlesque (Velvet Hammer, Lucha Va Voom). The sociological and philosophical divide separating Los Feliz, Silver Lake, Echo Park and downtown LA from the west side became so strong that by 2008, even Hollywood Boulevard had staged a major comeback with new restaurants, revived landmarks, and smarter clubs like The King King. Sunset Strip instead wallowed stubbornly in a self-serving obsolescence that has resulted in steadily diminishing public interest.

Several of the venues that thrived during the 1960s—including the Red Velvet, Bido Lito's, Stratford On Sunset, and the Melody Room—remain in operation under new names and management. Kurt Fisher took over the Red Velvet in 1969 and renamed it Soul'd Out. The club became a regular hangout for Ike & Tina Turner, The Chambers Brothers, Etta James, and many of the up-and-coming R&B and movie stars of the blaxploitation era. (Motown had moved in next door, so there was a lot of spillover from the label's office.) Brendan Mullen took over in the 1980s and 1990s, during which time the venue operated under the name Club Lingerie (and, briefly, Space 6507—a combination of its address on Sunset and an echo of Spaceland). With a track record that runs all the way back to its days as the Summit under Jimmy Maddin's management and as KRLA's Teenage Club—in spite of recent years of inactivity—that room maintains the longest history of consistently good rock'n'roll in town.

The Haunted House became a strip club called the Cave in the late 1960s. Pete's Wild Thing survived as a restaurant, Athenian Gardens, for over 30 years, before that too became a strip club (later burnt, then rebuilt as a restaurant). Bido Lito's continued as an alternative club called the Gaslight in the late 1980s and early 1990s, while the Melody Room was turned first into Filthy McNasty's (as seen of the sleeve of The Sweet's *Desolation Boulevard* LP) and then into the

Central. By the 1990s it had become the Viper Room, which, with Johnny Depp as host, echoed the movie industry connections of such clubs as the Trocadero back in the 1930s. (The Viper Room, however, is unlikely to ever present such consistently cool acts as Bobby Troup, Esquivel, Dizzy Gillespie, or Billy Ward & The Dominoes, as had the Melody Room.) The Aldous Huxley-inspired Brave New World at 7207 Melrose was most recently a vintage clothing shop, while its other location, on Cherokee, became Artists Recording Studio during the 1970s, according to engineer Mark Linett, but is now just an empty storefront.

The original location of the Renaissance—which became Stratford On Sunset during the 1960s—had closed down early, and served as the planning office for the Monterey Pop Festival. Arthur Blessitt, the Baptist preacher-turned-psychedelic 'Minister To Sunset Strip' then opened up His Place at the same location during the late 1960s. Blessitt made it his mission to coax kids off the hard drugs that had become prevalent by 1969, and also cut an album at his club with backing group The Eternal Rush. His Place then gave way to a coffeehouse and then a restaurant, Roy's, before being rebuilt from the inside out and turned into the House Of Blues, one of many uptight, corporate clubs opened in the 1990s in an attempt to 'bounce back' from the 80s abyss.

During the Reagan and Bush (Sr) years, Sunset Strip seemed like it had been hit by a neutron bomb of unconsciousness, vaporizing any remaining vestiges of cool. The 'prevailing wisdom' has since been to try to revive the glamour and glory of years gone by with movie industry hangouts such as Le Dome, Spago, the Standard, and a newly renovated Chateau Marmont. But those involved in the ultra-competitive television and movie industries wake up far too early in the morning to enjoy any kind of nightlife, and are too self-absorbed to seek out cutting-edge music. The metaphorical ridicule of Frank Zappa's 1966 song 'Plastic People' can now be applied in the literal sense.

The Trip, Pandora's Box, the Trocadero, and the Renaissance/Mocambo have all been vacant since the 1960s (the latter is now a parking lot). The Action, meanwhile, went 'high class' for a while as the Chez post-1966 but is now a Laundromat with a wooden floor. Neil Norman, son of GNP-Crescendo boss Gene Norman, sums up the situation well: "We could have rebuilt on the lot where the Crescendo/Interlude and Trip used to be, but the type of investment—and the acts we'd have to book to survive on Sunset Strip these days—would not be conducive to developing talent."

The Hollywood Palladium is one of the few Los Angeles venues to maintain a sense of class and style. Its wooden dance floor, circular art deco balcony, and exterior signage have all been maintained well. The building that housed Ciro's and It's Boss still stands with majestic, vintage dignity—perhaps because it avoided the rigors of 'rock' when it was turned into the Comedy Store. The Ash Grove on Melrose has also become a comedy club, Bud Friedman's Improvisation. McCabe's Guitar Shop in Santa Monica and the Folk Music Center in Claremont are definite traditionalist holdouts; McCabe's recently played host to the recording of a live album by Van Dyke Parks. Out by the beach, the Insomniac Cafe and the Gas House are long gone, but the Venice West location did re-open as Sponto Gallery, which lasted for a while, and now the building has been given Historical Landmark status. Maverick's Flat is still open on Crenshaw Boulevard, and retains the integrity and design of its original form better than any other nightclub in Los Angeles.

PJ's closed its doors in 1971, shortly after Rufus Thomas cut a 'live at' album there. The venue spent ten years as Starwood, which played host to some interesting bands, including The Jam, but in its later years was most notable for its violent atmosphere and aggressive security staff. Owner Eddie Nash was later depicted on the big screen as an incompetent, murderous cocaine-freak in both *Boogie Nights* (1998) and *Wonderland* (2003). By the time Starwood shut down in 1981, the Standells/Bobby Fuller Four era at PJ's had long been forgotten. The club has since been turned into a mini-mall.

The original Gazzarri's on La Cienega closed years ago when the hippie scene became too blitzed to go-go. The club's other location on the Strip hung on much longer, its musical acts and clientele deteriorating with each passing year. Owner Bill Gazzarri began to call himself the 'Godfather Of Rock'n'Roll'—perhaps ironically, as it was in front of that very building that mobster Mickey Cohen was shot on July 19th 1949. Gazzarri's was then given a corporate facelift and a new name: Billboard Live, intended as the first in a series of Hard Rock Cafe-style themed venues. The renovation cost around $5.5 million, but much of that money was ill spent. A clue to the out-of-touch mentality of the investors was the $2 million spent on a proposed 'Babe Cam' that would allow the club's patrons to 'check out' other guests anonymously. Club-goers were not impressed, nor were they by the soulless, major label performers. *Billboard* magazine quickly dismissed itself from the licensing deal that linked it to the venue, which was most recently known as the Key Club.

Then there is the building that was known, variously, as Earl Carroll's Vanities, the Moulin Rouge, and the Hullabaloo. In its final days as a rock'n'roll venue, the Hullabaloo became the Kaleidoscope, before being bought out by The Smothers Brothers—the smash-hit television comedy duo—for the West Coast staging of the musical *Hair*. They renamed the venue the Aquarius Theater and commissioned The Fool—the Dutch art team that had painted The Beatles' Apple building, John Lennon's Rolls Royce, and Janis Joplin's Jaguar—to decorate the exterior. This was an amazing sight, but didn't last long before being painted over (in a drab, earthy brown). Episodes of The *Midnight Special* were shot at the Aquarius, but by the 1980s it had become the home of the cheesy *Star Search*. More recently, the building has been used by the children's cable television network Nickelodeon.

At Earl Carroll's Vanities, cement blocks with movie star signatures graced the Sunset Boulevard side of the building. These were retained through the Moulin Rouge, Hullabaloo, and Kaleidoscope years, but removed to make way for The Fool's artwork outside the Aquarius Theater. They were never replaced; Brendan Mullen last recalls seeing them on display at the Variety Arts Center during the punk era. (One cement block was discovered more recently in the building's basement, bearing the signature of television minstrels Amos & Andy. It had been removed when the duo's show was banished from television by the NAACP in 1966.)

When the Aquarius was sold to become a television studio, the entire hall was gutted except for the base of the revolving stage. Only the foyer of the original Earl Carroll's remains, complete with mirrored bar embossed with nudes. The last vital public use of this landmark building was to present *Zoot Suit*, a play that meant everything to Mexican-Americans but was barely understood on Broadway because of its strong East LA dialect. In a fitting echo of the past, the play—and the subsequent movie version—was sponsored by Lou Adler; Edward James Olmos, whose band Pacific Ocean had played at Gazzarri's during the 1960s, took the role of El Pachuco.

During the course of the 1990s, Sunset Strip went through a major transformation, when this previously unincorporated area became the City Of West Hollywood (often referred to as WeHo). After 30 years in the wilderness, the Strip began to come back to life as a hot spot, echoing its position during the 1930s and 40s at the center of the movie world with deals being struck at Le Dome, cocktails enjoyed at Bar Marmont and Skybar, and moneyed folk holed up at the Argyle (formerly Sunset Tower), Chateau Marmont, and the Standard (formerly the Hollywood Sunset Hotel, and briefly the Golden Crest Retirement Hotel). One positive indicator was when the Standard was renovated to embellish—rather than demolish—the original, *Jetsons*-like design. Another sign of improvement was when the Ben Frank's building was saved from the wrecking ball in order to preserve its vintage appearance, complete with orange roof.

The popularity of these nouveau-Hollywood hangouts will remain as long as there are movie openings to attend. But some are not convinced. "It looks OK," says Roger McGuinn, "but all the billboards around there now are for sports and films—there's not much music—and everyone's got a BMW or a Mercedes-Benz. It's kind of like *Blade Runner*, you know?"

In terms of the current LA music scene, the Strip is even less representative than it might seem on the surface. As *New Times* columnist Jim Freek put it in response to readers' letters asking why he never writes about the Viper Room: "The thought of seeing Paul Stanley or Steven Tyler jump on stage to belt out some classic rock staple sounds like something that's more up the alley of vacationing Midwesterners. ... [And] if we really want to get shoved around or yelled at by a bunch of overweight security swine with fast food drive-thru headsets strapped onto their faces, we could certainly find a better way to do so." On all but the most conservative corners, *Maxim* guys and bimbo girls replaced the hard rock contingent of the 1980s. But these, too, came from a slick version of the frat boy/jock mentality; for them, politics and world affairs are not a comfortable conversational topic.

There is perhaps no better representation of Sunset Strip then and now than the building that once housed Dino's Lodge and the Sea Witch. LA's two most distinctive elements—beachcomber culture and Hollywood nightlife—were summed up in this single structure, which sat across the street from Fred C. Dobbs' and Ben Frank's, and right alongside the Playboy Club and the Trip. Behind the building, looking south, one glimpsed a panoramic view of city lights stretching out on the horizon below the hills; to the east sat Ciro's (or It's Boss) and Stratford On Sunset. This was the absolute center of Sunset Strip and, by extension, Los Angeles. Now, however, the building is a drab, gray office. A demarcation in cement notes that the television series *77 Sunset Strip* was filmed at the same location, but the street itself is silent, aside from the clicking heels of the businesspeople that inhabit these sterile premises, oblivious to the history echoing around them.

* * *

On December 5th 1996, *The Los Angeles Times Magazine* published a special issue on 'The Strip,' which closed with a quote from one of Sunset Plaza's managers of the time, Mark Montgomery: "We don't have any kings in this country, so there's no one to put the slaves to work, to build our Colosseums and Forums and Parthenons." *The Los Angeles Times* seemed fine with these sentiments. Hollywood, it would appear, is still stuck in the Reagan era—a time when 'liberal' became a dirty word. The music scene of Sunset Strip 1965–66, however, had brought conservative inertia and repression to its knees. *Laugh In*, produced by 1950s Ciro's booker George Schlatter (and an obvious play on the idea of a love-in) was the Number 1-rated network television show for three years in a row, despite leveling harsh criticisms at then-current Presidents Johnson and Nixon and the entire operation of the United States Government. As Tom Smothers, one half of *The Smothers Brothers Comedy Hour*, points out: "There's no political satire on television now, except at 11:30pm on HBO, or at 12:00 for *Politically Incorrect.* … There's no real discourse [on] television today, and it parallels what was happening in the mid 1960s during the Vietnam War." Smothers feels that his *Comedy Hour* was one the few shows to reflect what people were actually thinking. "That's still going on," he says. "I think if there was a way of taking a pulse, or a morality check, or ethic check on this country, I think most people are [rooting] for the underdog. We are basically revolutionaries at heart."

The momentum of LA's youth scene rapidly brought it to the attention of the mass media and the public at large. The nightclubs of the Sunset Strip were inspired by the black community's struggle for civil rights and love of rhythm & blues, and fuelled by the music of The Beatles, Bob Dylan, and The Rolling Stones. They brought together folk ethics, beat poetics, pop art, and rock'n'roll, in a mix that gave birth to The Byrds, Love, The Mothers Of Invention, The Doors, Buffalo Springfield, and the rest.

The media revolution inspired by these artists and musicians influenced everything that followed in television, radio, and the movies, and brought to light an entire social movement. The 1960s Sunset Strip underground scene gripped mainstream culture, and even radicalized it—at least for one brief, shining moment.

For what it's worth

In 2010, Domenic Priore interviewed Stephen Stills for Hans Fjellestad's documentary Sunset Strip, *a history of the scene from the 1920s to the present day. Here are his recollections of the events that inspired Buffalo Springfield's milestone single of the era, 'For What It's Worth' …*[1]

"If you've ever seen *American Graffiti*, the Strip used to be like that. There would be bad-to-the-bone cars that would come up and cruise, and so on. It was the same as every high school in America in the late 50s and early 60s; look at the girls, look at the boys in the cars. Finding a place to park was really hard, so you spent a lot of time in your car looking for a place, picking out the club you want to go to.

That's where Buffalo Springfield came together. The idea of the group was already formed back east, but I lost Neil. I called his mom, and she said, "Well, if you find him, tell him to call his mother." He had broken up the band and ran off with this girl. So I get out to LA, I call Richie Furay, and we're flopping around trying to have a band, if you will. Herbie Cohen, who managed Lenny Bruce and The Modern Folk Quartet—they were all very supportive. I actually got to open for Lenny during his pre-trial reunion show. He was really funny, and really trying hard. It was a great environment. I mean, it was just popping.

I was running around with Richie Furay, we were in a white van, going east on Sunset Strip. I pull up behind a hearse with Ontario plates, and the only guy that I ever—it could only be one person—because we had buried his first hearse in Thunder Bay when it died. So we wait for a stoplight, I run out, pound on the door … it's Neil. And he goes, "Oh Jesus!" We pull off on a side street and out tumbles Bruce Palmer: there was The Buffalo Springfield.

It took us a couple months to find a drummer that suited us. We started out as a house band, we lucked into it, I think. We practiced with acoustic guitars around Barry Friedman's house until somebody got us an audition at Whisky A Go Go. They said, "Yeah, you're the house band, and you'll open for everybody." Then we become *thee* band, and The Doors opened for us. When we went to New York, they took over.

There are some groups that I can hear—Them, The Electric Prunes—I thought were just epic. Before making a record, we were asked to be on an opening slot [along with The Standells and The Byrds] at The Rolling Stones' Hollywood Bowl concert. Everybody went to see the Stones, because they had the glamour at every big show. We actually made it a little tough for them, because we were good. Bill Wyman showed up early and saw us; we have been friends ever since.

The whole courtship of managers and stuff on Sunset Strip was hilarious. I wanted Lou Adler to produce us, but we got fixed up with Charlie Greene and Brian Stone instead. They took credit for Sonny & Cher, so we didn't realize that Sonny Bono actually took care of Sonny & Cher. That was all Sonny ... he was really smart.

The scene was totally spontaneous; there was nothing organized about it. There were no plots, no conspiracies, nobody calling me on the phone, "Let's go mess this up." You know, the whole J. Edgar Hoover mentality. Just ... everybody was too ditzy. We were like, "What's happening, where's the cool party, where's the best band, who's holding?" And there were just so many great musicians that came through town.

You could feel these people writing songs, and we'd run over and share them with each other. I lived at a place on Orange Grove Avenue, and Frank Zappa lived a couple of blocks away. He would run me down, to the middle of the creek, and read me the lyrics to 'Who Are The Brain Police.' He was so excited ... and I was like, "You lost me on the third line." Then we all would fall by each other's sessions.

Dylan really influenced me a lot, and he was great. But when the imitators of Dylan came around, part of me thought, "We should turn down the meaning, it's just ... enough." They really started pounding on it.

A big hit when I was around was 'Eve Of Destruction,' Barry McGuire. It was a hilarious song. As a piece of poetry, it's just hysterical, it's graceless. It's like *Pirates Of The Caribbean*, but at the same time it's salient. I was very careful when I was writing 'For What It's Worth' to make it more like an essay—a philosophical essay that didn't have a timeframe on it. It's very hard to sing 'Four Days Gone' now, but I can still sing 'For What It's Worth' because it still applies somewhere. I had great professors and teachers, and I got letters from a couple of them saying, "Well done."

On the night of the riot, I was coming to the Strip from Laurel Canyon. We got about a block away, I see kids, and a line of cops, lined up like Roman Centurions. I turned the car around—didn't even want to go in there. I'd seen all I needed to see, and I wrote 'For What It's Worth' on the way back. Everything, it reminded me of … just … the politics of fear, like we're doing today. It also reminded me of the guys on the line over in 'nam. I had friends over there, and I was worried about them. They were my best friends who'd signed up for another tour and didn't tell me.

I grew up in Florida but I spent a lot of time in New Orleans. New Orleans cops are the meanest cops in the world. They got crowd control down. They will charge on you, but they don't do it that way. They don't line up on one side of the street in full Macedonian battle array; they just sort of slip up on you, and throw you to the pavement. But these guys in LA were mad, because all these longhairs were objecting to the war and all that. And they turned it into a whole argument that it wasn't. The sit-in demonstration was actually a funeral for a bar.

I hadn't been in LA that long—I think about eight months. The day I left New Orleans, we had had a funeral for a bar that was the favorite hang out for all of the after-hours people. All the people that'd get off work, they would close early and come to Pipe Joe's for a drink … and they were closing it. There were 7,000 people, it spilled over to Rampart Street, an entire block. The New Orleans cops didn't do nothing about it, because it's local scene. The kids on the Strip were locals, they were from the valley. They weren't like, "Let's come from Denver, let's go to the Sunset Strip." That hadn't happened yet.

Even though we know there are tax sheets on the books that have to do with obstructing public thoroughfare, the spillage wasn't that much in the triangle where Pandora's Box stood, because you're where it's at, centered on that triangle where Crescent Heights and Fairfax head up to Laurel Canyon. It wasn't that big of a deal, and we absolutely did not want that reaction, but there were political and social forces behind it from downtown … and we all know what a hothouse of brain power downtown LA is.

After the CAFF Benefit, David Crosby, Hugh Masekela, and I ended up at this fella's house named Alan Pariser, and we said, "Why don't we have a pop festival with all the San Francisco bands and the LA bands?"

Pariser said, "Where would you do it?"

"Well, where do they have the jazz festival? Go to Monterey."

The next day, Alan takes me to this guy named Sid Bernstein, who is looking for the money, seed money. Then I went on the road and pretty much, later I come back, Lou Adler and The Mamas & The Papas have taken it over, with Buffalo Springfield on the bill. Hugh, actually—I saw him in South Africa about five years ago, and he remembers. eah, we were sitting there and talking about pop music where the jazz is … that was the drum of the idea.

This city is so corrupt. Remember the Mulholland water thing? That's all true. The gas company tearing up that beautiful trolley going all the way from downtown to the beach. God, what if it was still there? I mean, it was gorgeous. For a quarter you could ride it all the way to the beach. You can see where they used to go. It's just tragic. They can have public transport underneath these freeways and get rid of so much congestion, but they got to sell them cars. They had their oil rigs … at least they were in shallow water. You look at it, keep complaining about it, but even before this business with the deep water, your Gulf Coast was just stinky and funky and brackish, and you can't see in it. So it's bad business all around.

The thing is … that the same argument's been going on, ever since the 40s. Just like the way Henry Flagler went into Florida with no foresight and no sense of cause and effect, built Miami, and the result was that the urban sprawl is now killing the everglades. It's all down to that guy building a railroad to Key West. OK, that was great, but they didn't pay any attention to cause and effect.**"**

Stephen Stills,
As told to Domenic Priore

The Scene

A thumbnail sketch of
pre-BS nightlife in the
Greater Los Angeles area

A Be And See Shoppe 522 Wilshire
Boulevard (Santa Monica). Seller of
"Accessories For Peaceful Living."
A Doll's House 617 N La Cienega
Boulevard. Mod boutique.
A Teen-Canteen 320 N Orange Place
(Azusa). Surf hot-spot and rec center.
Abstract 7810 Sunset Boulevard (just east of
the Strip). Beatnik-era folk den.
Action 8265 W Santa Monica Boulevard
(south of the Strip). Nightclub opened by
the owners of the Whisky and the Trip.
Ad-Lib 8300 Sunset Boulevard (Sunset
Strip). Jazz club in the Hollywood Sunset
Hotel; formerly the T Bird. Another
(unrelated) venue of same name in the San
Gabriel Valley.
Adolph Loewi 904 N La Cienega
Boulevard. Art gallery existent in various
forms since 1911.
Aerospace Hall 7660 Beverly Boulevard
(near Fairfax). Concert venue; now the
Erewhon Natural Foods Market.
Ah Fong's 8005 Sunset Boulevard (just east
of the Strip). Cantonese restaurant owned by
actor Benson Fong.
Akron 5120 Melrose Avenue. Chain
store selling modernist furnishings. Also
at 4400 Sunset Boulevard (Downtown
Hollywood), 3115 S Sepulveda (West LA),
3570 Rodeo Place (South LA), 18020
Hawthorne Boulevard (Torrance), 200
N Beach Boulevard (Anaheim), 3675 E
Colorado Boulevard (Pasadena), 215 N

Citrus (West Covina), 1033 N Hollywood
Way (Burbank), 19151 Ventura Boulevard
(Tarzana); service building at 9175 San
Fernando Road.
American Recording 6229 Sunset
Boulevard (Downtown Hollywood). Record
studio; moved to 11386 Ventura Boulevard
in 1962.
Anaheim Bowl, 'The Chariot Room' 1925
W Lincoln Avenue (Anaheim). Bowling
alley that served as a community center and
garage hangout, open 24 hours.
Angel's Camp 614 N Doheny Drive (south
of the Strip). Bric-a-brac store.
Aron Record Shop 7753 ½ Melrose
Avenue. Later moved to 1150 N Highlight
Avenue (near Santa Monica Boulevard).
Arthur 666 N La Cienega Boulevard.
Shortlived LA version of famed NYC club.
Ash Grove 8162 Melrose Avenue. Diverse
music venue (everything from folk to jazz
to raga).
Automobile Club Of Southern California
2601 S Figueroa Street. First port of call for
road maps and information. (Historian on
premises.)
Aware Inn 8828 Sunset Boulevard (Sunset
Strip). Health food store with loose
connection to Ferus Gallery.
Bank 19840 S Hamilton Boulevard
(Torrance). 1968-era garage/psych club.
**Barnes Park Community Center/Barnes
Park Bowl** 350 S McPherrin Avenue
(Monterey Park). Surf venue.

Barney's Beanery 8447 W Santa Monica Boulevard. Prime hangout for the Ferus Gallery contingent.

Basin Street West 1304 S Western Avenue (South LA). Jazz club co-owned by basketball legend Wilt Chamberlain.

Bead Game 517 N Fairfax. Seller of beaded accoutrements.

Beau Gentry 1523 N Vine Street (Downtown Hollywood). Mod boutique.

Beef'n'Beer 8921 Sunset Boulevard (Sunset Strip). Early-hours bar/cafe.

Belinda 8220 Sunset Boulevard (Sunset Strip). Seller of the first 'Hollywood minis.'

Ben Frank's 8585 Sunset Boulevard (Sunset Strip). Diner. Love and Buffalo Springfield formed in the parking lot.

Bestiary 8582 W Santa Monica Boulevard (south of the Strip). Clothing store.

Bido Lito's 1608 N Cosmo Street (Downtown Hollywood). Club that broke Love and The Seeds; formerly a folk den, Cosmo Alley, run by Herb Cohen.

Big Union Hall 2516 E 49th (Vernon, East LA). Prime live venue for Chicano rock'n'roll.

Bill Watkins' Rubaiyat Room 2022 W Adams (South LA). Nightclub in the Watkins Hotel.

Billy Gilbert's Tiger Room 930 Wilshire (Downtown). Burlesque club in the Statler Hilton Hotel.

Billy Gray's Band Box 123 N Fairfax. Music/comedy venue; briefly replaced by a Cinnamon Cinder franchise.

Bit Coffee House 7445 Sunset Boulevard (on the northeast corner of Gardner Street Jazz). Jazz club.

Bizarre Bazaar 6514 Selma Avenue (Downtown Hollywood). Coffeehouse that showed underground movies; later Gemini Psychedelic Supermarket.

Bizazz 553-F N Glendale Avenue (Downtown). Flower-power boutique with designs by Jean Pagliuso.

Black Panthers Office 4117 Central Avenue (Watts).

Blue Grotto 1010 N Fairfax. Coffeehouse.

Blue Law 19840 S Hamilton Boulevard (Torrance). Psychedelic club.

Bob Adler's Restaurant 940 N La Cienega Boulevard.

Bob DeWitt's Topanga Canyon. Coffeehouse, also known as the Job.

Body Shop 8250 Sunset Boulevard (Sunset Strip). Burlesque club.

Bognar Galleries 947 N La Cienega Boulevard.

Bonesville 7369 Melrose Avenue. 1960s jazz club for "Night People" and "Show Biz Hippies."

Brave New World 1644 N Cherokee Avenue (Downtown Hollywood). New location of pioneering psychedelic club (previously at 7207 Melrose).

Broadside Tavern 960 E Holt Avenue (Pomona, East LA). Rock'n'roll club.

Bunny A Go Go/Nikki's Too 8355 Sunset Boulevard (Sunset Strip). Restaurant.

Cafe Frankenstein 860 S Pacific Coast Highway (Laguna Beach). Folk/beat coffeehouse and bookstore.

Californian Club 1759 W Santa Barbara Avenue (South LA). Rhythm & blues venue.

Candy Happening 1209 Glendon (West LA). Boutique.

Candy Store 451 N Rodeo Drive (Beverly Hills) Members-only go-go club.

Canter's 417–19 N Fairfax. After-hours hangout and site of several drugs busts.

Canyon Country Store 2108 Laurel Canyon Boulevard. Grocery store frequented by many a local musician.

Canyon Inn two-and-a-half miles north of Azusa on San Gabriel Canyon Road.

Capitol Records 1750 N Vine Street (Downtown Hollywood). Record label offices and studio.

Capt'n Merriweather's Pickle Farm 4315 Melrose Avenue. 1967-era club.

Carolina Lanes 5601 Century Boulevard (by the International Airport). Rhythm & blues venue.

Drop In 3901 El Segundo Boulevard (Hawthorne). Dance club at the Hawthorne Recreation Center.

Carousel Theatre 3213 E Garvey Avenue (West Covina). Theater in the round.

Casa Escobar 13321 Moorpark Street (Sherman Oaks). Latin-jazz joint.

Casa Vega 13301 Ventura Boulevard (Sherman Oaks). Cocktail lounge; still open.

Casino Club 14027 S Vermont (Gardena).

Castle 2630 Glendower Avenue (Downtown). Rental property used by Bob Dylan, Andy Warhol, and others. Another Castle at 4320 Cedarhurst Circle, where Love lived.

Cat's Pajamas 166 E Huntington Drive (Arcadia). Early-1960s folk club.

Catacombs 77 N Fair Oaks (Pasadena). Live venue.

Chateau Marmont 8221 Sunset Boulevard (Sunset Strip). Hotel.

Cheetah 1 Navy Street (Venice). LA version of the famed NYC discotheque with in-built boutique; opened 1967, formerly the Aragon Ballroom.

Chez Jay 1657 Ocean Avenue (Santa Monica). Nautically themed bar, restaurant, and artists' hangout.

China Trader 4200 Riverside Drive (Burbank). Cocktail lounge.

Cinema 1122 N Western Avenue (north of Sunset). Underground movie theater.

Cinematheque-16 8816 Sunset Boulevard (Sunset Strip). Underground movie theater.

Cineramadome 6360 Sunset Boulevard (Downtown Hollywood). Modernist movie theater showing mainstream fare.

Cinnamon Cinder 11345 Ventura Boulevard (Studio City). Nightclub; formerly Larry Potter's Supper Club, later the Magic Mushroom.

Cinnamon Cinder 4401 Pacific Coast Highway (Long Beach). Nightclub, shared acts with the other Cinnamon Cinders in Studio City and at 600 W Main Street (Alhambra).

Ciro's LeDisc 8433 Sunset Boulevard (Sunset Strip). Legendary nightclub with the Living Room upstairs. Later became It's Boss, then Spectrum 2000, then the Comedy Store.

Classic Cat 8844 Sunset Boulevard (Sunset Strip). Burlesque club; formerly Jerry Lewis' Restaurant and Raymond Robaire's Le Parisienne.

Clay Vito 303 N Laurel Avenue (Beverly, near Fairfax). Studio of sculptor Vito Paulekas, used as rehearsal room by The Byrds and Love.

Cloister 8590 Sunset Boulevard (Sunset Strip). Jazz club above the Renaissance, formerly the Larry Finley Restaurant.

Club 49er 10715 E Valley Boulevard (El Monte). Rock'n'roll nightclub, with watusi contest.

Club Renaissance #1 8428 Sunset Boulevard (Sunset Strip). Jazz club managed by Ben Shapiro; once the Barrymore family home.

Club Renaissance #2 8588 Sunset Boulevard (Sunset Strip). Jazz club run by Ben Shapiro; formerly the Mocambo.

Club Tropicana 247 E Manchester Boulevard (Watts). Teen-friendly nightclub.

Club Virginia's Latin Dancing 2434 W 7th Street (Downtown). Latin-jazz club.

Cock'n'Bull 9170 Sunset Boulevard (Sunset Strip). British-themed restaurant.

Coffee Cup 505 N Fairfax. Bustling high-school hangout.

Colonial West Hotel 8351 Sunset Boulevard (Sunset Strip). Hotel of choice for visiting stars.

Columbia Recording Studio 6121 Sunset Boulevard (Downtown Hollywood). Used by Simon & Garfunkel, Brian Wilson, The Byrds, and others.

Comara Gallery 8475 Melrose Place—at La Cienega. Art gallery.

Coney Island Joe's 'On the Strip' 8301 Sunset Boulevard (Sunset Strip). Post-1967 club "for the groovy set only."

Copley Press Inc 801 Morgana Drive (Bel Air). Printing press.

Copper Skillet 6100 Sunset Boulevard (Downtown Hollywood). "Coffeeshop of the stars."

Coronet Theatre 366 N La Cienega Boulevard. Foreign/underground movie theater; formerly the Turnabout Theater, then Now Gallery.

Cosmo Alley *see* Bido Lito's

Cougar 9181 DeSoto (Chatsworth). 1967-era nightclub.

Coventry Inn 302 Foothill Boulevard (Arcadia). Sometime jazz venue.

Creative Complex 11304 Burbank Boulevard (North Hollywood). "Music. Games. Books. Art. Drink. Talk."

Crescendo/Interlude 8572 and 8568 Sunset Boulevard (Sunset Strip). 1950s/early 1960s jazz club; later became the Trip.

Cyrano 8711 Sunset Boulevard (Sunset Strip). Restaurant.

DJ Club 5955 Van Nuys Boulevard (Van Nuys). Post-1967 club.

Daisy 326 N Rodeo Drive (Beverly Hills). Popular members-only go-go club.

Darby Memorial Park Community Building 3400 W Arbor Vitae (Inglewood). Recreation center.

David Stuart Galleries 807 N La Cienega Boulevard. Art gallery.

Decca Records Inc 5505 Melrose Avenue. Recording studio and record-label offices.

Del-Fi Records 6277 Selma Avenue (Downtown Hollywood). Recording studio used by The Bobby Fuller Four.

deVoss 8637 Sunset Boulevard (Sunset Strip). Ultra-hip clothing store.

Di Gatis Di Go Go 230 W Whittier Boulevard (La Habra).

Dick Clark Productions 9121 Sunset Boulevard (Sunset Strip). Production offices for *Where the Action Is* and *American Bandstand*.

Digger 5050 E 3rd Street (East LA). Jazz club.

Dino's Lodge 8524 Sunset Boulevard (Sunset Strip). Restaurant at the epicenter of Sunset Strip.

Direct Line 434 N La Brea Avenue. Club with interlinked telephones on tables to encourage flirtation among patrons.

Discoteen 5136 N Citrus Avenue (Covina). Nightclub.

Disneyland 1313 Harbor Boulevard (Anaheim). Hosted the Pepsi Hootenanny in 1964.

Dog House 7971 Sunset Boulevard (just east of the Strip). Groovy hot-dog stand. Also at 6262 Hollywood Boulevard, 259 Wilshire Boulevard (Santa Monica), 7110

Melrose Avenue, 5450 S Sepulveda, 1270
N Vermont, 1849 S Western, 2614 W 6th,
319 and 616 S Alvarado, 208 S Central
(Glendale), 1024 Broxton (West LA).
Dolores Original Drive-In Restaurant 8531
Wilshire Boulevard (Beverly Hills). Brian
Wilson used to meet deejay Roger Christian
here at night to write hot-rod songs.
Dolphin's of Hollywood 1065 E Vernon
Avenue (Watts). Rhythm & blues record
store, from which Dick 'Huggy Boy' Hugg
broadcast on KGFW radio during the
1950s. Offices at 8606 S Broadway.
Don The Beachcomber 1727 N McCadden
Place (Downtown Hollywood). Prominent
tiki restaurant.
Donte's 4269 Lankershim Boulevard (North
Hollywood). Restaurant and cocktail bar
with live music.
Dootone Records 9512 S Central Avenue
(Watts). Doo-wop label; home of The
Penguins, Redd Foxx, and others. Also
located at 13440 S Central.
Dragonwyck Colorado Boulevard, two
blocks east of Lake (Pasadena). Coffeehouse
with live jazz.
Dwan Gallery 10846 Lindbrook Drive
(West LA).Art gallery; displayed the work of
Ed Kienholz.
Dwight's 201 Pacific Coast Highway
(Huntington Beach). Beachside snack bar
and surf-mat rental place.
Earl Bostic's Flying Fox 3724 W Santa
Barbara (South LA). Live venue run by King
Records rhythm & blues saxophonist.
Earl Warren Showgrounds 3400 Calle Real
(Santa Barbara). Live venue.
Earth Flower Shop 244 Ocean Park
Boulevard (Santa Monica). Also known
as Earth Books; seller of "Everything A
Psychedelic Shop Should Have."

East Los Angeles College 1301 Brooklyn
Avenue (Monterey Park, East LA). Put on
regular rock'n'roll shows.
Eastlandia 2714 E Garvey Avenue (West
Covina). Prime spot for local bands.
Eatin' Affair 8958 Sunset Boulevard (Sunset
Strip). Restaurant; referred to as "the Slop
Affair" in Love song.
El Monte Legion Stadium 11511 E Valley
Boulevard (El Monte, East LA). Where
Chicano musicians earned their chops.
El Toril 365 N La Cienega Boulevard.
Restaurant and jazz club.
Elson Robyns Gallery 1018 N Fairfax. Art
gallery.
Elysian Park Area 19 (Downtown). Site of
LA's first love-in.
Ephemera 1344 Washington Boulevard
(Venice). Boutique.
Epicurean 6842 Sunset Boulevard
(Downtown Hollywood). "Coffee.
Conversation. Chess. 'Til Dawn."
Esther Robles 665 N La Cienega
Boulevard. Art gallery.
Factory 662 N LaPeer Drive (near Beverly
Hills). High society version of a hipster club.
Fairfax Cinemas 7907 Beverly Boulevard
(Fairfax). Hosted a yearly Battle of the
Bands.
Feingarten 816 N La Cienega Boulevard.
Art gallery.
Felix Landau 702 N La Cienega Boulevard.
Gallery; provided modernist art to 1950s
jazz club the Tiffany.
Ferus Gallery 736-A N La Cienega
Boulevard. Art gallery; first to display
Warhol's soup cans.
Fifth Estate 8226 Sunset Boulevard (Sunset
Strip). Activist coffeehouse and underground
theater. *The Los Angeles Free Press* operated
out of the basement from 1964–66.

Gazzari's

Villa Nova Restaurant

The Phone Booth
(Above Largo)

Largo

Hamburger Hamlet

London Fog

The Galaxy

Whisky a Go Go

deVo

Sunset Boulevard

Sunset Strip

Melody Room

Jerry Lewis Club

Cinematheque-16 / Aware Inn

The Trip

Playboy

Troubadour

Doheny Boulevard

Santa Monica Boulevard

Ash Grove

RoCk & RoLL HOLLYWOOD '65 - '66

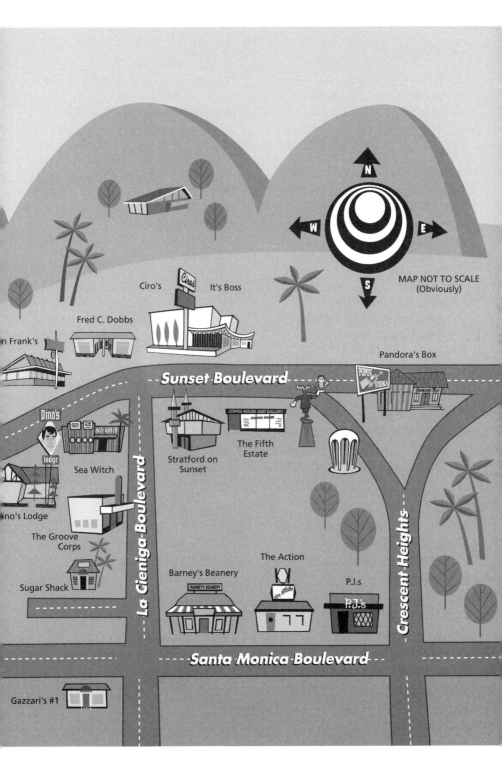

N
W · **E**
S

MAP NOT TO SCALE
(Obviously)

Ciro's · It's Boss

Fred C. Dobbs

Pandora's Box

n Frank's

Sunset Boulevard

Dino's · sea witch

COFFEE HOUSE AND GALLERY
COFFEE HOUSE

lodge

Sea Witch

Stratford on
Sunset

The Fifth
Estate

La Cieniga Boulevard

ino's Lodge

The Groove
Corps

The Action

P.J.s

Crescent Heights

Barney's Beanery

BARNEY'S BEANERY

P.J.s

Sugar Shack

Santa Monica Boulevard

Gazzari's #1

First National Nothing 4011 W Sunset Boulevard (Downtown). Art gallery.

Flying Jib 610 N Pacific (Redondo Beach). Pop/psych nightclub.

For-U 5877 Hollister Avenue (Goleta). 1967-era nightclub.

Foxe's Den 4272 Beverly Boulevard (near Fairfax). 1960s jazz club.

Frank Perls Gallery 9777 Wilshire Boulevard (Beverly Hills). Gallery on the 8th floor of the Life building.

Frascati Inn 1056 La Cienega (near Olympic). Restaurant, with two further locations on the Strip, including the Frascati Grill at 9131 Sunset.

Fred C. Dobbs' 8537 Sunset Boulevard (Sunset Strip). *The* mid-1960s Sunset coffeehouse of choice.

Free Press, the 5903 Melrose Avenue. Underground newspaper offices from 1966 onward.

Gaiety Delicatessen 9043 Sunset Boulevard (Sunset Strip). Popular kosher eatery.

Galaxy 8917 Sunset Boulevard (Sunset Strip). Lounge venue turned psych club.

Garret 925 N Fairfax. Coffeehouse, complete with fire pit.

Gas House 1501 Ocean Front Walk (Venice). Poetry and jazz club. Now a parking lot.

Gazzarri's 319 N La Cienega Boulevard. Go-go nightclub.

Gazzarri's On The Strip 9039 Sunset Boulevard (Sunset Strip). Garage-rock club, affiliated with *Hollywood A Go Go*.

Gee Gee's 8100 Sunset Boulevard (Sunset Strip). Restaurant; formerly Googie's (also at 501 W 5th Street, downtown).

Gene Autry's Continental West Hotel 8401 Sunset Boulevard (Sunset Strip). Run by the owner of the Los Angeles Angels.

Genesis IX 7551 Sunset Boulevard (Sunset Strip). 1967-era nightclub.

Genie The Tailor 9091 W Santa Monica Boulevard (south of the Strip). Clothing store run by *Where The Action Is* costume designer Genie Franklin.

Gigi Hall 3232 N Broadway (Lincoln Heights, East LA). Live venue.

Gilded Prune 116 Coral Way (Redondo Beach). Boutique.

Gilded Prune 859D Via de la Paz (Pacific Palisades). Outlet for 'Freaky Things' T-shirts, buttons, posters, etc.

Glass Crutch 3032 E Garvey Avenue (Covina).

GNP-Crescendo Records 9165 Sunset Boulevard (Sunset Strip). Home of jazz and The Seeds.

Go West 775 N Virgil Avenue (one block north of Melrose). Jazz, rock'n'roll, and folk club.

Gold Star Studios 6262 Santa Monica Boulevard (at Vine, Downtown Hollywood). Studio used by Spector, Buffalo Springfield, and others, notable for echo chamber.

Golden Bear 306 Pacific Coast Highway (Huntington Beach). Folk club.

Golden Gate Theatre 5176 E Whittier Boulevard (East LA). Top Chicano rock'n'roll venue. Thee Midniters had their office in the building next door.

Golden West Ballroom 12400 Studebaker Road at Imperial Highway (Norwalk).

Goldfinger Club 12528 La Cadena Drive (Colton). Late-1960s psych club.

Grandpa Takes A Trip 6367 Yucca Street (Downtown Hollywood). Gentlemen's outfitters, also at 8590 Melrose Avenue.

Granny Takes A Trip/West 836 N Fairfax Avenue. Mod boutique based on the Carnaby Street shop.

Great Linoleum Clothing Experiment 9093 Santa Monica Boulevard. Boutique.

Great Western Exhibit Center 2120 S Eastern Avenue (City Of Commerce, East LA). Live venue.

Greek Theater 2700 N Vermont Avenue (Griffith Park). Jazz concerts occasionally made it onto the summer schedule.

Greeko's Sandals 1128 Hermosa Avenue (Hermosa Beach). Custom-made belts, hats, handbags.

Griffith Park north of the Greek Theater. Site of LA's first Be-Ins.

Groove Company 1446 N Crescent Heights Boulevard. Record store.

Hamburger Hamlet 8931 Sunset Boulevard (Sunset Strip). Burger joint frequented by The Monkees.

Hangout 795 S Kellog Avenue (Goleta). Somewhere people hung out.

Happening 2905 Sunset (at Silver Lake, Downtown). Post-1967 psych club.

Harem Club 10821 Long Beach Boulevard (Lynwood). Breeding group for East LA rock'n'rollers.

Harmony Park Ballroom 1514 Broadway (Anaheim). Surf club; Dick Dale house band.

Harvey's Gold Street 8032 Garden Grove Boulevard (Garden Grove). Rock'n'roll club.

Hat 12121 E Valley Boulevard (El Monte). Burlesque club.

Haunted House 6315 Hollywood Boulevard. Go-go club with smoke monster stage; formerly Zardi's Jazzland.

Head East 8517 Sunset Boulevard (Sunset Strip). Boutique.

Headquarters 1144 Westwood Boulevard (West LA) Boutique and "psychedelicatessan."

Helgeson's Buick 3605 Market Street (Riverside). Deserted car dealership that played host to Battles of the Bands.

Hell Bent For Leather 6727 Hollywood Boulevard. Boutique frequented by Neil Young.

Heritage 724 N La Cienega Boulevard. Art gallery.

Hermosa Inn 22 Pier Avenue (Hermosa Beach). Jazz club adjacent to the Lighthouse and the Insomniac.

Hi Ho Club 3821 Van Buren Boulevard (Riverside). Part of a teen nightclub chain, with five other branches across SoCal.

Hieronymus 446 N Fairfax. Psychedelic coffeehouse and store.

Hippocampus 8826 Sunset Boulevard (Sunset Strip). Funky antique shop.

Hob Nob 621 E Arrow Highway (Covina).

Hole In The Wall 422 N La Cienega Boulevard. Mod boutique.

Hollywood Bowl 2301 N Highland Avenue (Downtown Hollywood). Hosted shows by The Beatles, Bob Dylan, The Rolling Stones, Beach Boys Summer Spectaculars, and more.

Hollywood Palace 1735 N Vine Street (Downtown Hollywood). Home of LA's answer to *The Ed Sullivan Show*.

Hollywood Palladium 6215 Sunset Boulevard (at Argyle, Downtown Hollywood). Concert venue; home of mid-1960s Teen-Age Fairs.

Hollywood Ranch Market 1248 N Vine Street (Downtown Hollywood). "We never close," said the sign out front.

House of Freberg Limited (But Not Very) 8720 Sunset Boulevard (Sunset Strip). Actor and comedian Stan Freberg's office.

House Of Sight & Sound 14513 Victory Boulevard (Van Nuys). Popular record store for Valley kids.

House Of The Rising Sun 1312 S Pacific Coast Highway (Redondo Beach). Folk club.

Huddle 2625 E Garvey Avenue (West Covina). Googie-esque diner.

Hullabaloo 6230 Sunset Boulevard (Downtown Hollywood). Nightclub; formerly Earl Carroll's Vanities, then the Moulin Rouge.

I Tafani 1951 Hillhurst Avenue (Downtown). Coffeehouse.

I'm A Hog For You Baby 424 N Fairfax. Boutique; also at 61 N Fair Oaks (Pasadena).

Ice House 24 N Mentor Alley (Pasadena). Folk/comedy club. Also at 234 S Brand (Glendale), also known as Savoy Light House.

Imperial Gardens 8225 Sunset Boulevard (Sunset Strip). Japanese restaurant; formerly Preston Sturges's Players.

In 133 Entrada (Santa Monica Canyon). Tiny, late-1960s go-go joint.

Infinite Mind 320 N Fairfax. Popular seller of drug paraphernalia etc.

Insomniac Cafe 53 Pier Avenue (Hermosa Beach). Folk/beat club with bookstore.

Interlude exact location unknown (Riverside). Nightclub for slightly older teens (16+).

Iopan Coffee House 1439 Chapala Street (Santa Barbara).

Islander 385 N La Cienega Boulevard. Tiki restaurant.

It Club 4731 W Washington Boulevard (two blocks east of La Brea). 1960s bebop venue.

It's Camp 5650 Vineland (North Hollywood). 1967-era club.

Itchy Foote/Moose 801 W Temple Avenue (Downtown). Teen dance club.

Jabberwock 3202 Sunset Boulevard (Downtown). Late-1960s bric-a-brac.

Jack Martin's AM-PM Undisclosed La Cienega location. Short-lived 1964 discotheque.

Jax 9667 Wilshire Boulevard (Beverly Hills). Mod boutique.

Jay Ward Animation Studio 8218 Sunset Boulevard (Sunset Strip). Home of the famous Rocky & Bullwinkle statue.

Jazz Go-Go 1952 W Adams Boulevard (South LA). Nightclub hosting black comedians, bebop, and rhythm & blues.

Jester's Club 10819 E Valley Boulevard (El Monte Mall).

KABC Television 4151 Prospect (Downtown). Studio where *Shindig!*, *American Bandstand*, and *Shivaree* were shot.

Kaleidoscope 6230 Sunset Boulevard (Downtown Hollywood). Post-1967 psychedelic club; previously had shortlived stints at 1228 Vine Street, 8433 Sunset Boulevard, and 3400 Wilshire Boulevard.

Kazoo, the/Free Press Bookstore 424? N Fairfax. Offshoot of the weekly underground newspaper.

KCOP Television 915 N La Brea Avenue. Used for *The Lloyd Thaxton Show* and *Bash!*

Kennedy Hall 451 S Atlantic Boulevard (East LA). Rock'n'roll club.

KHJ Television 5515 Melrose Avenue. Studio where *9th Street West, Hollywood A Go Go*, *Boss City*, and the indoor *Groovy* were shot.

King Banjo Pizza Parlor 7551 Sunset Boulevard (just east of the Strip). Bands, beer, wine, dancing, pool, no Cover.

Kiosk 7350 Sunset Boulevard (just east of the Strip). "Every Friday, 8:30pm—1:30am. Groovy Discussion for young adults over 18."

Kitten A Go Go 13065 E Valley Boulevard (El Monte). Burlesque club.

Knights Of Columbus Hall 1041 W Highland Avenue (Riverside). Live venue.

KPFK 3729 Cahuenga Boulevard (North Hollywood). 'Liberal' FM radio station.

KPFK Art Gallery 615 N Fairfax. Offshoot of Pacifica's underground radio station.

Kramer Gallery 635 N La Cienega Boulevard. Art gallery.

KTLA Television 5800 Sunset Boulevard (Downtown Hollywood). Where *Shebang* was shot.

La Cave Pigalle 3400 Wilshire Boulevard (South LA). Garage-rock venue inside the Ambassador Hotel. Also known simply as the Cave.

La Rue 8631 Sunset Boulevard (Sunset Strip). Legendary Hollywood restaurant, intended "For Elegant Dining."

Lalo Guerrero's Club 4209 Brooklyn Avenue (East LA). Adult-orientated rock'n'roll venue.

Largo 9009 Sunset Boulevard (Sunset Strip). Burlesque club, featured in *The Graduate*.

Lead Balloon 2559 Atlantic Boulevard (Long Beach). Flower-power store.

Ledbetters 1621 Westwood Boulevard (West LA). Early-1960s folk club.

Lemon Peel 4706 Van Nuys Boulevard (Van Nuys). Post-1967 dance club.

Lenny's Boot Parlor 1448 Gower Avenue (south of Sunset). Popular Mod boutique, adjacent to The Monkees' studio.

Leo Fender 500 S Raymond Avenue (Fullerton). Home of Fender Guitars; previously at 122 S Pomona Avenue and 107 S Spadra Avenue.

Lewin's Record Paradise 6507 Hollywood Boulevard. Record store specializing in hot British imports.

Liberty Custom Recorders 1560 N La Brea Avenue. 1950s studio home of Liberty Records.

Liberty Custom Recorders 6920 Sunset Boulevard (Downtown Hollywood). Studio used by Liberty Records.

Lighthouse 30 Pier Avenue (Hermosa Beach) Jazz club.

Lil' Abner's #6 9015 Long Beach Boulevard (South Gate). Live venue.

Lindy Opera House 5214 Wilshire Boulevard (South LA). The Mothers Of Invention played here.

Little Union Hall 1265 S Goodrich Boulevard (City Of Commerce, East LA). Rock'n'roll venue.

Living Room 5156 Sunset Boulevard (Downtown Hollywood). Coffeehouse, later part of It's Boss.

Location Recording Services 1440 N Highland Avenue (Downtown Hollywood). Studio where Shel Talmy learnt his trade.

London Fog 8919 Sunset Boulevard (Sunset Strip). Nightclub that featured The Doors as a house band; later Muthers.

Look 8849 Sunset Boulevard (Sunset Strip). Mod boutique, as seen in Jackie DeShannon's 'LA' promo.

Los Angeles Hippodrome 1853 Arlington at Washington Boulevard (South LA).

Los Angeles Oracle 840 N Fairfax. Underground newspaper offices.

Losers' 881 N La Cienega Boulevard. Bebop jazz, comedians, go-go dancers, and psychedelic light shows.

Luau, the 421 Rodeo Drive (Beverly Hills). Tiki restaurant.

Madman Muntz 8801 Sunset Boulevard (Sunset Strip). Early seller of personalized in-car music systems.

Magic Mushroom 11345 Ventura Boulevard (Studio City). Post-1967 nightclub.

Manchester Theater 322 W Manchester Boulevard (South LA).

Marina Palace Northeast corner of Pacific Coast Highway and First Street (Seal Beach).

Surf club, formerly the Airport Club; later the Quonsett Hut.

Mark-56 Records 1312 W Garvey Avenue (Monterey Park). Record label.

Martoni's 1523 N Cahuenga Boulevard (Downtown Hollywood). Italian restaurant and 'music biz' watering hole.

Marty's On The Hill 5005 S La Brea Avenue (Baldwin Hills). Jazz club.

Master Recorders 535 N Fairfax. Studio used by Little Richard, Fats Domino, Ricky Nelson, and others.

Maverick's Flat 4225 Crenshaw Boulevard (South LA). The premier soul music venue in Los Angeles.

McCabe's Guitar Shop 3015 Pico Boulevard (Santa Monica). Popular instrument retailer; now located at 3101 Pico Boulevard.

McGoo's 6651 Hollywood Boulevard. Pizzeria with jazz.

Mecca 7311 Orangethorpe Avenue (Buena Park). Among Orange County's finest folk venues; affiliated with the Forum at 5074 W Holt Boulevard (Montclair).

Melody Room 8852 Sunset Boulevard (Sunset Strip). 1950s swinger joint turned mid-1960s jazz club.

Melodyland 1700 S Harbor Boulevard (Anaheim). Prime rock'n'roll/garage club.

Middle Earth 18467 Ventura Boulevard (Tarzana). Post-1967 nightclub.

Mod Look 953 E Colorado Boulevard (Pasadena). Live venue.

Mod Shop 1420 W Santa Barbara. Boutique.

Mod Street West 11441 W Jefferson Boulevard (Culver City). Live venue; became the New Delhi Bath House in 1967.

Montebello Ballroom 104 S 10th at Whittier Boulevard (Montebello, East LA).

Rainbow Gardens 150 E Monterey Street (Pomona, East LA). Rock'n'roll nightclub.

Moonfire Inn 246 S Topanga Canyon Boulevard. Popular 1967-era live venue.

Moonfire Ranch Santa Monica Mountains. Experimental art haven, located near the top of Fernwood Pacific.

Mother Neptune's Coffee House 4319 Melrose Avenue. Jazz club; formerly the Coffe House and Xanadu.

Mother's Billiards 734 N Fairfax. Popular pool hall catering to the mid-1960s rock'n'roll set.

Music Box Theater 7080 Hollywood Boulevard (at La Brea Avenue). Jazz and comedy venue.

Mystic Eye 10045 Magnolia Avenue (Riverside). Showcase for local psychedelic acts during the late 1960s.

Nashville West 11910 E Valley Boulevard (El Monte). Country & western club.

New Balladeer 1566 Sawtelle Avenue (West LA). Early-1960s folk venue.

New Caves 14952 E Valley Boulevard (La Puente). Country & western club.

Nexus 5978 Hollister Avenue (Goleta). Live venue.

Nicholas Wilder 814 N La Cienega Boulevard. Art gallery, exhibited early minimalism and David Hockney.

Nikki's 6504 Hollywood Boulevard. Seller of cocktail dresses.

9000 Building 9000 Sunset Boulevard (Sunset Strip). Offices for The Byrds, Derek Taylor, and numerous labels, publishing companies, magazines, and fan clubs.

940 Club 940 N La Cienega Boulevard. Jazz club.

No War Toys Coffeehouse 2472 W Washington Boulevard at Arlington (South LA). The Doors once played a benefit here.

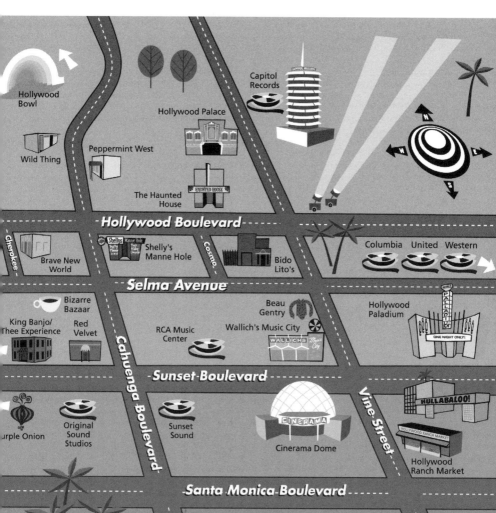

Hollywood Bowl

Wild Thing

Peppermint West

Hollywood Palace

The Haunted House

Capitol Records

Hollywood Boulevard

Cherokee

Brave New World

Shelly's Manne Hole

Cosmo

Bido Lito's

Columbia   United   Western

Selma Avenue

King Banjo/ Thee Experience

Bizarre Bazaar

Red Velvet

RCA Music Center

Beau Gentry

Wallich's Music City

Hollywood Paladium

Cahuenga Boulevard

Sunset Boulevard

Purple Onion

Original Sound Studios

Sunset Sound

Cinerama Dome

HULLABALOO!

Vine Street

Hollywood Ranch Market

Santa Monica Boulevard

Radio Recorders

Gold Star

HOLLYWOOD

Melrose Avenue

Canter's Deli

Original Brave New World

Maverick's Flat

Noctambulist 31 E Canon Perdido (Oxnard). Coffeehouse.

Norty's Music Center 436 N Fairfax. Record store that once employed Jerry Leiber. Still open as Hatikvah Music.

Oar House 2941 Main Street (Venice). Teen-orientated dance club.

Oasis 3801 S Western Avenue at 38th Street (South LA). 1950s jazz and rhythm & blues venue.

Old Time Movies 611 N Fairfax. Retro-movie theater, still in operation (as Silent Movie Theater).

Olde Worlde 8782 Sunset Boulevard (Sunset Strip). Belgian waffle shop.

Omnibus 75 N Fair Oaks (Pasadena). Boutique, home to Omega's Eye light show.

Omnibus Coffeehouse And Gallery 1835 N Cahuenga Boulevard (Downtown Hollywood). Formerly the Coffeehouse.

Orange Julius 8797 W Santa Monica Boulevard (south of the Strip). Refreshments stand popular with teenagers, also at 9601 Wilshire Boulevard (Beverly Hills), 210 N Virgil (Downtown), 1608 W Sunset Boulevard, 4131 W Santa Barbara (South LA), 6407 Pacific (Huntington Park), 6001 W Pico (South LA), 11106 Jefferson Boulevard (Culver City), 1445 S Atlantic Boulevard (East LA), 622 N Milpas (Santa Barbara).

Orange Street Parking Garage 3700 block of Orange Street (Riverside). Site of many a makeshift gig.

Original Sound Recorders 7120 Sunset Boulevard (just east of the Strip). Studio and label run by Art Laboe; employed Jack Nitzsche and Paul Buff.

Other Place 9680 Santa Monica Boulevard (Beverly Hills). Members-only go-go club.

PJ's 8151 W Santa Monica Boulevard (south of the Strip). Hollywood's main twist club.

Padded Cell 31 W Carrillo Street (Santa Barbara). Small teen dance club opposite Greyhound bus depot.

PAL Recording Studio 9040 Archibald (Cucamonga). Run by Paul Buff; later sold to Frank Zappa, who renamed it Studio Z.

Palace A Go Go! 500 Anacapa (Oxnard) Rock'n'roll and jazz shows with go-go dancing.

Palomino 6907 Lankershim Boulevard (North Hollywood) Country & western club.

Pandora's Box 8118 Sunset Boulevard (Sunset Strip). Jazz joint-turned-garage rock club. Shut down amid the protests of late 1966.

Papa Bach 11317 Santa Monica Boulevard (West LA). Bookstore.

Paradox/Merlin's Music Box 225 S Tustin Avenue (Orange County). Folk club.

Paragon Ballroom 403 Monterey Pass Road (Monterey Park). Lounge.

Paramount Ball Room 2706 Brooklyn Avenue (East LA). Rock'n'roll club.

Paramount Ranch Cornell Road near Thousand Oaks. Site of the first Renaissance Pleasure Faire events.

Paraphernalia 232 N Rodeo Drive (Beverly Hills). Mod boutique; also in NYC.

Paris 8163 Santa Monica Boulevard (near PJ's). Adult movie theater.

Pasadena Museum Of Art 411 W Colorado Boulevard (Pasadena). Ferus curator Walter Hopps was director here as well. Now known as the Norton Simon Museum.

Pasatano's Malibu. Folk/surf hangout, frequented by Henry Miller, Mia Farrow, and Peter Sellers.

Paul Kantor Gallery 348 N Camden Drive

(Beverly Hills). Art gallery; hosted Willem de Kooning show in 1966.

Pavalon Ballroom 317 Pacific Coast Highway (Huntington Beach). Surf club.

Peppermint Bandstand 17006 Bellflower Boulevard (Long Beach). Surf club.

Peppermint Lounge 201 W Pike (Long Beach). Shortlived teen-club that took its name from NYC's twist hotspot.

Peppermint Stick 15463 Ventura Boulevard (Sherman Oaks). Pre-Cinnamon Cinder teen dance-club.

Peppermint West 1754 N Cahuenga Boulevard (Downtown Hollywood). Dance club based on Manhattan's Peppermint Lounge; formerly the Tailspin.

Phil Harris Records 6723 Hollywood Boulevard. Pop record store.

Philles Records 9130 Sunset Boulevard (Sunset Strip). Phil Spector's business office.

Phone Booth 9011 Sunset Boulevard (Sunset Strip). Among the first LA bars to employ topless waitresses.

Pilgrimage Theater Cahuenga Boulevard East (Downtown Hollywood). Music venue across from the Hollywood Bowl.

Pink Pussycat 7969 W Santa Monica Boulevard (south of the Strip). Burlesque joint.

Pink's 709 N La Brea Avenue (corner of Melrose). Hot-dog stand frequented by Phil Spector and the Wrecking Crew.

Pix Theater 6126 Hollywood Boulevard. Movie theater, where The Byrds saw *A Hard Day's Night*. Currently a live venue, the Music Box Theater.

Place 11721 Valley Boulevard (El Monte). Dance club.

Playboy Club 8560 Sunset Boulevard (Sunset Strip). Four-story nightclub beneath Hugh Hefner's penthouse apartment.

Pleasure Dome Boutique 843 N Fairfax.

Plush Pup 8200 Sunset Boulevard (Sunset Strip). Minimalist hot-dog stand. Later became Dudley Do Right's Emporium.

Prison of Socrates 106 Main Street (Balboa). Early folk club.

Psychedelic Candle Shop 720 N Fairfax.

Psychedelic Center, Inc 36 W Dayton (Pasadena). Seller of funky accoutrements; later moved to 1622 E Colorado Boulevard (Pasadena).

Psychedelic Conspiracy corner of Sunset and Holloway (Sunset Strip). Boutique.

Pucci's 16065 Ventura Boulevard (Encino). Cocktail lounge.

Pupi's 8710 Sunset Boulevard (Sunset Strip). Pastry shop.

Purple Haze 10331 Magnolia Avenue (Riverside). Major live venue (1,000+ capacity); formerly the Riverside Youth Center.

Purple Onion 7290 Sunset Boulevard (Sunset Strip). 1950s jazz club turned 1960s rock'n'roll venue.

Queen's Arms 16352 Ventura Boulevard (Encino). Cocktail lounge.

Radiant Radish southwest corner of San Vicente & Melrose. Brian Wilson's Health Food Store (1969–71).

Radio Recorders 7000 Santa Monica Boulevard (Downtown Hollywood). Recording studio, known locally as the Annex. Used by Elvis Presley, Sam Cooke, The Coasters, and others.

RCA Music Center Of The World 6363 Sunset Boulevard (Downtown Hollywood). Recording studio; Dave Hassinger was engineer here.

Record Inn 4824 E Whittier Boulevard (East LA). Record store; the nerve center for Chicano rock'n'roll.

Record Rack 5160 E Whittier Boulevard (East LA). Record store owned by Tony Valdez, more recently a Channel 11 newscaster.

Red Velvet 6507 Sunset Boulevard (Downtown Hollywood). Celebrity hangout frequented by rock'n'rollers, including Elvis Presley, Righteous Brothers.

Rendezvous Ballroom 608 E Ocean Front (Balboa). Jazz club turned surf joint. Now located at 105 Main Street.

Retail Clerk's Hall 8550 Stanton Avenue (Buena Park). Surf music Mecca.

Rhythm Room 242 W Commonwealth Avenue (Fullerton). Recording studio, notably for East LA groups.

Ribs A Go Go 8826 Sunset Boulevard (Sunset Strip). Restaurant.

Righteous Source 1018 N Fairfax. Seller of candles, posters, black light, incense, etc.

Rip Tide 2424 Main Street (Santa Monica). Coffeehouse.

Riverside Municipal Auditorium 3485 Mission Inn Avenue (Riverside). Opened up to rock'n'roll during the mid 1960s.

Riverside National Guard Armory 2501 Fairmount Boulevard (Riverside). Live venue.

Riviera-Capri 7165 Beverly Boulevard (near Fairfax). Early underground-revival theater.

Roller Gardens 828 Buckaroo Avenue (Oxnard). Skating rink and site of many rock'n'roll gigs.

Rooster A Go Go 17424 S Lakewood Boulevard (Bellflower). Dance club.

Rouge Et Noir/Cosmos 143 Main Street (Seal Beach). Folk club.

Rowena Gallery 3043 Rowena (Downtown). Jazz/psych club with movie screen.

Royal Tahitian 2525 E Riverside Drive (Ontario). Live venue that played host to major out-of-town rhythm & blues acts.

Royal's World Countdown 1209 N Western Avenue (Downtown Hollywood). Underground newspaper.

Rubicon 517 N Fairfax. Boutique.

S Hurok Building 8255 Sunset Boulevard (Sunset Strip). Home of World Pacific and A&M Records.

Saints & Sinners E Holt Boulevard (Ontario). Rock'n'roll club.

Salty Cellar 304 Pacific Coast Highway (Huntington Beach). Teen-orientated rock'n'roll joint beneath Buzz Burger restaurant.

San Bernardino Municipal Auditorium 555 W 6th Street (San Bernardino). Live venue in Pioneer Park.

Sandal Maker 1093 ¼ Broxton (West LA).

Sandala Leather Shop/Studio Michel 424-426 Santa Monica Boulevard (Santa Monica). Seller of sandals and hand-made jewelry.

Sandalmaker 17 W Dayton (Pasadena). Footwear store.

Sandalsville 1016 N Fairfax. Shoe store with designs by Don Sargent.

Santa Monica Civic Auditorium 1855 Main Street (Santa Monica). One of the best-sounding live venues in Greater Los Angeles.

Scandia 9046 Sunset Boulevard (Sunset Strip). Modernist, chalet-style restaurant.

Scene 8171 Sunset Boulevard (Sunset Strip). Variety club.

Schwab's 8024 Sunset Boulevard (Sunset Strip). Pharmacy; also at the other end of the Strip, 9201 Sunset.

Screen Gems Columbia Studios 1438 Gower Avenue (corner of Sunset). Home of *The Monkees* (Stage 7).

Scrivner's Drive-In Restaurant 6407 Sunset Boulevard (at Cahuenga, Downtown Hollywood). 1950s drive-in from which Art Laboe broadcasted.

Sea Witch, the 8514 Sunset Boulevard (Sunset Strip). The Strip's first rock'n'roll club.

Sebring's exact location unknown (Fairfax). Chic hairdresser, the inspiration for Warren Beatty's *Shampoo*.

Self-Realization Fellowship 17190 Sunset Boulevard (Pacific Palisades). East Indian-inspired retreat; still open.

Seventh Veil 7180 Sunset Boulevard (just east of the Strip). Bar with nightly belly-dancing; formerly Mr Ken Ton's, after-hours jazz club.

Shap's 2565 E Colorado Boulevard (Pasadena). Live venue.

Shelly's Manne-Hole 1608 N Cahuenga Boulevard (Downtown Hollywood). Top 1960s jazz place.

Sherry's 8106 Sunset Boulevard (Sunset Strip). Jazz club. 31 Flavors Ice Cream was next door.

Shimmy Shack 18720 Van Buren Boulevard (Riverside). Rock'n'roll club.

Shrine Exposition Hall 665 W Jefferson Boulevard and 700 W 32nd Street (South LA). Concert hall.

Sid Zaro Gallery 835 N Fairfax. Framer and restorer, affiliated with the Ferus Group.

Sid's Blue Beet 107 21st Place (Newport Beach). Bohemian bar; formerly Stark's (since 1912) and the Lyceum Coffeehouse.

Sidereal Time 8582 W Santa Monica Boulevard. Clothing store; home of Larry Marty originals.

Silvan Simone 11579 Olympic Boulevard (South LA). Art Gallery.

Sitar 11270 W Santa Monica Boulevard (Beverly Hills). Musical instrument store.

Slate Bros 339 N La Cienega Boulevard. Lounge venue.

Smoke House 4420 Lakeside Drive (Burbank). Cocktail lounge; still open.

Smokey Joe's Hickory Barbeque Restaurant 157 N La Cienega Boulevard. 1950s rock'n'roll hangout; later Gay 90s, one of several jazz-themed restaurants owned by Paul Cummins (another was Roaring 20s, a few doors down as 133 N La Cienega).

Smokey Joe's Cafe 12851 Riverside Drive (North Hollywood). Opened following success on La Cienega, but lasted much longer (until the turn of the century).

Sneeky Pete's 8907 Sunset Boulevard (Sunset Strip). Restaurant and jazz club.

Sound Center 319 N Beverly Drive (Beverly Hills). Record store.

Sound House Recorders 2541 Merced Avenue (El Monte). Studio run by Les Paul's brother-in-law, Bob Summers.

Sound Labs 1800 Argyle Avenue (Downtown Hollywood). Armen Steiner's recording studio.

Specialty Records Inc 8300 W Santa Monica Boulevard (south of the Strip). Home of Little Richard, Larry Williams, and Don & Dewey.

Sportsmen's Lodge 12833 Ventura Boulevard (North Hollywood). Cocktail lounge; still open.

St Alphonsus School Hall 552 Amalia (East LA). Rock'n'roll club.

Stable 12515 Burbank Boulevard (North Hollywood). Boutique with fashions by Robert Duncan-Begg.

Stag Shop Of Hollywood 7862 W Santa Monica Boulevard (near Fairfax, south of the Strip). Clothes for the "MODern" man.

Starlight Ballroom exact location unknown (Oxnard). Rock'n'roll venue.

Stendahl Gallery 7055 Hillside Avenue (Downtown Hollywood). Art gallery in operation since 1915.

Stereo Masters 5538 Melrose Avenue. Recording studio used by East LA bands.

Stone Brothers Printing 1600 block of Sawtelle Boulevard (West LA). Print shop/studio space used by Wallace Berman to assemble *Semina*.

Stratford On Sunset 8428 Sunset Boulevard (Sunset Strip). Soul venue; later the Monterey Pop planning office.

Strawberry Fields (Decker Canyon). 'Tent city' just north of Malibu Canyon that became popular with teenyboppers and artists in the late 1960s.

Strip City 1304 S Western Avenue (South LA). Comedy, rhythm & blues, and "a bevy of dusky dolls."

Stripcombers 8301 Sunset Boulevard (Sunset Strip). Prime biker hangout; later the Source, a health food restaurant.

Studio Watts Workshop 10311 Grandee Avenue at 103rd Street (Watts). Community space for artists.

Studio Z 8040 Archibald (Cucamonga). Frank Zappa's studio, 1964–65; formerly Paul Buff's PAL Recording Studio.

Sugar Shack 5963 W Washington Boulevard. Short-lived nightclub.

Sundown, the 6507 Sunset Boulevard (at Wilcox). Jazz club; later the Summit, then the Red Velvet.

Sunset Sound 6650 Sunset Boulevard (Downtown Hollywood). Recording studio built by Tutti Camarata for Walt Disney; used by Love, The Doors, Buffalo Springfield, The Turtles, etc.

Sunset Tower 8358 Sunset Boulevard (Sunset Strip). Art-deco hotel with rich movie star history.

Swing Auditorium 689 SE Street (San Bernardino). Live venue; first US Rolling Stones gig here.

Swing Ventura Boulevard at Coldwater Canyon (Studio City). 1960s jazz joint for swinging couples.

Sy Devore Menswear 12930 Ventura Boulevard (North Hollywood). Boutique frequented by Nat 'King' Cole, Dean Martin, The Turtles.

Syndell Studio 11756 Gorham Avenue (Brentwood). Gallery affiliated with UCLA, managed by Walter Hopps and others.

Tail O' The Cock 12950 Ventura Boulevard (North Hollywood). Cocktail lounge; also at 477 S La Cienega Boulevard.

Tape Center 7550 Melrose Avenue. Car stereos and cartridge tapes, "made with love."

Tape City 8363 Sunset Boulevard (Sunset Strip). First port of call for car stereos.

Tarot Castle Psychedelic Print Shop 716 N Fairfax.

Tectron Records 7725 Melrose Avenue (four blocks east of Fairfax). Folk and jazz record store.

Ted Brinson's garage 2190 W 30th Street (South LA). Recording studio used by The Penguins, The Olympics, and others.

Thee Experience 7551 Sunset Boulevard (Sunset Strip). The last psych club on Sunset; opened and closed in 1969.

Third Eye 17150 Ventura Boulevard (Encino). Post-1967 nightclub.

Third i 312 S Catalina Avenue (Redondo Beach). Psychedelic club; formerly the Belair Club, then the Revelaire.

Tiki Ti 4427 W Sunset Boulevard (Downtown). The best tiki drinks in Los Angeles, since 1962.

Tikis 1001 N Potrero Grande Drive (Monterey Park). Tiki restaurant.

Tiny Naylor's 7105 Sunset Boulevard (northwest corner of LaBrea, just east of the Strip). Futuristic drive-in restaurant, as seen in *The Graduate*. Also at 3037 and 4014 Wilshire (South LA), 8620 S Western Avenue (Inglewood), 12056 Ventura Boulevard (Studio City).

Tio Ceasar's 7222 Sunset Boulevard (just east of the Strip). Coffeeshop with pool table and folk singers.

Topanga Corral 2034 N Topanga Canyon Boulevard. Site of many a post-Strip jam.

Topper Club 9018 E Garvey Avenue (South San Gabriel).

Trader Vic's 9876 Wilshire Boulevard (Beverly Hills). Tiki restaurant inside Welton Becket's Beverly Hilton Hotel.

Travaglini's 17500 Ventura Boulevard (Encino). Cocktail lounge.

Trip 8572 Sunset Boulevard (Sunset Strip). Nightclub; formerly the Crescendo/Interlude, then the Crescendo/Tiger Tail.

Tropicana Motel 8585 W Santa Monica Boulevard (south of the Strip). 'Groupie paradise' co-owned by LA Dodger Sandy Koufax.

Troubadour 364 N La Cienega Boulevard. Folk club; later moved to 9083 W Santa Monica Boulevard.

TTG Recording Studios 1441 N McCadden Place (off Sunset Boulevard). Recording studio, where The Mothers Of Invention cut *Freak Out*.

Turkey Joint West 116 Santa Monica Boulevard (Santa Monica). Nightclub.

Tustin Youth Center 600 W 6th Street (Tustin). Hosted an annual Battle of the Bands during the 1960s.

23 Skidoo 2116 Westwood Boulevard (West LA). Shortlived mid-1960s rock'n'roll venue.

Unicorn 8907 Sunset Boulevard (Sunset Strip). Beatnik-era folk/comedy club.

United Recorders 6050 Sunset Boulevard (Downtown Hollywood). Studio used by Jack Nitzsche.

Valley Music Theatre 20060 Ventura Boulevard (Woodland Hills). Space-age concert venue.

Valley Teen Center 6345 Victory Boulevard (Van Nuys). Recreation center that hosted teen dances.

Venice West 7 Dudley Avenue (Venice). Poetry and jazz club; later known as Sponto Gallery.

Via Veneto 8704 Sunset Boulevard (Sunset Strip). Restaurant named for a street in Rome.

Villa Frascati 8117 Sunset Boulevard (Sunset Strip). Restaurant.

Villa Nova 9015 Sunset Boulevard (Sunset Strip). Italian restaurant where DiMaggio met Monroe.

Wallichs Music City 1501 Vine Street (corner of Sunset Boulevard, Downtown Hollywood). Record and instrument store since 1930, also at 700 W 7th Street (Downtown), 17540 Hawthorne Boulevard (Torrance), 5255 Lakewood Boulevard (Lakewood), 2753 E Garvey Avenue (West Covina), 6600 Topanga Canyon Boulevard (Canoga Park); co-founder Glenn Wallichs later formed Capitol Records.

Wally Heider Sound 1604 N Cahuenga Boulevard (Downtown Hollywood). Studio used by The Beach Boys and CSN.

Warehouse IX 2214 Stoner Avenue (West LA).

Warner Playhouse 755 N La Cienega Boulevard. 400-seat theater, hosted shortlived Night Flight shows.

Water Wheel Inn 648 Sunset (West Covina). Notable for its watusi contests.

Watts Happening Coffee House 1802 E 103rd Street (Watts). Art center and home of the Watts Writer's Workshop.

Watts Towers Arts Center 1727 E 107th Street (Watts). Community arts center, also home to the Watts Towers Theater Workshop. Still open.

Weidman Gallery 811 N La Cienega Boulevard. Jay Ward artist, in business since 1963.

Wenzel's Music Town 13117 Lakewood Boulevard (Downey). Recording studio.

Western Recorders 6000 Sunset Boulevard (Downtown Hollywood). Studio used by The Beach Boys, The Mamas & The Papas, and others.

Whisky A Go Go 8901 Sunset Boulevard (Sunset Strip). Era-defining nightclub.

Whittinghill's 13562 Ventura Boulevard (Sherman Oaks). Cocktail lounge.

Wide World 6363 Hollywood Boulevard (Downtown Hollywood). Post-1967 record store.

Wil Wright's Ice Cream Parlor 8641 Sunset Boulevard (Sunset Strip). As frequented by Duke Ellington, David Crosby, Brian Wilson, and The Monkees.

Wild Goose 13302 Ventura Boulevard (Sherman Oaks). Cocktail lounge.

Wild Scene 13952 Ventura Boulevard (Sherman Oaks). Post-1967 folk club.

Wild Thing 1835 N Cahuenga Boulevard (Downtown Hollywood). Psych/garage club.

William Locy Sound Co 8207 Arlington Avenue (Riverside). Recording studio used by The Tornadoes, The Misunderstood.

Wilshire Ebell Theatre 4401 W 8th Street (South LA).

Wolper Productions Inc 8544 Sunset Boulevard (Sunset Strip). Documentary-maker David L. Wolper's HQ.

World Pacific Studios/Pacific Jazz Studios 8715 W 3rd Street (south of the Strip). Used by The Byrds, The Beach Boys, The Doors, and others early on.

Would You Believe Club 865 S Kellogg Avenue (Goleta). Youthful nightclub; formerly the Hangout.

Ye Mucky Duck 255 Wilshire Boulevard (Santa Monica). British-style pub, frequented by ex-pats.

Yesterday & Today exact location unknown (Fairfax). Boutique that took its name from the 1966 Beatles album.

Zeidler & Zeidler 1611 Crescent Heights Boulevard. Hip clothing store; also Downtown at 1611 S Western Avenue.

Zomba Cafe 11502 Ventura Boulevard (Studio City). Burlesque club.

Notes and sources

Chapter 1

1 Liner notes to *Where It's At: Cheetah*
2 Anthony Fawcett, Henry Diltz *California Rock, California Sound*
3 Frank Zappa, Peter Occhiogrosso *The Real Frank Zappa Book*
4 Francis Frascina *Art, Politics, And Dissent*

Chapter 2

1 David Clark *LA On Foot*
2 Johnny Otis *Upside Your Head*
3 *Shotgun Freeway: Drives Thru Lost LA*
4 John Gilmore *Laid Bare*
5 *Sing Out!* (1964)
6 Sam Hall Kaplan *LA Lost & Found*
7 Steve Propes
8 *Venture* (June 1965)
9 *Vanity Fair* (May 1995)
10 *Venture* (June 1965)
11 *Playboy* (1965)
12 Frank Zappa, Peter Occhiogrosso
13 *Mondo Hollywood*
14 *Downbeat* (December 1966)

Chapter 3

1 Magnificent Montague, Bob Baker *Burn, Baby! BURN!*
2 Lee Joseph, *Dionysis Records*
3 Jean Rosenbluth *Boulevard Of Golden Dreams*
4 Richard Kelly *The Andy Griffith Show*
5 Liner notes to *The Dillards Live! Almost!*
6 *Ugly Things*
7 *Ugly Things*

Chapter 4

1 Sundazed Records
2 Sundazed Records
3 *Lost & Found*
4 Derek Taylor *As Time Goes By*
5 'John Lennon (1940-1980)' from *Rolling Stone*, January 22, 1981. By Straight Arrow Publishers, Inc. 1981. All Rights Reserved. Reprinted by Permission.
6 *Hit Parader* (1966)
7 *Rolling Stone* (1970)
8 *Los Angeles Magazine* (December 1965)

Chapter 5

1 GNP-Crescendo Records
2 *American Bandstand*

Chapter 6

1 Eve Babitz *Slow Days, Fast Company*
2 Andres Chavez, Denise Chavez, Gerald Martinez *What It Is ... What It Was!*
3 Francis Frascina
4 Richard Cándida Smith *Utopia And Dissent*

Chapter 7

1 Ben Watson *Frank Zappa*
2 Frank Zappa, Peter Occhiogrosso
3 Liner notes to *Cucamonga*
4 Frank Zappa, Peter Occhiogrosso
5 Barry Miles, Chris Charlesworth *Frank Zappa In His Own Words*
6 Barry Miles, Chris Charlesworth
7 *Los Angeles Herald Examiner* (1965)

8 Don Waller
9 Jimmy Greenspoon, Mark Bego *One Is The Loneliest Number*
10 *The Guardian* (1972)
11 Derek Taylor

Chapter 8
1 *Sounds* (November 1973)

Chapter 9
1 Jim Ladd
2 John Einarson, Richie Furay *For What It's Worth*
3 Jim Ladd
4 Jim Ladd
5 Jim Ladd
6 Liner notes to *Buffalo Springfield: Neil Young, Stephen Stills, Richie Furay, Jim Messina, Bruce Palmer, Dewey Martin*
7 John Einarson, Richie Furay
8 Press kit for Randy *Meisner*
9 David and Larissa Beaudoin *The Hullabaloo*
10 *Sounds* (November 1973)
11 *Sounds* (November 1973)
12 *Sounds* (November 1973)
13 *Sounds* (November 1973)

Chapter 10
1 *Mojo* (1995)
2 Sundazed Records
3 Jean Rosenbluth
4 *Hit Parader* (1965)
5 Louis Chunovic *The Rocky And Bullwinkle Book*

Chapter 11
1 Dick Clark *Rock, Roll & Remember*
2 'A Hard Day's Night On The Strip,' *West* (October 16 1966)

Chapter 12
1 *LA Weekly* (2002)
2 Ray Manzarek *Light My Fire*
3 Derek Taylor
4 *Los Angeles Herald Examiner* (1971)
5 Francis Frascina

Chapter 13
1 Brendan Mullen, Marc Spitz *We Got The Neutron Bomb*

Epilogue
1 Author's interview, 2010, courtesy of Hans Fjellestad (edited for space and clarity).

Bibliography

Maury Allen, Bo Belinsky *Pitching And Wooing* (Bantam Books 1974)
Richard Alpert, Sidney Cohen, Lawrence Schiller *LSD* (New American Library 1966)
Pete Anderson, Mike Watkinson *Scott Walker: A Deep Shade Of Blue* (Virgin 1994)
Eve Babitz *Eve's Hollywood: A Confessional LA Novel* (Delacorte Press/Seymour Lawrence 1974)
Eve Babitz *Slow Days, Fast Company: The World, The Flesh, And LA Tales By Eve Babitz* (Knopf 1977)
Eve Babitz *LA Woman* (Linden Press 1982)
Andre Balazs *Hollywood Handbook* (Universe 1996)
Reyner Banham *Los Angeles: The Architecture Of Four Ecologies* (Penguin 1971)
Richard Barnes, Johnny Moke, Jan McVeigh *Mods!* (Plexus 1979)

David Beaudoin, Larissa Beaudoin *The Hullabaloo: A Little Bit of Heaven … A Whole Lot of Hell!* (Tru-Books 1997)

Wallace Berman *Support The Revolution* (Institute Of Contemporary Art 1992)

Alan Betrock *The I Was A Teenage Juvenile Delinquent Rock'n'Roll Horror Beach Party Movie Book: A Complete Guide To The Teen Exploitation Film: 1954-1969* (St Martin's Press 1986)

Ein Bilderbuch, Klaus Plaumann *The Beat Age: Die Fruhen Tage Des Rock In Deutschland Und Grofbritannien* (Zweitausendeins 1978)

Peter Biskind *Easy Riders, Raging Bulls: How The Sex'n'Drugs'n'Rock'n'Roll Generation Saved Hollywood* (Touchstone 1998)

Peter Brown, Steven Gaines *The Love You Make* (Signet 1984)

Rob Burt, Patsy North *West Coast Story* (Chartwell 1977)

Harry Castleman, Walter J. Podrazik *Watching TV: Four Decades Of American Television* (McGraw-Hill 1982)

Harry Castleman, Walter J. Podrazik *The TV Schedule Book: Four Decades Of Network Programming From Sign-on To Sign-off* (McGraw-Hill 1984)

Chris Charlesworth *Sex & Drugs & Rock & Roll* (Bobcat 1993)

Andres Chavez, Denise Chavez, Gerald Martinez *What It Is … What It Was!: The Black Film Explosion Of The '70s In Words And Pictures* (Miramax 1998)

Dominique Chevalier *Viva! Zappa* (St Martin's Press 1986)

Lawrence Christon *Tales Of Jay Ward And The Bullwinkle Gang—How The Subversive Silliness Of Rocky And Bullwinkle Sprang Into Our Living Rooms* (Los Angeles Times 1988)

Louis Chunovic *The Rocky And Bullwinkle Book* (Bantam 1996)

David Clark *LA On Foot: A Free Afternoon* (Camaro 1974)

Dick Clark, Richard Robinson *Rock, Roll & Remember* (Thomas Y. Crowell 1976)

William Claxton *Jazz* (Chronicle 1996)

Sally Wright Cobb, Mark G. Willems *The Brown Derby Restaurant: A Hollywood Legend* (Rizzoli 1996)

Jerry Cohen, William S. Murphy *Burn, Baby, Burn!: The Los Angeles Race Riot, August, 1965* (E.P. Dutton & Co 1966)

Lawrence Cohn *Nothing But The Blues: The Music And The Musicians* (Abbeville Press 1993)

Kim Cooper, David Smay *Bubblegum Music Is The Naked Truth: The Dark History Of Prepubescent Pop, From The Banana Splits To Britney Spears* (Feral House 2001)

Stephen Cox *The Beverly Hillbillies* (Contemporary 1988)

Marshall Crenshaw *Hollywood Rock: A Guide To Rock'n'Roll In The Movies* (Harper Perennial 1994)

Mike Davis *City Of Quartz* (Vintage 1992)

Jim Dawson, Steve Propes *What Was The First Rock'n'Roll Record* (Faber 1992)

Pamela Des Barres *I'm With The Band: Confessions Of A Groupie* (Beech Tree 1987)

David Ehrenstein, Bill Reed *Rock On Film* (Delilah 1982)

John Einarson *Desperados: The Roots Of Country Rock* (Cooper Square Press 2001)

John Einarson, Richie Furay *For What It's Worth: The Story Of Buffalo Springfield* (Quarry Press 1997)

Jonathan Eisen *Twenty-Minute Fandangos And Forever Changes: A Rock Bazaar* (Random House 1971)

Anthony Fawcett, Henry Diltz *California Rock California Sound* (Reed 1978)

Art Fein *The LA Rock'n'Roll History Tour* (2.13.61 1998)

Rob Finnis *The Phil Spector Story* (Rockon 1975)

Stuart Fischer *Kids TV: The First 25 Years* (Facts On File 1983)

Francis Frascina *Art, Politics And Dissent: Aspects Of The Art Left In Sixties America* (Manchester University Press 1999)

David Gebhard *A Guide To Architecture In Southern California* (LA County Museum Of Art 1965)

David Gebhard, Harriette Von Breton *Los Angeles In The Thirties: 1931-1941* (Hennessey & Ingalls 1989)

Charlie Gillett *The Sound Of The City: The Rise Of Rock And Roll* (Outerbridge & Dienstrfrey 1970)

John Gilmore *Laid Bare: A Memoir Of Wrecked Lives And The Hollywood Death Trip* (Amok 1997)

Michael Gray *Mother! The Frank Zappa Story* (Plexus 1994)

Jimmy Greenspoon, Mark Bego *One Is The Loneliest Number: On The Road And Behind The Scenes With The Legendary Rock Band Three Dog Night* (Pharos 1991)

Richard Goldstein *Goldstein's Greatest Hits: A Book Mostly About Rock'n'Roll* (Prentice-Hall 1970)

Jennifer Harris, Sarah Hyde, Greg Smith *1966 And All That* (Trefoil Design Library 1986)

Jim Heimann, Rip Georges *California Crazy* (Chronicle 1980)

Jim Heimann *Car Hops And Curb Service: A History Of American Drive-In Restaurants* (Chronicle 1996)

Jim Heimann *Hooray For Hollywood* (Chronicle 1983)

Jim Heimann *Out With The Stars: Hollywood Nightlife In The Golden Era* (Abbeville 1985)

Jim Heimann *Sins Of The City: The Real Los Angeles Noir* (Chronicle 1999)

James Henke, Parke Puterbaugh, Charles Perry, Barry Miles, Jon Savage, The Rock'n'Roll Hall Of Fame Museum *I Want To Take You Higher: The Psychedelic Era 1965-1969* (Chronicle 1997)

Alan Hess *Googie: Fifties Coffee Shop Architecture* (Chronicle 1985)

Alan Hess *Viva Las Vegas: After-Hours Architecture* (Chronicle 1993)

Clinton Heylin *Bootleg: The Secret History Of The Other Recording Industry* (St Martin's Griffin 1996)

Clinton Heylin *Bob Dylan: The Recording Sessions 1960-1994* (St Martin's Press 1995)

Clinton Heylin *A Life In Stolen Moments: Bob Dylan Day By Day 1941-1995* (Schirmer 1996)

Jerry Hopkins, Danny Sugerman *No One Here Gets Out Alive: The Biography Of Jim Morrison* (Warner 1981)

Jac Holzman, Gavan Daws *Follow The Music: The Life And High Times Of Elektra Records In The Great Years Of American Pop Culture* (FirstMedia 1998)

Barney Hoskyns *Waiting For The Sun: Strange Days, Weird Scenes, And The Sound Of Los Angeles* (St Martin's Press 1996)

John Javna, Gordon Javna *60s!* (St Martin's Press 1983)

Philip Jenkinson, Alan Warner *Celluloid Rock: Twenty Years Of Movie Rock* (Lorrimer 1974)

Paul C. Johnson *Los Angeles: Portrait Of An Extraordinary City* (Lane 1968)

Vernon Joynson *Fuzz, Acid, And Flowers: A Comprehensive Guide To American Garage, Psychedelic, And Hippie Rock* (1964–1975) (Borderline 1993)

Vernon Joynson *The Acid Trip: A Complete Guide To Psychedelic Music* (Babylon 1984)

Sam Hall Kaplan *LA Lost & Found: An Architectural History Of Los Angeles* (Crown 1987)

James Karnbach, Carol Bernson *It's Only Rock'n'Roll: The Ultimate Guide To The Rolling Stones* (Facts On File 1997)

Michael Kaye *Transverse City: Images Of Los Angeles In LA Rock'n'Roll And The Development Of The LA Sound* (Senior Honor Thesis for the Interdisciplinary Studies Field Major, University Of California 1993)

Richard Kelly *The Andy Griffith Show* (John F. Blair 1981)

Joe Kennelley, Roy Hankey *Sunset Boulevard: America's Dream Street* (Darwin Publications 1981)

Richard Kostelanetz *The Frank Zappa Companion: Four Decades Of Commentary* (Schirmer 1997)

Craig Krull *Photographing The LA Art Scene 1955–1975* (Smart Art Press 1996)

Lisa Law *Flashing On The Sixties: Photographs By Lisa Law* (Chronicle 1997)

Eric Lefcowitz *The Monkees Tale* (Last Gasp 1985)

Mark Lewisohn *The Beatles Live!* (Henry Holt & Co 1986)

Mark Lewisohn *The Beatles Recording Sessions: The Official Abbey Road Studio Session Notes 1962–1970* (Harmony 1988)

Mark Lewisohn *The Complete Beatles Chronicle* (Harmony 1992)

Lawrence Lipton *The Holy Barbarians* (Julian Messner 1959)

Guus Luijters, Gerard Timmer *Sexbomb: The Life And Death Of Jayne Mansfield* (Citadel Press 1988)

Leonard Maltin *TV Movies* (Signet 1982)

Ray Manzarek *Light My Fire: My Life With The Doors* (G.P. Putnam's Sons 1998)

Dave Marsh *Before I Get Old: The Story Of The Who* (St. Martin's Press 1983)

John Arthur Maynard *Venice West: The Beat Generation In Southern California* (Rutgers University Press 1991)

Martin McIntosh, Domenic Priore *Beatsville* (Outre Gallery Press 2003)

Carey McWilliams *Southern California: An Island On The Land* (Duell Sloane & Pearce 1946)

James A. Michener *Hawaii* (Bantam 1961)

Barry Miles, Chris Charlesworth *Frank Zappa: A Visual Documentary By Miles* (Omnibus 1993)

Barry Miles, Chris Charlesworth *Frank Zappa: In His Own Words* (Omnibus 1993)

Billy Miller, Miriam Linna *Kicks! #1–7* (Kicks 1989–92)

Billy Miller, Miriam Linna *The Great Lost Photographs Of Eddie Rocco* (Kicks 1997)

Magnificent Montague, Bob Baker *Burn, Baby! BURN! The Autobiography Of Magnificent Montague* (University Of Illinois Press 2003)

Tom Moran, Tom Sewell *Fantasy By The Sea* (Peace Press 1980)

Brendan Mullen, Marc Spitz *We Got The Neutron Bomb: The Untold Story Of LA Punk* (Three Rivers Press 2001)

Ed Naha *The Films Of Roger Corman: Brilliance On A Budget* (Arco 1982)

Stuart Nicholson *Remeniscing In Tempo: A Portrait Of Duke Ellington* (Northeastern University Press 1999)

Norbert Obermanns *Zappalog: The First Step Of Zappalogy* (Rhino 1981)

Johnny Otis *Upside Your Head: Rhythm And Blues On Central Avenue* (Wesleyan University Press 1993)

Tony Palmer *All You Need Is Love: The Story Of Popular Music* (Grossman 1976)

Gareth L. Pawlowski *How They Became The Beatles: A Definitive History Of The Early Years 1960–1964* (E.P. Dutton 1989)

Lisa Phillips *Beat Culture And The New America: 1950–1965* (Whitney Museum Of American Art 1966)

Michelle Phillips *California Dreamin': The True Story Of The Mamas & The Papas* (Warner 1986)

Domenic Priore *Look! Listen! Vibrate! SMILE!* (Last Gasp 1995)

Jerry Prochnicky, Joe Russo *Jim Morrison: My Eyes Have Seen You* (AM Graphics & Printing 1996)

Thomas Pynchon *The Crying Of Lot 49* (Bantam 1966)

The Queens Museum *Remembering The Future* (Rizzoli 1989)

A.J.S. Rayl, Curt Gunther *Beatles '64: A Hard Days Night In America* (Doubleday 1989)

Jeremy Reed *Another Tear Falls: An Appreciation Of Scott Walker* (Creation 1998)

Tom Reed *The Black Music History Of Los Angeles* (Black Accent 1992)

David Reyes, Tom Waldman *Land Of A Thousand Dances: Chicano Rock'n'Roll From Southern California* (University Of New Mexico Press 1998)

Lawrence S. Ritter *Lost Ballparks: A Celebration Of Baseball's Legendary Fields* (Viking Studio 1992)

Johnny Rogan *Timeless Flight: The Definitive Biography Of The Byrds* (Square One 1990)

Edward Ruscha *Every Building On The Sunset Strip* (Edward Ruscha 1966)

Ellen Sander *Trips: Rock Life In The Sixties* (Scribner's 1973)

William Sargent *Superstar In Masquerade: The Legendary Leon Russell*

Sara Scribner *Love Hurts* (Los Angles New Times, March 11–17 1999)

Bud Scoppa *The Byrds* (Scholastic 1971)

Jack Sargeant *Naked Lens: Beat Cinema* (Creation 1997)

Gene Sculatti *The Catalog Of Cool* (Warner 1982)

Gene Sculatti *Too Cool* (St. Martin's Press 1993)

Gene Sculatti, Davin Seay *San Francisco Nights: The Psychedelic Music Trip 1965–1968* (St. Martin's Press 1985)

Joel Selvin *San Francisco Musical History Tour: A Guide To Over 200 Of The Bay Area's Most Memorable Music Sites* (Chronicle 1996)

Joel Selvin, Jim Marshall *Monterey Pop* (Chronicle 1992)

Arnold Shaw *The Jazz Age: Popular Music In The 1920s* (Oxford University Press 1987)

Arnold Shaw *The Street That Never Slept: New York's Fabled 52nd Street* (Coward McCann & Geoghegan 1971)

Greg Shaw *The Doors On The Road: The Complete Live Performances Of The Doors* (Omnibus 1997)

Matin A. Sklar *Walt Disney's Disneyland* (Disney 1969)

Richard Cándida Smith *Utopia And Dissent: Art, Poetry, And Politics In California* (University Of California Press 1995)

Jeffrey Stanton *Venice Of America: Coney Island Of The Pacific* (Donahue 1990)

Jeffrey Stanton *Santa Monica Pier: A History From 1875 To 1990* (Donahue 1987)

John Steinbeck *The Grapes Of Wrath* (Viking 1939)

Jane Stern, Michael Stern *Sixties People* (Knopf 1990)

Danny Sugerman *The Doors: The Illustrated History* (William Morrow & Co 1983)

Derek Taylor *As Time Goes By: Living In The Sixties* (Straight Arrow 1973)

Nick Tosches *Country: Living Legends And Dying Metaphors In America's Biggest Music* (Scribner's 1977)

Nick Tosches *Unsung Heroes Of Rock'n'Roll: The Birth Of Rock'n'Roll In The Dark And Wild Years Before Elvis* (Scribner's 1984)

Track 16 Gallery *Forming: The Early Days Of LA Punk* (Smart Art Press 1999)

Steve Turner *Van Morrison: Too Late To Stop Now* (Viking 1993)

V. Vale, Andrea Juno *Incredibly Strange Films* (Re/Search Publications 1988)

Jurgen Vollmer *Rock'n'Roll Times* (Google Plex 1981)

David Walley *No Commercial Potential: The Saga Of Frank Zappa And The Mothers Of Invention* (Sunrise 1972)

Holly George Warren, Shawn Dahl, Greg Emanuel *The New Rolling Stone Encyclopedia Of Rock'n'Roll* (Fireside 1983)

Ben Watson *Frank Zappa: The Negative Dialectics Of Poodle Play* (St. Martin's Griffin 1996)

Steven Watson *The Birth Of The Beat Generation: Visionaries, Rebels, And Hipsters, 1944–1960* (Pantheon 1995)

Marc Weingarten *Station To Station: The History Of Rock'n'Roll On Television* (Pocket 2000)

Michael J. Weldon *The Psychotronic Encyclopedia Of Film* (Ballentine 1983)

Michael J. Weldon *The Psychotronic Video Guide* (St. Martin's Griffin 1996)

Alfred Wertheimer *Elvis '56: In The Beginning* (Collier 1979)

Liza Williams *Up The City Of Angels* (G.P. Putnam's Sons 1971)

Simon Wilson *Pop* (Barron's Educational Series 1978)

Seth Wimpfheimer *Fuz #1* (Seth Wimpfheimer 1997)

John G. Youmans *Social Dance* (Goodyear 1969)

Frank Zappa, Peter Occhiogrosso *The Real Frank Zappa Book* (Poseidon 1989)

Index

Acknowledgements

Author's thanks

Art Fein, who showed sincere interest in this project from its inception to its final edit. Mike Stax, who was always there with answers to questions and good conversation. Chris Nichols, who fed the kitty with research goodies all the time. Marc Gordon, who provided a place to stay in LA when I was living out of town. Most of this book was written in San Francisco, California, and New York City, New York, with the final edits taking place in Los Angeles. The New York Public Library on 5th Avenue is where most of the basic research for this book took place, and I'd like to thank my mother, Lillian Priore, for turning me on to it in the first place (plus taking me to the Los Angeles County Museum Of Art all the time during the 60s). Special dedication to Dino's Lodge—'77 Sunset Strip'—its cache as a tourist magnet for our New York relatives led me to witness the surrounding action one glorious weekend night in 1966. Cheers to my father, Carmine Priore, who experienced the Hollywood Canteen during World War II and eventually made the decision to move to Los Angeles from New York. Final thanks go to my wonderful girlfriend Becky Ebenkamp, for sharing the keenest sense of popular culture of anyone I've met to this day.

"The record biz was still singles-generated … the LP was not yet dominant. Zoning con … because of the freeway. Hard to preserve … impossible to catch the scene's flavor."—Harvey The K.

Here are those who helped: Josh Agle, Don Agrati, Gene Aguilera, Davie Allan, DJ Senor Amor, Alfred Archuleta Jr, Curtis Armstrong, Steve Auer, David Axelrod, Eve Babitz, Andy Babiuk, Gary Balaban, Ken Barnes, Kevin Barney, Stephan Bataillard, Ed Beardsley, Tosh Berman, Alan Betrock, Steve Binder, Rodney Bingenheimer—KROQ-FM 106.7, Michael Bishop, Dick Blackburn, Michael

Blodgett, Paul Body, Sean Boniwell, Book City Collectables—Hollywood Boulevard, Gary Bookasta, Randy Bookasta, Richard Bosworth, Rick Boyd, Chris Boyle, Harold Bronson, Hugh Brown—Rhino, Denny Bruce, Rob Burt, Al Burton, Bob Cabeen, Eric Caidin of Hollywood Book and Poster—Hollywood Boulevard, Billy Cardenas, Paul Carey, Logan Carr—Dick Clark Productions, Chuck Cecil—KKJZ-FM 88.1 in Long Beach, Brian Chidester, John Chilson, Bruce Ciero—*Bad Trip* magazine, Debbie Cohen—Jay Ward Productions Inc., Carolyn Kozo Cole—Los Angeles Public Library, Wendie Colter, Rick Coonce, Robert Tyson Cornell—Book Soup, Stan Coutant, Donna Crippen—El Monte Historical Museum, Vicki Curry—KCET, Bob Dalley, John Daniels—Maverick's Flat, Chris Darrow, Jennifer Davis, Saul Davis, Jim Dawson, Pamela Des Barres, Pam DeLacy, John Delgatto, Helen Demeestere, Dave Diamond, Ara Devian at Dickran Color Lab, Jim Dickson, Marie DiPadova, Dick Dodd, Kevin Donan—As The Record Turns, Mike Dormer, Joe Doyle, Rick Duboff, Owen Dugan, Mike Dugo, Jim Dunfrund, Bill Earl, Dawn Eden, John Einarson, Bob Eubanks, Alex Farman—Charlie's Chili in Newport Beach, Barry Feinstein, Gerry Fialka, Bobby Figueroa, Bill Finnerand, Kurt Fisher, Hans Fjellestad, Ben Fong-Torres, Kim Fowley, Peter Frame, Jim Freek, Richie Furay, Shelly Ganz, Bruce Gari, Jeff Gazzarri, Holly George-Warren, Mike Glass, Glenn Glenn, Chas Glynn, David Gordon, Michael Murphy Graham, Tim Granada, Paul Grant, Merrill Greene, Jimmy Greenspoon, Mike Griffiths, Mark Guerrero, Michael Hacker, Terry Hand, Bob Hare, Dave Hassinger, Jim Heimann, Skip Heller, Alan Hess, Chris

Hillman, Nick Hoffman, Frank Holmes, Danny Holloway, Jerry Hopkins, Brent Hosier, Danny Hutton, Brian Izen, Laurie Jacobson, Paul Johnson, Ken Kaffke, Jacaeber Kastor of Psychedelic Solution—Greenwich Village, Steve Kater, David Kessel, Terry Kirkman, Harvey Kubernik, Art Kunkin— *The Los Angeles Free Press*, Art Laboe, Jim Ladd, Alan Larman, Joseph Lanza, Bill Lebowitz of Golen Apple Comics—Melrose Ave., Arthur Lee, Johnny Legend, Jennifer Lewi—AP Images, June Lewin—Beverly Hills Public Library Historical Collection, Ted Liebler, Louie Lista, Michael Lloyd, Mark London, Dennis Loren, Zachariah Love—McCabe's Guitar Shop in Santa Monica, Eileen Lucero, Alan Lungstrum, Phil MacConnell—Sound Factory, Jimmy Maddin, Ray Manzarek, Mike Markesich, Brett Martin, Wink Martindale, Ann Marie Matheus, Bud Mathis, Larry McCormick, Gary McDougall, John McEuen, Gerry McGee, Mickey McGowan, Roger McGuinn, Gordon McLelland, Ana Medina of Archaic Idiot, Bart Mendoza, Pete Mhunzi, Jack Miller, Kingdom of Jehovah Witness (for Valley Music Theatre), Maria Montgomery, Audrey Moorehead, Bill Morinini, Victoria Morris, Brendan Mullen, Mark Neill, Patrick Neve, Earl Newman, Morgan Neville, Natalie Nichols, Gene Norman—Crescendo Records, Neil Norman, Dan Nowicki, Michael Ochs, Andrew Loog Oldham, Ernie Orosco, Alec Palao, Van Dyke Parks, Freddie Patterson, Tony Pascuzzo, Rosemarie Patronette, Christopher Peake, Jim Pewter, Kim Pickens, Paul Leo Politti, Jim Pons, Poo Bah Records—Pasadena, James Porter, Greg Prevost, Jerry Prochnicky, Steve Propes, *Psychotronic* magazine, Kit Rachlis—Los Angeles Magazine, Steve Rager, Vanessa

Ramsey, Mike Randle, Tom Reed, Nancy Retchin, Sam Riddle, Jerry Riopelle, George Rodriquez, Richard Rosas, Michael Rossman, Matthew W. Roth—Automobile Club of Southern California, Glenn Sadin, Jim Salzer, Tony Sanchez, Andrew Sandoval, William Sargent, David B. Saxen—Landscape Architecture in San Francisco, Sky Saxon, Jerry Schilling, Sue Schneider, Jay Schwartz, Sara Scribner, Gene Sculatti, Carolyn See, Joel Selvin, Ken Sharp, Greg Shaw, Doug Sheppard, Kirk Silsbee, Jim Simmons, Shannon Smith, Tom Smothers, Rick Snyder, Rick Spalla—Hollywood Newsreel, Sponto Gallery—Venice, Bob Stane and the staff at the Ice House—Pasadena, Gary Strobl, Danny Sugarman, Paul Surrat, Stuart Swezey—Amok Books, Lauren Taines— Barney's Beanery, Shel Talmy, Larry Tamblyn, Bryan Thomas, Johnny Thompson's Guitar Shop—Monterey Park, Gene Trindl, Lloyd Thaxton, Nancy Tyler, Ted Walbye, Karen Lanzoni, John Kiffe, Christine Nguyen, and Julio SIms—Getty Research Library, Erica Tyron of KSPC 88.7—Pomona, Mamie Van Doren, John Van Hamersveld, Jean Verney and Day J.C. Dacantibes from Whisky A GoGo in Juan Les Pins—France, Mark Volman, Don Waller, Mike Walsh, Marc Wanamaker, Tiffany Ward, Tim Warren— Crypt Records, Marc Weingarten, Danny Weizmann, Ian Whitcomb, Mike Wilkins, Mike Willard, Dino Williams, Gregory Williams, Jerry Yester.

"This town is a quiet town / For a riot town / Like this town."—Lee Hazlewood

Picture credits

The photographs used in this book come from the following sources, and we are grateful for their help. If you feel there has been a mistaken attribution, please contact the publisher. Maps of Sunset Strip and Downtown Hollywood c. 1965–66 illustrated by Josh Agle. All memorabilia scanned or photographed by Marc Wanamaker.

Jacket front Zoe Poore **2** Julian Wasser **97** Julain Wasser **98** Art Laboe **99** Julian Wasser **100** Chuck Boyd **101** *Love* Chuck Boyd *S&C* author's collection **102** *Vegas* George Rodriquez *surfers* author's collection **103** *Dale* Michael Ochs Archive *Midniters* George Rodriguez **104** *Them/Doors* George Rodriquez *Henske* Michael Ochs Archive **201** *both images* Julian Wasser **202** *Rising* Michael Ochs Archive *Hollies* Chuck Boyd **203** *Echols* Chuck Boyd *Sloan* Julian Wasser *Trip* Michael Ochs Archive **204** *both images* Michael Ochs Archive **205** *Fog* George Rodriquez *Chocolate* Michael Ochs Archive *Merry* Jasper Dailey, courtesy of Rodney Bingenheimer **206** *Mothers / Zappa* George Rodriguez **207** *both images* Michael Ochs Archive **208** *Kaleidoscope* Beth Changstrom **305** *Hazlewood* Michael Ochs Archive *Nitzsche* Chuck Boyd *Spector* Ray Avery **306** *Buffalo* Richie Furay *Stone* Michael Ochs Archive **307** *Mamas* Chuck Boyd **308** *Garr / Basil / Stones* Julian Wasser *Turtles* Michael Ochs Archive **309** Lisa Law **310** Julian Wasser **311** *Sea Witch* Julian Wasser *Lennon / McCartney* Chuck Boyd **312** *riot / Pandora's* Julian Wasser *Dino's* Sid Avery

ALSO AVAILABLE IN PRINT AND EBOOK EDITIONS FROM JAWBONE PRESS